ATTENTION DEFICIT DISORDERS INTERVENTION MANUAL

Second Edition

Stephen B. McCarney, Ed.D.

Copyright © 1989, 1994 by Hawthorne Educational Services, Inc.

Printed in the
United States of America.
4/98

H A W T H O R N E
Educational Services, Inc.
800 Gray Oak Drive
Columbia, MO 65201
Telephone: (573) 874-1710
FAX: 1-800-442-9509

Table of Contents

B. Hyperactive-Impulsive

Behavior
Number

V. Supplemental Interventions

Behavior
Number

I. Introduction

The **Attention Deficit Disorders Intervention Manual** (School Version) was developed after repeated requests from educators for a "strategies guide" to better meet the needs of students with Attention-Deficit Disorders in our schools today. The manual is the culmination of extensive efforts to provide classroom intervention strategies for the most common characteristics of Attention-Deficit Disorders exhibited by students in school situations.

The concept of identifying the most common Attention-Deficit Disorders intervention strategies grew out of years of staffings and in-service presentations where teachers earnestly asked the question over and over again, "What do you do with a student who . . .?" It is obvious that our educators genuinely want to provide an appropriate behavioral support program for those students with Attention-Deficit Disorders needs, and the **Attention Deficit Disorders Intervention Manual** is designed to provide the necessary intervention strategies.

The goals and objectives in this manual were developed to serve as samples which may be used in writing IEPs. Criteria for measuring the success of the student's attainment of the goals and objectives must be determined by those professional educators and parents who are aware of the student's current abilities and program recommendations.

The interventions in Section IV address behaviors associated with Attention-Deficit Disorders and correspond with the goals and objectives in Section III. Section V consists of supplemental intervention strategies for teaching students with Attention-Deficit Disorders who may exhibit learning or behavior problems in addition to those which are characteristic of Attention-Deficit Disorders. The interventions should serve as a guide for program development or change for any student in need of improvement. Interventions may be chosen by a team of professionals, a special educator in a self-contained class or functioning in a resource or consultant capacity, or by a regular education teacher. Professional judgment should dictate the choice of interventions for any particular student. The student's age, sex, and grade level are all to be considered in selecting appropriate intervention procedures. The interventions have been found appropriate for special education as well as regular education classroom environments.

The expectation is that the appropriate interventions will be selected, agreed upon, and consistently used by all instructional personnel working with the student. Use of the same interventions by all teachers in all settings greatly enhances the likelihood of student success in the educational environment. These interventions, appropriate for all educational environments, lend themselves particularly well to creating continuity across all the classes and educational settings in which the student functions.

In order to respond to the broad spectrum of implications related to behavior problems, the interventions contained in this manual are designed to represent solutions which are both preventive and reactive. Preventive interventions are environmental modifications used to reduce variables which may stimulate problem behavior. Such variables would be the amount of noise, movement, or another student who may prove particularly stimulating. Reactive interventions "teach" the student more appropriate ways to deal with his/her Attention-Deficit Disorder. These strategies include increased self-control, problem-solving skills, etc.

Some interventions in this manual apply to most students and should be considered first in order to provide a more general approach to Attention-Deficit Disorders. Other interventions are more specific and should be individually selected for students based on the appropriateness of the intervention to the specific problem the student exhibits.

For any behavior problem exhibited by students, it will be of value to assess the extent to which institutional variables influence the behavior and possibly contribute to the problem. Limited supervision in play areas, hallways, and during extracurricular activities, as well as arbitrary groupings and seating arrangements, are often examples of factors which are inherent in the institutional structure and often contribute to problem behavior. As a first step in improving a situation, these institutional variables should be evaluated and acted upon to reduce the influence of variables which result in unsuccessful or inappropriate behavior.

We understand that additional forms of intervention (i.e., medication) are appropriate and often necessary for the management of Attention-Deficit Disorders. This manual was designed to assist those other treatment methods by providing teachers and other care givers with intervention strategies which will prevent much Attention-Deficit behavior and facilitate the student's success by teaching the student to manage his/her own behavior.

The accompanying **Parent's Guide to Attention Deficit Disorders** was developed using the same format as this manual to be used by parents in meeting the behavioral needs of their child in the home. We hope the parent's manual will meet the same need in the homes of our children with Attention-Deficit Disorders as the school version does in the educational environment.

To all the people who have contributed to the development of the **Attention Deficit Disorders Intervention Manual**: Kathy Sharp, Waheeda Bilal, editing and proofreading; Mary Kay Murphy, graphics and publishing preparation; I extend my thanks for another job well done. And to Billy, who asks for so little and gives so much, I am truly thankful you came to be with us.

S.B.M.

II. Using the *Attention Deficit Disorders Intervention Manual* in Conjunction with the *Attention Deficit Disorders Evaluation Scale*

NOTE: If the **Attention Deficit Disorders Intervention Manual** is not being used in conjunction with the **Attention Deficit Disorders Evaluation Scale**, the following procedural steps need not be followed.

Step 1: The student is rated with the School Version of the **Attention Deficit Disorders Evaluation Scale**.

Step 2: Conversions of raw scores on the **Attention Deficit Disorders Evaluation Scale** are made, Subscale Standard Scores and Percentile Scores are determined, and the **Attention Deficit Disorders Evaluation Scale** Profile section is completed.

Step 3: Determine on which of the two characteristics (subscales) the student scores one or two standard deviations below the mean (subscale score below 7).

Step 4: Under each of those characteristics (subscales) on which the student scores one or two standard deviations below the mean, determine which behaviors constitute primary concern in the educational environment (the behaviors with the highest raw scores).

Step 5: Find Goals and Objectives from the **Attention Deficit Disorders Intervention Manual** (Section titled: III. Goals and Objectives) which represent each behavior indicated as a primary concern on the **Attention Deficit Disorders Evaluation Scale**.

Step 6: Determine those interventions from the **Attention Deficit Disorders Intervention Manual** (section IV) which are most appropriate in facilitating the student's success and meeting the Goals and Objectives chosen in Step 5. Section V contains supplemental intervention strategies for learning and behavior problems other than those on the **Attention Deficit Disorders Evaluation Scale**.

Step 7: If there are any behaviors which are of concern on subscales other than those subscales with scores one or two standard deviations below the mean; Goals, Objectives, and Interventions should be selected and written for those behaviors as well.

Step 8: Share those Goals, Objectives, and Intervention strategies selected for the student with all personnel involved in the student's educational program.

Step 9: Regular and special education teachers should implement those Intervention strategies selected to be most successful with the student. The student's progress should be monitored and regular consultation with parents and other educators should be conducted to evaluate the student's success.

A Reminder: It is not necessary to use the Goals and Objectives in this manual; Interventions may be implemented from ratings obtained from the **Attention Deficit Disorders Evaluation Scale** or from observations of the student's behavior.

III. Goals and Objectives

BEHAVIOR 1: Rushes through assignments with little or no regard for accuracy or quality of work

Goals:
1. The student will improve the accuracy of school assignments.
2. The student will improve the quality of school assignments.

Objectives:
1. The student will perform school assignments with _____% accuracy.
2. The student will check school assignments to correct errors on _____ out of _____ trials.
3. The student will turn in school assignments for the teacher to proofread and provide feedback for corrections and improvement on _____ out of _____ trials.
4. The student will re-do corrected school assignments with _____% accuracy.
5. The student will have a peer check his/her school assignments and correct errors found on _____ out of _____ trials.

BEHAVIOR 2: Is easily distracted by other activities in the classroom, other students, the teacher, etc.

Goal:
1. The student will remain on-task.

Objectives:
1. The student will demonstrate on-task behavior by sitting quietly at his/her seat, looking at his/her materials, and performing the task for _____ minutes at a time. (Gradually increase expectations as the student demonstrates success.)
2. The student will remain on-task for _____ minutes at a time. (Gradually increase expectations as the student demonstrates success.)
3. The student will remain on-task long enough to complete the task on _____ out of _____ tasks.
4. The student will remain on-task through its completion on _____ out of _____ tasks.
5. The student will maintain eye contact with the teacher for _____ minutes at a time.

BEHAVIOR 3: Does not listen to what other students are saying

Goals:
1. The student will improve listening skills in nonacademic settings.
2. The student will attend to what other students say.

Objectives:
1. The student will maintain eye contact when other students are speaking on _____ out of _____ occasions.
2. The student will listen quietly when other students are speaking on _____ out of _____ occasions.
3. The student will repeat what other students have said with _____% accuracy.
4. The student will respond appropriately to what other students say on _____ out of _____ occasions.

BEHAVIOR 4: Does not hear all of what is said

Goals:
1. The student will improve listening skills in academic settings.
2. The student will improve listening skills in nonacademic settings.

Objectives:
1. The student will maintain eye contact when information is being communicated _____% of the time.
2. The student will listen quietly when verbal directions are given _____% of the time.
3. The student will repeat what is said with _____% accuracy.
4. The student will respond appropriately to what is said, with reminders, _____% of the time.
5. The student will independently respond appropriately to what is said _____% of the time.

BEHAVIOR 5: **Does not direct attention or fails to maintain attention to important sounds in the immediate environment**

Goals:
1. The student will improve listening skills in academic settings.
2. The student will improve listening skills in nonacademic settings.
3. The student will attend more successfully to specific sounds in the environment.

Objectives:
1. The student will maintain eye contact when information is being communicated _____% of the time.
2. The student will listen quietly when verbal directions are given _____% of the time.
3. The student will repeat what is said with _____% accuracy.
4. The student will respond appropriately to what is said, with reminders, _____% of the time.
5. The student will independently respond appropriately to what is said _____% of the time.
6. The student will respond appropriately to environmental cues (e.g., bells, signs, etc.), when given verbal reminders, _____% of the time.
7. The student will independently respond appropriately to environmental cues (e.g., bells, signs, etc.) _____% of the time.

BEHAVIOR 6: **Is unsuccessful in activities requiring listening**

Goals:
1. The student will improve listening skills in academic settings.
2. The student will improve listening skills in nonacademic settings.

Objectives:
1. The student will maintain eye contact when information is being communicated _____% of the time.
2. The student will listen quietly when verbal directions are given _____% of the time.
3. The student will repeat what is said with _____% accuracy.
4. The student will respond appropriately to what is said, with reminders, with _____% accuracy.
5. The student will independently respond appropriately to what is said with _____% accuracy.
6. The student will follow one-step verbal directions with _____% accuracy.
7. The student will follow two-step verbal directions with _____% accuracy.
8. The student will follow multi-step verbal directions with _____% accuracy.

BEHAVIOR 7: **Needs oral questions and directions frequently repeated**

Goals:
1. The student will improve listening skills in academic settings.
2. The student will improve listening skills in nonacademic settings.

Objectives:
1. The student will maintain eye contact when information is being communicated _____% of the time.
2. The student will listen quietly when verbal directions are given _____% of the time.
3. The student will repeat what is said to him/her with _____% accuracy.

4. The student will respond appropriately to what is said, with reminders, with _____% accuracy.
5. The student will independently respond appropriately to what is said to him/her with _____% accuracy.

BEHAVIOR 8:   Attends more successfully when close to the source of sound

Goal:
1. The student will improve his/her awareness and attention to information and activities in the environment.

Objectives:
1. The student will maintain eye contact when information is being communicated _____% of the time.
2. The student will listen quietly when verbal directions are given _____% of the time.
3. The student will repeat what is said with _____% accuracy.
4. The student will respond appropriately to what is said, with reminders, _____% of the time.
5. The student will independently respond appropriately to what is said to him/her _____% of the time.
6. The student will follow one-step verbal directions with _____% accuracy.
7. The student will follow two-step verbal directions with _____% accuracy.
8. The student will follow multi-step verbal directions with _____% accuracy.

BEHAVIOR 9:   Requires eye contact in order to listen successfully

Goals:
1. The student will improve listening skills in academic settings.
2. The student will improve listening skills in nonacademic settings.
3. The student will attend more successfully to specific sounds in the environment.
4. The student will improve his/her awareness and attention to information and activities in the environment.

Objectives:
1. The student will maintain eye contact, when information is being communicated, _____% of the time.
2. The student will listen quietly, when verbal directions are given, _____% of the time.
3. The student will be able to repeat what is said to him/her with _____% accuracy.
4. The student will respond appropriately to what is said, with reminders, _____% of the time.
5. The student will independently respond appropriately to what is said to him/her _____% of the time.

BEHAVIOR 10:   Fails to demonstrate short-term memory skills

Goal:
1. The student will improve his/her short-term memory.

Objectives:
1. The student will follow two- or three-step directions independently with _____% accuracy.
2. The student will remember materials necessary for a task or assignment _____% of the time.
3. The student will memorize short poems or songs with _____% accuracy.
4. The student will remember information presented, removed, and presented again immediately with _____% accuracy.
5. The student will remember information after short intervals (10 to 15 minutes) with _____% accuracy.
6. The student will remember information after intervals of several hours with _____% accuracy.

BEHAVIOR 11:   Fails to remember sequences

Goals:
1. The student will improve his/her short-term memory.
2. The student will improve his/her long-term memory.

3. The student will improve his/her ability to remember sequences.

Objectives:
1. The student will remember the events in a daily routine with _____% accuracy.
2. The student will memorize sequential information (e.g., days of the week, months of the year, seasons, alphabet, etc.).
3. The student will follow an established routine in performing assignments, preparing for lunch, etc., _____% of the time.

BEHAVIOR 12:   Has difficulty concentrating

Goal:
1. The student will improve his/her ability to concentrate.

Objectives:
1. The student will work on a task for _____minutes.
2. The student will work on a task until completed on _____ out of _____ trials.
3. The student will attend to an activity for _____minutes.
4. The student will attend to an activity until it is completed on _____ out of _____ trials.
5. The student will attend to a lecture, conversation, or discussion for _____minutes.
6. The student will attend to a lecture, conversation, or discussion until it is completed on _____ out of _____ trials.

BEHAVIOR 13:   Loses place when reading

Goals:
1. The student will improve his/her ability to concentrate.
2. The student will improve his/her attention to reading activities.

Objectives:
1. The student will read lists of words without losing his/her place with _____% accuracy.
2. The student will read lines of words without losing his/her place with _____% accuracy.
3. The student will read sentences without losing his/her place with _____% accuracy.
4. The student will read paragraphs without losing his/her place with _____% accuracy.

BEHAVIOR 14:   Omits, adds, substitutes, or reverses letters, words, or sounds when reading

Goals:
1. The student will improve his/her ability to concentrate.
2. The student will improve his/her attention to writing activities.
3. The student will improve his/her writing skills.

Objectives:
1. The student will read complete phrases after he/she has been corrected by the teacher with _____% accuracy.
2. The student will independently read complete phrases with _____% accuracy.
3. The student will read complete sentences after he/she has been corrected by the teacher with _____% accuracy.
4. The student will independently read complete sentences with _____% accuracy.

BEHAVIOR 15:   Fails to copy letters, words, sentences, and numbers from a textbook, chalkboard, etc.

Goals:
1. The student will improve his/her ability to concentrate.

2. The student will improve his/her attention to information and activities in the environment.
3. The student will improve his/her ability to copy from the chalkboard, textbooks, etc.

Objectives:
1. The student will be able to form letters and numbers with _____% accuracy.
2. The student will trace letters and numbers from a model at a close distance replicating formation, size, and spacing with _____% accuracy.
3. The student will copy letters and numbers from a model at a close distance replicating formation, size, and spacing with _____% accuracy.
4. The student will copy words and sentences from a model at a close distance replicating formation, size, and spacing with _____% accuracy.

BEHAVIOR 16: Omits, adds, or substitutes words when writing

Goals:
1. The student will improve his/her attention to writing assignments.
2. The student will improve his/her concentration.
3. The student will improve his/her writing skills.

Objectives:
1. The student will use complete phrases when writing, after he/she has been corrected by the teacher, with _____% accuracy.
2. The student will independently use complete phrases when writing with _____% accuracy.
3. The student will complete sentences when writing, after he/she has been corrected by the teacher, with _____% accuracy.
4. The student will independently use complete sentences when writing with _____% accuracy.

BEHAVIOR 17: Fails to complete homework assignments and return them to school

Goal:
1. The student will complete homework assignments and return them to school.

Objectives:
1. The student will take homework assignments home on _____ out of _____ occasions.
2. The student will complete homework assignments at home on _____ out of _____ occasions.
3. The student will return completed homework assignments to school on _____ out of _____ occasions.
4. The student will complete homework assignments at school when he/she cannot complete the assignments at home on _____ out of _____ occasions.
5. The student will receive help at home when completing homework assignments on _____ out of _____ occasions.

BEHAVIOR 18. Does not perform or complete classroom assignments during class time

Goal:
1. The student will complete classroom assignments during class time.

Objectives:
1. The student will complete a task before going on to the next task on _____ out of _____ trials.
2. The student will complete _____ out of _____ assigned tasks per day.
3. The student will attempt _____ out of _____ assigned tasks per day.
4. The student will remain on-task for _____ out of _____ minutes per class period.

5. The student will use the time provided to work on assigned tasks in order to complete _____ tasks per day.

BEHAVIOR 19: **Is disorganized to the point of not having necessary materials, losing materials, being unable to find completed assignments, being unable to follow the steps of the assignment in order, etc.**

Goal:
1. The student will improve his/her organizational skills related to assignments.

Objectives:
1. The student will have the necessary materials for assigned activities on _____ out of _____ trials.
2. The student will carry his/her materials and assignments to and from activities in a book bag/backpack in order to prevent loss on _____ out of _____ trials.
3. The student will return materials to their specified locations on _____ out of _____ trials.
4. The student will place his/her completed work in a specified location (folder, "mailbox," etc.) on _____ out of _____ trials.
5. The student will be organized and prepared to work within _____ minutes of the beginning of class.
6. The student will complete one step of the task before going on to the next step on _____ out of _____ trials.
7. The student will complete the steps of the assigned task in sequential order on _____ out of _____ tasks.
8. The student will prioritize and complete assignments with the help of the teacher on _____ out of _____ opportunities.
9. The student will independently prioritize and complete assignments on _____ out of _____ opportunities.
10. The student will organize his/her materials at the beginning and end of each assigned task on _____ out of _____ trials.

BEHAVIOR 20: **Completes assignments with little or no regard to neatness**

Goal:
1. The student will perform assignments neatly.

Objectives:
1. The student will perform written tasks in a legible manner on _____ out of _____ trials.
2. The student will take his/her time when performing a written task in order to make it legible on _____ out of _____ tasks.
3. The student will turn in written work which is legible on _____ out of _____ trials.
4. The student will turn in written assignments that are clean, free of tears, neat, etc., on _____ out of _____ trials.
5. The student will re-copy his/her written assignments before turning them in on _____ out of _____ trials.

BEHAVIOR 21: **Fails to perform assignments independently**

Goal:
1. The student will independently perform assignments.

Objectives:
1. The student will attempt to perform a given assignment before asking for teacher assistance on _____ out of _____ trials.
2. The student will read necessary directions, instructions, explanations, etc., before asking for teacher assistance on _____ out of _____ trials.
3. The student will independently complete _____ out of _____ assignments per school day.
4. The student will ask for teacher assistance only when necessary when performing assignments on _____ out of _____ trials.

5. The student will work for _____ minutes without requiring assistance from the teacher on _____ out of _____ trials.

BEHAVIOR 22: Does not prepare for school assignments

Goal:
1. The student will be prepared for school assignments.

Objectives:
1. The student will study for _____ out of _____ tests.
2. The student will study for _____ out of _____ quizzes.
3. The student will study and perform classroom tests with _____% accuracy. (Gradually increase expectations as the student demonstrates success.)
4. The student will study and perform classroom quizzes with _____% accuracy. (Gradually increase expectations as the student demonstrates success.)
5. The student will be prepared for assigned activities by reading the assigned material for _____ out of _____ activities.
6. The student will complete his/her assigned tasks such as book reports, projects, etc., by the due date on _____ out of _____ trials.
7. The student will complete his/her homework prior to coming to the assigned activity on _____ out of _____ trials.
8. The student will correctly answer questions covering the assigned reading material on _____ out of _____ trials.
9. The student will read necessary information prior to coming to the assigned activity on _____ out of _____ trials.

BEHAVIOR 23: Does not remain on-task

Goal:
1. The student will remain on-task.

Objectives:
1. The student will demonstrate on-task behavior by sitting quietly at his/her seat, looking at his/her materials, and performing the task for _____ minutes at a time. (Gradually increase expectations as the student demonstrates success.)
2. The student will remain on-task for _____ minutes at a time. (Gradually increase expectations as the student demonstrates success.)
3. The student will remain on-task long enough to complete the task on _____ out of _____ tasks.
4. The student will remain on-task through its completion on _____ out of _____ tasks.
5. The student will maintain eye contact with the teacher for _____ minutes at a time.

BEHAVIOR 24: Does not perform academically at his/her ability level (i.e., performs below ability level or at a failing level)

Goal:
1. The student will perform academically at his/her ability level.

Objectives:
1. The student will perform academic tasks with _____% accuracy. (Gradually increase expectations as the student demonstrates success.)
2. The student will meet a _____% level of mastery on academic tasks. (Gradually increase expectations as the student demonstrates success.)

3. The student will perform academic tasks on his/her ability level on _____ out of _____ trials.
4. The student will perform tasks designed to meet his/her level of functioning with _____% accuracy. (Gradually increase expectations as the student demonstrates success.)

BEHAVIOR 25:   Does not listen to or follow verbal directions

Goal:
1. The student will follow verbal directions.

Objectives:
1. The student will follow verbal directions in correct sequential order on _____ out of _____ trials.
2. The student will follow _____ out of _____ verbal directions.
3. The student will demonstrate the ability to follow verbal directions by listening carefully and completing the task with _____ % accuracy.
4. The student will follow verbal directions with teacher assistance on _____ out of _____ trials.
5. The student will independently follow verbal directions on _____ out of _____ trials.
6. The student will complete one step of the verbal direction before going on to the next step on _____ out of _____ trials.
7. The student will follow one-step verbal directions on _____ out of _____ trials. (Gradually increase expectations as the student demonstrates success.)

BEHAVIOR 26:   Fails to make appropriate use of study time

Goal:
1. The student will make appropriate use of study time.

Objectives:
1. The student will begin assignments during study time on _____ out of _____ occasions.
2. The student will continue working on assignments during study time on _____ out of _____ occasions.
3. The student will complete assignments during study time on _____ out of _____ occasions.
4. The student will independently find school-related activities to engage in during study time on _____ out of _____ occasions.

BEHAVIOR 27:   Fails to follow necessary steps in math problems

Goal:
1. The student will improve his/her ability to follow the necessary steps in solving math problems.

Objectives:
1. The student will follow the necessary steps to solve addition problems not requiring regrouping with _____% accuracy.
2. The student will follow the necessary steps to solve addition problems requiring regrouping with _____% accuracy.
3. The student will follow the necessary steps to solve subtraction problems not requiring regrouping with _____% accuracy.
4. The student will follow the necessary steps to solve subtraction problems requiring regrouping with _____% accuracy.
5. The student will follow the necessary steps to solve multiplication problems not requiring regrouping with _____% accuracy.
6. The student will follow the necessary steps to solve multiplication problems requiring regrouping with _____% accuracy.
7. The student will follow the necessary steps to solve short division problems with _____% accuracy.
8. The student will follow the necessary steps to solve long division problems with _____% accuracy.

9. The student will follow the necessary steps to solve math word problems with _____% accuracy.
10. The student will follow the necessary steps to solve math problems involving fractions with _____% accuracy.
11. The student will follow the necessary steps to solve math problems involving decimals with _____% accuracy.
12. The student will follow the necessary steps to solve math problems involving time with _____% accuracy.
13. The student will follow the necessary steps to solve math problems involving measurement with _____% accuracy.

BEHAVIOR 28:   Does not read or follow written directions

Goal:
1. The student will follow written directions.

Objectives:
1. The student will follow written directions in correct sequential order on _____ out of _____ trials.
2. The student will follow _____ out of _____ written directions.
3. The student will demonstrate the ability to follow written directions by reading the directions carefully and completing the task with _____% accuracy.
4. The student will follow written directions with teacher assistance on _____ out of _____ trials.
5. The student will independently follow written directions on _____ out of _____ trials.
6. The student will read directions written on his/her ability level and follow them in correct sequential order on _____ out of _____ trials.
7. The student will complete one step of the written direction before going on to the next step on _____ out of _____ trials.
8. The student will follow one-step written directions on _____ out of _____ trials. (Gradually increase expectations as the student demonstrates success.)

BEHAVIOR 29:   Changes from one activity to another without finishing the first, without putting things away, before it is time to move on, etc.

Goal:
1. The student will be able to change from one activity to another without difficulty.

Objectives:
1. The student will change from one activity to another after finishing the first on _____ out of _____ occasions.
2. The student will change from one activity to another after putting things away on _____ out of _____ occasions.
3. The student will stop one activity and begin another when necessary on _____ out of _____ occasions.

BEHAVIOR 30:   Does not follow school rules

Goal:
1. The student will follow school rules.

Objectives:
1. The student will follow school rules on _____ out of _____ trials.
2. The student will walk in the halls when moving from one location to another on _____ out of _____ trials.
3. The student will refrain from throwing food in the cafeteria on _____ out of _____ trials.
4. The student will keep his/her food on his/her plate on _____ out of _____ trials.
5. The student will work quietly in the library on _____ out of _____ trials.
6. The student will talk quietly with a peer when in the library on _____ out of _____ trials.

7. The student will handle school property with care on _____ out of _____ trials.
8. The student will walk quietly through the halls on _____ out of _____ trials.
9. The student will interact appropriately with his/her peers during lunch, recess, break time, etc., on _____ out of _____ trials.

BEHAVIOR 31: Begins assignments before receiving directions or instructions or does not follow directions or instructions

Goals:
1. The student will begin assignments after receiving directions or instructions.
2. The student will follow directions.
3. The student will follow instructions.

Objectives:
1. The student will begin assignments after receiving directions, instructions, etc., with physical assistance on _____ out of _____ occasions.
2. The student will begin assignments after receiving directions, instructions, etc., with verbal prompts on _____ out of _____ occasions.
3. The student will independently begin assignments after receiving directions, instructions, etc., on _____ out of _____ occasions.
4. The student will begin assignments after receiving directions, instructions, etc., within _____ (indicate a given time period).
5. The student will begin assignments with peer assistance after receiving directions, instructions, etc., on _____ out of _____ occasions.

BEHAVIOR 32: Does not wait his/her turn in activities or games

Goals:
1. The student will allow others to take their turns.
2. The student will allow others to participate in activities and games.
3. The student will demonstrate appropriate interaction skills.

Objectives:
1. The student will allow others to take their turns on _____ out of _____ trials.
2. The student will demonstrate the ability to wait his/her turn by allowing others to take their turns on _____ out of _____ trials.
3. The student will take turns with a peer for _____ minutes at a time. (Gradually increase expectations as the student demonstrates success.)
4. The student will take turns with two peers for _____ minutes at a time. (Gradually increase expectations as the student demonstrates success.)
5. The student will take turns with four to six peers for _____ minutes at a time. (Gradually increase expectations as the student demonstrates success.)
6. The student will allow others to participate in activities and games on _____ out of _____ trials.
7. The student will demonstrate the ability to appropriately interact with others by allowing them to participate in activities and games on _____ out of _____ trials.
8. The student will participate with a peer in an activity or game for _____ minutes at a time. (Gradually increase expectations as the student demonstrates success.)
9. The student will participate with two peers in an activity or game for _____ minutes at a time. (Gradually increase expectations as the student demonstrates success.)
10. The student will participate with four to six peers in an activity or game for _____ minutes at a time. (Gradually increase expectations as the student demonstrates success.)
11. The student will demonstrate appropriate interaction skills during _____ out of _____ activities or games.
12. The student will demonstrate appropriate interaction skills when engaged in highly structured/supervised activities or games on _____ out of _____ trials.

13. The student will demonstrate appropriate interaction skills when engaged in structured activities and games with minimal supervision on _____ out of _____ trials.
14. The student will demonstrate appropriate interaction skills when engaged in unstructured activities such as free time, lunch, recess, etc., on _____ out of _____ trials.

BEHAVIOR 33:   Grabs things away from others

Goal:
1. The student will not grab things away from others.

Objectives:
1. The student will refrain from forcibly taking things from others on _____ out of _____ trials.
2. The student will ask the owner's permission before using materials, possessions, etc., on _____ out of _____ trials.
3. The student will ask the user's permission before using materials, equipment, etc., on _____ out of _____ trials.
4. The student will ask to use materials, will share materials, and will return materials in the same or better condition on _____ out of _____ trials.
5. The student will ask to borrow materials, equipment, possessions, etc., before taking them on _____ out of _____ trials.

BEHAVIOR 34:   Blurts out answers without being called on

Goals:
1. The student will answer only when called upon.
2. The student will communicate with others in an acceptable manner in the classroom.
3. The student will work quietly in the classroom.

Objectives:
1. The student will gain permission from the teacher to speak, by raising his/her hand, when he/she has an answer on _____ out of _____ trials.
2. The student will contribute his/her opinion/answer after being recognized by the teacher on _____ out of _____ trials.
3. The student will await his/her turn to talk when engaged, or attempting to engage, in interactions with others on _____ out of _____ trials.
4. The student will refrain from making sounds which are inappropriate for the situation on _____ out of _____ trials.

BEHAVIOR 35:   Interrupts the teacher

Goals:
1. The student will answer only when called upon.
2. The student will communicate with others in an acceptable manner in the classroom.
3. The student will work quietly in the classroom.

Objectives:
1. The student will gain permission from the teacher, by raising his/her hand, when he/she needs to talk with a peer on _____ out of _____ trials.
2. The student will contribute his/her opinion/answer after being recognized by the teacher on _____ out of _____ trials.
3. The student will await his/her turn to talk when engaged, or attempting to engage, in interactions with the teacher on _____ out of _____ trials.

4. The student will make comments to the teacher which are relevant to the situation on _____ out of _____ trials.
5. The student will refrain from making sounds which are inappropriate for the situation on _____ out of _____ trials.

BEHAVIOR 36:   Interrupts other students (e.g, talks while they are talking, makes noises, laughs, etc.)

Goals:
1. The student will refrain from bothering other students who are trying to work, listen, etc.
2. The student will stay on-task.

Objectives:
1. The student will refrain from interrupting other students who are trying to work, listen, etc., on _____ out of _____ trials.
2. The student will stay on-task for _____ minutes at a time. (Gradually increase expectations as the student demonstrates success.)
3. The student will interact with other students when appropriate on _____ out of _____ trials.
4. The student will interact with other students during free time, break time, lunch time, etc., on _____ out of _____ trials.
5. The student will ask the teacher's permission prior to interacting with a peer(s) on _____ out of _____ trials.
6. The student will remain appropriately seated until given teacher permission to do otherwise on _____ out of _____ trials.

BEHAVIOR 37:   Talks to others during quiet activity periods

Goals:
1. The student will communicate with others in an acceptable manner in the classroom.
2. The student will work quietly in the classroom.

Objectives:
1. The student will gain permission from the teacher, by raising his/her hand, when he/she needs to talk with a peer on _____ out of _____ trials.
2. The student will contribute his/her opinion/answer, after being recognized by the teacher, on _____ out of _____ trials.
3. The student will await his/her turn to talk when engaged, or attempting to engage, in interactions with others on _____ out of _____ trials.
4. The student will make comments which are relevant to the situation on _____ out of _____ trials.
5. The student will refrain from making sounds which are inappropriate for the situation on _____ out of _____ trials.

BEHAVIOR 38:   Moves about while seated, fidgets, squirms, etc.

Goals:
1. The student will engage in appropriate behaviors while seated.
2. The student will sit appropriately in his/her seat.

Objectives:
1. The student will demonstrate appropriate in-seat behavior by sitting quietly with his/her feet on the floor under the desk, keeping all four legs of the chair in contact with the floor, for _____ minutes at a time. (Gradually increase expectations as the student demonstrates success.)
2. The student will refrain from tipping his/her chair for _____ minutes at a time. (Gradually increase expectations as the student demonstrates success.)

3. The student will refrain from tipping his/her desk while seated for _____ minutes at a time. (Gradually increase expectations as the student demonstrates success.)
4. The student will keep his/her feet on the floor while seated for _____ minutes at a time. (Gradually increase expectations as the student demonstrates success.)
5. The student will sit quietly while seated for _____ minutes at a time. (Gradually increase expectations as the student demonstrates success.)
6. The student will refrain from touching others as they walk by on _____ out of _____ trials.
7. The student will refrain from tapping objects such as a pencil, paper clip, eraser, ruler, etc., for _____ minutes at a time. (Gradually increase expectations as the student demonstrates success.)

BEHAVIOR 39:   Appears restless

Goals:
1. The student will sit in his/her seat without moving about.
2. The student will wait for assistance without moving about.
3. The student will wait his/her turn without moving about.
4. The student will demonstrate body movements appropriate to the situation.

Objectives:
1. The student will demonstrate body movements appropriate to the situation on _____ out of _____ trials.
2. The student will refrain from making unnecessary body movements for _____ minutes at a time. (Gradually increase expectations as the student demonstrates success.)
3. The student will stop unnecessary body movements when cued by the teacher on _____ out of _____ trials.
4. The student will ask to have a break from the activity, go to a specific location in the classroom, etc., when he/she begins to feel anxious, upset, frustrated, etc., on _____ out of _____ trials.
5. The student will demonstrate appropriate in-seat behavior by sitting quietly with his/her feet on the floor under the desk, keeping all four legs of the chair in contact with the floor, for _____ minutes at a time. (Gradually increase expectations as the student demonstrates success.)
6. The student will keep his/her feet on the floor while seated for _____ minutes at a time. (Gradually increase expectations as the student demonstrates success.)
7. The student will sit quietly while seated for _____ minutes at a time. (Gradually increase expectations as the student demonstrates success.)

BEHAVIOR 40:   Is easily angered, annoyed, or upset

Goals:
1. The student will demonstrate appropriate behavior when angry.
2. The student will demonstrate appropriate behavior when annoyed with others.
3. The student will demonstrate appropriate behavior when upset.

Objectives:
1. The student will be able to settle minor conflicts with others without arguing, yelling, crying, hitting, etc., during _____ out of _____ interactions.
2. The student will tolerate a peer's inappropriate behavior by demonstrating patience and refraining from being verbally or physically aggressive during _____ out of _____ interactions.
3. The student will walk away from a peer or group situation when he/she becomes angry, annoyed, or upset during _____ out of _____ interactions.
4. The student will demonstrate self-control when angered, annoyed, or upset by a peer on _____ out of _____ trials.
5. The student will refrain from arguing, using a harsh tone of voice, yelling, etc., during _____ out of _____ interactions.
6. The student will continue to demonstrate appropriate behavior and interact with others when angry, annoyed, or upset during _____ out of _____ interactions.

BEHAVIOR 41:   Bothers other students who are trying to work, listen, etc.

Goals:
1. The student will refrain from bothering other students who are trying to work, listen, etc.
2. The student will stay on-task.

Objectives:
1. The student will refrain from bothering other students who are trying to work, listen, etc., on _____ out of _____ trials.
2. The student will stay on-task for _____ minutes at a time. (Gradually increase expectations as the student demonstrates success.)
3. The student will interact with other students when appropriate on _____ out of _____ trials.
4. The student will interact with other students during free time, break time, lunch time, etc., on _____ out of _____ trials.
5. The student will ask the teacher's permission prior to interacting with a peer(s) on _____ out of _____ trials.
6. The student will remain appropriately seated until given teacher permission to do otherwise on _____ out of _____ trials.

BEHAVIOR 42:   Makes unnecessary comments or noises in the classroom

Goals:
1. The student will communicate with others in an acceptable manner in the classroom.
2. The student will work quietly in the classroom.

Objectives:
1. The student will gain permission from the teacher, by raising his/her hand, when he/she needs to talk with a peer on _____ out of _____ trials.
2. The student will contribute his/her opinion/answer after being recognized by the teacher on _____ out of _____ trials.
3. The student will wait his/her turn to talk when engaged, or attempting to engage, in interactions with others on _____ out of _____ trials.
4. The student will make comments which are relevant to the situation on _____ out of _____ trials.
5. The student will refrain from making sounds which are inappropriate for the situation on _____ out of _____ trials.
6. The student will make positive comments about others on _____ out of _____ trials.

BEHAVIOR 43:   Makes unnecessary physical contact with others

Goal:
1. The student will make physical contact with others when appropriate.

Objectives:
1. The student will interact with others in a physically appropriate manner on _____ out of _____ trials.
2. The student will refrain from making unnecessary contact such as hugging, touching, etc., when interacting with others on _____ out of _____ trials.
3. The student will touch others in only designated areas such as the arm, shoulder, or hand on _____ out of _____ trials.
4. The student will gain others' attention in an appropriate manner by standing quietly or raising his/her hand until recognized on _____ out of _____ trials.
5. The student will demonstrate acceptable physical contact such as a handshake, pat on the back, "high five," etc., when appropriate on _____ out of _____ trials.

BEHAVIOR 44:   Is impulsive

Goal:
1. The student will demonstrate self-control.

Objectives:
1. The student will wait quietly for assistance from an instructor on _____ out of _____ trials.
2. The student will await his/her turn when engaged in activities with peers on _____ out of _____ trials.
3. The student will make decisions appropriate to the situation on _____ out of _____ trials.
4. The student will attempt a task before asking for assistance on _____ out of _____ trials.
5. The student will ask to use materials before taking them on _____ out of _____ trials.
6. The student will use materials appropriately and return them in the same or better condition on _____ out of _____ trials.
7. The student will stay in his/her seat for _____ minutes at a time. (Gradually increase expectations as the student demonstrates success.)
8. The student will raise his/her hand to leave his/her seat on _____ out of _____ trials.
9. The student will raise his/her hand to gain the teacher's attention on _____ out of _____ trials.
10. The student will listen to directions before beginning a task on _____ out of _____ trials.
11. The student will read directions before beginning a task on _____ out of _____ trials.
12. The student will refrain from touching others during _____ out of _____ interactions.
13. The student will demonstrate consideration/regard for others during _____ out of _____ trials.

BEHAVIOR 45:   Fails to comply with teachers or other school personnel

Goals:
1. The student will follow directives from teachers.
2. The student will follow directives from school personnel.

Objectives:
1. The student will follow through with teacher directives within _____ minutes. (Gradually increase expectations as the student demonstrates success.)
2. The student will follow through with directions given by school personnel within _____ minutes. (Gradually increase expectations as the student demonstrates success.)
3. The student will follow teacher directives when given _____ cues. (Gradually decrease number of cues as the student demonstrates success.)
4. The student will follow school personnel directives when given _____ cues. (Gradually decrease number of cues as the student demonstrates success.)
5. The student will stop an activity when told to do so by the teacher on _____ out of _____ trials.
6. The student will stop an activity when told to do so by school personnel on _____ out of _____ trials.

BEHAVIOR 46:   Ignores consequences of his/her behavior

Goals:
1. The student will consider consequences of his/her behavior.
2. The student will demonstrate consideration of consequences of his/her behavior.

Objectives:
1. The student will identify appropriate consequences of his/her behavior with the teacher on _____ out of _____ trials.
2. The student will behave in such a way as to demonstrate that he/she considered consequences of his/her behavior on _____ out of _____ trials.
3. The student will refrain from reacting impulsively on _____ out of _____ trials.

4. The student will demonstrate consideration of consequences of his/her behavior on _____ out of _____ trials.
5. The student will demonstrate behaviors that will result in positive consequences on _____ out of _____ trials.

BEHAVIOR 47: Fails to follow a routine

Goal:
1. The student will demonstrate the ability to follow a routine.

Objectives:
1. The student will follow a routine, with physical assistance, on _____ out of _____ trials.
2. The student will follow a routine, with verbal reminders, on _____ out of _____ trials.
3. The student will independently follow a routine on _____ out of _____ trials.
4. The student will rely on environmental cues to follow a routine (e.g., class schedule, school schedule, bells, lights turned off and on, clock) on _____ out of _____ trials.

BEHAVIOR 48: Does not follow the rules of games

Goal:
1. The student will follow the rules of games.

Objectives:
1. The student will take turns in group games on _____ out of _____ occasions.
2. The student will interact with peers in group games, with supervision, on _____ out of _____ occasions.
3. The student will interact without supervision, with peers, in group games on _____ out of _____ occasions.
4. The student will follow existing rules of group games, with verbal prompts, on _____ out of _____ occasions.
5. The student will independently follow existing rules of group games on _____ out of _____ occasions.
6. The student will share materials in group games on _____ out of _____ occasions.

BEHAVIOR 49: Leaves seat without permission

Goals:
1. The student will move about the classroom only when necessary.
2. The student will demonstrate body movements appropriate to the situation.

Objectives:
1. The student will leave his/her seat only when given permission by the teacher on _____ out of _____ trials.
2. The student will move about the classroom only when given permission by the teacher on _____ out of _____ trials.
3. The student will go directly to a specific location and immediately return to his/her seat when given permission by the teacher on _____ out of _____ trials.

BEHAVIOR 50: Does not work in a group situation

Goal:
1. The student will be productive when working in a group situation.

Objectives:
1. The student will participate verbally in a group situation on _____ out of _____ occasions.
2. The student will take turns while working in a group situation on _____ out of _____ occasions.

3. The student will share materials while working in a group situation on _____ out of _____ occasions.
4. The student will work with one other student in a group situation on _____ out of _____ occasions.
5. The student will work with all the members of a group on _____ out of _____ occasions.
6. The student will participate physically in a group situation on _____ out of _____ occasions.
7. The student will work independently in a group situation on _____ out of _____ occasions.
8. The student will work in a group situation with supervision on _____ out of _____ occasions.
9. The student will be productive in a group situation on _____ out of _____ occasions.
10. The student's work in a group situation will be done with _____% accuracy.

BEHAVIOR 51: Hops, skips, and jumps when moving from one place to another instead of walking

Goals:
1. The student will walk when moving from one place to another.
2. The student will demonstrate appropriate behavior when moving with a group.

Objectives:
1. The student will demonstrate appropriate behavior when moving on _____ out of _____ trials.
2. The student will stay in line when moving on _____ out of _____ trials.
3. The student will walk quietly on _____ out of _____ trials.
4. The student will keep his/her hands to his/her sides on _____ out of _____ trials.
5. The student will demonstrate appropriate behavior for _____ minutes at a time when walking.
6. The student will walk quietly by the teacher when moving with a group on _____ out of _____ trials.
7. The student will walk quietly by a peer when moving with a group on _____ out of _____ trials.

BEHAVIOR 52: Handles objects

Goals:
1. The student will engage in appropriate behaviors while seated.
2. The student will sit appropriately in his/her seat.
3. The student will demonstrate body movements appropriate to the situation.

Objectives:
1. The student will have in his/her possession only those materials necessary on _____ out of _____ occasions.
2. The student will use only those materials necessary on _____ out of _____ occasions.
3. The student will handle only those materials necessary on _____ out of _____ occasions.
4. The student will engage only in those behaviors necessary for an activity or assignment on _____ out of _____ occasions.

BEHAVIOR 53: Talks beyond what is expected or at inappropriate times

Goals:
1. The student will communicate to others in an acceptable manner in the classroom.
2. The student will talk quietly in the classroom.

Objectives:
1. The student will gain permission from the teacher, by raising his/her hand, when he/she needs to speak on _____ out of _____ trials.
2. The student will contribute his/her opinion/answer after being recognized by the teacher on _____ out of _____ trials.
3. The student will wait his/her turn to talk when engaged, or attempting to engage, in interactions with others on _____ out of _____ trials.

4. The student will make comments which are relevant to the situation on _____ out of _____ trials.
5. The student will end what he/she has to say within a reasonable length of time on _____ out of _____ occasions.

BEHAVIOR 54: Does not wait appropriately for assistance from an instructor

Goal:
1. The student will wait appropriately for assistance from an instructor.

Objectives:
1. The student will wait quietly for assistance from an instructor on _____ out of _____ occasions.
2. The student will continue working on parts of the assignment while waiting for assistance from the instructor on _____ out of _____ occasions.
3. The student will remain seated while waiting for assistance from an instructor on _____ out of _____ occasions.

BEHAVIOR 55: Does not adjust behavior to expectations of different situations

Goals:
1. The student will change his/her behavior from one situation to another.
2. The student will demonstrate flexibility in his/her behavior.

Objectives:
1. The student will change his/her behavior from one situation to another on _____ out of _____ trials.
2. The student will demonstrate flexibility in his/her behavior on _____ out of _____ trials.
3. The student will stop an activity when cued by the teacher on _____ out of _____ trials.
4. The student will stop an activity and begin another within _____ minutes. (Gradually increase expectations as the student demonstrates success.)
5. The student will demonstrate behavior appropriate for the situation on _____ out of _____ trials.
6. The student will calm down when he/she enters the building on _____ out of _____ trials.
7. At the end of recess, the student will calm down within _____ minutes and enter the building in a quiet manner.
8. The student will engage in a relaxation activity following a stimulating activity on _____ out of _____ trials.
9. The student will begin a task within _____ minutes. (Gradually increase expectations as the student demonstrates success.)

BEHAVIOR 56: Engages in inappropriate behaviors while seated

Goals:
1. The student will engage in appropriate behaviors while seated.
2. The student will sit appropriately in his/her seat.

Objectives:
1. The student will demonstrate appropriate in-seat behavior by sitting quietly with his/her feet on the floor under the desk, keeping all four legs of the chair in contact with the floor, for _____ minutes at a time. (Gradually increase expectations as the student demonstrates success.)
2. The student will refrain from tipping his/her chair for _____ minutes at a time. (Gradually increase expectations as the student demonstrates success.)
3. The student will refrain from tipping his/her desk while seated for _____ minutes at a time. (Gradually increase expectations as the student demonstrates success.)
4. The student will keep his/her feet on the floor while seated for _____ minutes at a time. (Gradually increase expectations as the student demonstrates success.)

5. The student will sit quietly while seated for _____ minutes at a time. (Gradually increase expectations as the student demonstrates success.)
6. The student will refrain from touching others as they walk by on _____ out of _____ trials.
7. The student will refrain from tapping objects such as a pencil, paper clip, eraser, ruler, etc., for _____ minutes at a time. (Gradually increase expectations as the student demonstrates success.)

BEHAVIOR 57: Becomes overexcited

Goal:
1. The student will maintain self-control in stimulating activities.

Objectives:
1. The student will temporarily remove himself/herself from an activity when he/she begins to become overexcited on _____ out of _____ trials.
2. The student will ask for teacher assistance when he/she becomes overexcited on _____ out of _____ trials.
3. The student will use a tone of voice appropriate to the situation on _____ out of _____ trials.
4. The student will maintain self-control when involved in _____ out of _____ stimulating activities.
5. The student will walk away from a stimulating situation and return when he/she has gained control of his/her behavior on _____ out of _____ trials.
6. The student will stop an activity when told to do so by the teacher on _____ out of _____ trials.
7. The student will physically interact with others in an appropriate manner on _____ out of _____ trials.
8. The student will refrain from reacting impulsively in _____ out of _____ stimulating activities.
9. The student will remain on-task in the presence of stimuli in the classroom on _____ out of _____ trials.
10. The student will remain quietly seated in the presence of stimuli on _____ out of _____ trials.
11. The student will follow rules in the presence of stimuli on _____ out of _____ trials.

BEHAVIOR 58: Demonstrates inappropriate behavior when moving with a group

Goal:
1. The student will demonstrate appropriate behavior when moving with a group.

Objectives:
1. The student will demonstrate appropriate behavior when moving with a group on _____ out of _____ trials.
2. The student will stay in line when moving with a group on _____ out of _____ trials.
3. The student will walk quietly when moving with a group on _____ out of _____ trials.
4. The student will keep his/her hands to his/her sides when moving with a group on _____ out of _____ trials.
5. The student will demonstrate appropriate behavior for _____ minutes at a time when moving with a group.
6. The student will walk quietly by the teacher when moving with a group on _____ out of _____ trials.
7. The student will walk quietly by a peer when moving with a group on _____ out of _____ trials.

BEHAVIOR 59: Moves about unnecessarily

Goals:
1. The student will move about the classroom only when necessary.
2. The student will demonstrate body movements appropriate to the situation.

Objectives:
1. The student will leave his/her seat only when given permission by the teacher on _____ out of _____ trials.
2. The student will move about the classroom only when given permission by the teacher on _____ out of _____ trials.
3. The student will go directly to a specific location and immediately return to his/her seat when given permission by the teacher on _____ out of _____ trials.

4. The student will demonstrate body movements appropriate to the situation on _____ out of _____ trials.
5. The student will refrain from making unnecessary body movements for _____ minutes at a time. (Gradually increase expectations as the student demonstrates success.)
6. The student will stop unnecessary body movements when cued by the teacher on _____ out of _____ trials.
7. The student will ask to have a break from the activity, go to a specific location in the classroom, etc., when he/she begins to feel anxious, upset, frustrated, etc., on _____ out of _____ trials.

BEHAVIOR 60: Engages in nervous habits

Goals:
1. The student will maintain self-control in stimulating activities.
2. The student will not engage in nervous habits.

Objectives:
1. The student will discontinue engaging in the nervous habit when cued by the teacher on _____ out of _____ trials.
2. The student will temporarily remove himself/herself from a stimulating activity on _____ out of _____ trials.
3. The student will maintain self-control when engaged in _____ out of _____ stimulating activities.
4. The student will refrain from biting his/her fingernails during _____ out of _____ stimulating activities.
5. The student will refrain from twirling his/her hair during _____ out of _____ stimulating activities.
6. The student will refrain from chewing the inside of his/her cheek during _____ out of _____ stimulating activities.
7. The student will refrain from chewing pencils or pens during _____ out of _____ stimulating activities.
8. The student will refrain from spinning/twirling objects during _____ out of _____ stimulating activities.

> **Note: The goals and objectives for the following behaviors have been included to supplement the goals and objectives for the original 60 behaviors which are found on the Attention Deficit Disorders Evaluation Scale. Related intervention strategies may be found in Section V.**

BEHAVIOR 61: Has difficulty with short-term or long-term memory

Goals:
1. The student will improve his/her short-term memory skills.
2. The student will improve his/her long-term memory skills.
3. The student will improve his/her information retrieval skills.

Objectives:
1. The student will independently follow one-step directions on __ out of __ trials.
2. The student will independently follow two- or three-step directions on __ out of __ trials.
3. The student will memorize a short poem and recite it word for word on __ out of __ trials.
4. The student will immediately remember information that was presented and removed on __ out of __ trials.
5. The student will recall information at short intervals of 10-15 minutes on __ out of __ trials.
6. The student will recall information at intervals of several hours or more on __ out of __ trials.
7. The student will recall information at intervals of several days or weeks on __ out of __ trials.

BEHAVIOR 62: Does not respond appropriately to environmental cues

Goals:
1. The student will improve his/her independent behavior.

2. The student will improve his/her independent behavior in academic settings.
3. The student will improve his/her independent behavior in nonacademic settings.
4. The student will improve his/her independent behavior outside the classroom.
5. The student will improve his/her independent behavior in the classroom.

Objectives:
1. The student will respond appropriately to environmental cues when given verbal reminders on ____ out of ____ occasions.
2. The student will respond independently to environmental cues on ____ out of ____ occasions.
3. The student will use environmental cues to move throughout the building when appropriate on ____ out of ____ occasions.
4. The student will use environmental cues in order to find locations in the building on __ out of ____ occasions.

BEHAVIOR 63:   Demonstrates difficulty with auditory memory

Goals:
1. The student will improve his/her auditory memory.
2. The student will improve his/her awareness and attention to information and activities in the environment.

Objectives:
1. The student will recognize information received auditorily (e.g., sounds, words, phrases, sentences, etc.) when presented, removed, and presented again with __% accuracy.
2. The student will recall information received auditorily (e.g., sounds, words, phrases, sentences, etc.) at short intervals (10-15 minutes) with __% accuracy.
3. The student will recall information received auditorily (e.g., sounds, words, phrases, sentences, etc.) at intervals of several hours with __% accuracy.
4. The student will recall information received auditorily (e.g., sounds, words, phrases, sentences, etc.) at intervals of days or weeks with __% accuracy.

BEHAVIOR 64:   Demonstrates difficulty with visual memory

Goals:
1. The student will improve his/her visual memory.
2. The student will improve his/her awareness and attention to information and activities in the environment.

Objectives:
1. The student will match visual images (e.g., pictures, letters, numbers, etc.) with __% accuracy.
2. The student will recognize visual images (e.g., pictures, letters, numbers, etc.) presented, removed, and presented again with __% accuracy.
3. The student will recall visual images (e.g., pictures, letters, numbers, words, etc.) at short intervals (10-15 minutes) with __% accuracy.
4. The student will recall visual images (e.g., pictures, letters, numbers, words, etc.) at intervals of several hours with __% accuracy.
5. The student will recall visual images (e.g., pictures, letters, numbers, words, etc.) at intervals of days or weeks with __% accuracy.

BEHAVIOR 65:   Has limited note-taking skills

Goals:
1. The student will improve his/her academic task-related behavior.

2. The student will improve his/her academic performance.
3. The student will improve his/her note-taking skills.

Objectives:
1. The student will write key words presented in lessons on __ out of __ trials.
2. The student will write key phrases presented in lessons on __ out of __ trials.
3. The student will tape record information presented in class and write notes from taped information on __ out of __ trials.
4. The student will take notes from information presented visually (e.g., chalkboard, overhead projector, etc.) on __ out of __ trials.
5. The student will take notes from information presented auditorally (e.g., tape recorder, lecture, etc.) on __ out of __ trials.
6. The student will take notes during class when necessary with verbal prompts on __ out of __ occasions.
7. The student will independently take notes during class when necessary on __ out of __ occasions.
8. The student will rely on environmental cues (e.g., other students, visual aids) to take notes during class when necessary on __ out of __ occasions.
9. The student will take notes related to the presentation on __ out of __ occasions.

BEHAVIOR 66:   Has limited memory skills

Goals:
1. The student will improve his/her short-term memory skills.
2. The student will improve his/her long-term memory skills.
3. The student will improve his/her information retrieval skills.

Objectives:
1. The student will independently follow one-step directions on __ out of __ trials.
2. The student will independently follow two- or three-step directions on __ out of __ trials.
3. The student will memorize a short poem and recite it word for word on __ out of __ trials.
4. The student will immediately remember information that was presented and removed on __ out of __ trials.
5. The student will recall information at short intervals of 10-15 minutes on __ out of __ trials.
6. The student will recall information at intervals of several hours or more on __ out of __ trials.
7. The student will recall information at intervals of several days or weeks on __ out of __ trials.
8. The student will remember the events in a daily routine on __ out of __ occasions.
9. The student will memorize sequential information (e.g., days of the week, months of the year, seasons, alphabet, etc.) with __% accuracy.
10. The student will remember materials necessary for a task or assignment on __ out of __ trials.

BEHAVIOR 67:   Requires repeated drill and practice to learn what other students master easily

Goals:
1. The student will improve his/her ability to grasp concepts at a faster pace.

Objectives:
1. The student will use visual cues to aid his/her ability to grasp concepts at a faster pace with __% accuracy.
2. The student will use auditory cues to aid his/her ability to grasp concepts at a faster pace with __% accuracy.
3. The student will use visual and auditory cues to aid his/her ability to grasp concepts at a faster pace with __% accuracy.
4. The student will learn __ new concepts per week. (Gradually increase expectations as the student demonstrates success.)
5. The student will independently review concepts and pass a weekly review with the teacher with __% accuracy.
6. The student will independently review concepts and pass a monthly review with the teacher with __% accuracy.

BEHAVIOR 68:   Does not demonstrate an understanding of spatial relationships

Goals:
1. The student will demonstrate an understanding of spatial relationships.

Objectives:
1. The student will imitate the actions of placing objects to demonstrate spatial relationships (e.g., near-far, above-below, over-under, etc.) with __% accuracy.
2. The student will independently demonstrate spatial relationships (e.g., near-far, above-below, over-under, etc.) with __% accuracy.
3. The student will recognize spatial relationships (e.g., near-far, above-below, over-under, etc.) with visual and verbal cues with __% accuracy.
4. The student will recognize spatial relationships (e.g., near-far, above-below, over-under, etc.) independently with __% accuracy.

BEHAVIOR 69:   Does not demonstrate an understanding of directionality

Goals:
1. The student will demonstrate an understanding of directionality.

Objectives:
1. The student will imitate the actions of placing objects to demonstrate directionality (e.g., left-right, forward-backward, east-west, etc.) with __% accuracy.
2. The student will independently demonstrate directionality (e.g., left-right, forward-backward, east-west, etc.) with __% accuracy.
3. The student will recognize directionality (e.g., left-right, forward-backward, east-west, etc.) with visual cues and verbal cues with __% accuracy.
4. The student will recognize directionality (e.g., left-right, forward-backward, east-west, etc.) independently with __% accuracy.

BEHAVIOR 70:   Demonstrates visual perception problems

Goals:
1. The student will improve his/her visual perception.

Objectives:
1. The student will identify objects in a picture with __% accuracy.
2. The student will recall information presented in visual form at an interval of ___ (indicate a length of time such as minutes, hours, days, weeks, etc.) with __% accuracy.
3. The student will follow written directions with __% accuracy.

BEHAVIOR 71:   Has difficulty classifying

Goals:
1. The student will demonstrate the ability to classify.

Objectives:
1. The student will recognize similarities of people, places, things, and concepts with __% accuracy.
2. The student will recognize differences of people, places, things, and concepts with __% accuracy.
3. The student will match similarities of people, places, things, and concepts with __% accuracy.

4. The student with match differences of people, places, things, and concepts with __% accuracy.
5. The student will verbally or in written form identify similarities of people, places, things, or concepts with __% accuracy.
6. The student will verbally or in written form identify differences of people, places, things, and concepts with __% accuracy.

BEHAVIOR 72: Demonstrates confusion

Goals:
1. The student will improve his/her awareness and attention to information and activities in the environment.
2. The student will improve his/her skills in logical thinking.

Objectives:
1. The student will find locations in the building, materials, etc., with verbal cues and directions __% of the time.
2. The student will use environmental cues (e.g., signs, labels, room numbers, etc.) to find locations in the building, materials, etc., __% of the time.
3. The student will independently find locations in the building, materials, etc., __% of the time.

BEHAVIOR 73: Perseverates - does the same thing over and over

Goals:
1. The student will improve his/her ability to determine when an activity or behavior is no longer appropriate.

Objectives:
1. The student will discontinue behaviors within __ minutes of the end of an activity, when told to stop, etc., on __ out of __ trials.
2. The student will discontinue behaviors at the end of an activity, when told to stop, etc., on __ out of __ trials.

BEHAVIOR 74: Fails to demonstrate logical thinking

Goals:
1. The student will improve his/her logical thinking skills.

Objectives:
1. The student will make appropriate decisions, with assistance, in __ out of __ situations.
2. The student will independently make appropriate decisions in __ out of __ situations.
3. The student will solve problems, with assistance, in __ out of __ situations.
4. The student will independently solve problems in __ out of __ situations.
5. The student will make correct inferences, with assistance, in __ out of __ situations.
6. The student will independently make correct inferences in __ out of __ situations.

BEHAVIOR 75: Does not follow directives from teachers or other school personnel

Goals:
1. The student will follow directives from teachers.
2. The student will follow directives from school personnel.

Objectives:
1. The student will follow through with teacher directives within __ minutes. (Gradually increase expectations as the student demonstrates success.)

2. The student will follow through with directions given by school personnel within __ minutes. (Gradually increase expectations as the student demonstrates success.)
3. The student will follow teacher directives when given __ cues. (Gradually decrease number of cues as the student demonstrates success.)
4. The student will follow school personnel directives when given __ cues. (Gradually decrease number of cues as the student demonstrates success.)
5. The student will stop an activity when told to do so by school personnel on __ out of __ trials.

BEHAVIOR 76:   Does not follow multistep verbal directions

Goals:
1. The student will improve his/her ability to follow multistep verbal directions.

Objectives:
1. The student will maintain eye contact when information is being communicated __% of the time.
2. The student will listen quietly when verbal directions are given __% of the time.
3. The student will repeat what is said with __% accuracy.
4. The student will follow multistep verbal directions, with reminders, with __% accuracy.
5. The student will independently follow multistep verbal directions with __% accuracy.
6. The student will ask for clarification of verbal directions not understood on __ out of __ occasions.
7. The student will follow multistep verbal directions within a given period of time on __ out of __ occasions.

BEHAVIOR 77:   Has limited test-taking skills

Goals:
1. The student will improve his/her test-taking skills.

Objectives:
1. The student will have necessary materials available for test-taking on __ out of __ trials.
2. The student will have a clear work area when taking a test on __ out of __ trials.
3. The student will remain on-task when completing a test on __ out of __ trials.
4. The student will follow directions for completion on the test on __ out of __ trials.
5. The student will take his/her time when completing a test on __ out of __ trials.
6. The student will engage in a relaxation activity prior to taking a test on __ out of __ occasions.
7. The student will perform classroom tests with __% accuracy.
8. The student will meet a __% level of mastery on classroom tests. (Gradually increase expectations as the student demonstrates success.)

BEHAVIOR 78:   Has limited task focus and task completion

Goals:
1. The student will complete assigned tasks.
2. The student will improve his/her ability to remain on-task.
3. The student will improve his/her awareness and attention to information and activities in the environment.

Objectives:
1. The student will work on a task for __ out of __ minutes per day.
2. The student will work on a task until completed on __ out of __ trials.
3. The student will attend to an activity for __ minutes.
4. The student will attend to an activity until it is completed on __ out of __ trials.
5. The student will complete a task before going on to the next task on __ out of __ trials.

6. The student will complete __ out of __ assigned tasks per day.
7. The student will use the time provided to work on assigned tasks in order to complete __ tasks per day.
8. The student will demonstrate on-task behavior by sitting quietly at his/her seat, looking at his/her materials, and performing the task for __ minutes at a time. (Gradually increase expectations as the student demonstrates success.)

BEHAVIOR 79:   Performs classroom tests or quizzes at a failing level

Goals:
1. The student will improve his/her performance on classroom tests.
2. The student will improve his/her performance on classroom quizzes.

Objectives:
1. The student will perform classroom tests with __% accuracy. (Gradually increase expectations as the student demonstrates success.)
2. The student will perform classroom quizzes with __% accuracy. (Gradually increase expectations as the student demonstrates success.)
3. The student will meet a __% level of mastery on classroom tests. (Gradually increase expectations as the student demonstrates success.)
4. The student will meet a __% level of mastery on classroom quizzes. (Gradually increase expectations as the student demonstrates success.)

BEHAVIOR 80:   Has difficulty retrieving or recalling concepts, persons, places, etc.

Goals:
1. The student will improve his/her short-term memory.
2. The student will improve his/her long-term memory.
3. The student will improve his/her awareness and attention to information and activities in the environment.

Objectives:
1. The student will recall or name objects, persons, places, etc., after they are presented and then removed with __% accuracy.
2. The student will recall or name objects, persons, places, etc., at short intervals (10-15 minutes) with __% accuracy.
3. The student will recall or name objects, persons, places, etc., at intervals of several hours with __% accuracy.
4. The student will recall or name objects, persons, places, etc., at intervals of days or weeks with __% accuracy.
5. The student will recall or name objects, persons, places, etc., with visual or verbal cues __% of the time.
6. The student will independently recall or name objects, persons, places, etc., __% of the time.

BEHAVIOR 81:   Fails to generalize knowledge from one situation to another

Goals:
1. The student will improve his/her ability to generalize knowledge from one situation to another.

Objectives:
1. The student will generalize basic concepts learned to application situations (e.g., will apply knowledge of word *stop* to a STOP sign set up in classroom, will use knowledge of counting by five's to add the value of nickels, etc.) with __% accuracy.
2. The student will generalize information given or learned to problem-solving situations with __% accuracy.
3. The student will generalize information learned to quizzes, tests, etc., with __% accuracy.

BEHAVIOR 82: **Remembers information one time but not the next**

Goals:
1. The student will improve his/her short-term memory.
2. The student will improve his/her long-term memory.
3. The student will improve his/her awareness and attention to information and activities in the environment.

Objectives:
1. The student will remember information presented, removed, and presented again immediately with __% accuracy.
2. The student will remember information at short intervals (10-15 minutes) with __% accuracy.
3. The student will remember information at intervals of several hours with __% accuracy.
4. The student will remember information at intervals of days or weeks with __% accuracy.

BEHAVIOR 83: **Requires slow, sequential, substantially broken-down presentation of concepts**

Goals:
1. The student will improve his/her ability to grasp new concepts.
2. The student will improve his/her awareness and attention to information and activities in the environment.

Objectives:
1. The student will understand what is said or presented to him/her at a slowed pace with __% accuracy.
2. The student will maintain eye contact when information is being communicated __% of the time.
3. The student will listen quietly when verbal directions are given __% of the time.
4. The student will be able to repeat what is said or presented to him/her with __% accuracy.
5. The student will respond appropriately to what is said or presented, with reminders, with __% accuracy.
6. The student will independently respond appropriately to what is said or presented to him/her with __% accuracy.

BEHAVIOR 84: **Turns in incomplete or inaccurately finished assignments**

Goals:
1. The student will increase the number of completed assignments turned in.
2. The student will improve the accuracy of assignments turned in.

Objectives:
1. The student will complete an assignment before turning it in on __ out of __ occasions.
2. The student will complete __ out of __ assignments per day.
3. The student will use the time provided to work on assigned tasks in order to complete __ assigned tasks per day.
4. The student will complete __ out of __ homework assignments each day.
5. The student will complete __ out of __ homework assignments each week.
6. The student will complete classroom assignments with a __% level of minimal accuracy (indicate a level of performance).
7. The student will complete homework assignments with a __% level of minimal accuracy (indicate a level of performance).

BEHAVIOR 85: **Has difficulty taking class notes**

Goals:
1. The student will improve his/her academic task-related behavior.

2. The student will improve his/her academic performance.
3. The student will improve his/her ability to take class notes.

Objectives:
1. The student will write key words presented in lessons on __ out of __ trials.
2. The student will write key phrases presented in lessons on __ out of __ trials.
3. The student will take notes from a tape recording of information presented in class on __ out of __ trials.
4. The student will take notes from information presented visually (e.g., chalkboard, overhead projector, etc.) on __ out of __ trials.
5. The student will take notes from information presented auditorally (e.g., tape recording, lecture, etc.) on ___ out of ___ trials.
6. The student will take notes during class when necessary with verbal prompts on __ out of __ occasions.
7. The student will independently take notes during class when necessary on __ out of __ occasions.
8. The student will rely on environmental cues (e.g., other students, visual aids) to take notes during class when necessary on __ out of __ occasions.
9. The student will take notes related to the presentation on __ out of __ occasions.

BEHAVIOR 86:   Is reluctant to attempt new assignments or tasks

Goals:
1. The student will attempt new assignments.
2. The student will attempt new tasks.

Objectives:
1. The student will attempt new assignments or tasks with teacher assistance on ___ out of ___ trials.
2. The student will independently attempt new assignments or tasks on ___ out of ___ trials.
3. The student will read the directions when attempting a new assignment or task on ___ out of ___ trials.
4. The student will perform a new assignment or task along with a peer on ___ out of ___ trials.
5. The student will attempt ___ out of ___ new assignments or tasks per day.
6. The student will begin a new assignment or task within ___ minutes.
7. The student will listen to directions prior to attempting a new assignment or task on ___ out of ___ trials.
8. The student will attempt to perform a new assignment or task before asking for teacher assistance on ___ out of ___ trials.
9. The student will work for ___ minutes without requiring teacher assistance on ___ out of ___ trials.

BEHAVIOR 87:   Does not turn in homework assignments

Goal:
1. The student will turn in homework assignments.

Objectives:
1. The student will complete ___ out of ___ homework assignments each day.
2. The student will complete ___ out of ___ homework assignments each week.
3. The student will bring ___ out of ___ of his/her completed homework assignments to school and turn them in each day.
4. The student will bring ___ out of ___ of his/her completed homework assignments to school and turn them in each week.
5. The student will carry his/her homework assignments to and from school in a book bag/backpack in order to prevent loss on ___ out of ___ trials.

6. The student will perform ___ out of ___ homework assignments at home and return them to school each day.
7. The student will perform ___ out of ___ homework assignments at home and return them to school each week.

BEHAVIOR 88: Is unable to work appropriately with peers in a tutoring situation

Goals:
1. The student will improve his/her interpersonal behavior.
2. The student will improve his/her interpersonal behavior in academic settings.

Objectives:
1. The student will follow directions given by a peer in a tutoring situation on __ out of __ occasions.
2. The student will share materials with peers in a tutoring situation on __ out of __ occasions.
3. The student will work quietly with peers in a tutoring situation on __ out of __ occasions.
4. The student will remain seated with peers in a tutoring situation on __ out of __ occasions.
5. The student will take turns with peers in a tutoring situation on __ out of __ occasions.
6. The student will take a leadership role with peers in a tutoring situation on __ out of __ occasions.
7. The student will verbally participate with peers in a tutoring situation on __ out of __ occasions.
8. The student will physically participate with peers in a tutoring situation on __ out of __ occasions.

BEHAVIOR 89: Does not take notes during class when necessary.

Goals:
1. The student will improve his/her academic task-related behavior.
2. The student will improve his/her academic performance.

Objectives:
1. The student will take notes during class when necessary with verbal prompts on __ out of __ occasions.
2. The student will independently take notes during class when necessary on __ out of __ occasions.
3. The student will rely on environmental cues (e.g., other students, visual aids) to take notes during class when necessary on __ out of __ occasions.
4. The student will take notes related to the presentation on __ out of __ occasions.

BEHAVIOR 90: Does not follow the rules of the classroom

Goal:
1. The student will follow the rules of the classroom.

Objectives:
1. The student will follow the rules of the classroom on ___ out of ___ trials.
2. The student will talk only after being given permission on ___ out of ___ trials.
3. The student will ask to leave his/her seat before doing so on ___ out of ___ trials.
4. The student will immediately respond to redirection on ___ out of ___ trials.
5. The student will follow the rules of the classroom with ___ reminders.
6. The student will independently follow the rules of the classroom on ___ out of ___ trials.

BEHAVIOR 91: Has unexcused absences

Goals:
1. The student will improve his/her attendance at school.
2. The student will improve his/her attendance in class.

Objectives:
1. The student will attend ___ out of ___ school days per week. (Gradually increase expectations as the student demonstrates success.)
2. The student will attend ___ out of ___ school days per month. (Gradually increase expectations as the student demonstrates success.)
3. The student will attend ___ out of ___ class periods per week. (Gradually increase expectations as the student demonstrates success.)
4. The student will attend ___ out of ___ class periods per month. (Gradually increase expectations as the student demonstrates success.)

BEHAVIOR 92:   Has unexcused tardiness

Goal:
1. The student will improve his/her punctuality.

Objectives:
1. The student will be on time to school on ___ out of ___ days per week. (Gradually increase expectations as the student demonstrates success.)
2. The student will be on time to school on ___ out of ___ days per month. (Gradually increase expectations as the student demonstrates success.)
3. The student will be on time to class on ___ out of ___ class periods per day. (Gradually increase expectations as the student demonstrates success.)
4. The student will be on time to class on ___ out of ___ class periods per week. (Gradually increase expectations as the student demonstrates success.)
5. The student will be on time to (specified activity) on ___ out of ___ days per week. (Gradually increase expectations as the student demonstrates success.)
6. The student will be on time to (specified activity) on ___ out of ___ days per month. (Gradually increase expectations as the student demonstrates success.)

BEHAVIOR 93:   Does not check completed work for accuracy

Goals:
1. The student will check completed assignments for accuracy.
2. The student will improve his/her academic performance.

Objectives:
1. The student will check his/her written language for capitalization errors on ___ out of ___ occasions.
2. The student will check his/her written language for punctuation errors on ___ out of ___ occasions.
3. The student will proofread his/her written language for errors on ___ out of ___ occasions.
4. The student will check his/her calculations on math assignments on ___ out of ___ occasions.
5. The student will check his/her work for legibility on ___ out of ___ occasions.
6. The student will check his/her work for spelling errors on ___ out of ___ occasions.
7. The student will review his/her responses on tests/quizzes on ___ out of ___ occasions.

BEHAVIOR 94:   Does not have necessary materials when needed

Goals:
1. The student will have necessary materials when needed.
2. The student will improve his/her organizational skills.

Objectives:
1. The student will put materials where they belong on ___ out of ___ occasions.

2. The student will carry his/her materials to and from activities in a book bag/backpack in order to prevent loss on __ out of __ occasions.
3. The student will organize his/her materials at the beginning and end of each assigned task on __ out of __ trials.
4. The student will demonstrate appropriate care and handling of school-related materials on __ out of __ trials.
5. The student will bring materials for projects on __ out of __ trials.

BEHAVIOR 95:   Does not demonstrate appropriate use of school-related materials

Goals:
1. The student will improve his/her independent behavior.
2. The student will improve his/her independent behavior in academic settings.
3. The student will improve his/her independent behavior in nonacademic settings.
4. The student will improve his/her independent behavior outside the classroom.
5. The student will improve his/her independent behavior in the classroom.

Objectives:
1. The student will use school-related materials for their designated purposes on __ out of __ occasions.
2. The student will use school-related materials according to accepted procedures on __ out of __ occasions.
3. The student will use school-related materials with supervision on __ out of __ occasions.
4. The student will independently use school-related materials on __ out of __ occasions.
5. The student will return school-related materials in the same or better condition on __ out of __ occasions.

BEHAVIOR 96:   Has difficulty differentiating speech sounds heard

Goals:
1. The student will improve listening skills in academic settings.
2. The student will improve listening skills in nonacademic settings.
3. The student will attend more successfully to specific sounds in the environment.

Objectives:
1. The student will produce different speech sounds (e.g., /ch/ and /sh/ sounds) with __% accuracy.
2. The student will produce different speech sounds (e.g., /ch/ and /sh/ sounds, vowel sounds, consonant sounds, rhyming words, etc.) with __% accuracy.
3. The student will recognize similar speech sounds (e.g., /ch/ and /sh/ sounds, vowel sounds, consonant sounds, rhyming words, etc.) with __% accuracy.
4. The student will differentiate speech sounds heard (e.g., /ch/ and /sh/ sounds, similar vowel sounds, similar consonant sounds, rhyming words, etc.) with __% accuracy.

BEHAVIOR 97:   Has difficulty imitating speech sounds

Goals:
1. The student will improve his/her production of speech sounds.

Objectives:
1. The student will recognize speech sounds with __% accuracy.
2. The student will imitate speech sounds with verbal prompting and assistance with __% accuracy.
3. The student will imitate speech sounds independently with __% accuracy.

BEHAVIOR 98: **Omits, adds, substitutes, or rearranges sounds or words when speaking**

Goals:
1. The student will improve his/her production of speech sounds.
2. The student will improve the ability to express himself/herself verbally.

Objectives:
1. The student will use complete phrases with assistance when speaking with __% accuracy.
2. The student will independently use complete phrases when speaking with __% accuracy.
3. The student will complete sentences with assistance when speaking with __% accuracy.
4. The student will independently use complete sentences when speaking with __% accuracy.

BEHAVIOR 99: **Distorts or mispronounces words or sounds when speaking (not attributed to dialect or accent)**

Goals:
1. The student will improve his/her conversational speech.
2. The student will improve the fluency of his/her speech.
3. The student will improve the ability to express himself/herself verbally.

Objectives:
1. The student will recognize words or sounds heard with __% accuracy.
2. The student will pronounce words or sounds made in isolation with __% accuracy.
3. The student will pronounce words or sounds when speaking with __% accuracy.

BEHAVIOR 100: **Does not use appropriate subject-verb agreement when speaking**

Goals:
1. The student will improve the ability to express himself/herself verbally.
2. The student will improve his/her grammatical speech.

Objectives:
1. The student will recognize correct subject-verb agreement with __% accuracy.
2. The student will use single subjects with single verbs with __% accuracy.
3. The student will use plural subjects with plural verbs with __% accuracy.
4. The student will demonstrate correct subject-verb agreement in written activities (e.g., worksheets) with __% accuracy.
5. The student will use correct subject-verb agreement when speaking with __% accuracy.

BEHAVIOR 101: **Does not carry on conversations with peers and adults**

Goals:
1. The student will improve his/her ability to carry on conversations with peers and adults.

Objectives:
1. The student will respond to conversational questions from peers __% of the time.
2. The student will respond to conversational questions from adults __% of the time.
3. The student will engage in conversation with peers __% of the time he/she is spoken to by a peer.
4. The student will engage in conversation with adults __% of the time he/she is spoken to by an adult.
5. The student will initiate conversations with peers (identify some criteria such as once a day, three times a day, etc.).

6. The student will initiate conversations with adults (identify some criteria such as once a day, three times a day, etc.).

BEHAVIOR 102: Has a limited speaking vocabulary

Goals:
1. The student will increase his/her speaking vocabulary.

Objectives:
1. The student will be able to verbally express his/her needs with __% accuracy.
2. The student will be able to verbally relate experiences with __% accuracy.
3. The student will respond to conversational questions on __ out of __ occasions.
4. The student will engage in conversation (identify some criteria such as once a day, three times a day, etc.).
5. The student will be able to verbally explain something to a peer or teacher with __% accuracy.

BEHAVIOR 103: Fails to use verb tenses correctly when speaking

Goals:
1. The student will improve his/her grammatical speech.

Objectives:
1. The student will use the present verb tense correctly when speaking with __% accuracy.
2. The student will use the past verb tense correctly when speaking with __% accuracy.
3. The student will use the future verb tense correctly when speaking with __% accuracy.

BEHAVIOR 104: Speaks dysfluently

Goals:
1. The student will improve the fluency of his/her speech.

Objectives:
1. The student will speak at a pace with repetitions and corrections in order to be understood by a listener __% of the time.
2. The student will correctly pause between words, phrases, and sentences on __ out of __ occasions.
3. The student will speak at a pace that can be understood by a listener __% of the time.

BEHAVIOR 105: Does not complete statements or thoughts when speaking

Goals:
1. The student will improve his/her conversational speech.
2. The student will improve the fluency of his/her speech.
3. The student will improve the ability to express himself/herself verbally.

Objectives:
1. The student will speak in single words which express thoughts with __% accuracy.
2. The student will speak in complete phrases which express thoughts with __% accuracy.
3. The student will speak in complete sentences which express thoughts with __% accuracy.
4. The student will adequately express thoughts (e.g., using correct words to express himself/herself) with __% accuracy.

BEHAVIOR 106: Fails to demonstrate word attack skills

Goals:
1. The student will improve his/her word attack skills.

Objectives:
1. The student will use picture clues to identify words in a story with __% accuracy.
2. The student will use context clues to identify words in a story with __% accuracy.
3. The student will use phonic clues to identify words with __% accuracy.
4. The student will use word attack skills to identify words with __% accuracy.

BEHAVIOR 107: Fails to correctly answer comprehension questions from reading activities

Goals:
1. The student will improve his/her reading comprehension.

Objectives:
1. The student will read and answer comprehension questions about individual words with __% accuracy.
2. The student will read and answer comprehension questions about individual phrases with __% accuracy.
3. The student will read and answer comprehension questions about individual sentences with __% accuracy.
4. The student will read and answer comprehension questions about individual paragraphs with __% accuracy.
5. The student will read and answer comprehension questions about short stories or chapters with __% accuracy.
6. The student will answer comprehension questions from reading activities with __% accuracy.

BEHAVIOR 108: Has difficulty with sound-symbol relationships

Goals:
1. The student will improve his/her ability to recognize sound-symbol relationships.

Objectives:
1. The student will recognize letters of the alphabet with __% accuracy.
2. The student, when presented a letter, will be able to recognize the sound that it makes with __% accuracy.
3. The student, when presented a sound, will be able to recognize the letter of the alphabet that represents the sound with __% accuracy.
4. The student will recognize sound-symbol relationships with __% accuracy.

BEHAVIOR 109: Has difficulty with phonic skills when reading

Goals:
1. The student will improve his/her phonic skills.

Objectives:
1. The student will orally produce short vowel sounds with __% accuracy.
2. The student will recognize short vowel sounds in words with __% accuracy.
3. The student will decode single syllable words with short vowel sounds with __% accuracy.
4. The student will orally produce long vowel sounds with __% accuracy.
5. The student will recognize long vowel sounds in words with __% accuracy.
6. The student will demonstrate the vowel-consonant silent *e* rule with __% accuracy.
7. The student will decode words following the vowel-consonant silent *e* pattern with __% accuracy.
8. The student will use phonic skills to sound out words when reading with __% accuracy.

BEHAVIOR 110: Does not discriminate between similar letters and words

Goals:
1. The student will improve his/her ability to discriminate between similar letters and words.

Objectives:
1. The student will recognize the letters of the alphabet with __% accuracy.
2. The student will recognize similar letters of the alphabet (e.g., *m* and *n*, *b* and *d*), when presented individually, with __% accuracy.
3. The student will recognize similar letters of the alphabet (e.g., *m* and *n*, *b* and *d*), when presented together, with __% accuracy.
4. The student will recognize similar letters of the alphabet (e.g., *m* and *n*, *b* and *d*), when they appear in words, with __% accuracy.
5. The student will recognize a sight word vocabulary, when the words are presented individually, with __% accuracy.
6. The student will recognize a sight word vocabulary, when the words are presented together, with __% accuracy.
7. The student will recognize a sight word vocabulary, when the word appears in reading material, with __% accuracy.

BEHAVIOR 111: Does not know all the letters of the alphabet

Goals:
1. The student will recognize and identify all the letters of the alphabet.

Objectives:
1. The student will recognize five lower case letters of the alphabet at a time until all letters are learned with __% accuracy.
2. The student will recognize five upper case letters of the alphabet at a time until all letters are learned with __% accuracy.

BEHAVIOR 112: Understands what is read to him/her but not what he/she reads silently

Goals:
1. The student will improve his/her reading comprehension skills.

Objectives:
1. The student will demonstrate comprehension of individual words he/she reads with __% accuracy.
2. The student will demonstrate comprehension of individual phrases he/she reads with __% accuracy.
3. The student will demonstrate comprehension of individual sentences he/she reads with __% accuracy.
4. The student will demonstrate comprehension of individual paragraphs he/she reads with __% accuracy.
5. The student will demonstrate comprehension of short stories, chapters, etc., he/she reads with __% accuracy.
6. The student will comprehend reading material with __% accuracy.

BEHAVIOR 113: Does not comprehend what he/she reads

Goal:
1. The student will improve his/her reading comprehension skills.

Objectives:
1. The student will read and correctly answer __ out of __ comprehension questions about sight words on his/her level of functioning.

2. The student will read and correctly answer __ out of __ comprehension questions covering individual phrases on his/her level of functioning.
3. The student will read and correctly answer ___ out of ___ comprehension questions covering individual sentences on his/her level of functioning.
4. The student will read and correctly answer ___ out of ___ comprehension questions covering individual paragraphs on his/her level of functioning.
5. After reading a short passage on his/her level of functioning, the student will correctly answer __ out of __ comprehension questions covering the material.
6. After reading a short passage on his/her level of functioning to the teacher, the student will be able to corrrectly answer __ out of __ comprehension questions.
7. After independently reading a three-page passage on his/her level of functioning, the student will correctly answer __ out of __ questions.

BEHAVIOR 114:   Does not read independently

Goals:
1. The student will increase the amount of time spent reading independently.

Objectives:
1. The student will independently read brief information in the environment (e.g., labels, signs, names of persons, etc.) on __ out of __ trials.
2. The student will independently read short selections of reading material (e.g., cartoons, comic books, sentences, etc.) on __ out of __ trials.
3. The student will independently read short stories on __ out of __ trials.
4. The student will independently read library books, books of interest in the classroom, magazine stories, etc., on __ out of __ trials.

BEHAVIOR 115:   Fails to demonstrate word comprehension

Goals:
1. The student will improve his/her word comprehension skills.

Objectives:
1. The student will use picture cues to comprehend words with __% accuracy.
2. The student will use visual or verbal cues to comprehend words with __% accuracy.
3. The student will use a dictionary to comprehend words with __% accuracy.
4. The student will independently read complete sentences with __% accuracy.

BEHAVIOR 116:   Has difficulty applying decoding skills when reading

Goals:
1. The student will improve his/her ability to apply decoding skills when reading.

Objectives:
1. The student will identify root words at his/her level with __% accuracy.
2. The student will identify suffixes at his/her level with __% accuracy.
3. The student will identify prefixes at his/her level with __% accuracy.
4. The student will use context clues to identify an unknown word with __% accuracy.
5. The student will use picture clues to identify an unknown word with __% accuracy.
6. The student will use phonic clues to identify an unknown word with __% accuracy.

BEHAVIOR 117:   Fails to recognize words on grade level

Goals:
1. The student recognizes words on grade level.

Objectives:
1. The student will recognize words on grade level, with assistance (e.g., verbal cues, picture cues, context cues, etc.), with __% accuracy.
2. The student will independently recognize words on grade level with __% accuracy.

BEHAVIOR 118:   Does not summarize/retell important concepts after reading a selection

Goals:
1. The student will improve his/her ability to summarize/retell important concepts from a reading selection.

Objectives:
1. The student will identify the main characters from a reading selection with __% accuracy.
2. The student will report the beginning, middle, and end of a story with __% accuracy.
3. The student will sequence the events of a story with __% accuracy.
4. The student will relate important facts from a reading selection with __% accuracy.
5. The student will outline a reading selection with __% accuracy.

BEHAVIOR 119:   Reads words correctly in one context but not in another

Goals:
1. The student will improve his/her sight word vocabulary.

Objectives:
1. The student will recognize a sight word from a series of words with __% accuracy.
2. The student will recognize sight words in phrases with __% accuracy.
3. The student will recognize sight words in sentences with __% accuracy.
4. The student will recognize words from one context to another, with assistance, with __% accuracy.
5. The student will independently recognize words from one context to another with __% accuracy.

BEHAVIOR 120:   Uses inappropriate spacing between words or sentences when writing

Goals:
1. The student will improve his/her ability to use appropriate spacing between words or sentences when writing.

Objectives:
1. The student will space correctly between letters and numbers with __% accuracy.
2. The student will space correctly between words when writing with __% accuracy.
3. The student will space correctly between sentences when writing with __% accuracy.

BEHAVIOR 121:   Reverses letters and numbers when writing

Goals:
1. The student will improve his/her ability to form letters and numbers correctly when writing.

Objectives:
1. The student will recognize letters and numbers with __% accuracy.

2. The student will be able to copy letters and numbers with __% accuracy.
3. The student will form letters and numbers correctly when writing with __% accuracy.

BEHAVIOR 122:   Fails to write within a given space

Goals:
1. The student will improve his/her ability to write within a given space.

Objectives:
1. The student will write within horizontal lines drawn on paper with __% accuracy.
2. The student will write within vertical lines drawn on paper with __% accuracy.
3. The student will write within horizontal lines drawn on primary paper with __% accuracy.
4. The student will write within vertical margins on paper with __% accuracy.
5. The student will write within a given space on standard lined paper with __% accuracy.

BEHAVIOR 123:   Fails to form letters correctly when printing or writing

Goals:
1. The student will improve his/her ability to form letters correctly when printing or writing.

Objectives:
1. The student will trace lowercase letters of the alphabet in manuscript, replicating formation with __% accuracy.
2. The student will trace uppercase letters of the alphabet in manuscript, replicating formation with __% accuracy.
3. The student will copy lowercase letters of the alphabet in manuscript at close range, replicating formation with __% accuracy.
4. The student will copy uppercase letters of the alphabet in manuscript at close range, replicating formation with __% accuracy.
5. The student will trace lowercase letters of the alphabet in cursive, replicating formation with __% accuracy.
6. The student will trace uppercase letters of the alphabet in cursive, replicating formation with __% accuracy.
7. The student will copy lowercase letters of the alphabet in cursive at close range, replicating formation with __% accuracy.
8. The student will copy uppercase letters of the alphabet in cursive at close range, replicating formation with __% accuracy.
9. The student will print lowercase letters of the alphabet, replicating formation with __% accuracy.
10. The student will print uppercase letters of the alphabet, replicating formation with __% accuracy.
11. The student will write lowercase letters of the alphabet, replicating formation with __% accuracy.
12. The student will write uppercase letters of the alphabet, replicating formation with __% accuracy.

BEHAVIOR 124:   Fails to use verb tenses correctly when writing

Goals:
1. The student will improve his/her ability to use the correct verb tenses when writing.

Objectives:
1. The student will use the present verb tense when writing with __% accuracy.
2. The student will use the past verb tense when writing with __% accuracy.
3. The student will use the future verb tense when writing with __% accuracy.

BEHAVIOR 125: **Uses inappropriate letter size when writing**

Goals:
1. The student will improve his/her ability to use appropriate letter size when writing.

Objectives:
1. The student will trace lowercase letters of the alphabet, replicating size with __% accuracy.
2. The student will trace uppercase letters of the alphabet, replicating size with __% accuracy.
3. The student will copy lowercase letters of the alphabet at close range, replicating size with __% accuracy.
4. The student will copy uppercase letters of the alphabet at close range, replicating size with __% accuracy.
5. The student will print lowercase letters of the alphabet, replicating size with __% accuracy.
6. The student will print uppercase letters of the alphabet, replicating size with __% accuracy.
7. The student will write lowercase letters of the alphabet in cursive, replicating size with __% accuracy.
8. The student will write uppercase letters of the alphabet in cursive, replicating size with __% accuracy.

BEHAVIOR 126: **Fails to use capitalization correctly when writing**

Goals:
1. The student will improve his/her use of capitalization when writing.

Objectives:
1. The student will write capital letters with __% accuracy.
2. The student will use capitalization in drill activities of capitalization rules (e.g., personal pronoun I, first letter of first word in a sentence, etc.) with __% accuracy.
3. The student will write capital letters at the beginning of words requiring capitalization from lists given orally (e.g., names of persons, rivers, cities, states, etc.) with __% accuracy.
4. The student will use capitalization when writing with __% accuracy.

BEHAVIOR 127: **Fails to punctuate correctly when writing**

Goals:
1. The student will improve his/her use of punctuation when writing.

Objectives:
1. The student will use periods when writing with __% accuracy.
2. The student will use question marks when writing with __% accuracy.
3. The student will use exclamation marks when writing with __% accuracy.
4. The student will use commas when writing with __% accuracy.
5. The student will use quotation marks when writing with __% accuracy.
6. The student will use colons when writing with __% accuracy.
7. The student will use semicolons when writing with __% accuracy.

BEHAVIOR 128: **Does not use appropriate subject-verb agreement when writing**

Goals:
1. The student will improve his/her grammatical skills when writing.

Objectives:
1. The student will orally conjugate common verbs with __% accuracy.
2. The student will conjugate common verbs in written form with __% accuracy.
3. The student will write sentences requiring subject-verb agreement with __% accuracy.

4. The student will use subject-verb agreement when writing with __% accuracy.

BEHAVIOR 129:   **Does not compose complete sentences or express complete thoughts when writing**

Goals:
1. The student will improve his/her written language skills.

Objectives:
1. The student will write single words which express thoughts with __% accuracy.
2. The student will write phrases which express thoughts with __% accuracy.
3. The student will write complete sentences which express thoughts with __% accuracy.

BEHAVIOR 130:   **Fails to correctly organize writing activities**

Goals:
1. The student will improve his/her ability to organize writing activities.

Objectives:
1. The student will write in sequence (e.g., numbers, letters, days, months, etc.), after he/she has been corrected by the teacher, with __% accuracy.
2. The student will independently sequence (e.g., numbers, letters, days, months, etc.) when writing with __% accuracy.
3. The student will write a complete sentence with subject-verb agreement on __ out of __ trials.
4. The student will write complete sentences with correct word order on __ out of __ trials.
5. The student will write two related complete sentences describing a single subject (e.g., event, personal experience, etc.) on __ out of __ trials.
6. The student will write three related complete sentences describing a single subject (e.g., event, personal experience, etc.) on __ out of __ trials.
7. The student will write a series of three or more sentences which correctly sequence a series of events on __ out of __ trials.
8. The student will write a paragraph of three or more related sentences with introduction and closing sentences on __ out of __ trials.

BEHAVIOR 131:   **Fails to use spelling rules**

Goals:
1. The student will improve his/her spelling skills.

Objectives:
1. The student will use the spelling rule "*i* before *e* except after *c*" with __% accuracy.
2. The student will use the spelling rule "words which end with a vowel plus *y*, add *s* to make plural" with __% accuracy.
3. The student will use the spelling rule "words which end with a consonant plus *y*, change the *y* to *i* and add *es* to make plural" with __% accuracy.
4. The student will use the spelling rule "words with one syllable, one vowel, and one consonant at the end, double the final consonant when adding an ending" with __% accuracy.

BEHAVIOR 132:   **Has difficulty spelling words that do not follow the spelling rules**

Goals:
1. The student will improve his/her spelling skills.

Objectives:
1. The student will spell an identified sight word vocabulary with __% accuracy.
2. The student will spell words that do not follow spelling rules with __% accuracy.

BEHAVIOR 133: Spells words correctly in one context but not in another

Goals:
1. The student will improve his/her spelling skills.

Objectives:
1. The student will spell words in more than one context, with assistance, with __% accuracy.
2. The student will independently spell words in more than one context with __% accuracy.

BEHAVIOR 134: Requires continued drill and practice in order to learn spelling words

Goals:
1. The student will improve his/her spelling skills.

Objectives:
1. The student will increase the number of spelling words learned in a given time period (indicate one week, two weeks, a month, etc.)

BEHAVIOR 135: Fails to correctly solve math problems requiring addition

Goals:
1. The student will improve his/her ability to solve addition problems.

Objectives:
1. The student will demonstrate understanding of number values to 100 with __% accuracy.
2. The student will demonstrate understanding of number values above 100 with __% accuracy.
3. The student will demonstrate understanding of place value with __% accuracy.
4. The student will solve addition problems which do not require regrouping with __% accuracy.
5. The student will solve addition problems requiring regrouping with __% accuracy.

BEHAVIOR 136: Fails to correctly solve math problems requiring subtraction

Goals:
1. The student will improve his/her ability to solve subtraction problems.

Objectives:
1. The student will demonstrate understanding of number values to 100 with __% accuracy.
2. The student will demonstrate understanding of number values above 100 with __% accuracy.
3. The student will demonstrate understanding of place value with __% accuracy.
4. The student will solve subtraction problems which do not require regrouping with __% accuracy.
5. The student will solve subtraction problems requiring regrouping with __% accuracy.

BEHAVIOR 137: Fails to correctly solve math problems requiring multiplication

Goals:
1. The student will improve his/her ability to solve multiplication problems.

Objectives:
1. The student will demonstrate understanding of number values to 100 with __% accuracy.
2. The student will demonstrate understanding of number values above 100 with __% accuracy.
3. The student will demonstrate understanding of place value with __% accuracy.
4. The student will solve multiplication problems which do not require regrouping with __% accuracy.
5. The student will solve multiplication problems requiring regrouping with __% accuracy.

BEHAVIOR 138: Fails to correctly solve math problems requiring division

Goals:
1. The student will improve his/her ability to solve division problems.

Objectives:
1. The student will demonstrate understanding of number values to 100 with __% accuracy.
2. The student will demonstrate understanding of number values above 100 with __% accuracy.
3. The student will demonstrate understanding of place value with __% accuracy.
4. The student will solve division problems which do not require regrouping with __% accuracy.
5. The student will solve division problems requiring regrouping with __% accuracy.

BEHAVIOR 139: Does not remember math facts

Goals:
1. The student will improve his/her ability to recall math facts.

Objectives:
1. The student will add two numbers with sums of nine or less with __% accuracy.
2. The student will solve subtraction problems of one-digit numbers with __% accuracy.
3. The student will use a number line to solve simple addition problems involving the basic math facts with __% accuracy.
4. The student will use a number line to solve simple subtraction problems involving the basic math facts with __% accuracy.
5. The student will add two one-digit numbers with __% accuracy.
6. The student will solve subtraction problems involving the basic math facts with __% accuracy.
7. The student will solve addition problems with more than one column, not requiring regrouping, with __% accuracy.
8. The student will solve subtraction problems with more than one column, not requiring regrouping, with __% accuracy.
9. The student will multiply two one-digit numbers with __% accuracy.
10. The student will solve division problems involving one-digit divisors and one-digit quotients with __% accuracy.

BEHAVIOR 140: Does not make use of columns when working math problems

Goals:
1. The student will improve his/her use of columns when working math problems.

Objectives:
1. The student will recognize the ones place value with __% accuracy.
2. The student will recognize the tens place value with __% accuracy.
3. The student will recognize the hundreds place value with __% accuracy.
4. The student will recognize the thousands place value with __% accuracy.
5. The student will use the ones place column when working math problems with __% accuracy.

6. The student will use the tens place column when working math problems with __% accuracy.
7. The student will use the hundreds place column when working math problems with __% accuracy.
8. The student will use the thousands place column when working math problems with __% accuracy.
9. The student will work math problems from right to left with __% accuracy.

BEHAVIOR 141: Has difficulty solving math word problems

Goals:
1. The student will improve his/her ability to solve math word problems.

Objectives:
1. The student will solve addition math word problems not requiring regrouping with __% accuracy.
2. The student will solve subtraction math word problems not requiring regrouping with __% accuracy.
3. The student will solve math word problems involving simple multiplication with __% accuracy.
4. The student will solve math word problems involving simple division with __% accuracy.
5. The student will solve addition math word problems requiring regrouping with __% accuracy.
6. The student will solve subtraction math word problems requiring regrouping with __% accuracy.
7. The student will solve math word problems involving multiplication requiring regrouping with ___% accuracy.
8. The student will solve math word problems involving long division with __% accuracy.
9. The student will solve math word problems involving fractions with __% accuracy.
10. The student will solve math word problems involving decimals with __% accuracy.
11. The student will solve math word problems involving time with __% accuracy.
12. The student will solve math word problems involving measurement with __% accuracy.
13. The student will solve math word problems involving more than one operation with __% accuracy.

BEHAVIOR 142: Fails to change from one math operation to another

Goals:
1. The student will improve his/her ability to change from one operation to another.

Objectives:
1. The student will recognize math operation symbols with __% accuracy.
2. The student will describe or demonstrate the operation required of math operation symbols with __% accuracy.
3. The student will change from one math operation to another, with assistance (e.g., written and verbal cues), with __% accuracy.
4. The student will change from one math operation to another independently with __% accuracy.

BEHAVIOR 143: Does not understand abstract math concepts without concrete examples

Goals:
1. The student will improve his/her ability to understand abstract math concepts without concrete examples.

Objectives:
1. The student will demonstrate knowledge of one-to-one relationships of numbers to objects with __% accuracy.
2. The student will use manipulatives to solve math problems with __% accuracy.
3. The student will solve math problems independently and then check his/her work using manipulatives with __% accuracy.
4. The student will solve math problems independent of manipulatives, with verbal assistance, with __% accuracy.

5. The student will solve math problems independently with __% accuracy.

BEHAVIOR 144:   Fails to correctly solve math problems requiring regrouping

Goals:
1. The student will improve his/her ability to correctly solve math problems requiring regrouping.

Objectives:
1. The student will solve addition math problems which do not require regrouping with __% accuracy.
2. The student will solve subtraction math problems which do not require regrouping with __% accuracy.
3. The student will solve multiplication math problems which do not require regrouping with __% accuracy.
4. The student will solve addition math problems requiring regrouping with __% accuracy.
5. The student will solve subtraction math problems requiring regrouping with __% accuracy.
6. The student will solve multiplication math problems requiring regrouping with __% accuracy.

BEHAVIOR 145:   Fails to correctly solve math problems involving fractions or decimals

Goals:
1. The student will improve his/her ability to solve problems involving fractions or decimals.

Objectives:
1. The student will be able to recognize fractional values with __% accuracy.
2. The student will be able to recognize decimal values with __% accuracy.
3. The student will be able to solve addition problems involving fractions, which do not require regrouping, with __% accuracy.
4. The student will be able to solve addition problems involving decimals, which do not require regrouping, with __% accuracy.
5. The student will be able to solve subtraction problems involving fractions, which do not require regrouping, with __% accuracy.
6. The student will be able to solve subtraction problems involving decimals, which do not require regrouping, with __% accuracy.
7. The student will be able to solve multiplication problems involving fractions, which do not require regrouping, with __% accuracy.
8. The student will be able to solve multiplication problems involving decimals, which do not require regrouping, with __% accuracy.
9. The student will be able to solve simple division problems involving fractions, which do not require regrouping, with __% accuracy.
10. The student will be able to solve simple division problems involving decimals, which do not require regrouping, with __% accuracy.
11. The student will be able to solve long division problems involving fractions, which do not require regrouping, with __% accuracy.
12. The student will be able to solve long division problems involving decimals, which do not require regrouping, with __% accuracy.
13. The student will be able to solve addition problems involving fractions, which require regrouping, with __% accuracy.
14. The student will be able to solve addition problems involving decimals, which require regrouping, with __% accuracy.
15. The student will be able to solve subtraction problems involving fractions, which require regrouping, with __% accuracy.
16. The student will be able to solve subtraction problems involving decimals, which require regrouping, with __% accuracy.
17. The student will be able to solve multiplication problems involving fractions, which require regrouping, with __% accuracy.

18. The student will be able to solve multiplication problems involving decimals, which require regrouping, with __% accuracy.
19. The student will be able to solve simple division problems involving fractions, which require regrouping, with __% accuracy.
20. The student will be able to solve simple division problems involving decimals, which require regrouping, with __% accuracy.
21. The student will be able to solve long division problems involving fractions, which require regrouping, with __% accuracy.
22. The student will be able to solve long division problems involving decimals, which require regrouping, with __% accuracy.

BEHAVIOR 146:   Fails to correctly solve problems involving money

Goals:
1. The student will improve his/her ability to apply math skills to the use of money.

Objectives:
1. The student will solve money problems involving coins, which do not require regrouping, with __% accuracy.
2. The student will solve money problems involving coins, which require regrouping, with __% accuracy.
3. The student will solve money problems involving dollars, which do not require regrouping, with __% accuracy.
4. The student will solve money problems involving dollars, which require regrouping, with __% accuracy.
5. The student will solve money problems involving dollars and coins, which do not require regrouping, with __% accuracy.
6. The student will solve money problems involving dollars and coins, which require regrouping, with __% accuracy.

BEHAVIOR 147:   Fails to correctly solve problems using measurement

Goals:
1. The student will improve his/her ability to apply math skills to the use of measurement.

Objectives:
1. The student will solve math problems involving length (e.g., inches, feet, yards, or miles) with ____% accuracy.
2. The student will solve math problems involving liquid measurement (e.g., ounces, cups, pints, quarts, gallons, etc.) with __% accuracy.
3. The student will solve math problems involving dry weight (e.g., ounces, pounds, or tons) with __% accuracy.

BEHAVIOR 148:   Fails to demonstrate knowledge of place value

Goals:
1. The student will increase his/her knowledge of place value.

Objectives:
1. The student will recognize the ones place value with __% accuracy.
2. The student will recognize the tens place value with __% accuracy.
3. The student will recognize the hundreds place value with __% accuracy.
4. The student will recognize the thousands place value with __% accuracy.

BEHAVIOR 149: Confuses operational signs when working math problems

Goals:
1. The student will improve his/her ability to discriminate various operational signs when working math problems.

Objectives:
1. The student will recognize operational signs (e.g., +, -, ÷, ×) with __% accuracy.
2. The student will change from one math operation to another, when two operations are involved, with __% accuracy.
3. The student will change from one math operation to another, when three operations are involved, with __% accuracy.
4. The student will change from one math operation to another, when four operations are involved, with __% accuracy.

BEHAVIOR 150: Has difficulty understanding abstract concepts

Goals:
1. The student will improve his/her ability to understand abstract concepts.

Objectives:
1. The student will match pictures of abstract concepts (e.g., dimensionality, size, space, shape, etc.) with tangible representations with __% accuracy.
2. The student will identify abstract concepts (e.g., dimensionality, size, space, shape, etc.), with visual and verbal cues, with __% accuracy.
3. The student will identify abstract concepts (e.g., dimensionality, size, space, shape, etc.) independently with __% accuracy.

IV. Interventions

1 Rushes through assignments with little or no regard to accuracy or quality of work

1. Allow the student to perform schoolwork in a quiet place (e.g., study carrel, library, resource room, etc.) in order to reduce distractions.

2. Assign the student shorter tasks while increasing accuracy and quality expectations.

3. Supervise the student while he/she is performing schoolwork in order to monitor accuracy and quality.

4. Provide the student with clearly stated criteria for acceptable work.

5. Have the student read/go over schoolwork with the teacher in order that the student can become more aware of the accuracy and quality of his/her work.

6. Provide the student with samples of work which may serve as models for acceptable levels of accuracy and quality (e.g., the student is to match the quality of the sample before turning in the assignment).

7. Provide the student with additional time to perform schoolwork in order to achieve increased accuracy and quality.

8. Teach the student procedures for improving accuracy and quality of work (e.g., listen to directions, make certain directions are understood, work at an acceptable pace, check for errors, correct for neatness, copy the work over, etc.).

9. Recognize accuracy and quality (e.g., display student's work, congratulate the student, etc.).

10. Conduct a preliminary evaluation of the work, requiring the student to make necessary corrections before final grading.

11. Establish levels of expectations for accuracy and quality of performance and require the student to correct or repeat assignments until the expectations are met.

12. Provide the student with quality materials to perform the assignment (e.g., pencil with eraser, paper, dictionary, handwriting sample, etc.).

13. Make certain that all educators who work with the student maintain consistent expectations of accuracy and quality.

14. Have the student question any directions, explanations, and instructions not understood.

15. Assess student performance in a variety of ways (e.g., have the student give verbal explanations, simulations, physical demonstrations, etc.).

16. Give shorter assignments, but give them more frequently. Increase the length of assignments as the student demonstrates success.

17. Structure the environment in such a way as to provide the student with increased opportunities for help or assistance on academic or homework tasks (e.g., peer tutors, seat the student near the teacher or aide, etc.).

18. Provide the student with clearly stated written directions for homework in order that someone at home may be able to provide assistance.

19. Teach the student study skills.

20. Reduce distracting stimuli (e.g., place the student in the front row, provide a carrel or "office" space away from distractions, etc.). This is to be used as a means of reducing distracting stimuli and not as a form of punishment.

21. Interact frequently with the student to monitor task performance.

22. Have the student maintain a chart representing the number of tasks completed and the accuracy rate of each task.

23. Assess quality and clarity of directions, explanations, and instructions given to the student.

24. Provide time at school for the completion of homework if homework assigned has not been completed or has resulted in failure. (The student's failure to complete homework assignments may be the result of variables in the home over which he/she has no control.)

25. Teach the student note-taking skills.

26. Assess the appropriateness of assigning homework to the student.

27. Teach the student direction-following skills: (a) listen carefully, (b) ask questions, (c) use environmental cues, (d) rely on examples provided, etc.

28. Identify resource personnel from whom the student may receive additional assistance (e.g., librarian, special education teacher, other personnel with expertise or time to help, etc.).

29. Deliver reinforcement for any and all measures of improvement.

30. Mastery should not be expected too soon after introducing new information, skills, etc.

31. Provide the student with self-checking materials, requiring correction before turning in assignments.

32. Should the student consistently fail to complete assignments with minimal accuracy, evaluate the appropriateness of tasks assigned.

33. Provide instruction and task format in a variety of ways (e.g., verbal instructions, written instructions, demonstrations, simulations, manipulative, drill activities with peers, etc.).

34. Provide the student with opportunities for review prior to grading assignments.

35. Make certain the assignments measure knowledge of content and not related skills such as reading or writing.

36. Have the student respond to tasks orally.

37. Have the assignments tape recorded, allowing the student to listen to questions as often as necessary.

38. If the student has difficulty completing homework assignments with minimal accuracy, provide a time during the day when assistance can be given at school.

39. Teach the student to practice basic study skills (e.g., reading for the main idea, note taking, summarizing, highlighting, studying in a good environment, using time wisely, etc.).

40. Arrange a time for the student to study with a peer tutor before completing a graded assignment.

41. Provide multiple opportunities for the student to learn information covered by assignments (e.g., films, visitors, community resources, etc.).

42. Allow the student to respond to alternative assignment questions (e.g., more generalized questions that represent global understanding).

43. Provide parents with information regarding appropriate ways in which to help their child with homework (e.g., read directions with the student, work a few problems together, answer questions, check the completed assignment, etc.).

44. Modify instructions to include more concrete examples in order to enhance student learning.

45. Monitor student performance in order to detect errors and determine where learning problems exist.

46. Reduce the emphasis on competition. Students who compete academically and fail to succeed may cease to try to do well and do far less than they are able.

47. Allow/require the student to make corrections after assignments have been checked the first time.

48. Provide the student with evaluative feedback for assignments completed (i.e., identify what the student did successfully, what errors were made, and what should be done to correct the errors).

49. Maintain consistency in assignment format and expectations so as not to confuse the student.

50. Provide adequate repetition and drill to assure minimal accuracy of assignments presented (i.e., require mastery/minimal accuracy before moving to the next skill level).

51. It is not necessary to grade every assignment performed by the student. Assignments may be used to evaluate student ability or knowledge and provide feedback. Grades may not need to be assigned until mastery/minimal accuracy has been attained.

52. Provide the student with a selection of assignments and require him/her to choose a minimum number from the total amount (e.g., present the student with 10 academic tasks from which 6 must be finished that day).

53. Allow the student to put an assignment away and return to it at a later time if this helps the student be more successful.

54. Have the student practice an assignment with the teacher, an aide, or a peer before performing the assignment for a grade.

55. Monitor the first problem or part of the assignment in order to make certain the student knows what is expected.

56. Provide frequent interactions and encouragement to support the student's confidence and optimism for success (e.g., make statements such as, "You're doing great." "Keep up the good work." "I'm really proud of you." etc.).

57. Build varying degrees of difficulty into assignments in order to ensure the student's self-confidence and at the same time provide a challenge (e.g., easier problems are intermingled with problems designed to measure knowledge gained).

58. Communicate with parents (e.g., notes home, phone calls, etc.) in order to share information concerning the student's progress and so that they can reinforce the student at home for improving the accuracy and quality of assignments at school.

59. Modify academic tasks (e.g., format, requirements, length, etc.).

60. Provide the student with clearly stated step-by-step directions for homework in order that someone at home may be able to provide assistance.

61. Make certain that homework relates to concepts already taught rather than introducing a new concept.

62. Ask parents to set aside an established length of time each evening (e.g., 45 minutes, one hour, etc.) for homework rather than allowing the student to watch TV or play "as soon as the homework is finished."

63. Make certain that your comments take the form of constructive criticism rather than criticism that can be perceived as personal, threatening, etc. (e.g., instead of saying, "You always make the same mistake." say,"A better way to do that might be . . .").

64. Along with a directive, provide an incentive statement (e.g., "When you finish your work neatly, you may have free time." etc.).

65. Assign a peer to work with the student in order to provide an acceptable model for the student to imitate.

66. Evaluate the appropriateness of the task to determine: (a) if the task is too difficult and (b) if the length of time scheduled for the task is appropriate.

67. Work the first few problems of an assignment with the student in order to make certain that he/she knows what to do, how to perform the assignment, etc.

68. Write a contract with the student specifying what behavior is expected (e.g., improving the accuracy and quality of assignments) and what reinforcement will be made available when the terms of the contract have been met. (See Appendix for Behavioral Contract.)

69. Reinforce those students in the classroom who turn in assignments which are accurate and of high quality.

70. Reinforce the student for improving the accuracy and quality of his/her work based on ability. Gradually increase the amount of improvement expected for reinforcement as the student demonstrates success.

71. Establish classroom rules:
1. Work on-task.
2. Work quietly.
3. Remain in your seat.
4. Finish task.
5. Meet task requirements.

Reiterate rules often and reinforce the student for following rules.

72. Speak with the student to explain: (a) what the student is doing wrong (e.g., turning in work which has spelling errors, work which has spacing errors, work that is illegible, etc.) and (b) what the student should be doing (e.g., taking time to check for spelling, spacing errors, etc.).

73. Reinforce conscientiousness in improving accuracy and quality of assignments (e.g., double checking spelling, proper positioning of letters, adequate spacing, etc.): (a) give the student a tangible reward (e.g., classroom privileges, line leading, passing out materials, five minutes free time, etc.) or (b) give the student an intangible reward (e.g., praise, handshake, smile, etc.).

2   Is easily distracted by other activities in the classroom, other students, the teacher, etc.

1. Reinforce the student for staying on-task in the classroom: (a) give the student a tangible reward (e.g., classroom privileges, line leading, passing out materials, five minutes free time, etc.) or (b) give the student an intangible reward (e.g., praise, handshake, smile, etc.).

2. Speak to the student to explain: (a) what he/she is doing wrong (e.g., failing to attend to tasks), and (b) what he/she should be doing (e.g., attending to tasks).

3. Establish classroom rules (e.g., work on-task, work quietly, remain in your seat, finish task, meet task expectations). Reiterate rules often and reinforce students for following rules.

4. Reinforce those students in the classroom who demonstrate on-task behavior.

5. Reinforce the student for attending to task based on the length of time he/she can be successful. Gradually increase the length of time required for reinforcement as the student demonstrates success.

6. Write a contract with the student specifying what behavior is expected (establish a reasonable length of time to stay on-task) and what reinforcement will be made available when the terms of the contract have been met.

7. Communicate with parents (e.g., notes home, phone calls, etc.) in order to share information concerning the student's progress and so that they may reinforce the student at home for staying on-task in the classroom.

8. Identify a peer to act as a model for the student to imitate on-task behavior.

9. Have the student question any directions, explanations, instructions he/she does not understand.

10. Evaluate the auditory and visual stimuli in the classroom in order to determine the level of stimuli to which the student can respond in an appropriate manner.

11. Reduce auditory and visual stimuli to a level at which the student can successfully function. Gradually allow auditory and visual stimuli to increase as the student demonstrates that he/she can successfully tolerate the increased levels.

12. Seat the student so that he/she experiences the least amount of auditory and visual stimuli possible.

13. Provide the student with a quiet place in which to work where auditory and visual stimuli are reduced. This is used to reduce distracting stimuli and not as a form of punishment.

14. Seat the student away from those peers who create the most auditory and visual stimulation in the classroom.

15. Provide the student with a carrel or divider at his/her desk to reduce auditory and visual stimuli.

16. Make certain that all auditory and visual stimuli in the classroom are reduced as much as possible for all learners.

17. Provide the student with the opportunity to move to a quiet place in the classroom any time that auditory and visual stimuli interfere with his/her ability to function successfully.

18. Provide the student with earphones to wear if auditory stimuli interfere with his/her ability to function. Gradually remove the earphones as the student can more successfully function in the presence of auditory stimuli.

19. Allow the student to close the door or windows in order to reduce auditory and visual stimuli outside of the classroom.

20. Require the student to be productive in the presence of auditory and visual stimuli for short periods of time. Gradually increase the length of time the student is required to be productive as he/she becomes successful.

21. Provide the student with shorter tasks which do not require extended attention in order to be successful. Gradually increase the length of the tasks as the student demonstrates success.

22. Have the student engage in small group activities (e.g., free time, math, reading, etc.) in order to reduce the level of auditory and visual stimuli in the group. Gradually increase group size as the student can function successfully.

23. Model for the student appropriate behavior in the presence of auditory and visual stimuli in the classroom (e.g., continuing to work, asking for quiet, moving to a quieter part of the classroom, etc.).

24. Remove the student from an activity until he/she can demonstrate appropriate on-task behavior.

25. Assign the student shorter tasks but more of them (e.g., modify a 20-problem math activity to 4 activities of 5 problems each to be performed at various times during the day). Gradually increase the number of problems for each activity as the student demonstrates success.

26. Present tasks in the most attractive and interesting manner possible.

27. Assess the degree of task difficulty in relation to the student's ability to successfully perform the task.

28. Interact frequently with the student in order to maintain his/her involvement in the activity (e.g., ask the student questions, ask the student's opinions, stand close to the student, seat the student near the teacher's desk, etc.).

29. Provide the student with a timer which he/she may use to increase the amount of time during which he/she maintains attention (e.g., have the student work on the activity until the timer goes off).

30. Provide the student with a predetermined signal (e.g., hand signal, verbal cue, etc.) when he/she begins to display off-task behaviors.

31. Structure the environment to reduce the opportunity for off-task behavior. Reduce lag time by providing the student with enough activities to maintain productivity.

32. Have the student work with a peer tutor in order to maintain attention to task.

33. Make certain the student has all necessary materials to perform assignments.

34. Make certain the student knows what to do when he/she cannot successfully perform assignments (e.g., raise hand, ask for assistance, go to the teacher, etc.).

35. Maintain visibility to and from the student. The teacher should be able to see the student and the student should be able to see the teacher, making eye contact possible at all times.

36. Make certain to recognize the student when his/her hand is raised, in order to convey that assistance will be provided as soon as possible.

37. Teach the student how to manage his/her time until the teacher can provide assistance (e.g., try the problem again, go on to the next problem, wait quietly, etc.).

3 Does not listen to what other students are saying

1. Make certain the student's hearing has been checked recently.

2. Reinforce the student for listening to what is said to him/her by other students (e.g., making eye contact, putting aside materials, answering the students, etc.): (a) give the student a tangible reward (e.g., classroom privileges, line leading, passing out materials, five minutes free time, etc.) or (b) give the student an intangible reward (e.g., praise, handshake, smile, etc.).

3. Reinforce the students in the classroom who listen to what other students are saying.

4. Speak to the student to explain: (a) what the student is doing wrong (e.g., failing to listen to what other students are saying), and (b) what the student should be doing (e.g., listening to other students when they speak to him/her, listening to other students when they speak to a group, etc.).

5. Reinforce the student for listening to what other students are saying based on the length of time the student can be successful. Gradually increase the number of times or length of time the student is required to listen as he/she demonstrates success.

6. Have the student repeat or paraphrase what other students are saying in order to determine what was heard.

7. Make certain the student is attending to what other students are saying (e.g., making eye contact, stopping other activities, responding appropriately, etc.).

8. Make certain that other students speak clearly and concisely when speaking to the student.

9. Make certain the student is near the students who are speaking.

10. Make certain that competing sounds (e.g., talking, noises, motion in the classroom, etc.) are silenced when other students are talking, in order to enhance the student's ability to listen to what others are saying.

11. Reduce the emphasis on competition in the classroom. Competition may cause the student to be excited or distracted and fail to listen to what other students are saying.

12. Have other students stand directly in front of the student when speaking to him/her in order for the student to be more likely to listen to what others are saying.

13. Have other students call the student by name before speaking to him/her.

14. Teach the student listening skills (e.g., listen carefully, write down important points, ask for clarification, wait until all directions are received before beginning).

15. Have the student practice listening to what other students are saying (e.g., following simple instructions, sharing information, etc.).

16. Have the student silently repeat information just heard from other students in order to help in remembering important information.

17. Teach the student to respect others and what they are saying by respecting the student and what he/she says.

18. Do not force the student to interact with someone when he/she is not completely comfortable.

19. Treat the student with respect. Talk in an objective manner at all times.

20. Encourage the student to interact with others.

21. Provide the student with frequent opportunities to meet new people.

4 Does not hear all of what is said

1. Make certain the student's hearing has been checked recently.

2. Have the student repeat or paraphrase what is said to him/her in order to determine what was heard.

3. Give the student short directions, explanations, and instructions to follow. Gradually increase the length of the directions, explanations, and instructions as the student demonstrates success.

4. Maintain consistency in the verbal delivery of information.

5. Make certain the student is attending to the source of information (e.g., making eye contact, hands free of writing materials, looking at assignment, etc.).

6. Provide the student with written directions and instructions to supplement verbal directions and instructions.

7. Emphasize or repeat word endings, key words, etc.

8. Speak clearly and concisely when delivering directions, explanations, and instructions.

9. Place the student near the source of information.

10. Reduce distracting stimuli (e.g., noise and motion in the classroom) in order to enhance the student's ability to listen successfully.

11. Stop at key points when delivering directions, explanations, and instructions in order to determine student comprehension.

12. Use multiple modalities (e.g., auditory, visual, tactile, etc.) when presenting directions, explanations, and instructional content. Determine which modality is stronger and utilize the results.

13. Reduce the emphasis on competition in the classroom. Competition may cause the student to begin an activity before hearing all of what is said.

14. Deliver directions, explanations, and instructions at an appropriate pace.

15. Identify a list of word endings, key words, etc., that the student will practice listening for when someone is speaking.

16. Stop at various points during the presentation of information to check the student's comprehension.

17. Teach the student listening skills (e.g., stop working, look at the person delivering questions and directions, have necessary note-taking materials, etc.).

18. Tell the student what to listen for when being given directions, receiving information, etc.

19. Make certain that all directions, questions, explanations, and instructions are delivered in the most clear and concise manner, at an appropriate pace for the student, and loudly enough to be heard.

20. Play games to teach listening skills (e.g., *Red Light-Green Light, Mother May I?, Simon Says*).

21. Have the student silently repeat information just heard to help him/her remember the important facts.

22. Have the student question any directions, explanations, and instructions he/she does not understand.

23. Evaluate the level of difficulty of information to which the student is expected to listen (e.g., be sure information is communicated on the student's ability level).

24. Reinforce the student for listening carefully based on the length of time the student can be successful. Gradually increase the length of time the student is required to listen as the student demonstrates success.

25. Speak to the student to explain: (a) what the student is doing wrong (e.g., failing to listen to word endings, key words, etc.) and (b) what the student should be doing (e.g., listening for word endings, key words, etc.).

26. Reinforce the student for listening to what is said (e.g., making eye contact, hands free of writing materials, looking at assignment, etc.): (a) give the student a tangible reward (e.g., classroom privileges, line leading, passing out materials, five minutes free time, etc.) or (b) give the student an intangible reward (e.g., praise, handshake, smile, etc.).

5   Does not direct attention or fails to maintain attention to important sounds in the immediate environment

1. Make certain the student's hearing has been recently checked.

2. Make certain the student is attending (e.g., making eye contact, hands free of materials, etc.) before delivering directions, explanations, and instructions.

3. Make certain that competing sounds (e.g., talking, movement, noises, etc.) are silenced when directions are being given, public address announcements are being made, etc.

4. Deliver a predetermined signal (e.g., hand signal, turning lights off and on, etc.) prior to bells ringing, announcements being made, directions being given, etc.

5. Give a verbal cue in order to gain the student's attention prior to bells ringing, announcements being made, etc.

6. Stand directly in front of the student when delivering information.

7. Call the student by name prior to bells ringing, announcements being made, directions being delivered, etc.

8. Seat the student next to a peer who directs and maintains attention to sounds in the immediate environment.

9. Have a peer provide the student with the information not heard.

10. Provide the student with public announcements, directions, and instructions in written form.

11. Maintain visibility to and from the student at all times in order to ensure he/she is attending.

12. Have the student verbally repeat information heard.

13. Reduce distracting stimuli in the immediate environment (e.g., place the student on the front row, provide the student with a carrel or "office" space away from distractions, etc.). This is used as a form of reducing distracting stimuli and not as a form of punishment.

14. Teach the student listening skills (e.g., listen carefully, write down important points, ask for clarification, wait until all directions are received before beginning).

15. Have the student engage in practice activities designed to develop listening skills (e.g., following one-, two-, or three-step directions; listening for the main point; etc.).

16. Make certain that directions, public announcements, etc., are delivered in a clear and concise manner (e.g., keep phrases and sentences short).

17. Give directions in a variety of ways in order to enhance the student's ability to attend.

18. Stop at various points when delivering directions, public announcements, etc., in order to ensure that the student is attending.

19. Deliver directions one step at a time. Gradually increase the number of steps as the student demonstrates the ability to direct and maintain attention.

20. Maintain consistency of the format in which auditory information is delivered (e.g., morning announcements, recess bell, delivery of directions, etc.).

21. Seat the student far enough away from peers in order to ensure the ability to successfully attend to sounds in the immediate environment.

22. Stop at various points during the presentation of information to check the student's comprehension.

23. Tell the student what to listen for when being given directions, receiving information, etc.

24. Make certain that all directions, questions, explanations, and instructions are delivered in the most clear and concise manner and at an appropriate pace for the student.

25. Use pictures, diagrams, the chalkboard, and gestures when delivering information.

26. When delivering directions, explanations, and information be certain to use vocabulary that is within the student's level of comprehension.

27. Seat the student close to the source of sound.

28. Have the student question any directions, explanations, and instructions he/she does not understand.

29. Identify a peer to act as a model for the student to imitate directing and maintaining of attention to important sounds in the immediate environment.

30. Reinforce the student for directing and maintaining his/her attention to important sounds in the immediate environment based on the length of time the student can be successful. Gradually increase the length of time required for reinforcement as the student demonstrates success.

31. Reinforce those students in the classroom who direct and maintain their attention to important sounds in the immediate environment.

32. Reinforce the student for directing and maintaining attention to important sounds in the environment: (a) give the student a tangible reward (e.g., classroom privileges, line leading, passing out materials, five minutes free time, etc.) or (b) give the student an intangible reward (e.g., praise, handshake, smile, etc.).

6 Is unsuccessful in activities requiring listening

1. Make certain the student's hearing has been checked recently.

2. Seat the student close to the source of directions explanations, and instructions.

3. Make certain the student is attending (e.g., making eye contact, hands free of writing materials, etc.) before delivering directions, explanations, and instructions.

4. Make certain that competing sounds (e.g., talking, movement, noises, etc.) are silenced when directions are being given, public address announcements are being made, etc.

5. Deliver a predetermined signal (e.g., hand signal, turning off and on lights, etc.) prior to bells ringing, announcements being made, etc.

6. Stand directly in front of the student when delivering directions, explanations, and instructions.

7. Call the student by name prior to bells ringing, announcements being made, directions being given, etc.

8. Have a peer provide the information the student does not hear.

9. Provide the student with public announcements, directions, and instructions in written form.

10. Maintain visibility to and from the student at all times to ensure he/she is attending.

11. Reduce distracting stimuli in the immediate environment (e.g., place the student on the front row, provide the student with a carrel or "office" space away from distractions, etc.). This is used as a form of reducing distracting stimuli and not as a form of punishment.

12. Have the student verbally repeat or paraphrase information heard.

13. Teach the student listening skills (e.g., listen carefully, write down important points, ask for clarification, wait until all directions are received before beginning).

14. Have the student engage in practice activities designed to develop his/her listening skills (e.g., following one-, two-, or three-step directions; listening for the main point; etc.).

15. Give directions in a variety of ways in order to enhance the student's ability to attend.

16. Stop at various points when delivering directions, public announcements, etc., in order to ensure that the student is attending.

17. Deliver directions to the student individually.

18. Demonstrate directions, explanations, and instructions as they are presented orally (e.g., use the chalkboard to work a problem for the student, begin playing a game with the student, etc.).

19. Use pictures, diagrams, and gestures when delivering information.

20. Deliver information slowly to the student.

21. Present one concept at a time. Make certain the student understands each concept before presenting the next.

22. Rephrase directions, explanations, and instructions in order to increase the likelihood of the student understanding what is being presented.

23. Present directions, explanations, and instructions as simply and clearly as possible (e.g., "Get your book. Turn to page 29. Do problems 1 through 5.").

24. When delivering directions, explanations, and instructions be certain to use vocabulary that is within the student's level of comprehension.

25. Have the student practice listening skills by taking notes when directions, explanations, and instructions are presented.

26. Play games designed to teach listening skills (e.g., *Simon Says, Red Light-Green Light, Mother May I?*, etc.).

27. Have the student practice group listening skills (e.g., "Everyone take out a piece of paper. Write your name on the paper. Number your paper from 1 to 20.").

28. Teach the student when to ask questions, how to ask questions, and what types of questions obtain what types of information.

29. Have the student silently repeat information just heard to help him/her remember the important facts.

30. Use multiple modalities (e.g., auditory, visual, tactile, etc.) when presenting directions, explanations, and instructional content. Determine which modality is stronger and utilize the results.

31. Teach the student direction-following skills (e.g., stop doing other things, listen carefully, write down important points, wait until all directions are given, question any directions not understood, etc.).

32. Interact frequently with the student. Make certain that eye contact is being made in order to ensure the student is attending.

33. Have the student tape record directions, explanations, and instructions in order that he/she may apply information as often as needed.

34. Identify the student's most efficient learning mode and use it consistently to increase the probability of understanding (e.g., if the student fails to understand directions or information presented verbally, present it in written form).

35. Have the student question any directions, explanations, and instructions he/she does not understand.

36. Identify a peer to act as a model for the student to imitate appropriate listening skills.

37. Evaluate the level of difficulty of information to which the student is expected to listen (e.g., information communicated on the student's ability level).

38. Write a contract with the student specifying what behavior is expected (e.g., listening to directions, explanations, and instructions) and what reinforcement will be made available when the terms of the contract have been met.

39. Reinforce those students in the classroom who listen to directions, explanations, and instructions.

40. Speak to the student to explain: (a) what he/she is doing wrong (e.g., not listening to directions, explanations, and instructions) and (b) what he/she should be doing (e.g., listening to directions, explanations, and instructions).

41. Reinforce the student for listening: (a) give the student a tangible reward (e.g., classroom privileges, line leading, passing out materials, five minutes free time, etc.) or (b) give the student an intangible reward (e.g., praise, handshake, smile, etc.).

7 Needs oral questions and directions frequently repeated

1. Make certain the student's hearing has been checked recently.

2. Present oral questions and directions in a clear and concise manner and at an appropriate pace for the student.

3. Reduce distracting stimuli (e.g., place the student on the front row, provide a carrel or "office" space away from distractions, etc.). This is used as a form of reducing distracting stimuli and not as a form of punishment.

4. Have the student take notes relative to oral questions and directions.

5. Have a peer help the student follow oral questions and directions.

6. Maintain mobility in order to provide assistance to the student.

7. Present oral questions and directions in a variety of ways in order to increase the probability of understanding (e.g., if the student fails to understand verbal directions, present them in written form).

8. Maintain consistency in the manner in which oral questions and directions are delivered.

9. Deliver oral questions that involve only one concept or step. Gradually increase the number of concepts or steps as the student demonstrates success.

10. Stand close to or directly in front of the student when delivering oral questions and directions.

11. Teach the student listening skills (e.g., stop working, look at the person delivering questions and directions, have necessary note-taking materials, etc.).

12. Deliver questions and directions in written form.

13. Identify a peer to deliver and/or repeat oral questions and directions.

14. Tell the student that oral questions and directions will be given only once.

15. Give a signal prior to delivering directions orally to the student.

16. Deliver oral directions prior to handing out materials.

17. Teach the student direction-following skills (e.g., listen carefully, write down important points, etc.).

18. Interact frequently with the student in order to help the student follow directions for an activity.

19. Have the student orally repeat or paraphrase the directions to the teacher.

20. Establish assignment rules (e.g., listen to directions, wait until all oral directions have been given, ask questions about anything you do not understand, begin the assignment when you are certain about what you are supposed to do, make certain you have all necessary materials, etc.).

21. Make certain the student is attending while you deliver oral questions and directions (e.g., making eye contact, hands free of writing materials, looking at assignment, etc.).

22. Maintain visibility to and from the student when delivering oral questions and directions. The teacher should be able to see the student and the student should be able to see the teacher, making eye contact possible at all times in order to make certain the student is attending.

23. Call the student by name prior to delivering oral questions and directions.

24. Make certain that eye contact is being made between you and the student when delivering oral questions and directions.

25. Stop at various points during the presentation of directions to check the student's comprehension.

26. Give the student one task to perform at a time. Introduce the next task only when the student has successfully completed the previous task by following directions correctly.

27. Provide visual information (e.g., written directions, instructions, etc.) to support the information the student receives auditorily.

28. Tell the student what to listen for when being given directions, receiving information, etc.

29. Use pictures, diagrams, the chalkboard, and gestures when delivering information.

30. When delivering directions, explanations, and information be certain to use vocabulary that is within the student's level of comprehension.

31. Deliver information to the student on a one-to-one basis or employ a peer tutor.

32. Make it pleasant and positive for the student to ask questions about things not understood. Reinforce the student by assisting, congratulating, praising, etc.

33. Evaluate the appropriateness of requiring the student to respond to oral questions and directions without needing repetition.

34. Have the student question any directions, explanations, and instructions he/she does not understand.

35. Identify a peer to act as a model for the student to imitate responding to oral questions and directions without requiring repetition.

36. Communicate with parents (e.g., notes home, phone calls, etc.) in order to share information concerning the student's progress and so that they can reinforce the student at home for responding to oral questions and directions without requiring repetition at school.

37. Write a contract with the student specifying what behavior is expected (e.g., following directions with one cue) and what reinforcement will be made available when the terms of the contract have been met. (See Appendix for Behavioral Contract.)

38. Reinforce the student for responding to oral questions and directions without requiring repetition based on the number of times the student can be successful. Gradually increase the number of times required for reinforcement as the student demonstrates success.

39. Reinforce those students in the classroom who respond to oral questions and directions without requiring repetition.

40. Establish classroom rules:
1. Work on-task.
2. Work quietly.
3. Remain in your seat.
4. Finish task.
5. Meet task expectations.
Reiterate rules often and reinforce students for following rules.

41. Speak with the student to explain: (a) what the student is doing wrong (e.g., needing oral questions and directions repeated) and (b) what the student should be doing (e.g., responding to oral questions and directions without requiring repetition).

42. Reinforce the student for responding to oral questions and directions without requiring frequent repetition: (a) give the student a tangible reward (e.g., classroom privileges, line leading, passing out materials, five minutes free time, etc.) or (b) give the student an intangible reward (e.g., praise, handshake, smile, etc.).

8 Attends more successfully when close to the source of sound

1. Make certain the student's hearing has been checked recently.

2. Maintain mobility in order to provide assistance to the student, be frequently near the student, etc.

3. Maintain consistency in the manner in which oral questions and directions are given.

4. Deliver oral questions and directions that involve only one step. Gradually increase the number of concepts or steps as the student demonstrates success.

5. Stand close to or directly in front of the student when delivering oral questions and directions.

6. Teach the student listening skills (e.g., stop working, look at the person delivering questions and directions, have necessary note-taking materials, etc.).

7. Tell the student that oral questions and directions will only be given once.

8. Give a signal to the student before delivering directions, explanations, or instructions (e.g., clap hands, turn lights off and on, etc.).

9. Have the student repeat or paraphrase the directions orally to the teacher.

10. Teach the student direction-following skills (e.g., listen carefully, write down important points, etc.).

11. Interact frequently with the student in order to help him/her follow directions for an activity.

12. Make certain the student is attending before delivering directions, explanations, or instructions (e.g., maintaining eye contact, hands free of writing materials, looking at the assignment, etc.).

13. Establish assignment rules (e.g., listen carefully, wait until all oral directions have been given, ask questions about anything you do not understand, begin the assignment only when you are certain about what you are to do, make certain you have all necessary materials, etc.).

14. Maintain visibility to and from the student when delivering directions, explanations, or instructions (i.e., the teacher should be able to see the student and the student should be able to see the teacher, making eye contact possible at all times) in order to make certain the student is attending.

15. Call the student by name prior to delivering directions, explanations, or instructions.

16. Seat the student close to the source of information in the classroom. Gradually move the student away from the source of information as he/she demonstrates success.

17. Make certain that directions, explanations, or instructions are delivered loudly enough to be heard by the student.

18. Move the student away from other students who may interfere with his/her ability to attend to directions, explanations, or instructions.

19. Stop at key points when delivering directions, explanations, or instructions in order to determine student comprehension.

20. Present directions, explanations, or instructions as simply and clearly as possible (e.g., "Get your book. Turn to page 29. Do problems 1 through 5.").

21. Stop at various points during the presentation of information to check the student's comprehension.

22. Make certain that the student has adequate opportunities for repetition of information through different experiences.

23. Teach the student listening skills (e.g., stop working, look at the person delivering questions and directions, have necessary note-taking materials, etc.).

24. Identify the student's most efficient learning mode and use it consistently to increase the probability of understanding (e.g., if the student fails to understand information presented verbally, present it in written form).

25. Make certain that all directions, questions, explanations, and instructions are delivered in the most clear and concise manner, at an appropriate pace, and loudly enough for the student to hear.

26. Maintain mobility in order to provide assistance to the student, be frequently near the student, etc.

27. Have the student take notes relative to oral questions and directions.

28. Present oral questions and directions in a clear and concise manner.

29. Reduce distracting stimuli (e.g., make certain the classroom is quiet, reduce movement in the classroom, etc.).

30. Identify a peer to act as a model for the student to imitate responding to information from any location in the classroom.

31. Write a contract with the student specifying what behavior is expected (e.g., attending to information from any location in the classroom) and what reinforcement will be made available when the terms of the contract have been met.

32. Reinforce the student for attending to information presented from any location in the classroom: (a) give the student a tangible reward (e.g., classroom privileges, line leading, passing out materials, five minutes free time, etc.) or (b) give the student an intangible reward (e.g., praise, handshake, smile, etc.).

1. Make certain the student's hearing has been checked recently.

2. Remove the distracting stimuli in the student's immediate environment (e.g., books, writing materials, personal property, etc.).

3. Reduce visual and auditory stimuli in and around the classroom which interfere with the student's ability to listen successfully (e.g., close the classroom door and windows, draw the shades, etc.).

4. Deliver information to the student on a one-to-one basis. Gradually include more students in the group with the student as he/she demonstrates the ability to listen successfully.

5. Maintain eye contact when delivering information to the student. Gradually decrease the amount of eye contact as the student demonstrates the ability to listen successfully.

6. Reinforce the student for attending to the source of information. Continuous eye contact is not necessary for reinforcement.

7. Deliver information in a clear and concise manner.

8. Deliver information in both verbal and written form.

9. Evaluate the level of information presented to the student to determine if the information is presented at a level the student can understand.

10. Maintain visibility to and from the student at all times in order to ensure that the student is attending.

11. Make certain information is delivered loudly enough to be heard by the student.

12. Seat the student close to the source of information in the classroom. Gradually move the student away from the source of information as the student demonstrates success.

13. Make certain the student is not engaged in activities that interfere with directions, explanations, and instructions (e.g., looking at other materials, putting away materials, talking to others, etc.).

14. Require the student to repeat or paraphrase information heard in order to determine successful listening.

15. Teach the student listening skills (e.g., have hands free of writing materials, clear desk of nonessential materials, attend to the source of information, etc.) in order to enhance his/her ability to listen successfully.

16. Deliver a predetermined signal to the student (e.g., hand signal, turn lights off and on, etc.) prior to delivering information.

17. Verbally present information that is necessary for the student to have in order to perform successfully.

18. Have the student take notes when information is verbally presented.

19. Maintain consistency in the format in which information is verbally presented.

20. Call the student by name prior to delivering information.

21. Allow natural consequences to occur as a result of the student's failure to listen (e.g., the inability to respond correctly, a failing grade, etc.).

22. Make certain that the student is seated close enough to see and hear the teacher when information is being delivered.

23. Use multiple modalities (e.g., auditory, visual, tactile, etc.) when presenting directions, explanations, and instructional content. Determine which modality is stronger and utilize the results.

24. Make the subject matter meaningful to the student (e.g., explain the purpose of an assignment, relate the subject matter to the student's environment, etc.).

25. Stop at various points during the presentation of information to check the student's comprehension.

26. Tell the student what to listen for when given directions, receiving information, etc.

27. Have the student question any directions, explanations, or instructions he/she does not understand.

28. Write a contract with the student specifying what behavior is expected (e.g., listening to directions, explanations, and instructions) and what reinforcement will be made available when the terms of the contract have been met.

29. Reinforce the student for listening based on the length of time the student can be successful. Gradually increase the length of time required for reinforcement as the student demonstrates success.

30. Reinforce those students in the classroom who listen to directions, explanations, and instructions.

31. Speak to the student to explain: (a) what the student is doing wrong (e.g., failing to listen to directions, explanations, and instructions) and (b) what the student should be doing (e.g., listening to directions, explanations, and instructions).

32. Reinforce the student for listening: (a) give the student a tangible reward (e.g., classroom privileges, line leading, passing out materials, five minutes free time, etc.) or (b) give the student an intangible reward (e.g., praise, handshake, smile, etc.).

10 Fails to demonstrate short-term memory skills

1. Make certain the student's hearing has been recently checked.

2. Reinforce the student for demonstrating short-term memory skills: (a) give the student a tangible reward (e.g., classroom privileges, line leading, passing out materials, five minutes free time, etc.) or (b) give the student an intangible reward (e.g., praise, handshake, smile, etc.).

3. Reinforce the student for demonstrating short-term memory skills based on the length of time he/she can be successful. Gradually increase the length of time required for reinforcement as the student demonstrates success.

4. Write a contract with the student specifying what behavior is expected (e.g., following two-step directions, etc.) and what reinforcement will be made available when the terms of the contract have been met.

5. Evaluate the appropriateness of the memory activity to determine: (a) if the task is too difficult and (b) if the length of time scheduled to complete the task is appropriate.

6. Have the student question any directions, explanations, instructions he/she does not understand.

7. Have the student act as a classroom messenger. Give the student a verbal message to deliver to another teacher, the secretary, an administrator, etc. Increase the length of the messages as the student demonstrates success.

8. Review the schedule of the morning or afternoon activities with the student and have him/her repeat the sequence. Increase the length of the sequence as the student demonstrates success.

9. Have the student engage in concentration game activities with a limited number of symbols. Gradually increase the number of symbols as the student demonstrates success.

10. Reinforce students for remembering to have materials such as pens, pencils, paper, textbooks, notebooks, etc.

11. At the end of the school day, have the student recall three activities in which he/she was engaged during the day. Gradually increase the number of activities the student is required to recall as he/she demonstrates success.

12. After a field trip or special event, have the student sequence the activities which occurred.

13. After reading a short story, have the student identify the main characters, sequence the events, and report the outcome of the story.

14. Have the student deliver the schedule of daily events to other students.

15. Teach the student to use associative memory clues.

16. Use multiple modalities (e.g., auditory, visual, tactile, etc.) when presenting directions, explanations, and instructional content.

17. Assign a peer tutor to engage in short-term memory activities with the student (e.g., concentration games, following directions, etc.).

18. Record a message on a tape recorder. Have the student write the message after he/she has heard the message. Increase the length of the message as the student demonstrates success.

19. Involve the student in activities to enhance his/her short-term memory skills (e.g., carry messages from one location to another; act as group leader, teacher assistant; etc.).

20. Have the student practice short-term memory skills by engaging in activities which are purposeful to him/her (e.g., delivering messages, being in charge of room cleanup, acting as custodian's helper, operating equipment, etc.).

21. Informally assess the student's auditory and visual short-term memory skills in order to determine which is the stronger. Utilize the results when presenting directions, explanations, and instructional content.

22. Have the student practice repetition of information in order to increase short-term memory skills (e.g., repeating names, telephone numbers, dates of events, etc.).

23. Teach the student how to organize information into smaller units (e.g., break the number sequence 132563 into units of 13, 25, 63).

24. Use sentence dictation to develop the student's short-term memory skills. Begin with sentences of three words and increase the length of the sentences as the student demonstrates success.

25. Show the student an object or a picture of an object for a few seconds. Ask the student to recall specific attributes of the object (e.g., color, size, shape, etc.).

26. Deliver directions, explanations, and instructional content in a clear manner and at an appropriate pace.

27. Have the student practice making notes for specific information he/she wants and/or needs to remember.

28. Teach the student to recognize key words and phrases related to information in order to increase his/her short-term memory skills.

29. Make certain the student is attending to the source of information (e.g., eye contact is being made, hands are free of materials, student is looking at assignment, etc.).

30. Reduce distracting stimuli when information is being presented, the student is studying, etc.

31. Stop at various points during the presentation of information to check for student comprehension.

32. Give the student one task to perform at a time. Introduce the next task only when the student has successfully completed the previous task.

33. Have the student memorize the first sentence or line of poems, songs, etc. Require more to be memorized as the student experiences success.

34. Teach the student information-gathering skills (e.g., listen carefully, write down important points, ask for clarification, wait until all information is received before beginning, etc.).

35. Have the student repeat/paraphrase directions, explanations, and instructions.

36. Reduce the emphasis on competition. Competitive activities may cause the student to hurry and begin without listening carefully.

37. Provide the student with environmental cues and prompts designed to enhance his/her success in the classroom (e.g., posted rules, schedule of daily events, steps for performing tasks, etc.).

38. Provide the student with written lists of things to do, materials he/she will need, etc.

39. Establish a regular routine for the student to follow in performing activities, assignments, etc. (e.g., listen to the person speaking to you, wait until directions are given before starting the assignment, make certain you have all needed materials, etc.).

11 Fails to remember sequences

1. Have the student question any directions, explanations, and instructions not understood.

2. Break the sequence into units and have the student learn one unit at a time.

3. Give the student short sequences (e.g., two components, three components, etc.) to remember. Gradually increase the length of the sequence as the student demonstrates success.

4. Provide the student with environmental cues and prompts (e.g., lists of jobs to perform, schedule of daily events, bell, timer, etc.).

5. Maintain consistency in sequential activities in order to increase the likelihood of student success (e.g, the student has math every day at one o'clock, recess at two o'clock, etc.).

6. Teach the student to use associative cues or mnemonic devices to remember sequences.

7. Have the student maintain notes, written reminders, etc., in order to remember sequences.

8. Actively involve the student in learning to remember sequences by having the student physically perform sequential activities (e.g., operating equipment, following recipes, solving math problems, etc.).

9. Have the student be responsible for helping a peer remember sequences.

10. Have the student practice remembering sequences by engaging in sequential activities which are purposeful (e.g., operating equipment, following recipes, opening a combination lock, etc.).

11. Teach the student to use environmental resources to remember sequences (e.g., calendar, dictionary, etc.).

12. Have the student maintain a notebook in which to keep notes regarding necessary sequential information (e.g., lists of things to do, schedule of events, days of the week, months of the year, etc.).

13. Provide the student with frequent opportunities to recite sequences throughout the day in order to increase memory skills.

14. Assign the student additional activities which require the use of sequences in order to enhance the ability to remember sequences.

15. Practice sequential memory activities each day for those sequences which the student needs to memorize (e.g., important telephone numbers, addresses, etc.).

16. Provide the student with a schedule of daily events for each day's activities at school. (See Appendix for Schedule of Daily Events.)

17. Teach the student to make reminders for himself/herself (e.g., notes, lists, etc.).

18. Make it pleasant and positive for the student to ask questions about things he/she does not understand. Reinforce the student by assisting the student, congratulating, praising, etc.

19. Have the student repeat to himself/herself information just heard to help him/her remember the important facts.

20. Tell the student what to listen for when being given directions, receiving information, etc.

21. Stop at various points during the presentation of information to check the student's comprehension.

22. Help the student employ memory aids.

23. Evaluate the appropriateness of the task to determine: (a) if the task is too difficult and (b) if the length of time scheduled to complete the task is appropriate.

24. Reinforce the student for remembering sequences based on the number of times the student can be successful. Gradually increase the length of the sequences required for reinforcement as the student demonstrates success.

25. Reinforce those students in the classroom who remember sequences.

26. Reinforce the student for remembering sequences: (a) give the student a tangible reward (e.g., classroom privileges, line leading, passing out materials, five minutes free time, etc.) or (b) give the student an intangible reward (e.g., praise, handshake, smile, etc.).

12 Has difficulty concentrating

1. Teach the student to use basic concentration and study skills (e.g., reading for the main idea, note taking, highlighting, outlining, summarizing, studying in an appropriate environment, etc.).

2. Make the subject matter meaningful to the student (e.g., explain the purpose of an assignment, relate the subject matter to the student's environment, etc.).

3. Structure the environment in such a way as to reduce distracting stimuli (e.g., place the student on the front row, provide a carrel or quiet place away from distractions, etc.). This is used as a means of reducing stimuli and not as a form of punishment.

4. Follow a less desirable task with a more desirable task, making the completion of the first necessary to perform the second.

5. Break down large tasks into smaller tasks (e.g., assign the student to write an outline for a book report, then the first rough draft, etc.).

6. Assign a peer tutor to work with the student to serve as a model for appropriate work habits.

7. Allow natural consequences to occur as a result of the student's inability to concentrate (e.g., work not done or completed inaccurately must be made up during recreational time, not concentrating while people are talking results in not knowing what to do, etc.).

8. Give directions in a variety of ways to increase the probability of understanding (e.g., if the student fails to understand verbal directions, present them in written form).

9. Provide clearly stated directions, written or verbal (i.e., make directions as simple and concrete as possible).

10. Reduce directions to steps (e.g., give the student each additional step after completion of the previous step).

11. Make certain the student knows that directions will only be given once.

12. Try various groupings in order to determine the situation in which the student can concentrate most easily.

13. Separate the student from the peers who may be encouraging or stimulating the inappropriate behavior.

14. Reinforce the student for beginning, staying on, and completing assignments.

15. Assign the student shorter tasks and gradually increase the number over time as the student demonstrates success.

16. Use a variety of high-interest means to communicate with the student (e.g., auditory, visual, manipulatives, etc.).

17. Present assignments in small amounts (e.g., assign 10 problems, use pages removed from workbooks, etc.).

18. Make certain that the student's academic tasks are on his/her ability level.

19. Teach the student note-taking skills (e.g., copy main ideas from the chalkboard, identify main ideas from lectures, condense statements into a few key words, etc.).

20. Maintain physical contact with the student while talking to him/her (e.g., touch the student's hand or shoulder).

21. Require the student to make eye contact while delivering information to him/her.

22. Deliver one-, two-, and three-step directions to the student, increasing the number of steps as the student demonstrates success in concentrating.

23. Have the student participate in games requiring varying lengths of concentration (e.g., tic-tac-toe, checkers, chess, etc.).

24. Seat the student close to the source of information.

25. Reduce distracting stimuli in and around the student's desk (e.g., materials in the desk, on the desk, etc.).

26. Highlight or underline important information the student reads (e.g., directions, reading assignments, math word problems, etc.).

27. Tell the student what to listen for when being given directions, receiving information, etc.

28. Make certain the student knows what to look for when reading (e.g., main characters, main ideas, sequence of events, etc.).

29. Provide the student with appropriate time limits for the completion of assignments.

30. Maintain visibility to and from the student at all times in order to monitor the student's concentration.

31. Provide the student with a prompt when the student is off-task (e.g., move close to the student, speak to the student, etc.).

32. Use multiple modalities (e.g., auditory, visual, tactile, etc.) when presenting directions, explanations, and instructional content. By using multiple modalities, the information may hold the student's interest for a longer period of time.

33. Make certain the student is attending to the source of information (e.g., eye contact is being made, hands are free of materials, student is looking at the assignment, etc.).

34. Stop at various points during a presentation of information to check the student's comprehension.

35. Give the student one task to perform at a time. Introduce the next task only when the student has successfully completed the previous task.

36. Teach the student listening skills (e.g., stop working, look at the person delivering questions and directions, have necessary note-taking materials, etc.).

37. Reduce the amount of information on a page if it is causing visual distractions for the student (e.g., less print to read, fewer problems, isolate information that is presented to the student).

38. Use pictures, diagrams, the chalkboard, and gestures when delivering information in order to hold the student's attention.

39. Have the student repeat to himself/herself information just heard to help him/her remember the important facts.

40. Deliver information to the student on a one-to-one basis or employ a peer tutor.

41. Communicate clearly with the student the length of time he/she has to complete the assignment and when the assignment should be completed. The student may want to use a timer in order to complete the tasks within a given period of time.

42. Assess the quality and clarity of directions, explanations, and instructions given to the student.

43. Write a contract with the student specifying what behavior is expected (e.g., concentrating on a task) and what reinforcement will be made available when the terms of the contract have been met.

44. Reinforce the student for concentrating on a task for the length of time the student can be successful. Gradually increase the length of time required for reinforcement.

45. Establish classroom rules:
1. Work on-task.
2. Work quietly.
3. Remain in your seat.
4. Finish task.
5. Meet task expectations.
Reiterate rules often and reinforce students for following rules.

46. Reinforce the student for concentrating: (a) give the student a tangible reward (e.g., classroom privileges, line leading, passing out materials, five minutes free time, etc.) or (b) give the student an intangible reward (e.g., praise, handshake, smile, etc.).

47. Present directions following the outline of : (1) What, (2) How, (3) Materials, and (4) When.

48. Have the student take notes when directions are being given following the "What, How, Materials, and When" format. (See Appendix for Assignment Form.)

49. While concepts are presented, have the student listen and take notes for "Who, What, Where, When, How, and Why." (See Appendix for Outline Form.)

50. Present concepts following the outline of: (1) Who, (2) What, (3) Where, (4) When, (5) How, and (6) Why.

1. Make certain the student's vision has been checked recently.

2. Modify or adjust reading materials to the student's ability level.

3. Use a highlight marker to identify key syllables, words, etc., for the student. These words and phrases become the student's sight word vocabulary.

4. Have the student point to syllables, words, etc., while reading them in order to recognize omissions.

5. Tape record the student's reading in order that he/she can hear omissions.

6. Reduce the emphasis on competition. Competitive activities may cause the student to hurry and omit words.

7. Have the student read aloud to the teacher each day in order to provide evaluative feedback relative to omissions.

8. Verbally correct the student's omissions as often as possible in order that he/she hears the correct version of the reading material.

9. Make a list of those words on which the student makes omissions. Have the student practice reading these words.

10. Have the student use a paper strip to move down the page as he/she reads each line.

11. Make a reading "window" for each textbook the student uses. The student moves the reading "window" down and across the page as he/she reads.

12. Reduce the amount of material the student reads at one time (e.g., reduce reading material to single sentences on a page, a single paragraph, etc.).

13. Enlarge the print the student is reading.

14. Provide a quiet place for the student to work (e.g., "office" space, a study carrel, etc.).

15. Have the student highlight or underline the material he/she reads.

16. Have the student read aloud in order to maintain his/her place.

17. Have the student place a ruler under each line as he/she reads. The student then moves the ruler to the next line and so on.

18. Give the student time to read a selection more than once, emphasizing comprehension rather than speed.

19. Make certain that the reading demands of all subjects and assignments are within the ability level of the student. If not, modify or adjust the reading material to the student's ability level.

20. Make certain that the student's knowledge of a particular skill is being assessed rather than the student's ability to read directions, etc.

21. Reduce the amount of information on a page if it is causing visual distractions for the student (e.g., less print to read, fewer pictures, etc.).

22. Avoid subjecting the student to uncomfortable reading situations (e.g., reading aloud in a group, identifying that the student's reading group is the lowest level, etc.).

23. Have the student point to every word read in order to hold his/her place.

24. Have the student read orally, working for 95%-100% accuracy with no substitutions.

25. In a small group setting, have all students point to all words being read orally. Proceed by having each student read just one sentence, then move automatically to the next student without a break for discussion.

14 Omits, adds, substitutes, or reverses letters, words, or sounds when reading

1. Make certain the student's vision has been checked recently.

2. Set up a system of reinforcers, either tangible (e.g., extra computer time, helper for the day, etc.) or intangible (e.g., smile, handshake, praise, etc.), to encourage the student to be more successful in reading.

3. Make a list of words and phrases from the student's reading material which he/she does not recognize (e.g., have the science teacher identify the words and phrases the student would not recognize in the following week's assignment). These words and phrases will become the student's reading activities for the following week.

4. Modify or adjust reading materials to the student's ability level.

5. Have the student identify words and phrases that he/she does not recognize. Make these words the student's word list to be learned.

6. Emphasize that the student learn a root-word sight vocabulary in order to be able to add various prefixes and suffixes to develop word attack skills.

7. Use a highlight marker to identify key syllables, words, etc., for the student. These words and phrases become the student's sight word vocabulary.

8. Use a sight word vocabulary approach in order to teach the student key words and phrases when reading directions and instructions (e.g., key words such as *circle, underline, match,* etc.).

9. Tape record pronunciations of words on which the student commonly makes errors in order that he/she can hear all the sounds.

10. Tape record the student's reading in order that he/she can hear omissions, additions, substitutions, or reversals.

11. Have the student point to syllables while reading them in order to help him/her recognize omissions, additions, substitutions, or reversals.

12. Make certain the student is learning basic word lists to assist in reading.

13. Reduce the emphasis on competition. Competitive activities may cause the student to omit, add, substitute, or reverse letters, words, or sounds when reading.

14. Have the student read aloud to the teacher each day in order to provide evaluative feedback relative to omissions, additions, substitutions, and reversals.

15. Verbally correct the student's omissions, additions, substitutions, and reversals as often as possible in order that he/she hears the correct version of the reading material.

16. Make a list of those words for which the student has omission, addition, substitution, or reversal errors. Have the student practice reading these words.

17. Have the student write those letters, words, or sounds in which he/she omits, adds, substitutes, or reverses in order to have a greater opportunity to see the correct version.

18. Make certain the student has an alphabet strip at his/her desk to use as a reference for the correct form of letters in order to reduce reversal-related errors when reading.

19. Teach the student to use context clues in reading. These skills will be particularly helpful when he/she is experiencing difficulty with reversals.

20. Tape record difficult reading material for the student to listen to while he/she reads along.

21. Teach reading, spelling, and handwriting simultaneously with all students at the chalkboard.

22. Make certain that the reading demands of all subjects and assignments are within the ability level of the student. If not, modify or adjust the reading material to the student's ability level.

23. Make certain that the student's knowledge of a particular skill is being assessed rather than the student's ability to read directions, instructions, etc. Reading directions, instructions, etc., to the student can increase success.

24. In a small group, require all students to point, look, and listen when other group members read orally.

25. Reduce the amount of material the student reads at one time (e.g., reduce reading material to single sentences on a page, a single paragraph, etc.). Gradually increase the amount of material as the student experiences success.

26. Reduce the amount of information on a page if it is causing visual distractions for the student (e.g., less print to read, fewer pictures on a page, etc.).

27. Use a kinesthetic approach by having the child point to every word and read orally. Stop the student for immediate correction if necessary, while continuing with ample praise for hard work and success.

28. Keep a simple picture-coded sound chart available at all times for the student to use in checking and comparing.

15 Fails to copy letters, words, sentences, and numbers from a textbook, chalkboard, etc.

1. Make certain the student's vision has been recently checked.

2. Enlarge the print from which the student is copying.

3. Change the format of the material from which the student copies (e.g., less material to be copied, enlarge the print, etc.).

4. Seat the student closer to the material being copied.

5. Highlight or underline the material the student is copying.

6. Have the student copy small amounts of material (e.g., a sentence or line) at a time.

7. Make certain that the student has only those materials necessary for copying (e.g., pencil, pen, paper, etc.) on his/her desk.

8. Provide the student with a private place to work (e.g., study carrel, "office," etc.). This is used to reduce distracting stimuli and not as a form of punishment.

9. Employ a variety of ways for the student to obtain information without copying it (e.g., teacher-made material, commercially-produced material, photocopy of the material, etc.).

10. Have a peer assist the student in copying the material (e.g., by reading the material aloud as the student copies it, copying the material for the student, etc.).

11. Make certain that the material to be copied has a clear background/foreground contrast in order to maximize visibility (e.g., black on white projections, white chalk on green chalkboard, etc.).

12. Place the material from which the student is to copy close to him/her. Gradually move the material away from the student as long as he/she can be successful.

13. Maintain consistency of the format from which the student copies.

14. Make certain that there is no glare on the material to be copied from a distance.

15. Provide the student with material to copy at his/her desk if he/she is unable to copy it from a distance.

16. Identify any particular letters or numbers the student has difficulty copying and have him/her practice copying those letters and numbers.

17. Have the student practice writing letters, words, and sentences by tracing over a series of dots.

18. Make certain the student has a number line and alphabet strip on his/her desk to use as a reference for the correct form of letters and numbers in order to reduce errors.

19. Require the student to proofread all written work. Reinforce the student for each correction made.

20. Recognize quality work (e.g., display the student's work, congratulate the student, etc.).

21. Provide the student with quality materials to perform assignments (e.g., pencil with eraser, paper, dictionary, handwriting sample, etc.). Be certain that the student has only the necessary materials on his/her desk.

22. Assess the appropriateness of giving the student assignments which require copying if the student's ability makes it impossible to complete the assignment.

23. Reduce the emphasis on competition. Competitive activities may cause the student to hurry and commit any number of errors.

24. Use the computer and monitor as an alternative writing tool.

25. If the student wears glasses, encourage him/her to wear them for board work.

26. Reduce distracting stimuli (e.g., noise and motion in the classroom) in order to enhance the student's ability to copy letters, words, sentences, and numbers from a model.

27. Have the student question any directions, explanations, and instructions not understood.

28. Evaluate the appropriateness of the task to determine: (a) if the task is too difficult and (b) if the length of time scheduled to complete the task is appropriate.

29. Reinforce the student for copying letters, words, sentences, and numbers from a model: (a) give the student a tangible reward (e.g., classroom privileges, line leading, passing out materials, five minutes free time, etc.) or (b) give the student an intangible reward (e.g., praise, handshake, smile, etc.).

1. Speak to the student to explain what he/she is doing wrong (e.g., not writing in clear and complete sentences, leaving words out, etc.) and what he/she should be doing (e.g., writing in clear and complete sentences, rereading written work, etc.).

2. Reduce the emphasis on competition. Competitive activities may cause the student to hurry and omit, add, or substitute words when writing.

3. Have the student proofread all written work for omissions, additions, or substitutions. Reinforce the student for correcting omissions, additions, or substitutions.

4. Encourage the student to read all written work aloud in order to detect omissions, additions, or substitutions.

5. Give the student several sentences and have him/her combine them to practice making a complete sentence (e.g., *The car is new. The car is red. The car is mine.* becomes *The new, red car is mine.*).

6. Give the student a list of transition words (e.g., *therefore, although, because,* etc.) and have him/her make sentences using each word.

7. Have the student write a daily log or diary expressing thoughts in complete sentences.

8. Encourage the student to create stories about topics which interest him/her in order to provide more experiences in writing.

9. Have the student complete "fill-in-the-blank" stories and sentences and then read them aloud.

10. Make certain the student is aware of the types of errors made (e.g., omits *is*, omits final *s,* etc.) in order to be more conscious of them when writing.

11. Make certain the student is not interrupted or hurried when engaged in writing activities.

12. Have the student assist in grading or proofreading other students' written work in order to become more aware of omissions, additions, and substitutions.

13. Have the student engage in writing activities designed to cause him/her to want to be successful in writing (e.g., writing a letter to a friend, rock star, famous athlete, etc.).

14. When correcting or grading the student's writing, be certain to provide evaluative feedback which is designed to be instructional (e.g., point out all omissions, additions, and substitutions; suggest more appropriate words or phrases; help the student rewrite work to make corrections in the omissions, additions, and substitutions; etc.).

15. Give the student scrambled words from a sentence and have him/her put them in the correct order to form the sentence.

16. Give the student a group of related words (e.g., *baseball, fans, glove, strikeout,* etc.) and have him/her make up a paragraph including each word.

17. Reduce distracting stimuli when the student is engaged in writing activities by placing the student in a carrel or "office" space. This is used as a means of reducing the distracting stimuli and not as a form of punishment.

18. Make a list of the student's most common omissions, additions, and substitutions and have him/her refer to the list when engaged in writing activities in order to check for errors.

19. Have the student practice writing simple sentences successfully without omissions, additions, and substitutions.

20. Make certain the student has written work proofread by someone (e.g., aide, peer, etc.) for omissions, additions, and substitutions before turning in the completed assignment.

21. Recognize quality work (e.g., display the student's work, congratulate the student, etc.).

22. Check the student's work at various points throughout a writing assignment in order to detect any omissions, additions, or substitutions.

23. Require the student to proofread all written work. Reinforce the student for each correction made.

24. Dictate sentences to the student to encourage successful writing of simple sentences.

25. Have the student read simple passages and tape record them. Then have the student underline passages that were omitted.

17 Fails to complete homework assignments and return them to school

1. Reinforce the student for completing homework assignments and returning them to school: (a) give the student a tangible reward (e.g., classroom privileges, line leading, passing out materials, five minutes free time, etc.) or (b) give the student an intangible reward (e.g., praise, handshake, smile, etc.).

2. Speak to the student to explain: (a) what he/she is doing wrong (e.g., not completing homework assignments, not returning homework to school, etc.) and (b) what he/she should be doing (e.g., completing homework assignments and returning them to school).

3. Establish homework assignment rules (e.g., work on-task, finish task, meet task expectations). Reiterate rules often and reinforce students for following rules.

4. Reinforce those students in the classroom who complete their homework assignments and return them to school.

5. Reinforce the student for completing homework assignments based on the number of assignments the student can successfully complete. Gradually increase the number of assignments required for reinforcement as the student demonstrates success.

6. Write a contract with the student specifying what behavior is expected (e.g., completing homework assignments and returning them to school) and what reinforcement will be made available when the terms of the contract have been met.

7. Communicate with parents (e.g., notes home, phone calls, etc.) in order to share information concerning the student's progress and so that they can reinforce the student at home for returning completed homework to school.

8. Evaluate the appropriateness of the task to determine: (a) if the task is too easy, (b) if the task is too difficult, and (c) if the length of time scheduled to complete the task is appropriate.

9. Identify a peer to act as a model for the student to imitate completing homework assignments and returning them to school.

10. Have the student keep a chart or graph representing the number of homework assignments completed and returned to school.

11. Have the student question any directions, explanations, instructions he/she does not understand.

12. Assess the appropriateness of assigning the student homework if his/her ability or circumstances at home make it impossible to complete and return the assignments.

13. Meet with parents to instruct them in appropriate ways to help the student with homework.

14. Assign a peer to help the student with homework.

15. Present the tasks in the most attractive and interesting manner possible.

16. Allow the student additional time to turn in homework assignments.

17. Deliver directions orally in order to increase the probability of the student's understanding of homework assignments.

18. Chart homework assignments completed.

19. Repeat directions in order to increase the student's probability of understanding.

20. Allow the student to perform a highly desirable task when his/her homework has been completed.

21. Give directions in a variety of ways in order to increase the probability of understanding (e.g., if the student fails to understand verbal directions, present them in written form).

22. Provide the parents with information necessary for them to help the student with homework (e.g., what the assignments are and how to help with the assignments).

23. Provide the student with written directions for doing homework assignments.

24. Allow natural consequences to occur for failure to complete homework assignments (e.g., students who do not finish their homework do not get to engage in more desirable activities).

25. Encourage the parents to provide the student with a quiet, comfortable place and adequate time to do homework.

26. Introduce the student to other resource persons who may be of help in performing homework assignments (e.g., librarian, special education teacher, other personnel with expertise or time to help, etc.).

27. Make certain the student understands that assignments not completed during work time will have to be completed during other times (e.g., break time, recreational time, before school, after school, etc.).

28. Take proactive steps to deal with student refusal to perform a homework assignment in order that the rest of the group will not be exposed to contagion (e.g., refrain from arguing with the student, place the student at a carrel or other quiet place to work, remove the student from the group or classroom, etc.).

29. Maintain consistency of expectations and keep the expectations within the ability level of the student.

30. Work a few problems with the student on homework assignments in order to serve as a model and start the student on the assignment.

31. Make certain to provide the student with a selection of assignments, requiring him/her to choose a minimum number from the total (e.g., present the student with 10 academic tasks from which he/she must finish 6 that day).

32. Make certain that homework is designed to provide drill activities rather than introduce new information.

33. Develop a contract with the student and his/her parents requiring that homework be done before more desirable activities take place at home (e.g., playing, watching television, going out for the evening, etc.).

34. Should the student fail to take necessary materials home, provide a set of these materials to be kept at home and send directions for homework with the student.

35. Provide a reinforcing activity at the beginning of the day, contingent upon the completion and return of homework assignments.

36. Assign small amounts of homework initially, gradually increasing the amount over time (e.g., one or two problems to perform may be sufficient to begin the homework process).

37. Find a tutor (e.g., peer, volunteer, etc.) to work with the student at home.

38. Provide time at school for homework completion when the student cannot be successful in performing assignments at home.

39. Provide the student with a book bag, backpack, etc., to take homework assignments and materials to and from home.

40. Send homework assignments and materials directly to the home with someone other than the student (e.g., brother or sister, neighbor, etc.).

41. Create a learning center at school with time available before school begins, the last hour of each school day, etc., and where professional educators are available to help with homework assignments.

42. Do not use homework as a punishment (i.e., additional work should not be assigned as a consequence for inappropriate behavior at school).

18 Does not perform or complete classroom assignments during class time

1. Reinforce the student for attempting and completing classroom assignments during class time: (a) give the student a tangible reward (e.g., classroom privileges, line leading, passing out materials, five minutes free time, etc.) or (b) give the student an intangible reward (e.g., praise, handshake, smile, etc.).

2. Speak with the student to explain: (a) what the student is doing wrong (e.g., not completing assignments) and (b) what the student should be doing (e.g., completing assignments during class).

3. Establish classroom rules:
1. Work on-task.
2. Work quietly.
3. Remain in your seat.
4. Finish task.
5. Meet task requirements.
Reiterate rules often and reinforce students for following rules.

4. Reinforce the student for attempting and completing assignments based on the amount of work he/she can successfully complete. Gradually increase the amount of work required for reinforcement as the student demonstrates success.

5. Write a contract with the student specifying what behavior is expected (e.g., attempting and completing class assignments) and what reinforcement will be made available when the terms of the contract have been met. (See Appendix for Behavioral Contract.)

6. Have the student keep a chart or graph representing the number of class assignments completed.

7. Evaluate the appropriateness of the task to determine: (a) if the task is too difficult and (b) if the length of time scheduled for the task is appropriate.

8. Assign a peer to help the student with class assignments.

9. Assess the degree of task difficulty in comparison with the student's ability to perform the task.

10. Assign the student shorter tasks (e.g., modify a 20-problem math activity to 4 activities of 5 problems each, to be done at various times during the day). Gradually increase the number of problems over time.

11. Present tasks in the most attractive and interesting manner possible.

12. Reduce distracting stimuli (e.g., place the student in the front row, provide a carrel or quiet place away from distractions). This is used as a means of reducing stimuli and not as a form of punishment.

13. Interact frequently with the student in order to maintain involvement with class assignments (e.g., ask the student questions, ask the student's opinion, stand close to the student, seat the student near the teacher's desk, etc.).

14. Allow the student additional time to complete class assignments.

15. Supervise the student during class assignments in order to maintain on-task behavior.

16. Deliver directions orally in order to increase the probability of the student's understanding of class assignments.

17. Repeat directions in order to increase the probability of the student's understanding.

18. Encourage the student to ask for clarification of directions for classroom assignments.

19. Follow a less desirable task with a highly desirable task, making the completion of the first necessary to perform the second.

20. Give directions in a variety of ways to increase the probability of understanding (e.g., if the student fails to understand verbal directions, present them in written form).

21. Provide the student with step-by-step written directions for doing class assignments.

22. Make certain the student understands the natural consequences of failing to complete assignments (e.g., students who do not finish their work are not allowed to do more desirable activities).

23. Allow the student to perform alternative assignments. Gradually introduce more components of the regular assignments until those assignments are routinely performed.

24. Explain to the student that work not done during work time will have to be done during other times (e.g., break time, recreational time, after school, etc.).

25. Take steps to deal with student refusal to perform an assignment in order that the rest of the group will not be exposed to contagion (e.g., refrain from arguing with the student, place the student at a carrel or other quiet place to work, remove the student from the group or classroom, etc.).

26. Maintain consistency of expectations while keeping expectations within the ability level of the student.

27. Allow the student the option of performing the assignment at another time (e.g., earlier in the day, later, on another day, or at home).

28. Provide the student with a selection of assignments and require him/her to choose a minimum number from the total (e.g., present the student with 10 academic tasks from which 6 must be finished that day.).

29. Maintain consistency in daily routine.

30. Work a few problems with the student on an assignment in order to serve as a model and help the student begin a task.

31. Reinforce the student for beginning, staying on, and completing assignments.

32. Communicate with parents (e.g., notes home, phone calls, etc.) in order to share information concerning the student's progress and so that they can reinforce the student at home for completing assignments at school.

33. Identify a peer to act as a model for the student to imitate appropriate completion of assignments.

34. Have the student question any directions, explanations, and instructions not understood.

35. Assess the quality and clarity of directions, explanations, and instructions given to the student.

36. Structure the environment in such a way as to provide the student with increased opportunity for help or assistance.

37. Communicate clearly to the student the length of time he/she has to complete the assignment.

38. Communicate clearly to the student when the assignment should be completed.

39. Have the student time assignments in order to monitor his/her own behavior and accept time limits.

40. Structure time units in order that the student knows exactly how long he/she has to work and when to be finished.

41. Provide the student with more than enough time to finish an activity, and decrease the amount of time as the student demonstrates success.

42. Have the student repeat the directions orally to the teacher.

43. Rewrite directions at a lower reading level.

44. Provide the student with shorter tasks given more frequently.

45. Provide the student with a schedule of daily events in order that he/she knows exactly what and how much there is to do in a day. (See Appendix for Schedule of Daily Events.)

46. Prevent the student from becoming over-stimulated by an activity (e.g., frustrated, angry, etc.).

47. Specify exactly what is to be done for the completion of the task (e.g., indicate definite starting and stopping points, indicate a minimum requirement, etc.).

48. Require the student to begin each assignment within a specified period of time (e.g., three minutes, five minutes, etc.).

49. Provide clearly stated directions in written or verbal form (i.e., make the directions as simple and concrete as possible).

50. Interact frequently with the student in order to help him/her follow directions for the assignments.

51. Provide alternatives for the traditional format of directions (e.g., tape record directions, summarize directions, directions given by peers, etc.).

52. Practice direction-following skills on nonacademic tasks (e.g., recipes, games, etc.).

53. Reduce directions to steps (e.g., give the student each additional step after completion of the previous step).

54. Make certain the student achieves success when following directions.

55. Reduce the emphasis on early completion. Hurrying to complete assignments may cause the student to fail to follow directions.

56. Have the student use a timer in order to complete tasks within a given period of time.

57. Present one assignment at a time. As each assignment is completed, deliver reinforcement along with the presentation of the next assignment.

58. Establish assignment rules:
  1. Listen to directions.
  2. Wait until all directions have been given.
  3. Ask questions about anything not understood.
  4. Make certain you have all necessary materials.
  5. Begin assignment when you are certain about what to do.
Reiterate rules often and reinforce students for following rules.

59. Allow the student access to pencils, pens, etc., only after directions have been given.

60. Make certain that the student is attending to the teacher when directions are given (e.g., making eye contact, hands free of writing materials, looking at assignment, etc.).

61. Maintain visibility to and from the student in order to make certain the student is attending. The teacher should be able to see the student and the student should be able to see the teacher, making eye contact possible at all times.

62. Along with the student, chart those assignments that have been completed in a given period of time.

63. Reduce the emphasis on academic and social competition. Fear of failure may cause the student to not want to complete the required number of assignments in a given period of time.

64. Have the student complete assignments in a private place (e.g., carrel, "office," quiet study area, etc.) in order to reduce the anxiety of public failure.

65. Provide the student with the opportunity to perform assignments in a variety of ways (e.g., on tape, with a calculator, orally, etc.).

66. Have the student explain to the teacher what should be done in order to perform the assignments.

67. Make it pleasant and positive for the student to ask questions about things he/she does not understand. Reinforce the student by assisting, congratulating, praising, etc.

68. Provide the student with quality material to perform the assignment (e.g., pencil with eraser, paper, dictionary, handwriting sample, etc.). Be certain that the student has only the necessary material on his/her desk.

69. Make certain the student is not required to learn more information than he/she is capable of at any one time.

70. Provide the student with increased opportunities for help or assistance on academic tasks (e.g., peer tutoring, directions for work sent home, frequent interactions, etc.).

71. Reduce the amount of information on a page if it is causing visual distractions for the student (e.g., less print to read, fewer problems, isolate information that is presented to the student).

19 Is disorganized to the point of not having necessary materials, losing materials, failing to find completed assignments, failing to follow the steps of the assignment in order, etc.

1. Reinforce the student for being organized/prepared for specified activities: (a) give the student a tangible reward (e.g., classroom privileges, line leading, passing out materials, five minutes free time, etc.) or (b) give the student an intangible reward (e.g., praise, handshake, smile, etc.).

2. Speak to the student to explain: (a) what he/she is doing wrong (e.g., failing to bring necessary materials for specified activities) and (b) what he/she should be doing (e.g., having necessary materials for specified activities).

3. Establish classroom rules (e.g., have necessary materials, work on-task, work quietly, remain in your seat, finish task, and meet task expectations). Reiterate rules often and reinforce students for following rules.

4. Reinforce those students in the classroom who are organized/prepared for specified activities.

5. Reinforce the student for being organized/prepared for specified activities based on the number of times he/she can be successful. Gradually increase the number of times required for reinforcement as the student demonstrates success.

6. Write a contract with the student specifying what behavior is expected (e.g., having necessary materials for specified activities) and what reinforcement will be made available when the terms of the contract have been met.

7. Communicate with parents (e.g., notes home, phone calls, etc.) in order to share information concerning the student's progress and so that they may reinforce the student at home for being organized/prepared for specified activities at school.

8. Evaluate the appropriateness of the task to determine: (a) if the task is too easy, (b) if the task is too difficult, and (c) if the length of time scheduled to complete the task is appropriate.

9. Identify a peer to act as a model for the student to imitate being organized/prepared for specified activities.

10. Have the student question any directions, explanations, instructions he/she does not understand.

11. Assign a peer to accompany the student to specified activities in order to make certain the student has the necessary materials.

12. Provide the student with a list of necessary materials for each activity of the day.

13. Provide the student with verbal reminders of necessary materials required for each activity.

14. Provide time at the beginning of each day for the student to organize his/her materials.

15. Provide time at various points throughout the day for the student to organize his/her materials (e.g., before school, recess, lunch, end of the day, etc.).

16. Provide storage space for materials the student is not using at any particular time.

17. Act as a model for being organized/prepared for specified activities.

18. Make certain that work not completed because necessary materials were not brought to the specified activity must be completed during recreational or break time.

19. Have the student chart the number of times he/she is organized/prepared for specified activities.

20. Remind the student at the end of the day when materials are required for specified activities for the next day (e.g., note sent home, verbal reminder, etc.).

21. Have the student establish a routine to follow before coming to class (e.g., check which activity is next, determine which materials are necessary, collect materials, etc.).

22. Have the student leave necessary materials at specified activity areas.

23. Provide the student with a container in which to carry necessary materials for specified activities (e.g., backpack, book bag, briefcase, etc.).

24. Provide adequate transition time between activities for the student to organize his/her materials.

25. Establish a routine to be followed for organization and appropriate use of work materials. Provide the routine for the student in written form, or verbally reiterate often.

26. Provide adequate time for the completion of activities.

27. Assess the quality and clarity of directions, explanations, and instructions given to the student.

28. Provide the student with structure for all academic activities (e.g., specific directions, routine format for tasks, time units, etc.).

29. Minimize materials needed for specified activities.

30. Provide an organizer for materials inside the student's desk.

31. Provide the student with an organizational checklist (e.g., routine activities, materials needed, and steps to follow).

32. Make certain that all personal property is labeled with the student's name.

33. Teach the student how to conserve rather than waste materials (e.g., amount of glue, paper, tape, etc., to use; putting lids, caps, tops on such materials as markers, pens, bottles, jars, cans, etc.).

34. Teach the student to maintain care of personal property and school materials (e.g., keep property with him/her, know where property is at all times, secure property in lockers, leave valuable property at home, etc.).

35. Provide the student with an appropriate place to store/secure personal property (e.g., desk, locker, closet, etc.) and require that the student store all property when not in use.

36. Limit the student's freedom to take property from school if he/she is unable to remember to return such items.

37. Make certain that failure to have necessary materials results in loss of opportunity to participate in activities or a failing grade for that day's activity.

38. Reduce the number of materials for which the student is responsible. Increase the number as the student demonstrates appropriate use of property.

39. Require that lost or damaged property be replaced by the student. If the student cannot replace the property, restitution can be made by working at school.

40. Make certain that the student is not inadvertently reinforced for losing materials. Provide the student with used materials, copies of the materials, etc., rather than new materials if he/she fails to care for the materials in an appropriate manner.

41. Provide the student with more work space (e.g., a larger desk or table at which to work).

42. Reduce distracting stimuli (e.g., place the student on the front row, provide a carrel or quiet place away from distractions, etc.). This is to be used as a means of reducing distracting stimuli and not as a form of punishment.

43. Interact frequently with the student in order to prompt organizational skills and appropriate use of materials.

44. Assign the student organizational responsibilities in the classroom (e.g., equipment, software materials, etc.).

45. Limit the student's use of materials (i.e., provide the student with only those materials necessary at any given time).

46. Act as a model for organization and appropriate use of work materials (e.g., putting materials away before getting others out, having a place for all materials, maintaining an organized desk area, following a schedule for the day, etc.).

47. Have the student maintain an assignment notebook which indicates those materials needed for each activity.

48. Provide the student with a schedule of daily events in order that he/she knows exactly what and how much there is to do in a day. (See Appendix for Schedule of Daily Events.)

49. Supervise the student while he/she is performing school work in order to monitor quality.

50. Allow natural consequences to occur as the result of the student's inability to organize or use materials appropriately (e.g., work not done during work time must be made up during recreational time, materials not maintained will be lost or not serviceable, etc.).

51. Assist the student in beginning each task in order to reduce impulsive behavior.

52. Provide the student with structure for all academic activities (e.g., specific directions, routine format for tasks, time units, etc.).

53. Provide a color coded organizational system (e.g., notebook, folders, etc.).

54. Teach the student to prioritize assignments (e.g., according to importance, length, etc.).

55. Provide adequate time for completion of activities.

56. Develop monthly calendars to keep track of important events, due dates, assignments, etc.

20 Completes assignments with little or no regard to neatness

1. Allow the student to perform schoolwork in a quiet place (e.g., study carrel, library, resource room, etc.) in order to reduce distractions.

2. Assign the student shorter tasks while increasing the quality of expectations.

3. Supervise the student while he/she is performing schoolwork in order to monitor handwriting quality.

4. Provide the student with clearly stated criteria for acceptable work.

5. Have the student read/go over schoolwork with the teacher in order that the student can become aware of the quality of his/her work.

6. Provide the student with samples of work which may serve as models for acceptable quality (e.g., the student is to match the quality of the sample before turning in the assignment).

7. Provide the student with additional time to perform schoolwork in order to achieve quality.

8. Teach the student procedures for doing quality work (e.g., listen to directions, make certain directions are understood, work at an acceptable pace, check for errors, correct for neatness, copy the work over, etc.).

9. Recognize quality (e.g., display the student's work, congratulate the student, etc.).

10. Conduct a preliminary evaluation of the work, requiring the student to make necessary corrections before final grading.

11. Establish levels of expectations for quality handwriting performance, and require the student to correct or repeat assignments until the expectations are met.

12. Provide the student with quality materials to perform assignments (e.g., pencil with eraser, paper, dictionary, handwriting sample, etc.).

13. Provide the student with ample opportunity to master handwriting skills (e.g., instruction in letter positioning, direction, spacing, etc.).

14. Provide the student with an appropriate model of handwriting (e.g., other students' work, teacher samples, commercial samples, etc.) to use at his/her desk.

15. Model appropriate handwriting at all times.

16. Provide a multitude of handwriting opportunities for the student to practice handwriting skills (e.g., writing letters to sports and entertainment figures, relatives, or friends; writing for free information on a topic in which the student is interested, etc.).

17. Have the student trace handwriting models and fade the models as the student develops the skill.

18. Gradually reduce the space between lines as the student's handwriting improves.

19. Use primary paper to assist the student in sizing upper-case and lower-case letters. Use standard-lined paper when the student's skills improve.

20. Use lined paper that is also vertically lined (e.g., | | | | |) to teach the student appropriate spacing skills (e.g., K|a|t|h|y).

21. Use adhesive material (e.g., tape, Dycem material, etc.) to keep paper positioned appropriately for handwriting.

22. Use a pencil grip (e.g., three-sided, foam rubber, etc.) in order to provide the student assistance in appropriate positioning of the pencil or pen.

23. Use handwriting models with arrows that indicate the direction in which the student should correctly form the letters.

24. Provide older students with functional handwriting opportunities (e.g., job application forms, reinforcer surveys, order forms, checks to write, etc.).

25. Make certain that all educators who work with the student maintain consistent expectations of handwriting quality.

26. Make certain the student has a number line and alphabet strip on his/her desk to use as a reference for the correct form of letters and numbers in order to reduce errors.

27. Make certain the student understands that work not done neatly must be redone until it is neat.

28. Recognize quality work (e.g., display student's work, congratulate the student, etc.).

29. Provide the student with shorter tasks, but more of them throughout the day (e.g., 4 assignments of 5 problems each rather than one assignment of 20 problems).

30. Reduce the emphasis on competition. Competitive activities may cause the student to rush through work.

31. If the student does not complete his/her work according to teacher directions and expectations, it must be completed during recreational or break time.

32. Have the student chart the number of times his/her handwriting is acceptable during a given week.

33. Use a different-sized pencil or pencil grip to assist the student with fine motor skills in order to produce acceptable handwriting.

34. Check the student's grip on the pencil to make certain that he/she is holding the pencil correctly.

35. Assign a peer to work with the student in order to provide an acceptable model for the student to imitate.

36. Evaluate the appropriateness of the task to determine: (a) if the task is too easy, (b) if the task is too difficult, and (c) if the length of time scheduled to complete the task is appropriate.

37. Communicate with parents (e.g., notes home, phone calls, etc.) in order to share information concerning the student's progress and so that they can reinforce the student at home for improving the quality of his/her handwriting at school.

38. Write a contract with the student specifying what behavior is expected (e.g., improving the quality of his/her handwriting) and what reinforcement will be made available when the terms of the contract have been met.

39. Reinforce the student for improving the quality of handwriting based on ability. Gradually increase the amount of improvement expected for reinforcement as the student demonstrates success.

40. Reinforce those students in the classroom who turn in assignments which are legible.

41. Establish classroom rules:
1. Work on-task.
2. Work quietly.
3. Remain in your seat.
4. Finish task.
5. Meet task expectations.
Reiterate rules often and reinforce students for following rules.

42. Speak with the student to explain: (a) what the student is doing wrong (e.g., turning in work which has spelling errors or spacing errors, work that is illegible, etc.) and (b) what he/she should be doing (e.g., taking time to check for spelling, spacing errors, etc.).

43. Reinforce conscientiousness in improving handwriting (e.g., double-checking spelling, proper positioning of letters, correct spacing, etc.): (a) give the student a tangible reward (e.g., classroom privileges, line leading, passing out materials, five minutes free time, etc.) or (b) give the student an intangible reward (e.g., praise, handshake, smile, etc.).

1. Establish classroom rules:
1. Work on-task.
2. Work quietly.
3. Request assistance when needed.
4. Remain in your seat.
5. Finish task.
6. Meet task expectations.

Reiterate rules often and reinforce students for following rules.

2. Reinforce those students in the classroom who communicate needs to others when necessary.

3. Reinforce the student for communicating needs to others based on the number of times he/she can be successful. Gradually increase the number of times required for reinforcement as the student demonstrates success.

4. Write a contract with the student specifying what behavior is expected (e.g., asking for teacher assistance when necessary) and what reinforcement will be made available when the terms of the contract have been met. (See Appendix for Behavioral Contract.)

5. Communicate with parents (e.g., notes home, phone calls, etc.) in order to share information concerning the student's progress and so that they can reinforce the student at home for communicating needs to others when necessary at school.

6. Identify a peer to act as a model for the student to imitate communication of needs to others.

7. Encourage the student to question any directions, explanations, and instructions not understood.

8. Evaluate the appropriateness of expecting the student to communicate needs to others when necessary.

9. Maintain mobility throughout the classroom in order to determine the student's needs.

10. Offer the student assistance frequently throughout the day.

11. Make certain that directions, explanations, and instructions are delivered on the student's ability level.

12. Structure the environment in order that the student is not required to communicate all needs to others (i.e., make certain the student's tasks are on his/her ability level, be sure that instructions are clear, and maintain frequent interactions with the student in order to ensure success).

13. In order to detect the student's needs, communicate with the student as often as opportunities permit.

14. Demonstrate accepting behavior (e.g., willingness to help others, making criticisms constructive and positive, demonstrating confidentiality in personal matters, etc.).

15. Communicate to the student an interest in his/her needs.

16. Communicate to the student that he/she is a worthwhile individual.

17. Call on the student often in order to encourage communication.

18. Teach the student communication skills (e.g., hand raising, expressing needs in written and/or verbal forms, etc.).

19. Encourage communication skills in the classroom.

20. Communicate your own personal needs and feelings to the student.

21. Encourage the student to communicate needs to other personnel in the educational environment (e.g., school counselor, school psychologist, principal, etc.).

22. Communicate with parents, agencies, or appropriate parties in order to inform them of the problem, determine the cause of the problem, and find solutions to the problem.

23. Teach the student to communicate needs in an appropriate manner (e.g., raise hand, use a normal tone of voice when speaking, verbally express problems, etc.).

24. Recognize the student's attempts to communicate needs (e.g., facial expressions, gestures, inactivity, self-depreciating comments, etc.).

25. Have the student interact with a peer in order to encourage him/her to communicate needs to others. Gradually increase the number of peers the student interacts with as he/she demonstrates success in communicating needs to others.

26. Pair the student with a nonthreatening peer, a peer with similar interests and ability level, etc.

27. Give the student responsibilities in the classroom in order to increase the probability of communication (e.g., passing out materials, collecting lunch money, collecting schoolwork, etc.).

28. Give the student responsibilities in the classroom that require communication (e.g., peer tutor, group leader, teacher assistant, etc.).

29. Have the student keep a chart or graph representing the number of assignments performed independently.

30. Assess the degree of task difficulty in comparison with the student's ability to perform the task.

31. Assign the student shorter tasks (e.g., modifying a 20-problem math activity to 4 activities of 5 problems each, to be done at various times during the day). Gradually increase the number of problems as the student demonstrates success.

32. Present the task in the most interesting manner possible.

33. Reduce distracting stimuli (e.g., place the student in the front row, provide a carrel or quiet place away from distractions, etc.). This is to be used as a means of reducing stimuli and not as a form of punishment.

34. Allow the student additional time to complete assignments when working independently.

35. Encourage the student to ask for clarification of directions for assignments.

36. Provide the student with step-by-step written directions for assignments.

37. Allow the student to perform alternative assignments. Gradually introduce more components of the regular assignments until those assignments are routinely performed.

38. Explain to the student that work not done during work time will have to be done during other times (e.g., break time, recreational time, after school, etc.).

39. Maintain consistency of expectations while keeping expectations within the ability level of the student.

40. Maintain consistency in daily routine.

41. Work a few problems with the student on an assignment in order to serve as a model and help the student begin a task.

42. Reinforce the student for beginning, working on, and completing assignments.

43. Provide the student with a selection of assignments and require him/her to choose a minimum number of assignments to perform independently (e.g., present the student with 10 academic tasks from which six must be finished that day).

44. Communicate clearly with the student the length of time he/she has to complete the assignment and when the assignment should be completed. The student may want to use a timer in order to complete tasks within a given period of time.

45. Specify exactly what is to be done for the completion of the task (e.g., indicate definite starting and stopping points, indicate the minimum requirements, etc.).

46. Reinforce the student for performing assignments independently.

47. Speak to the student to explain: (a) what the student is doing wrong (e.g., asking for teacher assistance when not necessary) and (b) what the student should be doing (e.g., asking for teacher assistance when necessary).

48. Reinforce the student for communicating needs to others when necessary: (a) give the student a tangible reward (e.g., classroom privileges, line leading, passing out materials, five minutes free time, etc.) or (b) give the student an intangible reward (e.g., praise, handshake, smile, etc.).

22 Does not prepare for school assignments

1. Reinforce the student for turning in homework. Gradually increase the number of times required for reinforcement as the student demonstrates success.

2. Write a contract with the student specifying what behavior is expected (e.g., turning in homework) and what reinforcement will be made available when the terms of the contract have been met. (See Appendix for Behavioral Contract.)

3. Communicate with the parents (e.g., notes home, phone calls, etc.) in order to share information concerning the student's progress and so that they can reinforce the student at home for turning in homework at school.

4. Evaluate the appropriateness of the homework assignment to determine: (a) if the task is too difficult and (b) if the length of time scheduled to complete the task is appropriate.

5. Identify a peer to act as a model for the student to imitate turning in homework assignments.

6. Have the student keep a chart or graph of the number of homework assignments turned in to the teacher.

7. Have the student question any directions, explanations, and instructions not understood.

8. Assess the appropriateness of assigning the student homework if his/her ability or circumstances at home make it impossible to complete and return the assignments.

9. Meet with parents to instruct them in appropriate ways to help the student with homework.

10. Assign a peer to help the student with homework.

11. Present the tasks in the most attractive and interesting manner possible.

12. Allow the student additional time to turn in homework assignments.

13. Deliver directions orally in order to increase the probability of the student's understanding of homework assignments.

14. Chart homework assignments completed.

15. Repeat directions in order to increase the student's probability of understanding.

16. Allow the student to perform a highly desirable task when homework has been turned in.

17. Give directions in a variety of ways in order to increase the probability of understanding (e.g., if the student fails to understand verbal directions, present them in written form).

18. Provide the student with written directions for doing homework assignments.

19. Allow natural consequences to occur for failure to turn in homework assignments (e.g., students who do not finish their homework do not get to engage in more desirable activities).

20. Encourage the parents to provide the student with a quiet, comfortable place and adequate time to do homework.

21. Introduce the student to other resource persons who may be of help in doing homework (e.g., other teachers, the librarian, etc.).

22. Allow the student to perform alternative homework assignments. Gradually introduce more components of the regular homework assignment until the assignments are routinely performed and returned to school.

23. Take proactive steps to deal with student refusal to perform a homework assignment in order that the rest of the group will not be exposed to contagion (e.g., refrain from arguing with the student, place the student in a carrel or other quiet place to work, remove the student from the group or classroom, etc.).

24. Reinforce those students who complete their assignments at school during the time provided.

25. Maintain consistency of expectations and keep the expectations within the ability level of the student.

26. Work a few problems with the student on homework assignments in order to serve as a model and start the student on a task.

27. Make certain that homework is designed to provide drill activities rather than introduce new information.

28. Develop a contract with the student and his/her parents requiring that homework be done before more desirable activities take place at home (e.g., playing, watching television, going out for the evening, etc.).

29. Should the student fail to take necessary materials home, provide a set of these materials to be kept at home and send directions for homework with the student.

30. Assign small amounts of homework initially, gradually increasing the amount as the student demonstrates success (e.g., one or two problems may be sufficient to begin the homework process).

31. Find a tutor (e.g., peer, volunteer, etc.) to work with the student at home.

32. Maintain consistency in assigning homework (i.e., assign the same amount of homework each day).

33. Provide time at school for homework completion when the student cannot be successful in performing assignments at home.

34. Provide the student with a book bag, backpack, etc., to take homework assignments and materials to and from home.

35. Send homework assignments and materials directly to the home with someone other than the student (e.g., brother or sister, neighbor, bus driver, etc.).

36. Schedule the student's time at school in order that homework will not be absolutely necessary if he/she takes advantage of the school time provided to complete assignments.

37. Create a learning center at school, open the last hour of each school day, where professional educators are available to help with homework.

38. Do not use homework as a punishment (i.e., homework should not be assigned as a consequence for inappropriate behavior at school).

39. Arrange with the student's parents to pick up homework each day if the student has difficulty "remembering" to take it home.

40. Set up a homework system for the student (e.g., two days a week work with drill flash cards, three days a week work on book work sent home, etc.). This will add some variety to homework.

41. Specify exactly what is to be done for the completion of the homework task (e.g., indicate definite starting and stopping points, indicate the minimum requirements, etc.).

42. Make certain the student has mastered the concepts presented at school. All homework should be a form of practice for what has been learned at school.

43. Reinforce those students in the classroom who turn in their homework assignments.

44. Establish homework assignment rules:
1. Work on-task.
2. Finish task.
3. Meet task expectations.
4. Turn in task.
Reiterate rules often and reinforce students for following rules.

45. Speak to the student to explain: (a) what the student is doing wrong (e.g., not turning in homework assignments) and (b) what the student should be doing (e.g., completing homework assignments and returning them to school).

46. Reinforce the student for turning in homework assignments: (a) give the student a tangible reward (e.g., classroom privileges, line leading, passing out materials, five minutes free time, etc.) or (b) give the student an intangible reward (e.g., praise, handshake, smile, etc.).

23 Does not remain on-task

1. Evaluate the auditory and visual stimuli in the classroom in order to determine the level of stimuli to which the student can respond in an appropriate manner.

2. Reduce auditory and visual stimuli to a level at which the student can successfully function. Gradually allow auditory and visual stimuli to increase as the student demonstrates that he/she can successfully tolerate the increased levels.

3. Seat the student so that he/she experiences the least amount of auditory and visual stimuli.

4. Provide the student with a quiet place in which to work where auditory and visual stimuli are reduced. This is used to reduce distracting stimuli and not as a form of punishment.

5. Seat the student away from those peers who create the most auditory and visual stimulation in the classroom.

6. Provide the student with a carrel or divider at his/her desk to reduce auditory and visual stimuli.

7. Make certain that all auditory and visual stimuli in the classroom are reduced as much as possible for all learners.

8. Provide the student with the opportunity to move to a quiet place in the classroom any time that auditory and visual stimuli interfere with the ability to function successfully.

9. Provide the student with earphones to wear if auditory stimuli interfere with the ability to function. Gradually remove the earphones as the student can more successfully function in the presence of auditory stimuli.

10. Allow the student to close the door or windows in order to reduce auditory and visual stimuli from outside of the classroom.

11. Remove the student from an activity until he/she can demonstrate appropriate on-task behavior.

12. Require the student to be productive in the presence of auditory and visual stimuli for short periods of time. Gradually increase the length of time the student is required to be productive as he/she becomes successful.

13. Provide the student with shorter tasks which do not require extended attention in order to be successful. Gradually increase the length of the tasks as the student demonstrates success.

14. Have the student engage in small group activities (e.g., free time, math, reading, etc.) in order to reduce the level of auditory and visual stimuli in the group. Gradually increase group size as the student can function successfully.

15. Model for the student appropriate behavior in the presence of auditory and visual stimuli in the classroom (e.g., continuing to work, asking for quiet, moving to a quieter part of the classroom, etc.).

16. Assign the student shorter tasks but more of them (e.g., modify a 20-problem math activity to 4 activities of 5 problems each, to be performed at various times during the day). Gradually increase the number of problems for each activity as the student demonstrates success.

17. Present tasks in the most attractive and interesting manner possible.

18. Assess the degree of task difficulty in relation to the student's ability to successfully perform the task.

19. Interact frequently with the student in order to maintain involvement in the activity (e.g., ask the student questions, ask the student's opinion, stand close to the student, seat the student near the teacher's desk, etc.).

20. Provide the student with a timer to be used to increase the amount of time during which he/she maintains attention (e.g., have the student work on the activity until the timer goes off).

21. Provide the student with a predetermined signal (e.g., hand signal, verbal cue, etc.) when he/she begins to display off-task behaviors.

22. Structure the environment to reduce the opportunity for off-task behavior. Reduce lag time by providing the student with enough activities to maintain productivity.

23. Have the student work with a peer tutor in order to maintain attention to task.

24. Make certain the student has all necessary materials to perform assignments.

25. Make certain the student knows what to do when he/she cannot successfully perform assignments (e.g., raise hand, ask for assistance, go to the teacher, etc.).

26. Maintain visibility to and from the student. The teacher should be able to see the student and the student should be able to see the teacher, making eye contact possible at all times.

27. Make certain to recognize the student when his/her hand is raised in order to convey that assistance will be provided as soon as possible.

28. Teach the student how to manage time until the teacher can provide assistance (e.g., try the problem again, go on to the next problem, wait quietly, etc.).

29. Communicate clearly with the student the length of time he/she has to complete the assignment and when the assignment should be completed. The student may want to use a timer in order to complete tasks within a given period of time.

30. Specify exactly what is to be done for the completion of the task (e.g., indicate definite starting and stopping points, indicate the minimum requirements, etc.).

31. Make certain the student understands that work not done during work time must be completed at other times such as recess, free time, after school, etc.

32. Provide the student with increased opportunities for help or assistance on academic tasks (e.g., peer tutoring, directions for work, frequent interactions, etc.).

33. Identify the student's most efficient learning mode and use it consistently to increase the probability of understanding and remaining on-task for longer periods of time.

34. Give the student one task to perform at a time. Introduce the next task only when the student has successfully completed the previous task.

35. Have the student question any directions, explanations, and instructions not understood.

36. Identify a peer to act as a model for the student to imitate on-task behavior.

37. Communicate with parents (e.g., notes home, phone calls, etc.) in order to share information concerning the student's progress and so that they can reinforce the student at home for staying on-task in the classroom.

38. Write a contract with the student specifying what behavior is expected (e.g., establish a reasonable length of time to stay on-task) and what reinforcement will be made available when the terms of the contract have been met. (See Appendix for Behavioral Contract.)

39. Reinforce the student for attending to task based on the length of time he/she can be successful. Gradually increase the length of time required for reinforcement as the student demonstrates success.

40. Reinforce those students in the classroom who demonstrate on-task behavior.

41. Establish classroom rules:
1. Work on-task.
2. Work quietly.
3. Remain in your seat.
4. Finish task.
5. Meet task expectations.

Reiterate rules often and reinforce students for following rules.

42. Speak to the student to explain: (a) what the student is doing wrong (e.g., failing to attend to tasks) and (b) what the student should be doing (e.g., attending to tasks).

43. Reinforce the student for staying on-task in the classroom: (a) give the student a tangible reward (e.g., classroom privileges, line leading, passing out materials, five minutes free time, etc.) or (b) give the student an intangible reward (e.g., praise, handshake, smile, etc.).

24 Does not perform academically at his/her ability level

NOTE: Make certain that the academic programming is appropriate for the student's ability level.

1. Assess student performance in a variety of ways (e.g., have the student give verbal explanations, simulations, physical demonstrations, etc.).

2. Give shorter assignments, but give them more frequently. Increase the length of the assignments as the student demonstrates success.

3. Structure the environment in such a way as to provide the student with increased opportunity for help or assistance on academic or homework tasks (e.g., provide peer tutors, seat the student near the teacher or aide, etc.).

4. Provide the student with clearly stated written directions for homework in order that someone at home may be able to provide assistance.

5. Teach the student study skills.

6. Reduce distracting stimuli (e.g., place the student in the front row, provide a carrel or "office" space away from distractions, etc.). This is used as a means of reducing distracting stimuli and not as a form of punishment.

7. Interact frequently with the student to monitor task performance.

8. Have the student maintain a chart representing the number of tasks completed and the accuracy rate of each task.

9. Provide time at school for the completion of homework if homework assigned has not been completed or has resulted in failure. (The student's failure to complete homework assignments may be the result of variables in the home over which he/she has no control.)

10. Assess the quality and clarity of directions, explanations, and instructions given to the student.

11. Teach the student note-taking skills.

12. Assess the appropriateness of assigning homework to the student.

13. Teach the student direction-following skills: (a) listen carefully, (b) ask questions, (c) use environmental cues, (d) rely on examples provided, etc.

14. Identify resource personnel from whom the student may receive additional assistance (e.g., librarian, special education teacher, other personnel with expertise or time to help, etc.).

15. Establish a level of minimum accuracy which will be accepted as a level of mastery.

16. Deliver reinforcement for any and all measures of improvement.

17. Mastery should not be expected too soon after introducing new information, skills, etc.

18. Provide the student with self-checking materials, requiring correction before turning in assignments.

19. Should the student consistently fail to complete assignments with minimal accuracy, evaluate the appropriateness of tasks assigned.

20. Provide instruction and task format in a variety of ways (e.g., verbal instructions, written instructions, demonstrations, simulations, manipulatives, drill activities with peers, etc.).

21. If the student has difficulty completing homework assignments with minimal accuracy, provide a time during the day when he/she can receive assistance at school.

22. Make certain the assignments measure knowledge of content and not related skills such as reading or writing.

23. Have assignments read to the student.

24. Have the student respond to tasks orally.

25. Have the assignments tape recorded, allowing the student to listen to questions as often as necessary.

26. Provide the student with opportunities for review prior to grading assignments.

27. Teach the student to practice basic study skills (e.g., reading for the main idea, note taking, summarizing, highlighting, studying in a good environment, using time wisely, etc.). (See Appendix for various study skill areas.)

28. Arrange a time for the student to study with a peer tutor before completing a graded assignment.

29. Provide multiple opportunities for the student to learn the information covered by assignments (e.g., films, visitors, community resources, etc.).

30. Allow the student to respond to alternative assignment questions (e.g., more generalized questions that represent global understanding).

31. Provide parents with information regarding appropriate ways in which to help their child with homework (e.g., read directions with the student, work a few problems together, answer questions, check the completed assignment, etc.).

32. Modify instruction to include more concrete examples in order to enhance student learning.

33. Monitor student performance in order to detect errors and determine where learning problems exist.

34. Reduce the emphasis on competition. Students who compete academically and fail to succeed may cease to try to do well and do far less than they are able.

35. Allow/require the student to make corrections after assignments have been checked the first time.

36. Maintain consistency in assignment format and expectations so as not to confuse the student.

37. Provide the student with evaluative feedback for assignments completed (i.e., identify what the student did successfully, what errors were made, and what should be done to correct the errors).

38. Provide adequate repetition and drill to assure minimal accuracy of assignments presented (i.e., require mastery/minimal accuracy before moving to the next skill level).

39. It is not necessary to grade every assignment performed by the student. Assignments may be used to evaluate student ability or knowledge and provide feedback. Grades may not need to be assigned until mastery/minimal accuracy has been attained.

40. Provide the student with a selection of assignments and require him/her to choose a minimum number from the total amount (e.g., present the student with 10 academic tasks from which 6 must be finished that day).

41. Allow the student to put an assignment away and return to it at a later time if he/she could be more successful.

42. Have the student practice an assignment with the teacher, aide, or peer before performing the assignment for a grade.

43. Monitor the student's performance of the first problem or part of the assignment in order to make certain the student knows what is expected.

44. Provide frequent interactions and encouragement to support the student's confidence and optimism for success (e.g., make statements such as "You're doing great." "Keep up the good work." "I'm really proud of you." etc.).

45. Build varying degrees of difficulty into assignments in order to ensure the student's self-confidence and at the same time provide a challenge (e.g., easier problems are intermingled with problems designed to measure knowledge gained).

46. Work the first few problems of an assignment with the student in order to make certain that he/she knows what to do, how to perform the assignment, etc.

47. Modify academic tasks (e.g., format, requirements, length, etc.).

48. Provide the student with clearly stated step-by-step directions for homework in order that someone at home may be able to provide assistance.

49. Make certain that homework relates to concepts already taught rather than introducing a new concept.

50. Allow the student to perform alternative versions of the assignments. Gradually introduce more components of the regular assignments until those can be performed successfully.

51. Communicate clearly with the student the length of time he/she has to complete the assignment and when the assignment should be completed. The student may want to use a timer in order to complete tasks within a given period of time.

52. Have the student act as a peer tutor to teach another student a concept he/she has mastered. This can serve as reinforcement for the student.

53. Make certain the student has mastery of concepts at each level before introducing a new skill level.

54. Make certain the student is not required to learn more information than he/she is capable of at any one time.

55. Identify the student's most efficient learning mode and use it consistently to increase the probability of understanding.

56. Have the student question any directions, explanations, and instructions not understood.

57. Evaluate the appropriateness of the task to determine: (a) if the task is too difficult and (b) if the length of time scheduled to complete the task is appropriate.

58. Communicate with parents (e.g., notes home, phone calls, etc.) in order to share information concerning the student's progress and so that they can reinforce the student at home for improving his/her academic task and homework performance.

59. Write a contract with the student specifying what behavior is expected (e.g., completing an assignment with __% accuracy) and what reinforcement will be made available when the terms of the contract have been met.

60. Reinforce those students in the classroom who show improvement on academic task and homework performance.

61. Establish classroom rules:
1. Work on-task.
2. Work quietly.
3. Remain in your seat.
4. Finish task.
5. Meet task expectations.
Reiterate rules often and reinforce students for following rules.

62. Speak to the student to explain: (a) what the student is doing wrong (e.g., performing below his/her ability level, failing assignments, etc.) and (b) what the student should be doing (e.g., improving his/her academic task and homework performance).

63. Reinforce the student for improving academic task and homework performance: (a) give the student a tangible reward (e.g., classroom privileges, line leading, passing out materials, five minutes free time, etc.) or (b) give the student an intangible reward (e.g., praise, handshake, smile, etc.).

Please note: If the student continues to fail in spite of the above interventions and is not being served by special education personnel, he/she should be referred for consideration for special education services.

25 Does not listen to or follow verbal directions

1. Teach the student skills for following verbal directions (e.g., listen carefully, write down important points, use environmental cues, wait until all directions are received before beginning, etc.).

2. Give directions in a variety of ways in order to increase the probability of understanding (e.g., if the student fails to understand verbal directions, present them in written form).

3. Provide clearly stated verbal directions (e.g., make the directions as simple and concrete as possible).

4. Reduce distracting stimuli in order to increase the student's ability to follow verbal directions (e.g., place the student on the front row, provide a carrel or "office" space away from distractions, etc.). This is used as a means of reducing distracting stimuli and not as a form of punishment.

5. Interact frequently with the student in order to help him/her follow verbal directions for an activity.

6. Structure the environment in such a way as to provide the student with increased opportunity for help or assistance on academic tasks (e.g., peer tutoring, directions for work sent home, frequent interactions, etc.).

7. Provide alternatives for the traditional format of presenting verbal directions (e.g., tape record directions, summarize directions, directions given by peers, etc.).

8. Assess the quality and clarity of verbal directions, explanations, and instructions given to the student.

9. Have the student practice following verbal directions on nonacademic tasks (e.g., recipes, games, etc.).

10. Have the student repeat directions or give an interpretation after receiving verbal directions.

11. Give verbal directions before handing out materials.

12. Reduce verbal directions to steps (e.g., give the student each additional step after completion of the previous step).

13. Deliver a predetermined signal (e.g., clapping hands, turning lights off and on, etc.) before giving verbal directions.

14. Require that assignments done incorrectly, for any reason, be redone.

15. Make certain the student achieves success when following verbal directions.

16. Reduce the emphasis on competition. Competitive activities may cause the student to hurry to begin the task without verbal directions.

17. Have the student maintain a record (e.g., chart or graph) of his/her performance in following verbal directions.

18. Communicate clearly to the student when it is time to listen to verbal directions.

19. Provide the student with a predetermined signal when he/she is not following verbal directions (e.g., lights turned off and on, hand signals, etc.).

20. Follow a less desirable task with a highly desirable task, making the following of verbal directions and completion of the first task necessary to perform the second task.

21. Prevent the student from becoming overstimulated by an activity (e.g., frustrated, angry, etc.).

22. Make certain the student has all the materials needed to perform the assignment/activity.

23. Require the student to wait until the teacher gives him/her a signal to begin a task (e.g., give a hand signal, ring a bell, etc.).

24. Have a designated person be the only individual to deliver verbal directions to the student.

25. Make certain the student is attending to the teacher (e.g., making eye contact, hands free of writing materials, looking at assignment, etc.) before verbal directions are given.

26. Stand next to the student when giving verbal directions.

27. Maintain visibility to and from the student. The teacher should be able to see the student and the student should be able to see the teacher, making eye contact possible at all times when verbal directions are given.

28. Make certain that verbal directions are delivered in a nonthreatening manner (e.g., positive voice, facial expression, language, etc.).

29. Make certain that verbal directions are delivered in a supportive rather than threatening manner (e.g., "Will you please . . ." or "You need . . ." rather than "You better . . ." or "If you don't . . .").

30. Present directions in both written and verbal forms.

31. Provide the student with a written copy of verbal directions.

32. Tape record directions for the student to listen to individually and repeat as necessary.

33. Maintain consistency in the format of verbal directions.

34. Develop direction-following assignments/activities (e.g., informal activities designed to have the student carry out verbal directions in steps, with increasing degrees of difficulty).

35. Have a peer help the student with any verbal directions he/she does not understand.

36. Seat the student close to the source of the verbal directions (e.g., teacher, aide, peer, etc.).

37. Seat the student far enough away from peers to ensure increased opportunities for attending to verbal directions.

38. Work the first problem or problems with the student in order to make certain that he/she follows the verbal directions accurately.

39. Work through the steps of the verbal directions as they are delivered in order to make certain the student follows the directions accurately.

40. Have the student carry out one step of the verbal directions at a time, checking with the teacher to make certain that each step is successfully followed before attempting the next.

41. Make certain that verbal directions are given on a level at which the student can be successful (e.g., two-step or three-step directions are not given to students who can only successfully follow one-step directions).

42. Give the student one task to perform at a time. Introduce the next task only when the student has successfully completed the previous task.

43. When delivering directions, explanations, and information, be certain to use vocabulary that is within the student's level of comprehension.

44. Assign a peer to work with the student to help him/her follow verbal directions.

45. Have the student question any verbal directions, explanations, and instructions he/she does not understand.

46. Identify a peer to act as a model for the student to imitate the appropriate following of verbal directions.

47. Evaluate the appropriateness of the task to determine: (a) if the task is too difficult and (b) if the length of time scheduled to complete the task is appropriate.

48. Communicate with parents (e.g., notes home, phone calls, etc.) in order to share information concerning the student's progress and so that they can reinforce the student at home for following verbal directions at school.

49. Reinforce those students in the classroom who follow verbal directions.

50. Write a contract with the student specifying what behavior is expected (e.g., following verbal directions) and what reinforcement will be made available when the terms of the contract have been met. (See Appendix for Behavioral Contract.)

51. Establish classroom rules:
1. Work on-task.
2. Work quietly.
3. Remain in your seat.
4. Finish task.
5. Meet task expectations.

Reiterate rules often and reinforce students for following rules.

52. Reinforce the student for following verbal directions based on the length of time the student can be successful. Gradually increase the length of time required for reinforcement as the student demonstrates success.

53. Speak to the student to explain: (a) what the student is doing wrong (e.g., ignoring verbal directions) and (b) what the student should be doing (e.g., listening to and following verbal directions).

54. Reinforce the student for following verbal directions: (a) give the student a tangible reward (e.g., classroom privileges, line leading, passing out materials, five minutes free time, etc.) or (b) give the student an intangible reward (e.g., praise, handshake, smile, etc..

1. Assess the degree of task difficulty in comparison with the student's ability to perform the task.

2. Assign the student shorter tasks (e.g., modify a 20-problem math activity to 4 activities of 5 problems each, to be done at various times during the day). Gradually increase the number of problems over time.

3. Present tasks in the most attractive and interesting manner possible.

4. Reduce distracting stimuli (e.g., place the student in the front row, provide a carrel or quiet place away from distractions). This is used as a means of reducing stimuli and not as a form of punishment.

5. Interact frequently with the student in order to maintain involvement with class assignments (e.g., ask the student questions, ask the student's opinion, stand close to the student, seat the student near the teacher's desk, etc.).

6. Allow the student additional time to complete class assignments.

7. Supervise the student during study time in order to maintain on-task behavior.

8. Deliver directions orally in order to increase the probability of the student's understanding of class assignments.

9. Repeat directions in order to increase the probability of understanding.

10. Encourage the student to ask for clarification of directions for classroom assignments.

11. Follow a less desirable task with a highly desirable task, making the completion of the first necessary to perform the second.

12. Give directions in a variety of ways to increase the probability of understanding (e.g., if the student fails to understand verbal directions, present them in written form).

13. Provide the student with step-by-step written directions for doing class assignments.

14. Make certain the student understands the natural consequences of failing to complete assignments (e.g., students who do not finish their work will not be allowed to do more desirable activities).

15. Allow the student to perform alternative assignments during study time. Gradually introduce more components of the regular assignments until those assignments are routinely performed.

16. Explain to the student that work not done during work time (study time) will have to be done during other times (e.g., break time, recreational time, after school, etc.).

17. Take steps to deal with student refusal to perform assignments during study time in order that the rest of the group will not be exposed to contagion (e.g., refrain from arguing with the student, place the student at a carrel or other quiet place to work, remove the student from the group or classroom, etc.).

18. Maintain consistency of expectations while keeping expectations within the ability level of the student.

19. Allow the student the option of performing assignments during another study time (e.g., earlier in the day, later, on another day, or at home).

20. Provide the student with a selection of assignments and require him/her to choose a minimum number from the total amount (e.g., present the student with 10 academic tasks from which 6 must be finished that day).

21. Maintain consistency in daily routine.

22. Work a few problems with the student on an assignment in order to serve as a model and help the student begin a task.

23. Practice direction-following skills on nonacademic tasks.

24. Reinforce the student for beginning, staying on, and completing assignments during study time.

25. Communicate with parents (e.g., notes home, phone calls, etc.) in order to share information concerning the student's progress and so that they can reinforce the student at home for completing assignments at school.

26. Identify a peer to act as a model for the student to imitate appropriate completion of assignments.

27. Have the student question any directions, explanations, and instructions not understood.

28. Assess the quality and clarity of directions, explanations, and instructions given to the student.

29. Structure the environment in such a way as to provide the student with increased opportunities for help or assistance.

30. Communicate clearly to the student the length of time available to complete the assignment.

31. Communicate clearly to the student when the assignment should be completed.

32. Have the student time his/her assignments in order to monitor personal behavior and accept time limits.

33. Structure time units in order that the student knows exactly how much time is available to work and when work should be finished.

34. Provide the student with more than enough time to finish an activity and decrease the amount of time as the student demonstrates success.

35. Have the student repeat the directions orally to the teacher.

36. Rewrite directions at a lower reading level.

37. Provide the student with shorter tasks given more frequently.

38. Provide the student with a schedule of daily events in order that he/she knows exactly what and how much there is to do in a day. (See Appendix for Schedule of Daily Events.)

39. Prevent the student from becoming over- stimulated by an activity (e.g., frustrated, angry, etc.).

40. Specify exactly what is to be done for the completion of the task (e.g., indicate definite starting and stopping points, indicate a minimum requirement, etc.).

41. Require the student to begin each assignment within a specified period of time (e.g., three minutes, five minutes, etc.).

42. Provide clearly stated directions in written or verbal form (i.e., make the directions as simple and concrete as possible).

43. Interact frequently with the student in order to help him/her follow directions for the assignments.

44. Provide alternatives for the traditional format of directions (e.g., tape record directions, summarize directions, directions given by peers, etc.).

45. Reduce directions to steps (e.g., give the student each additional step after completion of the previous step).

46. Make certain the student achieves success when following directions.

47. Reduce the emphasis on early completion. Hurrying to complete assignments may cause the student to fail to follow directions.

48. Establish assignment rules (e.g., listen to directions, wait until all directions have been given, ask questions about anything you do not understand, make certain you have all necessary materials, begin assignments only when you are certain about what you are supposed to do, etc.).

49. Allow the student access to pencils, pens, etc., only after directions have been given.

50. Make certain that the student is attending to the teacher when directions are given (e.g., making eye contact, hands free of writing materials, looking at assignment, etc.).

51. Maintain visibility to and from the student in order to make certain the student is attending. The teacher should be able to see the student and the student should be able to see the teacher, making eye contact possible at all times.

52. With the student, chart those assignments that have been completed in a given period of time.

53. Present one assignment at a time. As each assignment is completed, deliver reinforcement along with the presentation of the next assignment.

54. Have the student use a timer in order to complete the tasks within a given period of time.

55. Reduce emphasis on academic and social competition. Fear of failure may cause the student to not want to complete assignments in a given period of time.

56. Have the student complete assignments in a private place (e.g., carrel, "office," quiet study area, etc.) in order to reduce the anxiety of public failure.

57. Provide the student with the opportunity to perform assignments/activities in a variety of ways (e.g., on tape, with a calculator, orally, etc.).

58. Have the student explain to the teacher what should be done in order to perform the assignments.

59. Along with a directive, provide an incentive statement (e.g., "If you make appropriate use of study time, you may have free time." etc.).

60. Use a timer to help the student know how much time he/she has to study.

61. Make certain the student has assignments to work on during study time.

62. Assign a peer to help the student with class assignments during study time.

63. Evaluate the appropriateness of the task to determine: (a) if the task is too difficult and (b) if the length of time scheduled to complete the task is appropriate.

64. Have the student keep a chart or graph representing the number of class assignments completed during study time.

65. Write a contract with the student specifying what behavior is expected (e.g., working on class assignments during study time) and what reinforcement will be made available when the terms of the contract have been met. (See Appendix for Behavioral Contract.)

66. Reinforce the student for attempting and completing assignments based on the amount of work the student successfully completes. Gradually increase the amount of work required for reinforcement as the student demonstrates success.

67. Reinforce those students in the classroom who attempt and complete assignments during study time.

68. Establish classroom rules:
1. Work on-task.
2. Work quietly.
3. Remain in your seat.
4. Finish task.
5. Meet task requirements.
Reiterate rules often and reinforce students for following rules.

69. Speak with the student to explain: (a) what the student is doing wrong (e.g., not working during study time) and (b) what the student should be doing (e.g., completing assignments during study time, studying, etc.).

70. Reinforce the student for attempting and completing class assignments during study time: (a) give the student a tangible reward (e.g., classroom privileges, line leading, passing out materials, five minutes free time, etc.) or (b) give the student an intangible reward (e.g., praise, handshake, smile, etc.).

1. Reinforce the student for following necessary steps in math problems: (a) give the student a tangible reward (e.g., classroom privileges, line leading, passing out materials, five minutes free time, etc.) or (b) give the student an intangible reward (e.g., handshake, praise, smile, etc.).

2. Evaluate the appropriateness of the task to determine: (a) if the task is too easy, (b) if the task is too difficult, and (c) if the length of time scheduled for the task is appropriate.

3. Reduce the emphasis on competition. Competitive activities may cause the student to hurry and fail to follow the necessary steps in math problems.

4. Make certain the student recognizes all math operation symbols (e.g., ×, −, +, ÷).

5. Use written reminders by math problems to indicate which step is to be done. Gradually reduce the use of reminders as the student demonstrates success.

6. Put all math problems involving the same steps on a single line, on a separate sheet of paper, etc.

7. Make the math operation symbols next to the problems extra large in order that the student will be more likely to observe the symbol.

8. List the steps in solving math problems on the chalkboard, bulletin board, etc.

9. Have the student check his/her answers to math problems on a calculator.

10. Use a separate piece of paper for each type of math problem, gradually introducing different types of problems on the same page.

11. Provide the student with a list of steps necessary for the problems he/she is attempting to solve. Have the student keep a list at his/her desk for a reference while solving math problems.

12. Color code math operation symbols next to math problems in order that the student will be more likely to observe the symbol.

13. Have a peer tutor work with the student while he/she learns to follow the steps in math problems.

14. Work the first problem or two of a math assignment for the student in order that he/she will know which steps to use.

15. Have the student act as a peer tutor for another student who is learning new math concepts. Explaining steps in basic math problems will help the student cement his/her own skills.

16. Have the student equate math problems to real life situations in order that he/she will better understand the steps involved in solving the problem (e.g., 4×25 is the same as 4 baskets of apples with 25 apples in each basket. How many apples do you have?).

17. Be certain to assign the student math problems requiring the same operation to make it easier for the student to follow steps in solving the problems. More than one operation may be required in an assignment as the student demonstrates success.

28 Does not read or follow written directions

1. Have the student question any written directions, explanations, and instructions he/she does not understand.

2. Assign a peer to work with the student to help him/her follow written directions.

3. Teach the student skills for following written directions (e.g., read carefully, write down important points, ask for clarification, wait until all directions are received before beginning, etc.).

4. Give directions in a variety of ways to increase the probability of understanding (e.g., if the student fails to understand written directions, present them in verbal form).

5. Provide clearly stated written directions (e.g., make the directions as simple and concrete as possible).

6. Reduce distracting stimuli in order to increase the student's ability to follow written directions (e.g., place the student on the front row, provide a carrel or "office" space away from distractions, etc.). This is used as a means of reducing distracting stimuli and not as a form of punishment.

7. Interact frequently with the student in order to help him/her follow written directions.

8. Structure the environment in such a way as to provide the student with increased opportunities for help or assistance on academic tasks (e.g., peer tutoring, directions for work sent home, frequent interactions, etc.).

9. Provide alternatives for the traditional format of presenting written directions (e.g., tape record directions, summarize directions, directions given by peers, etc.).

10. Assess the quality and clarity of written directions, explanations, and instructions given to the student.

11. Practice the following of written directions on nonacademic tasks (e.g., recipes, games, etc.).

12. Have the student repeat written directions orally to the teacher.

13. Reduce written directions to individual steps (e.g., give the student each additional step after completion of the previous step).

14. Deliver a predetermined signal (e.g., clapping hands, turning lights off and on, etc.) before giving written directions.

15. Deliver written directions before handing out materials.

16. Require that assignments done incorrectly, for any reason, be redone.

17. Make certain the student achieves success when following written directions.

18. Reduce the emphasis on competition. Competitive activities may cause the student to hurry to begin the task without following written directions.

19. Have the student maintain a record (e.g., chart or graph) of his/her performance in following written directions.

20. Follow a less desirable task with a highly desirable task, making the completion of the first necessary to perform the second.

21. Prevent the student from becoming over- stimulated by an activity (e.g., frustrated, angry, etc.).

22. Require the student to wait until the teacher gives him/her a signal to begin an activity after receiving written directions (e.g., hand signal, bell ringing, etc.).

23. Make certain that the student is attending to the teacher (e.g., making eye contact, hands free of writing materials, looking at assignment, etc.) before giving written directions.

24. Make certain that written directions are presented on the student's reading level.

25. Maintain visibility to and from the student. The teacher should be able to see the student and the student should be able to see the teacher, making eye contact possible at all times in order to make certain the student is attending to written directions.

26. Present directions in both written and verbal form.

27. Provide the student with a copy of written directions at his/her desk rather than on the chalkboard, posted in the classroom, etc.

28. Tape record directions for the student to listen to individually and repeat as necessary.

29. Develop assignments/activities for following written directions (e.g., informal activities designed to have the student carry out directions in steps, increasing the degree of difficulty).

30. Maintain consistency in the format of written directions.

31. Have a peer help the student with any written directions not understood.

32. Seat the student close to the source of the written directions (e.g., chalkboard, projector, etc.).

33. Make certain that the print is large enough to increase the likelihood of following written directions.

34. Transfer directions from texts and workbooks when pictures or other stimuli make it difficult to attend to or follow written directions.

35. Work through the steps of written directions as they are delivered in order to make certain the student follows the directions accurately.

36. Work the first problem or problems with the student to make certain that he/she follows the written directions accurately.

37. Have the student repeat to himself/herself information just read to help in remembering the important facts.

38. Have the student carry out written directions one step at a time, checking with the teacher to make certain that each step is successfully followed before attempting the next.

39. Make certain that directions are given at the level at which the student can be successful (e.g., two-step or three-step directions should not be given to students who can only successfully follow one-step directions).

40. Use visual cues such as *green dot* to start, *red dot* to stop, arrows, etc., in written directions.

41. Highlight, circle, or underline key words in written directions (e.g., key words such as *match, circle, underline*).

42. Make certain that all directions, questions, explanations, and instructions are delivered in a clear and concise manner and at an appropriate pace for the student.

43. Identify a peer to act as a model for the student to imitate appropriate following of written directions.

44. Evaluate the appropriateness of the task to determine: (a) if the task is too easy, (b) if the task is too difficult, and (c) if the length of time scheduled to complete the task is appropriate.

45. Communicate with parents (e.g., notes home, phone calls, etc.) in order to share information concerning the student's progress and so that they can reinforce the student at home for following written directions at school.

46. Write a contract with the student specifying what behavior is expected (e.g., following written directions) and what reinforcement will be made available when the terms of the contract have been met.

47. Reinforce the student for following written directions based on the length of time he/she can be successful. Gradually increase the length of time required for reinforcement as the student demonstrates success.

48. Reinforce those students in the classroom who follow written directions.

49. Establish classroom rules:
1. Work on-task.
2. Work quietly.
3. Remain in your seat.
4. Finish task.
5. Meet task expectations.

Reiterate rules often and reinforce students for following rules.

50. Speak to the student to explain: (a) what the student is doing wrong (e.g., ignoring written directions) and (b) what the student should be doing (e.g., following written directions).

51. Reinforce the student for following written directions: (a) give the student a tangible reward (e.g., classroom privileges, line leading, passing out materials, five minutes free time, etc.) or (b) give the student an intangible reward (e.g., praise, handshake, smile, etc.)

29 Changes from one activity to another without finishing the first, without putting things away, before it is time to move on, etc.

1. Reinforce the student for changing from one activity to another without difficulty: (a) give the student a tangible reward (e.g., classroom privileges, line leading, passing out materials, five minutes free time, etc.) or (b) give the student an intangible reward (e.g., praise, handshake, smile, etc.).

2. Speak to the student to explain: (a) what he/she is doing wrong (e.g., failing to stop one activity and begin another) and (b) what he/she should be doing (e.g., changing from one activity to another).

3. Establish classroom rules (e.g., work on-task, work quietly, remain in your seat, finish task, meet task expectations). Reiterate rules often and reinforce students for following rules.

4. Reinforce those students in the classroom who change from one activity to another without difficulty.

5. Reinforce the student for demonstrating acceptable behavior based on the length of time the student can be successful. Gradually increase the length of time required for reinforcement as the student demonstrates success.

6. Write a contract with the student specifying what behavior is expected (e.g., putting materials away and getting ready for another activity) and what reinforcement will be made available when the terms of the contract have been met.

7. Communicate with parents (e.g., notes home, phone calls, etc.) in order to share information concerning the student's progress and so that they can reinforce the student at home for demonstrating acceptable behavior at school.

8. Evaluate the appropriateness of the task to determine: (a) if the task is too difficult and (b) if the length of time scheduled to complete the task is appropriate.

9. Have the student question any directions, explanations, instructions he/she does not understand.

10. Assign a peer to work with the student to provide an appropriate model.

11. Explain to the student that he/she should be satisfied with his/her best effort rather than insisting on perfection.

12. Prevent the student from becoming overstimulated by an activity. Supervise student behavior in order to limit overexcitement in physical activities, games, parties, etc.

13. Have the student time his/her activities in order to monitor his/her own behavior and accept time limits.

14. Convince the student that work not completed in one sitting can be completed later. Provide the student with ample time to complete earlier assignments in order to guarantee closure.

15. Provide the student with more than enough time to finish an activity. Decrease the amount of time provided as the student demonstrates success.

16. Structure time limits in order that the student knows exactly how long he/she has to work and when he/she must be finished.

17. Allow a transition period between activities in order that the student can make adjustments in his/her behavior.

18. Employ a signal technique (e.g., turning the lights off and on) to warn that the end of an activity is near.

19. Establish definite time limits and provide the student with this information before the activity begins.

20. Assign the student shorter activities and gradually increase the length of the activities as the student demonstrates success.

21. Maintain consistency in daily routine.

22. Maintain consistency of expectations and keep expectations within the ability level of the student.

23. Allow the student to finish an activity unless it will be disruptive to the schedule.

24. Schedule activities so the student has more than enough time to finish an activity if he/she works consistently.

25. Provide the student with a list of materials needed for each activity (e.g., pencil, paper, textbook, workbook, etc.).

26. Present instructions/directions before handing out necessary materials.

27. Collect the student's materials (e.g., pencil, paper, textbook, workbook, etc.) when it is time to change from one activity to another.

28. Provide the student with clearly stated expectations for all situations.

29. Provide adequate transition time for the student to finish an activity and get ready for the next activity.

30. Prevent the student from becoming so stimulated by an event or activity that he/she cannot control his/her behavior.

31. Establish rules that are to be followed in various parts of the school building (e.g., lunchroom, music room, art room, gymnasium, library, playground, etc.).

32. Identify the expectations of different environments and help the student develop the skills to be successful in those environments.

33. In conjunction with other school personnel, develop as much consistency across the various environments as possible (e.g., rules, criteria for success, behavioral expectations, consequences, etc.).

34. Reduce the student's involvement in activities which prove too stimulating for him/her.

35. Have the student engage in relaxing transitional activities designed to reduce the effects of stimulating activities (e.g., put head on desk, listen to the teacher read a story, put headphones on and listen to relaxing music, etc.).

36. Use a timer to help the student know when it is time to change to a new activity.

30 Does not follow school rules

1. Maintain maximum supervision of the student and gradually decrease supervision as the student is able to follow school rules.

2. Have the student maintain a chart representing the amount of time spent following school rules, with reinforcement given for increasing acceptable behavior.

3. Practice mobility to be frequently near the student.

4. Provide the student with many social and academic successes.

5. Provide the student with positive feedback that indicates he/she is successful.

6. Post school rules in various places, including on the student's desk, in the hallways, etc.

7. Be a consistent authority figure (e.g., be consistent in relationship with students).

8. Provide the student with optional courses of action in order to prevent total refusal to obey school rules (e.g., may return to the classroom).

9. Intervene early to prevent the student's behavior from leading to contagion of other students.

10. Require the student to verbalize the school rules at designated times throughout the day (e.g., before school, during recess, at lunch, at the end of the day, etc.).

11. Have a peer act as a model for following school rules.

12. Interact with the student frequently to determine if school rules are being followed.

13. Make certain that all educators maintain consistent enforcement of school rules.

14. Have the student question any school rules not understood.

15. Provide the student with a list of school rules and/or behavior expectations to carry with him/her at all times in the school environment.

16. Help the student identify specific school rules he/she has difficulty following and make these rules into goals for behavior improvement.

17. Separate the student from the peer(s) who stimulates his/her inappropriate behavior.

18. Make certain that rules and behavior expectations are consistent throughout the school and classroom.

19. Model for the student those behaviors he/she is expected to display in the school environment.

20. Have a peer accompany the student in nonacademic settings.

21. Make certain that behavioral demands are appropriate for the student's ability level (e.g., staying in line, waiting a turn, moving with a group, sitting at a table with a group, moving about the building alone, etc.).

22. Make certain the student is actively involved in the environment (i.e., give the student responsibilities, activities, and errands to run in order to provide purposeful behavior).

23. Reinforce the student for moving from one place to another in an appropriate length of time.

24. Have the student carry a point card at all times so that he/she can be reinforced anywhere in the school environment for following rules.

25. Inform other personnel of any behavior problem that the student may have in order that supervision and assistance may be provided.

26. Be consistent in applying consequences for behavior (e.g., appropriate behavior receives positive consequences while inappropriate behavior receives negative consequences).

27. Reinforce the student for going directly from one location to another.

28. Reinforce the student for remaining in assigned areas (e.g., play areas, student lounge, recreational area, etc.).

29. Use related consequences for the student's inappropriate behavior (e.g., running in the halls results in having to walk with an adult, throwing food in the cafeteria results in having to sit next to an adult when eating, disruption in the library requires additional adult supervision, etc.).

30. Along with a directive, provide an incentive statement (e.g., "When you finish your math, you may go outside to play." "You may have free time after you finish your work.").

31. Intervene early when there is a problem in order to prevent more serious problems from occurring.

32. Before beginning a new activity, make sure the student knows the rules.

33. Teach the student to "think" before acting (e.g., ask himself/herself: "What is happening?" "What am I doing?" "What should I do?" "What will be best for me?").

34. Maintain visibility to and from the student. The teacher should be able to see the student and the student should be able to see the teacher, making eye contact possible at all times.

35. Structure the environment in such a way that the student remains active and involved.

36. Have the student question any directions, explanations, and instructions not understood.

37. Evaluate the appropriateness of the task to determine: (a) if the task is too difficult and (b) if the length of time scheduled to complete the task is appropriate.

38. Communicate with parents (e.g., notes home, phone calls, etc.) in order to share information concerning the student's progress and so that they can reinforce the student at home for following school rules.

39. Write a contract with the student specifying what behavior is expected (e.g., walking in the halls) and what reinforcement will be made available when the terms of the contract have been met. (See Appendix for Behavioral Contract.)

40. Reinforce the student for following school rules based on the length of time the student can be successful. Gradually increase the length of time required for reinforcement as the student demonstrates success.

41. Reinforce those students in the classroom who follow school rules.

42. Establish school rules:
1. Walk in halls.
2. Arrive for class on time.
3. Respect the privacy of others.
4. Talk quietly in the halls.
Reiterate rules often and reinforce students for following rules.

43. Speak to the student to explain: (a) what the student is doing wrong (e.g., failing to follow school rules) and (b) what the student should be doing (e.g., following school rules).

44. Reinforce the student for following school rules: (a) give the student a tangible reward (e.g., classroom privileges, line leading, passing out materials, five minutes free time, etc.) or (b) give the student an intangible reward (e.g., praise, handshake, smile, etc.).

31 Begins assignments before receiving directions or instructions or does not follow directions or instructions

1. Evaluate the appropriateness of the task to determine: (a) if the task is too difficult and (b) if the length of time scheduled to complete the task is appropriate.

2. Have the student question any directions, explanations, and instructions not understood.

3. Assess the quality and clarity of directions, explanations, and instructions given to the student.

4. Assign a peer or volunteer to help the student begin a task.

5. Structure the environment in such a way as to provide the student with increased opportunities for help or assistance.

6. Reduce distracting stimuli (e.g., place the student in the front row, provide a carrel or "office" space away from distractions, etc.). This is used as a means of reducing distracting stimuli and not as a form of punishment.

7. Have the student maintain a record (e.g., chart or graph) of performance in attempting new assignments/activities.

8. Communicate clearly to the student when it is time to begin.

9. Have the student time his/her activities in order to monitor personal behavior and accept time limits.

10. Present the task in the most interesting and attractive manner possible.

11. Maintain mobility in order to provide assistance to the student.

12. Structure time units in order that the student knows exactly how long to work and when to be finished.

13. Provide the student with more than enough time to finish an activity, and decrease the amount of time as the student demonstrates success.

14. Give directions in a variety of ways to increase the probability of understanding (i.e., if the student fails to understand verbal directions, present them in written form).

15. Have the student repeat the directions orally to the teacher.

16. Give a signal (e.g., clapping hands, turning lights off and on, etc.) before giving verbal directions.

17. Provide the student with a predetermined signal when he/she is not beginning a task (e.g., turning lights off and on, hand signals, etc.).

18. Tell the student that directions will be given only once.

19. Rewrite directions at a lower reading level.

20. Deliver verbal directions in a more basic way.

21. Help the student with the first few items on a task and gradually reduce the amount of help over time.

22. Follow a less desirable task with a highly desirable task, making the completion of the first necessary to perform the second.

23. Provide the student with a schedule of activities in order to know exactly what and how much there is to do in a day.

24. Specify exactly what is to be done for the completion of the task (e.g., make definite starting and stopping points, identify a minimum requirement, etc.).

25. Prevent the student from becoming overstimulated by an activity (e.g., frustrated, angry, etc.).

26. Require the student to begin each assignment within a specified period of time (e.g., three minutes, five minutes, etc.).

27. Provide the student with shorter tasks given more frequently.

28. Provide the student with a selection of assignments, requiring him/her to choose a minimum number from the total (e.g., present the student with 10 academic tasks from which 6 must be finished that day).

29. Provide the student with a certain number of problems to do for the assignment, requiring him/her to choose a minimum number from the total (e.g., present the student with 10 math problems from which 7 must be completed).

30. Start with a single problem and add more problems to the task over time.

31. Reduce emphasis on competition (e.g., academic or social). Fear of failure may cause the student to refuse to attempt new assignments/activities.

32. Provide the student with self-checking materials in order to check work privately, reducing the fear of public failure.

33. Have the student attempt the new assignment/activity in a private place (e.g., carrel, "office," quiet study area, etc.) in order to reduce the fear of public failure.

34. Have the student practice a new skill (e.g., jumping rope, dribbling a basketball) alone, with a peer, or with the teacher before the entire group attempts the activity.

35. Provide the student the opportunity to perform the assignment/activity in a variety of ways (e.g., on tape, with a calculator, orally, etc.).

36. Deliver directions/instructions before handing out materials.

37. Allow the student to perform new assignments/activities in a variety of places in the building (e.g., resource room, library, learning center, etc.).

38. Provide the student with a sample of the assignment/activity which has been partially completed by a peer or teacher (e.g., book reports, projects).

39. Do not require the student to complete the assignment/activity in one sitting.

40. Allow the student the option of performing the assignment at another time (e.g., earlier in the day, later, on another day).

41. Make certain that the student has all materials needed in order to perform the assignment/activity.

42. Have the student explain to the teacher what is to be done in order to perform the assignment.

43. Explain to the student that work not done during work time will have to be made up at other times (e.g., during recess, before school, after school, during lunch time).

44. Teach the student direction-following skills (e.g., listen carefully, write down important points, ask for clarification, wait until all directions are received before beginning).

45. Provide clearly stated directions, written or verbal (e.g., make the directions as simple and concrete as possible).

46. Interact frequently with the student in order to help him/her follow directions for the activity.

47. Provide alternatives to the traditional format for directions (e.g., tape record directions, summarize directions, directions given by peers, etc.).

48. Practice direction-following skills on nonacademic tasks.

49. Deliver directions and instructions before handing out materials.

50. Structure the environment in such a way as to provide the student with increased opportunities for help or assistance on academic tasks (e.g., peer tutoring, directions for work sent home, frequent interactions, etc.).

51. Reduce the number of directions given at one time (i.e., give the student each additional step after completion of the previous step).

52. Require that assignments done incorrectly, for any reason, be redone.

53. Make certain the student achieves success when following directions.

54. Reduce the emphasis on competition. Competitive activities may cause the student to hurry into the assignment without following the directions.

55. Establish assignment rules (e.g., listen to directions, wait until all directions have been given, ask questions about anything you do not understand, begin assignments only when you are certain about what is required, make certain you have all necessary materials, etc.).

56. Reinforce those students who receive directions before beginning a new task.

57. Require the student to wait until the teacher gives a signal to begin (e.g., hand signal, ringing of bell, etc.).

58. Require the student to wait until other students begin the task.

59. Require the student to have all necessary materials before beginning the task.

60. Allow the student access to pencils, pens, etc., only after directions have been given.

61. Make certain that the student is attending to the teacher (e.g., making eye contact, hands free of writing materials, looking at assignment, etc.) before directions are given.

62. Stand next to the student when giving directions.

63. Require the student to ask permission from the teacher to begin.

64. Maintain visibility to and from the student (i.e., the teacher should be able to see the student and the student should be able to see the teacher, making eye contact possible at all times) in order to make certain the student is attending.

65. Along with a directive, provide an incentive statement (e.g., "If you wait to begin your work, I will come around to help you with the first problem." etc.).

66. Communicate with parents (e.g., notes home, phone calls, etc.) in order to share information concerning the student's progress and so that they can reinforce the student at home for beginning assignments after receiving directions at school.

67. Write a contract with the student specifying what behavior is expected (e.g., beginning assignments after listening to directions) and what reinforcement will be made available when the terms of the contract have been met. (See Appendix for Behavioral Contract.)

68. Reinforce the student for beginning assignments after receiving directions, instructions, etc., based on the length of time the student can be successful. Gradually decrease the amount of time to begin the task in order for the student to be reinforced.

69. Establish classroom rules:
1. Work on-task.
2. Work quietly.
3. Remain in your seat.
4. Finish task.
5. Meet task expectations.
Reiterate rules often and reinforce students for following rules.

70. Speak with the student to explain: (a) what the student is doing wrong (e.g., not following directions when performing academic tasks) and (b) what he/she should be doing (e.g., listening to directions, asking for clarification if not understood, taking notes, following one step at a time, etc.).

71. Reinforce the student for beginning assignments after receiving directions or instructions; (a) give the student a tangible reward (e.g., classroom privileges, line leading, passing out materials, five minutes free time, etc.) or (b) give the student an intangible reward (e.g., praise, handshake, smile, etc.).

32 Does not wait his/her turn in activities or games

1. Reinforce the student for taking turns: (a) give the student a tangible reward (e.g., classroom privileges, line leading, passing out materials, five minutes free time, etc.) or (b) give the student an intangible reward (e.g., praise, handshake, smile, etc.).

2. Speak with the student to explain: (a) what he/she is doing wrong (e.g., failing to give others opportunities to have a turn) and (b) what he/she should be doing (e.g., allowing others to have a turn).

3. Reinforce those students in the classroom who take turns.

4. Write a contract with the student specifying what behavior is expected (e.g., taking turns) and what reinforcement will be made available when the terms of the contract have been met.

5. Communicate with the parents (e.g., notes home, phone calls, etc.) in order to share information concerning the student's progress and so that they may reinforce the student at home for taking turns at school.

6. Assess the appropriateness of the task or social situation in relation to the student's ability to perform successfully.

7. Encourage group participation by giving students assignments which require working together to complete the activity (e.g., making murals, bulletin boards, maps, art projects, etc.).

8. Encourage peers to take turns with the student.

9. Have the student work directly with a peer in order to model taking turns, and gradually increase group size over time.

10. Reduce competitiveness in the school environment (e.g., avoid situations where refusing to take turns contributes to winning; avoid situations where winning or "beating" someone else becomes the primary objective of a game, activity, or academic exercise; etc.).

11. Create and reinforce activities (e.g., school bulletin board, class project, bake sale, etc.) in which students work together for a common goal rather than individual success or recognition. Point out that larger accomplishments are realized through group effort rather than by individuals.

12. Allow the student to have many turns and enough materials to satisfy immediate needs, and gradually require sharing and taking turns.

13. Provide special activities for the entire class at the end of the day, which are contingent upon taking turns throughout the day.

14. Structure the classroom environment in such a way as to take advantage of natural opportunities to take turns (e.g., allow more group activities, point out natural consequences when a student takes turns, etc.).

15. Capitalize on opportunities to work together (e.g., when there is a spill, assign students different responsibilities for cleaning it up; when a new student enters the classroom, assign different students responsibilities for orientation; etc.).

16. Discourage students from bringing personal possessions to school which others desire. Encourage the use of communal school property.

17. Require the student to practice taking turns if he/she is unable to willingly do so.

18. Provide enough materials, activities, etc., in order that taking turns will not always be necessary.

19. Provide the student with many opportunities to take turns in order to help him/her learn the concept of taking turns.

20. Make certain that every student gets to use materials, take a turn, etc., and that there is no opportunity for selfishness.

21. Point out to the student the natural rewards of taking turns (e.g., personal satisfaction, friendships, companionship, etc.).

22. Make certain that those students who are willing to take turns are not taken advantage of by their peers.

23. Make certain that other students are taking turns with the student in order that a reciprocal relationship can be expected.

24. Maintain a realistic level of expectation for taking turns.

25. Have the student engage in an activity with one peer and gradually increase the size of the group as the student demonstrates success.

26. Determine the peers with whom the student would most prefer to interact and attempt to facilitate the interaction.

27. Assign an outgoing, nonthreatening peer to interact with the student.

28. Assign the student to interact with younger peers.

29. Assign the student to engage in activities in which he/she is likely to interact successfully with peers.

30. Make certain that the student understands that interacting with peers is contingent upon appropriate behavior.

31. Teach the student appropriate ways to interact with peers in group games (e.g., suggest activities, share materials, problem solve, take turns, follow game rules, etc.).

32. Supervise activities closely in order that the peer(s) with whom the student interacts does not stimulate his/her inappropriate behavior.

33. Make certain that activities are not so stimulating as to make successful interactions with peers difficult.

34. Involve the student in extracurricular activities in order to encourage appropriate interaction with peers.

35. Find the peer with whom the student is most likely to be able to successfully interact (e.g., a student with similar interests, background, classes, behavior patterns, nonacademic schedule, etc.).

36. Make certain, beforehand, that the student is able to successfully engage in the activity (e.g., the student understands the rules, the student is familiar with the game, the student will be compatible with the other students playing the game, etc.).

37. Make certain that the student understands that failing to interact appropriately with peers during activities may result in termination of the game and/or loss of future opportunities to engage in activities.

38. Establish a set of standard behavior rules for group games (e.g., follow the rules of the game, take turns, make positive comments, work as a team member, be a good sport). Reiterate rules often and reinforce students for following the rules.

39. Design activities in which each student takes short turns. Increase the length of each student's turn as the student demonstrates success at taking turns.

40. Allow natural consequences to occur when the student fails to take turns (e.g., other students will not want to interact with him/her, other students will not be willing to take turns, etc.).

41. Talk to the student before playing a game and remind the student of the importance of taking turns.

42. Intervene early when there is a problem in order to prevent more serious problems from occurring.

43. Make certain there is adult supervision when the student is playing games with others.

44. Do not force the student to interact with someone with whom he/she is not completely comfortable.

45. Make certain the student does not become involved in overstimulating activities in which he/she gets excited and cannot settle down.

46. Treat the student with respect. Talk in an objective manner at all times.

47. Provide the student with a predetermined signal when he/she begins to display inappropriate manners.

48. Teach the student to "take turns" (e.g., each student may use the colored pencils for 15 minutes, each student may have three turns, etc.).

33 Grabs things away from others

1. Structure the environment so that time does not permit inappropriate behavior.

2. Teach the student the concept of borrowing by loaning and requiring the return of those things the student has been taking from others.

3. Identify those things the student has been grabbing from others and provide the student with those items as reinforcers for appropriate behavior.

4. Reduce the opportunity to take things from other students by restricting students from bringing unnecessary items to school.

5. Maintain visibility to and from the student. The teacher should be able to see the student and the student should be able to see the teacher, making eye contact possible at all times.

6. Supervise the student in order to monitor behavior.

7. Encourage all students to monitor their own belongings.

8. Make certain the student has his/her own necessary school-related items (e.g., pencil, ruler, paper, etc.).

9. Use a permanent marker to label all property brought to school by students and teachers.

10. Secure all school items of value (e.g., cassette tapes, lab materials, industrial arts and home economics supplies, etc.).

11. Make certain the student understands the natural consequences of inappropriate behavior (e.g., the student must make restitution for taking things which belong to others).

12. Communicate with the student's family to establish procedures whereby the student may earn those things he/she would otherwise take from other students.

13. Teach the student to share (e.g., schedule activities daily which require sharing).

14. Help the student build or create a prized possession to satisfy the need for ownership (e.g., this can be done in art, home economics, industrial arts, etc.).

15. Deal with the grabbing of belongings privately rather than publicly.

16. Provide multiples of the items which are being taken in order to have enough for all or most students to use (e.g., pencils, erasers, rulers, etc.).

17. Intervene early when there is a problem in order to prevent more serious problems from occurring.

18. Teach the student to respect others and their belongings by respecting the student's belongings.

19. Make certain the student does not become involved in overstimulating activities when playing with others.

20. Find a peer to play with the student who will be a good influence (e.g., someone younger, older, of the same sex, of the opposite sex, etc.).

21. Teach the student acceptable ways to communicate displeasure, anger, frustration, etc.

22. Do not assume the student is being treated nicely by others. Peers may be stimulating inappropriate behavior.

23. Teach the student to ask for things in a positive manner. Teach key words and phrases (e.g., "May I borrow your pencil?" "Do you mind if I play with your ball?" etc.).

24. Teach the student the concept of borrowing by allowing the student to borrow things from you and requiring him/her to ask permission before doing so.

25. Teach the student to "take turns" sharing possessions (e.g., each child may use the markers for 15 minutes, one child bats while the other throws the ball, players change places after three hits, etc.).

26. Provide the student with enough "things" that sharing will not be necessary. Gradually reduce the number of things as the student learns to share.

27. Teach the student to "think" before acting (e.g., ask himself/herself: "What is happening?" "What am I doing?" "What should I do?" "What will be best for me?" etc.).

28. Communicate with the parents (e.g., notes home, phone calls, etc.) in order to share information concerning the student's appropriate behavior and so that they can reinforce the student at home for appropriate use or consideration of others' belongings at school.

29. Write a contract with the student specifying what behavior is expected (e.g., not grabbing things away from others) and what reinforcement will be made available when the terms of the contract have been met. (See Appendix for Behavioral Contract.)

30. Remove the student from the group or activity until he/she can demonstrate appropriate behavior and self-control.

31. Reinforce the student for demonstrating appropriate behavior based on the length of time the student can be successful. Gradually increase the length of time required for reinforcement as the student demonstrates success.

32. Reinforce those students in the classroom who demonstrate appropriate behavior in reference to others' belongings.

33. Establish classroom rules:
1. Work on-task.
2. Remain in your seat.
3. Finish task.
4. Meet task expectations.
Reiterate rules often and reinforce students for following rules.

34. Speak with the student to explain: (a) what the student is doing wrong (e.g., grabbing things from others) and (b) what the student should be doing (e.g., asking to use things, borrowing, sharing, returning, etc.).

35. Reinforce the student for demonstrating appropriate behavior: (a) give the student a tangible reward (e.g., classroom privileges, line leading, passing out materials, five minutes free time, etc.) or (b) give the student an intangible reward (e.g., praise, handshake, smile, etc.).

1. Reinforce the student for waiting to be called on before speaking: (a) give the student a tangible reward (e.g., classroom privileges, line leading, passing out materials, five minutes free time, etc.) or (b) give the student an intangible reward (e.g., praise, handshake, smile, etc.).

2. Speak with the student to explain: (a) what the student is doing wrong (e.g., blurting out answers) and (b) what the student should be doing (e.g., waiting until it is appropriate to speak, waiting to be called on before speaking, etc.).

3. Establish classroom rules:
1. Work on-task.
2. Remain in your seat.
3. Finish task.
4. Meet task expectations.
5. Raise your hand.
Reiterate rules often and reinforce students for following rules.

4. Reinforce those students in the classroom who wait to be called on before speaking.

5. Reinforce the student for waiting to be called on before speaking based on the number of times the student can be successful. Gradually increase the number of times required for reinforcement as the student demonstrates success.

6. Remove the student from the group or activity until he/she can demonstrate appropriate behavior and self-control.

7. Write a contract with the student specifying what behavior is expected (e.g., waiting to be called on before speaking) and what reinforcement will be made available when the terms of the contract have been met. (See Appendix for Behavioral Contract.)

8. Evaluate the appropriateness of the task to determine: (a) if the task is too difficult and (b) if the length of time scheduled to complete the task is appropriate.

9. Communicate with parents (e.g., notes home, phone calls, etc.) in order to share information concerning the student's appropriate behavior and so that they can reinforce the student at home for waiting to be called on before speaking.

10. Make certain that reinforcement is not inadvertently given for inappropriate behavior (e.g., blurting out answers without being called on).

11. Give adequate opportunities to respond (i.e., enthusiastic students need many opportunities to contribute).

12. Have the student be the leader of a small group activity if he/she possesses mastery of a skill or has an interest in that area.

13. Provide the student with a predetermined signal if he/she begins to blurt out answers without being called on.

14. Structure the environment in such a way as to limit opportunities for inappropriate behaviors (e.g., keep the student engaged in activities, have the student seated near the teacher, etc.).

15. Give the student responsibilities in the classroom (e.g., running errands, opportunities to help the teacher, etc.).

16. Reduce activities which might threaten the student (e.g., reduce peer pressure, academic failure, teasing, etc.).

17. Provide the student with many social and academic successes.

18. Make the necessary adjustments in the environment to prevent the student from experiencing stress, frustration or anger (e.g., reduce peer pressure, academic failure, teasing, etc.).

19. Maintain visibility to and from the student. The teacher should be able to see the student and the student should be able to see the teacher, making eye contact possible at all times.

20. Interact frequently with the student to reduce the need to blurt out answers without being called on.

21. Assess the appropriateness of the social situation in relation to the student's ability to function successfully.

22. Try various groupings in order to determine the situation in which the student is most comfortable.

23. Reinforce the student for raising his/her hand in order to be recognized.

24. Call on the student when he/she is most likely to be able to respond correctly.

25. Have the student work in small groups in which there are frequent opportunities to speak. Gradually increase the size of the group as the student learns to wait longer for a turn to speak.

26. Make certain that the student's feelings are considered when it is necessary to deal with inappropriate comments (i.e., handle comments in such a way as to not diminish the student's enthusiasm for participation).

27. Encourage the student to model the behavior of peers who are successful.

28. Help the student improve concentration skills (e.g., listening to the speaker, taking notes, preparing comments in advance, making comments in the appropriate context, etc.).

29. Have the student question any directions, explanations, and instructions not understood.

30. Deliver directions, explanations, and instructions in a clear and concise manner in order to reduce the student's need to ask questions.

31. Have the student practice waiting for short periods of time for a turn to speak. Gradually increase the length of time required for reinforcement as the student demonstrates success.

32. Explain to the student the reasons why blurting out answers without being called on is inappropriate (e.g., is impolite, hurts others' feelings, etc.).

33. Attempt to provide equal attention to all students in the classroom.

34. Make the student aware of the number of times he/she blurts out answers without being called on.

35. Do not criticize when correcting the student; be honest yet supportive. Never cause the student to feel bad about himself/herself.

36. Make certain the student does not become overstimulated by an activity.

37. Treat the student with respect. Talk in an objective manner at all times.

38. Provide the student with a predetermined signal when he/she begins to display inappropriate manners.

1. Make certain that reinforcement is not inadvertently given for inappropriate behavior (e.g., interrupting the teacher).

2. Give adequate opportunities to respond (i.e., enthusiastic students need many opportunities to contribute).

3. Provide the student with a predetermined signal if he/she begins to interrupt.

4. Structure the environment in such a way as to limit opportunities for interrupting the teacher (e.g., keep the student engaged in activities, have the student seated near the teacher, etc.).

5. Reduce activities which might cause the student to interrupt or talk out (e.g., announcing test score ranges or test scores aloud, emphasizing the success of a particular student or students, etc.).

6. Provide the student with many social and academic successes.

7. Make the necessary adjustments in the environment to prevent the student from experiencing stress, frustration, or anger (e.g., reduce peer pressure, academic failure, teasing, etc.).

8. Maintain visibility to and from the student. The teacher should be able to see the student and the student should be able to see the teacher, making eye contact possible at all times.

9. Interact frequently with the student to reduce the need to interrupt the teacher.

10. Reinforce the student for raising his/her hand in order to be recognized.

11. Call on the student when he/she is most likely to be able to respond correctly.

12. Teach the student to recognize the appropriate time to speak (e.g., when the teacher has finished speaking, after raising his/her hand, to make comments within the context of the situation, to make comments that are a follow-up to what has just been said, etc.).

13. Have the student work in small groups in which there are frequent opportunities to speak. Gradually increase the size of the group as the student learns to wait longer for a turn to speak.

14. Make certain that the student's feelings are considered when it is necessary to deal with his/her interruptions (i.e., handle comments in such a way as to not diminish the student's enthusiasm for participation).

15. Encourage the student to model the behavior of peers who are successful.

16. Help the student improve concentration skills (e.g., listening to the speaker, taking notes, preparing comments in advance, making comments in the appropriate context, etc.).

17. Have the student question any directions, explanations, and instructions not understood.

18. Deliver directions, explanations, and instructions in a clear and concise manner in order to reduce the student's need to ask questions.

19. Have the student practice waiting for short periods of time for a turn to speak. Gradually increase the length of time required for reinforcement as the student demonstrates success.

20. Explain to the student why it is inappropriate to interrupt the teacher (e.g., is impolite, is unfair to other students, others cannot hear what the teacher is saying, etc.).

21. Attempt to provide equal attention to all students in the classroom.

22. Make the student aware of the number of times he/she interrupts the teacher.

23. Do not criticize when correcting the student, be honest yet supportive. Never cause the student to feel bad about himself/herself.

24. Talk to the student before beginning an activity and remind him/her of the importance of listening and not interrupting.

25. Treat the student with respect. Talk in an objective manner at all times.

26. Provide the student with a predetermined signal when he/she begins to display inappropriate manners.

27. Make certain the student knows when it is acceptable to interrupt others (e.g., in an emergency).

28. Acknowledge the student's presence and/or need to talk with you (e.g., by saying, "Just a minute"; putting your arm around the student; smiling and nodding your head; etc.).

29. Evaluate the appropriateness of the task to determine: (a) if the task is too difficult and (b) if the length of time scheduled to complete the task is appropriate.

30. Communicate with parents (e.g., notes home, phone calls, etc.) in order to share information concerning the student's appropriate behavior and so that they can reinforce the student at home for waiting his/her turn to speak at school.

31. Write a contract with the student specifying what behavior is expected (e.g., waiting for a turn to speak) and what reinforcement will be made available when the terms of the contract have been met. (See Appendix for Behavioral Contract.)

32. Remove the student from the group or activity until he/she can demonstrate appropriate behavior and self-control.

33. Reinforce the student for waiting for a turn to speak based on the length of time the student can be successful. Gradually increase the length of time required for reinforcement as the student demonstrates success.

34. Reinforce those students in the classroom who wait their turn to speak.

35. Establish classroom rules:
1. Work on-task.
2. Remain in your seat.
3. Finish task.
4. Meet task expectations.
5. Raise your hand.
Reiterate rules often and reinforce students for following rules.

36. Speak with the student to explain: (a) what the student is doing wrong (e.g., interrupting the teacher) and (b) what the student should be doing (e.g., waiting until it is appropriate to speak, waiting to be called on, etc.).

37. Reinforce the student for waiting for a turn to speak: (a) give the student a tangible reward (e.g., classroom privileges, line leading, passing out materials, five minutes free time, etc.) or (b) give the student an intangible reward (e.g., praise, handshake, smile, etc.).

1. Reinforce the student for demonstrating appropriate behavior: (a) give the student a tangible reward (e.g., classroom privileges, line leading, passing out materials, five minutes free time, etc.) or (b) give the student an intangible reward (e.g., praise, handshake, smile, etc.).

2. Speak to the student to explain: (a) what the student is doing wrong (e.g., interrupting other students who are trying to work, listen, etc.) and (b) what the student should be doing (e.g., waiting for a turn to speak, working quietly, etc.).

3. Establish classroom rules:
1. Work on-task.
2. Remain in your seat.
3. Finish task.
4. Meet task expectations.
5. Raise your hand.
Reiterate rules often and reinforce students for following rules.

4. Reinforce those students in the classroom who wait their turn to speak, work quietly, etc.

5. Reinforce the student for demonstrating appropriate behavior (e.g., waiting for a turn to speak, working quietly, etc.) based on the length of time the student can be successful. Gradually increase the length of time required for reinforcement as the student demonstrates success.

6. Write a contract with the student specifying what behavior is expected (e.g., waiting for a turn to speak, working quietly, etc.) and what reinforcement will be made available when the terms of the contract have been met. (See Appendix for Behavioral Contract.)

7. Communicate with parents (e.g., notes home, phone calls, etc.) in order to share information concerning the student's appropriate behavior and so that they can reinforce the student at home for not bothering other students at school.

8. Identify a peer to act as a model for the student to imitate appropriate behavior.

9. Have the student question any directions, explanations, and instructions not understood.

10. Reinforce those students in the classroom who demonstrate on-task behavior.

11. Reduce distracting stimuli (e.g., place the student on the front row, provide a carrel or "office" away from distractions, etc.). This is used as a means of reducing distracting stimuli and not as a form of punishment.

12. Interact frequently with the student in order to maintain his/her involvement in the activity (e.g., ask the student questions, ask the student's opinion, stand close to the student, seat the student near the teacher's desk, etc.).

13. Maintain visibility to and from the student. The teacher should be able to see the student and the student should be able to see the teacher, making eye contact possible at all times.

14. Assess the degree of task difficulty in relation to the student's ability to perform the task successfully.

15. Provide a full schedule of activities. Prevent lag time from occurring when the student can bother other students.

16. Remove the student from the group or activity until he/she can demonstrate appropriate behavior and self-control.

17. Teach the student appropriate ways to communicate needs to others (e.g., waiting a turn, raising his/her hand, etc.).

18. Provide the student with enjoyable activities to perform when he/she completes a task early.

19. Seat the student near the teacher.

20. Provide the student with frequent opportunities to participate, share, etc.

21. Provide students with frequent opportunities to interact with one another (e.g., before and after school, between activities, etc.).

22. Seat the student away from those students he/she is most likely to bother.

23. Do not criticize when correcting the student; be honest yet supportive. Never cause the student to feel bad about himself/herself.

24. Talk to the student before beginning an activity and remind him/her of the importance of listening to others.

25. Treat the student with respect. Talk in an objective manner at all times.

26. Provide the student with a predetermined signal when he/she begins to display inappropriate manners.

27. Make sure the student knows when it is acceptable to interrupt others (e.g., in an emergency).

37 Talks to others during quiet activity periods

1. Reinforce the student for working quietly: (a) give the student a tangible reward (e.g., classroom privileges, line leading, passing out materials, five minutes free time, etc.) or (b) give the student an intangible reward (e.g., praise, handshake, smile, etc.).

2. Speak with the student to explain: (a) what the student is doing wrong (e.g., talking to others during quiet activity periods) and (b) what the student should be doing (e.g., waiting until it is appropriate to speak, working quietly, etc.).

3. Establish classroom rules:
1. Work on-task.
2. Remain in your seat.
3. Finish task.
4. Meet task expectations.
5. Raise your hand.
Reiterate rules often and reinforce students for following rules.

4. Reinforce those students in the classroom who work quietly.

5. Reinforce the student for working quietly based on the length of time the student can be successful. Gradually increase the length of time required for reinforcement as the student demonstrates success.

6. Remove the student from the group or activity until he/she can demonstrate appropriate behavior and self-control.

7. Write a contract with the student specifying what behavior is expected (e.g., working quietly) and what reinforcement will be made available when the terms of the contract have been met. (See Appendix for Behavioral Contract.)

8. Communicate with parents (e.g., notes home, phone calls, etc.) in order to share information concerning the student's appropriate behavior and so that they can reinforce the student at home for working quietly at school.

9. Have the student be the leader of a small group activity if he/she possesses mastery of skills or an interest in that area.

10. Evaluate the appropriateness of the task to determine: (a) if the task is too difficult and (b) if the length of time scheduled to complete the task is appropriate.

11. Make certain that reinforcement is not inadvertently given for inappropriate behavior (e.g., making inappropriate comments, talking to others during quiet activity periods, etc.).

12. Give the student adequate opportunities to speak in the classroom, talk to other students, etc. (i.e., enthusiastic students need many opportunities to contribute).

13. Provide the student with a predetermined signal if he/she begins to talk to other students during quiet activity periods.

14. Explain to the student that he/she may be trying too hard to fit in and should relax and wait until more appropriate times to interact.

15. Structure the environment in such a way as to limit opportunities for talking to other students during quiet activity periods (e.g., keep the student engaged in activities, have the student seated near the teacher, etc.).

16. Give the student responsibilities in the classroom (e.g., running errands, opportunities to help the teacher, etc.).

17. Reduce activities which might threaten the student (e.g., announcing test score ranges or test scores aloud, making students read aloud in class, emphasizing the success of a particular student or students, etc.).

18. Provide the student with many social and academic successes.

19. Make the necessary adjustments in the environment to prevent the student from experiencing stress, frustration or anger (e.g., reduce peer pressure, academic failure, teasing, etc.).

20. Interact frequently with the student to reduce the need to talk to other students.

21. Maintain visibility to and from the student. The teacher should be able to see the student and the student should be able to see the teacher, making eye contact possible at all times.

22. Assess the appropriateness of the social situation in relation to the student's ability to function successfully.

23. Try various groupings in order to determine the situation in which the student is most comfortable.

24. Reinforce the student for raising his/her hand in order to be recognized.

25. Call on the student when he/she is most likely to be able to respond correctly.

26. Teach the student to recognize appropriate times to talk to other students (e.g., between activities, during breaks, at recess, etc.).

27. Have the student work in small groups in which there are frequent opportunities to speak. Gradually increase the size of the group as the student learns to wait longer for a turn to speak.

28. Provide the student with a predetermined signal when he/she begins to display inappropriate behavior.

29. Encourage the student to model the behavior of peers who are successful.

30. Help the student improve concentration skills (e.g., listening to the speaker, taking notes, preparing comments in advance, making comments in the appropriate context, etc.).

31. Have the student question any directions, explanations, and instructions not understood in order that he/she does not have to ask other students for information.

32. Deliver directions, explanations, and instructions in a clear and concise manner in order to reduce the student's need to ask other students for information.

33. Make certain that the student's feelings are considered when it is necessary to deal with his/her talking to other students (i.e., handle comments in such a way as to not diminish the student's enthusiasm for participation).

34. After telling the student why he/she should not be talking, explain the reason.

35. Do not leave a lot of unstructured time for the student.

38 Moves about while seated, fidgets, squirms, etc.

1. Reinforce the student for sitting appropriately in his/her seat: (a) give the student a tangible reward (e.g., classroom privileges, line leading, passing out materials, five minutes free time, etc.) or (b) give the student an intangible reward (e.g., praise, handshake, smile, etc.).

2. Speak to the student to explain: (a) what he/she is doing wrong (e.g., tipping chair) and (b) what he/she should be doing (e.g., sitting appropriately in his/her chair).

3. Establish classroom rules (e.g., work on-task, work quietly, remain in your seat, finish task, meet task expectations). Reiterate rules often and reinforce students for following rules.

4. Reinforce those students in the classroom who sit appropriately in their seats.

5. Reinforce the student for sitting appropriately in his/her seat based on the length of time he/she can be successful. Gradually increase the length of time required for reinforcement as the student demonstrates success.

6. Write a contract with the student specifying what behavior is expected (e.g., sitting appropriately in his/her seat) and what reinforcement will be made available when the terms of the contract have been met.

7. Communicate with parents (e.g., notes home, phone calls, etc.) in order to share information concerning the student's progress and so that they may reinforce the student at home for sitting appropriately in his/her seat at school.

8. Evaluate the appropriateness of the task to determine: (a) if the task is too easy, (b) if the task is too difficult, and (c) if the length of time scheduled to complete the task is appropriate.

9. Identify a peer to act as a model for the student to imitate appropriate ways in which to sit in his/her seat.

10. Have the student question any directions, explanations, instructions he/she does not understand.

11. Have desks and/or chairs that can be fastened to the floor or which are designed to prevent tipping.

12. Provide the student with a specific description of appropriate in-seat behavior (e.g., face forward, feet on floor, back straight, etc.).

13. Implement logical consequences for students who fail to sit appropriately in their seats (e.g., the student would have to sit on the floor, stand next to his/her desk to work, sit in a chair without a desk, etc.).

14. Maintain consistency of expectations for having the student sit appropriately in his/her seat.

15. Make certain the student is aware of the natural consequences that may occur from sitting inappropriately in his/her seat (e.g., injury, damaging property, hurting others, etc.).

16. Place the student in a carrel in order to reduce distracting stimuli which may cause him/her to sit inappropriately in his/her seat.

17. Seat the student next to a peer who sits appropriately in his/her seat.

18. Deliver a predetermined signal (e.g., hand signal, bell ringing, etc.) when the student begins to sit inappropriately in his/her seat.

19. Model for the student appropriate ways in which to sit in a chair or at a desk.

20. Provide activities which are interesting to the student in order to keep him/her on-task and sitting appropriately in his/her seat.

21. Seat the student near the teacher.

22. Seat the student away from peers in order to reduce the likelihood that he/she will sit inappropriately in his/her seat.

23. Evaluate the necessity of having the student sit facing forward, feet on floor, back straight, etc.

24. Make certain that the chair or desk to which the student is assigned is appropriate and/or comfortable for him/her (e.g., the desk is not too high, the chair is not too big, etc.).

25. Remove any materials the student uses to make noises while seated.

26. Use natural consequences when the student touches others as they walk by (e.g., move the student to another location in the room, have others walk away from the student, etc.).

1. Reinforce the student for demonstrating physical self-control: (a) give the student a tangible reward (e.g., classroom privileges, line leading, passing out materials, five minutes free time, etc.) or (b) give the student an intangible reward (e.g., praise, handshake, smile, etc.).

2. Speak with the student to explain: (a) what he/she is doing wrong (e.g., moving in seat, moving about the room, running, etc.) and (b) what he/she should be doing (e.g., practicing self-control, following rules, etc.).

3. Establish classroom rules (e.g., work on-task, work quietly, remain in your seat, finish task, meet task expectations). Reiterate rules often and reinforce students for following rules.

4. Reinforce those students in the classroom who demonstrate physical self-control.

5. Reinforce the student for demonstrating appropriate behavior based on the length of time he/she can be successful. Gradually increase the length of time required for reinforcement as the student demonstrates success.

6. Remove the student from the group or activity until he/she can demonstrate appropriate behavior and self-control.

7. Write a contract with the student specifying what behavior is expected (e.g., demonstrating physical self-control) and what reinforcement will be made available when the terms of the contract have been met.

8. Communicate with the parents (e.g., notes home, phone calls, etc.) in order to share information concerning the student's progress and so that they may reinforce the student at home for demonstrating physical self-control at school.

9. Evaluate the appropriateness of the task to determine: (a) if the task is too easy, (b) if the task is too difficult, and (c) if the length of time scheduled for the task is appropriate.

10. Try various groupings in order to determine the situation in which the student is most comfortable.

11. Make the necessary adjustments in the environment to prevent the student from experiencing stress, frustration, anger, etc., as much as possible.

12. Interact frequently with the student to prevent excessive or unnecessary body movements.

13. Maintain visibility to and from the student. The teacher should be able to see the student and the student should be able to see the teacher, making eye contact possible at all times.

14. Facilitate on-task behavior by providing a full schedule of daily events. Prevent lag time when the student is free to engage in excessive or unnecessary body movements. (See Appendix for Schedule of Daily Events.)

15. Reduce stimuli which would contribute to unnecessary or excessive behavior.

16. Interact frequently with the student in order to maintain his/her attention to the activity (e.g., ask the student questions, ask the student's opinions, stand close to the student, seat the student near the teacher's desk, etc.).

17. Give the student additional responsibilities (e.g., chores, errands, etc.) to keep him/her actively involved and give him/her a feeling of success or accomplishment.

18. Modify or eliminate situations at school which cause the student to experience stress or frustration.

19. Maintain supervision at all times and in all parts of the school environment.

20. Prevent the student from becoming overly stimulated by an activity (i.e., monitor or supervise student behavior to limit overexcitement in physical activities, games, parties, etc.).

21. Provide the student with a predetermined signal when he/she exhibits inappropriate behavior.

22. Make certain that reinforcement is not inadvertently given for inappropriate behavior (e.g., attending to the student only when he/she engages in excessive/unnecessary body movements).

23. Separate the student from the peer who stimulates the inappropriate behavior.

24. Provide the student with the most attractive and interesting activities possible.

25. Provide the student with a calm, quiet environment in which to work.

26. Provide the student with a quiet place in the environment where he/she may go when he/she becomes upset. This is not meant as punishment, but as a means of helping the student be able to function more successfully in his/her environment.

27. Provide the student frequent opportunities to participate, take a turn, etc., in order to keep him/her involved in the activity.

28. Avoid discussion of topics sensitive to the student (e.g., divorce, death, unemployment, alcoholism, etc.).

29. Seat the student near the teacher.

30. Have the student question any directions, explanations, instructions he/she does not understand.

31. Schedule short activities for the student to perform while seated. Gradually increase the length of the activities as the student demonstrates success at staying in his/her seat.

32. Give the student frequent opportunities to leave his/her seat for appropriate reasons (e.g., getting materials, running errands, assisting the teacher, etc.).

33. Identify a peer to act as a model for the student to imitate staying in his/her seat.

34. Make certain the student has all necessary materials at his/her desk in order to reduce the need to leave his/her seat.

35. Have the student chart the length of time he/she is able to remain in his/her seat.

36. Work the first few problems of an assignment with the student in order that he/she will know what is expected.

40 Is easily angered, annoyed, or upset

1. Prevent frustrating or anxiety-producing situations from occurring (e.g., give the student tasks only on his/her ability level, give the student only the number of tasks that can be tolerated in one sitting, reduce social interactions which stimulate the student to become physically abusive, etc.).

2. Teach the student problem-solving skills: (a) identify the problem, (b) identify goals and objectives, (c) develop strategies, (d) develop a plan of action, and (e) carry out the plan.

3. Provide the student with positive feedback which indicates he/she is successful, important, respected, etc.

4. Maintain maximum supervision of the student. Gradually decrease supervision over time as the student demonstrates self-control.

5. Maintain visibility to and from the student. The teacher should be able to see the student and the student should be able to see the teacher, making eye contact possible at all times.

6. Be mobile in order to be frequently near the student.

7. Reduce activities which might threaten the student (e.g., announcing test score ranges or test scores aloud, making students read aloud in class, emphasizing the success of a particular student or students, etc.).

8. Try various groupings in order to determine the situation in which the student is most successful.

9. Make the necessary adjustments in the environment to prevent the student from experiencing stress, frustration, and anger.

10. Reduce the emphasis on competition and perfection. Repeated failure and frustration may cause the student to become angered, annoyed, or upset.

11. Teach the student alternative ways to deal with situations which make him/her frustrated, angry, etc. (e.g., withdrawing, talking, etc.).

12. Facilitate on-task behavior by providing a full schedule of daily events. Prevent lag time from occurring when the student would be likely to become involved in activities which would cause him/her to be angered, annoyed, or upset. (See Appendix for Schedule of Daily Events.)

13. Maintain supervision in order that the student is not left alone or allowed to be unsupervised with other students.

14. Provide the student with as many high-interest activities as possible.

15. Provide the student with opportunities for social and academic success.

16. Make other personnel aware of the student's tendency to become easily angered, annoyed, or upset.

17. Provide a quiet place for the student to work independently, away from peer interactions. This is not to be used as a form of punishment but as an opportunity to increase the student's success in his/her environment.

18. Place reinforcement emphasis on academic productivity and accuracy to divert the student's attention away from others who cause him/her to become angered, annoyed, or upset.

19. Make the student aware of the natural consequences for becoming easily angered, annoyed, or upset (e.g., loss of friendships, injury, more restrictive environment, legal action, etc.).

20. Separate the student from the peer(s) who may be encouraging or stimulating the student to become angered, annoyed, or upset.

21. Do not force the student to interact or remain in a group if he/she is likely to become angered, annoyed, or upset.

22. Provide the student with a selection of optional activities to be performed if he/she becomes angered, annoyed, or upset.

23. Maintain consistency in expectations.

24. Maintain consistency in daily routine.

25. Remove the student from the group or activity until he/she can demonstrate self-control.

26. Maintain a positive/calm environment (e.g., positive comments, acknowledgment of successes, quiet communications, etc.).

27. Allow flexibility in meeting academic demands when the student becomes angered, annoyed, or upset (e.g., allow more time, modify assignments, provide help with assignments, etc.).

28. Present tasks in the most attractive and interesting manner possible.

29. Make certain to ask the student why he/she becomes easily angered, annoyed, or upset. The student may have the most accurate perception as to why he/she becomes easily angered, annoyed, or upset.

30. Teach the student decision-making steps: (a) think about how others may be influenced, (b) think about consequences, (c) carefully consider the unique situation, (d) think of different courses of action which are possible, (e) think about what is ultimately best, etc.

31. Avoid topics, situations, etc., that may cause the student to become easily angered, annoyed, or upset (e.g., divorce, death, unemployment, alcoholism, etc.).

32. Discourage the student from engaging in those activities that cause him/her to become easily angered, annoyed, or upset.

33. Teach the student to verbalize his/her feelings before losing self-control (e.g., "The work is hard." "Please leave me alone; you're making me angry." etc.).

34. Deliver directions in a supportive rather than a threatening manner (e.g., "Please finish your math assignment before going to recess." rather than "You had better finish your math or else!").

35. Do not criticize. When correcting the student, be honest yet supportive. Never cause the student to feel bad about himself/herself.

36. Intervene early when the student becomes angered, annoyed, or upset in order to prevent more serious problems from occurring.

37. Make certain the student does not become involved in overstimulating activities which cause him/her to become angered, annoyed, or upset.

38. Treat the student with respect. Talk in an objective manner at all times.

39. Be careful to avoid embarrassing the student by giving him/her orders, demands, etc., in front of others.

40. Find a peer to work with the student who would be a good influence (e.g., someone younger, older, of the same sex, of the opposite sex, etc.).

41. Allow the student to attempt something new in private before doing so in front of others.

42. Teach the student acceptable ways to communicate displeasure, anger, frustration, etc.

43. Do not force the student to interact with others.

44. Encourage the student to use problem-solving skills: (a) identify the problem, (b) identify goals and objectives, (c) develop strategies, (d) develop a plan of action, and (c) carry out the plan.

45. Make sure you express your feelings in a socially acceptable way.

46. Make certain the student is allowed to voice an opinion in a situation in order to avoid becoming angry or upset.

47. Teach the student to "think" before acting (e.g., ask himself/herself: "What is happening?" "What am I doing?" "What should I do?" "What will be best for me?").

48. Talk to the student about ways of handling situations successfully without conflict (e.g., walk away from a situation, change to another activity, ask for help, etc.).

49. Have the student question any directions, explanations, and instructions not understood.

50. Identify a peer to act as a model for the student to imitate self-control.

51. Evaluate the appropriateness of the academic task to determine: (a) if the task is too difficult and (b) if the length of time scheduled to complete the task is appropriate.

52. Communicate with parents, agencies, or appropriate parties in order to inform them of the problem, determine the cause of the problem, and find solutions to the problem.

53. Communicate with parents (e.g., notes home, phone calls, etc.) in order to share information concerning the student's progress and so that they will reinforce the student at home for demonstrating self-control at school.

54. Write a contract with the student specifying what behavior is expected (e.g., problem solving, moving away from the situation, asking for assistance from the teacher, etc.) and what reinforcement will be made available when the terms of the contract have been met. (See Appendix for Behavioral Contract.)

55. Reinforce the student for demonstrating self-control based on the length of time the student can be successful. Gradually increase the length of time required for reinforcement as the student demonstrates success.

56. Reinforce those students in the classroom who demonstrate self-control.

57. Establish classroom rules:
1. Work on-task.
2. Work quietly.
3. Remain in your seat.
4. Finish task.
5. Meet task expectations.
Reiterate rules often and reinforce students for following rules.

58. Speak to the student to explain: (a) what the student is doing wrong (e.g., hitting, arguing, throwing things, etc.) and (b) what the student should be doing (e.g., moving away from the situation, asking for assistance from the teacher, etc.).

59. Reinforce the student for demonstrating self-control in those situations in which he/she is likely to become angry, annoyed, or upset: (a) give the student a tangible reward (e.g., classroom privileges, line leading, passing out materials, five minutes free time, etc.) or (b) give the student an intangible reward (e.g., praise, handshake, smile, etc.).

41 Bothers other students who are trying to work, listen, etc.

1. Reduce distracting stimuli (e.g., place the student on the front row, provide a carrel or "office" away from distractions, etc.). This is used as a means of reducing distracting stimuli and not as a form of punishment.

2. Interact frequently with the student in order to maintain his/her involvement in the activity (e.g., ask the student questions, ask the student's opinion, stand close to the student, seat the student near the teacher's desk, etc.).

3. Maintain visibility to and from the student. The teacher should be able to see the student and the student should be able to see the teacher, making eye contact possible at all times.

4. Assess the degree of task difficulty in relation to the student's ability to perform the task successfully.

5. Provide a full schedule of activities. Prevent lag time from occurring when the student can bother other students.

6. Remove the student from the group or activity until he/she can demonstrate appropriate behavior and self-control.

7. Teach the student appropriate ways to communicate needs to others (e.g., waiting a turn, raising his/her hand, etc.).

8. Provide the student with enjoyable activities to perform when he/she completes a task early.

9. Seat the student near the teacher.

10. Provide the student with frequent opportunities to participate, share, etc.

11. Provide students with frequent opportunities to interact with one another (e.g., before and after school, between activities, etc.).

12. Seat the student away from those students he/she is most likely to bother.

13. Intervene early when there is a problem in order to prevent a more serious problem from occurring.

14. Teach the student to respect others and their belongings by respecting the student and his/her belongings.

15. Identify a peer who would be a good influence to interact with the student (e.g., someone younger, older, of the same sex, of the opposite sex, etc.).

16. Make certain the student knows when it is acceptable to interrupt others (e.g., an emergency).

17. Do not leave a lot of unstructured time for the student.

18. Reinforce those students in the classroom who demonstrate on-task behavior.

19. Have the student question any directions, explanations, and instructions not understood.

20. Identify a peer to act as a model for the student to imitate appropriate behavior.

21. Evaluate the appropriateness of the task to determine: (a) if the task is too difficult and (b) if the length of time scheduled to complete the task is appropriate.

22. Communicate with parents (e.g., notes home, phone calls, etc.) in order to share information concerning the student's progress and so that they can reinforce the student at home for demonstrating appropriate behavior at school.

23. Write a contract with the student specifying what behavior is expected (e.g., demonstrating appropriate behavior) and what reinforcement will be made available when the terms of the contract have been met. (See Appendix for Behavioral Contract.)

24. Reinforce the student for demonstrating appropriate behavior based on the length of time the student can be successful. Gradually increase the length of time required for reinforcement as the student demonstrates success.

25. Reinforce those students in the classroom who demonstrate appropriate behavior.

26. Establish classroom rules:
1. Work on-task.
2. Work quietly.
3. Remain in your seat.
4. Finish task.
5. Meet task expectations.

Reiterate rules often and reinforce students for following rules.

27. Speak to the student to explain: (a) what the student is doing wrong (e.g., bothering other students who are trying to work, listen, etc.) and (b) what the student should be doing (e.g., demonstrating appropriate behavior).

28. Reinforce the student for demonstrating appropriate behavior: (a) give the student a tangible reward (e.g., classroom privileges, line leading, passing out materials, five minutes free time, etc.) or (b) give the student an intangible reward (e.g., praise, handshake, smile, etc.).

42 Makes unnecessary comments or noises in the classroom

1. Remove the student from the group or activity until he/she can demonstrate appropriate behavior and self-control.

2. Write a contract with the student specifying what behavior is expected (e.g., making appropriate comments) and what reinforcement will be made available when the terms of the contract have been met. (See Appendix for Behavioral Contract.)

3. Communicate with the parents (e.g., notes home, phone calls, etc.) in order to share information concerning the student's progress and so that they can reinforce the student at home for making appropriate comments at school.

4. Evaluate the appropriateness of the task to determine: (a) if the task is too long and (b) if the length of time scheduled for the task is appropriate.

5. Make certain that reinforcement is not inadvertently given for inappropriate behavior (e.g., making inappropriate comments or unnecessary noises).

6. Give adequate opportunities to respond (i.e., enthusiastic students need many opportunities to contribute).

7. Have the student be the leader of a small group activity if he/she possesses mastery of skills or an interest in that area.

8. Provide the student with a predetermined signal if he/she begins to make inappropriate comments or unnecessary noises.

9. Explain to the student that he/she may be trying too hard to fit in and that he/she should relax and make more appropriate comments.

10. Structure the environment in such a way as to limit opportunities for inappropriate behaviors (e.g., keep the student engaged in activities, have the student seated near the teacher, etc.).

11. Give the student responsibilities in the classroom (e.g., running errands, opportunities to help the teacher, etc.).

12. Reduce activities which might threaten the student (e.g., announcing test score ranges or test scores aloud, making students read aloud in class, emphasizing the success of a particular student or students, etc.).

13. Provide the student with many social and academic successes.

14. Make the necessary adjustments in the environment to prevent the student from experiencing stress, frustration or anger (e.g., reduce peer pressure, academic failure, teasing, etc.).

15. Maintain visibility to and from the student. The teacher should be able to see the student and the student should be able to see the teacher, making eye contact possible at all times.

16. Interact frequently with the student to reduce his/her need to make inappropriate comments or unnecessary noises.

17. Assess the appropriateness of the social situation in relation to the student's ability to function successfully.

18. Try various groupings in order to determine the situation in which the student is most comfortable.

19. Reinforce the student for raising his/her hand in order to be recognized.

20. Call on the student when he/she is most likely to be able to respond correctly.

21. Teach the student to recognize and make appropriate comments (e.g., comments within the context of the situation, comments that are a follow-up to what has just been said, etc.).

22. Encourage the student to model the behavior of peers who are successful.

23. Have the student work in small groups in which he/she will have frequent opportunities to speak. Gradually increase the size of the group as the student learns to wait longer for a turn to speak.

24. Make certain that the student's feelings are considered when it is necessary to deal with his/ her inappropriate comments (i.e., handle comments in such a way as to not diminish the student's enthusiasm for participation).

25. Help the student improve concentration skills (e.g., listening to the speaker, taking notes, preparing comments in advance, making comments in the appropriate context, etc.).

26. Have the student question any directions, explanations, and instructions not understood.

27. Deliver directions, explanations, and instructions in a clear and concise manner in order to reduce the student's need to ask questions.

28. Have the student practice waiting for a turn to speak for short periods of time. Gradually increase the length of time required for reinforcement as the student demonstrates success.

29. Explain to the student the reasons why making inappropriate comments and unnecessary noise is not acceptable (e.g., is impolite, might hurt others' feelings, etc.).

30. Attempt to provide equal attention to all students in the classroom.

31. Make the student aware of the number of times he/she makes inappropriate comments and unnecessary noises.

32. Allow natural consequences to occur due to the student making inappropriate comments or unnecessary noises in the classroom (e.g., making noises and inappropriate comments during class time will cause the student to have to make up the work during recreational time).

33. Do not inadvertently reinforce the student's inappropriate behavior by laughing when the student is silly, rude, etc.

34. Make certain the student sees the relationship between his/her behavior and the consequences which may follow (e.g., failing to listen to directions and making distracting noises will cause the student to not understand what to do).

35. Remove the student from the situation until he/she can demonstrate appropriate behavior.

36. Provide the student with a predetermined signal when he/she begins to display inappropriate behavior.

37. Make certain the student knows when it is acceptable to interrupt others (e.g., an emergency).

38. Teach the student acceptable ways to communicate displeasure, anger, frustration, etc.

39. Have the student put himself/herself in someone else's place (e.g., "How would you feel if someone called you dumb or stupid?").

40. Do not force the student to interact with others.

41. Reinforce the student for making appropriate comments based on the length of time the student can be successful. Gradually increase the length of time required for reinforcement as the student demonstrates success.

42. Reinforce those students in the classroom who make appropriate comments.

43. Establish classroom rules:
1. Work on-task.
2. Work quietly.
3. Remain in your seat.
4. Finish task.
5. Meet task expectations.
Reiterate rules often and reinforce students for following rules.

44. Speak with the student to explain: (a) what the student is doing wrong (e.g., making inappropriate comments or unnecessary noises) and (b) what the student should be doing (e.g., waiting until it is appropriate to speak, thinking of comments which relate to the situation, etc.).

45. Reinforce the student for making appropriate comments in the classroom: (a) give the student a tangible reward (e.g., classroom privileges, line leading, passing out materials, five minutes free time, etc.) or (b) give the student an intangible reward (e.g., praise, handshake, smile, etc.).

43 Makes unnecessary physical contact with others

1. Reinforce the student for respecting the norms of physical proximity based on the length of time the student can be successful. Gradually increase the length of time required for reinforcement as the student demonstrates success.

2. Remove the student from the group or activity until the student can demonstrate appropriate behavior and self-control.

3. Write a contract with the student specifying what behavior is expected (e.g., shaking hands rather than hugging) and what reinforcement will be made available when the terms of the contract have been met. (See Appendix for Behavioral Contract.)

4. Communicate with parents (e.g., notes home, phone calls, etc.) in order to share information concerning the student's progress and so that they can reinforce the student at home for respecting the norms of physical proximity at school.

5. Separate the student from the person who is the primary focus of the student's attempts to make frequent physical contact.

6. Reduce the opportunity for the student to engage in inappropriate physical contact (e.g., stand an appropriate distance from the student when interacting).

7. Model socially acceptable physical contact for the student (e.g., handshake, pat on the back, etc.).

8. Provide the student with many social and academic successes.

9. Indicate to the student that public displays of frequent physical contact are inappropriate.

10. When working directly with the student, always be in the presence of others.

11. Provide the student with verbal recognition and reinforcement for social and academic successes.

12. Give the student your full attention when communicating with him/her in order to prevent the student's need for physical contact.

13. Provide the student with social interaction in place of physical interaction (e.g., call the student by name, speak to the student, praise, congratulate, etc.).

14. Provide the student with high-interest activities (e.g., academic activities which are inherently interesting, activities during free time, etc.).

15. Try various groupings to find a situation in which the student's need for physical attention can be satisfied by socially acceptable interactions (e.g., holding hands while dancing in an extracurricular activity, a hug for an accomplishment, handshake or "high five" in sports, etc.).

16. Acknowledge the student when he/she seeks attention verbally instead of making it necessary for the student to gain attention through physical contact.

17. Allow natural consequences to occur as a result of the student's inappropriate behavior (e.g., excessive physical contact may cause people to stay away from the student or may result in pushing, shoving, etc.).

18. Make certain that reinforcement is not inadvertently given for inappropriate behavior (e.g., attending to the student only when he/she makes unnecessary physical contact).

19. Prevent the student from becoming overstimulated by an activity (e.g., monitor or supervise student behavior to limit overexcitement in physical activities, games, parties. etc.).

20. Teach the student appropriate ways to interact with others (e.g., verbal and physical introductions, interactions, etc.).

21. Avoid inadvertently stimulating the student's unnecessary physical contact (e.g., attire, language used, physical proximity, etc.).

22. Make certain the student sees the relationship between his/her behavior and the consequences which may follow (e.g., touching and hugging people all of the time may result in others not wanting to be around him/her).

23. Find a peer to play with the student who would be a good influence (e.g., someone younger, older, of the same sex, of the opposite sex, etc.).

24. Establish classroom rules:
1. Work on-task.
2. Work quietly.
3. Remain in your seat.
4. Finish task.
5. Meet task expectations.

Reiterate rules often and reinforce students for following rules.

25. Reinforce those students in the classroom who interact appropriately with other students or teachers.

26. Speak with the student to explain: (a) what the student is doing wrong (e.g., touching, hugging, etc.) and (b) what the student should be doing (e.g., talking, exchanging greetings, etc.). Discuss appropriate ways to seek attention.

27. Reinforce the student for respecting the norms of physical proximity: (a) give the student a tangible reward (e.g., classroom privileges, line leading, passing out materials, five minutes free time, etc.) or (b) give the student an intangible reward (e.g., praise, handshake, smile, etc.).

44 Is impulsive

1. Reduce the opportunity to act impulsively by limiting decision making. Gradually increase opportunities for decision making as the student demonstrates success.

2. Maintain supervision at all times and in all areas of the school environment.

3. Maintain visibility to and from the student. The teacher should be able to see the student and the student should be able to see the teacher, making eye contact possible at all times.

4. Be mobile in order to be frequently near the student.

5. Assign additional responsibilities to the student (e.g., chores, errands, etc.) to give him/her a feeling of success or accomplishment.

6. Prevent the student from becoming overstimulated by an activity (e.g., monitor or supervise student behavior to limit overexcitement in physical activities, games, parties, etc.).

7. Provide the student with adequate time to perform activities in order to reduce his/her impulsive behavior.

8. Provide the student with a routine to be followed when making decisions (e.g., place a list of decision-making strategies on the student's desk).

9. Explain to the student that he/she should be satisfied with personal best effort rather than expecting perfection.

10. Provide the student with clear, simply stated explanations, instructions, and directions so that he/she knows exactly what is expected.

11. Assist the student in beginning each task in order to reduce impulsive responses.

12. Have a peer work with the student in order to model deliberate and responsible behavior in academic and social settings.

13. Reduce distracting stimuli (e.g., place the student on the front row, provide a carrel or quiet place away from distractions, etc.). This is used as a means of reducing distracting stimuli and not as a form of punishment.

14. Teach the student decision-making steps: (a) think about how other persons may be influenced, (b) think about consequences, (c) carefully consider the unique situation, (d) think of different courses of action which are possible, and (e) think about what is ultimately best for him/her.

15. Make the student aware of the reasons we all must practice responsibility (e.g., others' rights are not infringed upon, others are not hurt, order is not lost, property is not damaged or destroyed, etc.).

16. Reduce the emphasis on competition. Competition may result in impulsive behavior in order to win or be first.

17. Emphasize individual success or progress rather than winning or "beating" other students.

18. Make certain that all students get equal opportunities to participate in activities (e.g., students take turns, everyone has an equal opportunity to be first, etc.).

19. Allow natural consequences to occur in order that the student can learn that persons who take turns and act in a deliberate fashion are more successful than those who act impulsively (e.g., if you begin an activity before understanding the directions, you will finish early, but you may perform the assignment incorrectly and receive a failing grade, you may have to repeat the assignment, etc.).

20. Deliver a predetermined signal (e.g., hand signal, verbal cue, etc.) when the student begins to demonstrate impulsive behaviors.

21. Make certain the student does not become involved in overstimulating activities on the playground, during P.E., during lunch, etc.

22. Make certain the student has an adequate amount or number of activities scheduled in order to prevent the likelihood of impulsively engaging in unplanned activities. (See Appendix for Schedule of Daily Events.)

23. Assign the student to an area of the classroom where he/she is to remain at any one time.

24. Maintain consistency in the daily routine of activities.

25. Make certain the student knows which areas in the classroom are "off limits" to him/her.

26. In order to determine if the student heard a direction, have the student repeat it.

27. Do not criticize the student. When correcting the student, be honest yet supportive. Never cause the student to feel bad about himself/herself.

28. Intervene early when there is a problem in order to prevent a more serious problem from occurring.

29. Do not leave a lot of unstructured time for the student.

30. Teach the student to "think" before acting (e.g., ask himself/herself: "What is happening?" "What am I doing?" "What should I do?" "What is best for me?").

31. Evaluate the appropriateness of the task to determine: (a) if the task is too difficult and (b) if the length of time scheduled to complete the task is appropriate.

32. Communicate with parents (e.g., notes home, phone calls, etc.) in order to share information concerning the student's progress and so that they can reinforce the student at home for acting in a deliberate and responsible manner at school.

33. Write a contract with the student specifying what behavior is expected (e.g., acting in a deliberate and responsible manner) and what reinforcement will be made available when the terms of the contract have been met. (See Appendix for Behavioral Contract.)

34. Remove the student from the group or activity until he/she can demonstrate appropriate behavior and self-control.

35. Reinforce the student for demonstrating appropriate behavior based on the length of time the student can be successful. Gradually increase the length of time required for reinforcement as the student demonstrates success.

36. Reinforce those students in the classroom who act in a deliberate and responsible manner.

37. Establish classroom rules:
1. Work on-task.
2. Work quietly.
3. Remain in your seat.
4. Finish task.
5. Meet task expectations.
Reiterate rules often and reinforce students for following rules.

38. Speak with the student to explain: (a) what the student is doing wrong (e.g., taking action before thinking about what he/she is doing) and (b) what the student should be doing (e.g., considering consequences, thinking about the correct response, considering others, etc.).

39. Reinforce the student for acting in a deliberate and responsible manner: (a) give the student a tangible reward (e.g., classroom privileges, line leading, passing out materials, five minutes free time, etc.) or (b) give the student an intangible reward (e.g., praise, handshake, smile, etc.).

A Reminder: Do not confuse impulsive behavior with enthusiasm. Impulsive behavior should be controlled while enthusiasm should be encouraged.

45 Fails to comply with teachers or other school personnel

1. Reinforce the student for following directives from teachers or other school personnel: (a) give the student a tangible reward (e.g., classroom privileges, line leading, passing out materials, five minutes free time, etc.) or (b) give the student an intangible reward (e.g., praise, handshake, smile, etc.).

2. Speak with the student to explain: (a) what he/she is doing wrong (e.g., failing to follow directions or observe rules) and (b) what he/she should be doing (e.g., following established guidelines or expectations).

3. Establish classroom rules (e.g., work on-task, work quietly, remain in your seat, finish task, meet task expectations). Reiterate rules often and reinforce students for following rules.

4. Reinforce those students in the classroom who follow directives from teachers and other school personnel.

5. Reinforce the student for following the directives of teachers and other school personnel based on the length of time he/she can be successful. Gradually increase the amount of time required for reinforcement as the student demonstrates success.

6. Remove the student from the group or activity until he/she can demonstrate appropriate behavior and self-control.

7. Write a contract with the student specifying what behavior is expected (e.g., following teacher directives) and what reinforcement will be made available when the terms of the contract have been met.

8. Communicate with the parents (e.g., notes home, phone calls, etc.) in order to share information concerning the student's progress and so that they may reinforce the student at home for following directives from teachers and other school personnel.

9. Evaluate the appropriateness of the task to determine: (a) if the task is too easy, (b) if the task is too difficult, and (c) if the length of time scheduled for the task is appropriate.

10. Structure the environment in such a way that the student remains active and involved in appropriate behavior.

11. Maintain visibility to and from the student. The teacher should be able to see the student and the student should be able to see the teacher, making eye contact possible at all times.

12. Give the student preferred responsibilities.

13. Present the tasks in the most interesting and attractive manner possible.

14. Maintain maximum supervision of the student and gradually decrease supervision as the student becomes successful at following directives.

15. Have the student maintain a chart representing the amount of time spent following teacher directives or rules, with reinforcement for increasing appropriate behavior.

16. Be mobile in order to be frequently near the student.

17. Provide the student with many social and academic successes.

18. Provide the student with positive feedback that indicates he/she is successful.

19. Post rules in various places, including the student's desk.

20. Make certain the student receives the information necessary to perform activities (e.g., written information, verbal directions, reminders, etc.).

21. Teach the student direction-following skills: (a) listen carefully, (b) ask questions, (c) use environmental cues, (d) rely on examples provided, (e) wait until all directions are given before beginning, etc.

22. Maintain a positive, professional relationship with the student (i.e., an adversary relationship is likely to result in failure to follow directions).

23. Be a consistent authority figure (e.g., be consistent in relationship with student).

24. Provide the student with optional courses of action in order to prevent total refusal to obey directives from teachers and other school personnel.

25. Intervene early to prevent the student's behavior from leading to contagion for other students.

26. Deliver directions in a step-by-step sequence.

27. Have a peer act as a model for following teacher directives.

28. Interact with the student frequently to determine if directives are being followed.

29. Maintain consistency in rules, routine, and general expectations of conduct and procedure.

30. Allow natural consequences to occur as a result of not following directives from teachers and other school personnel (e.g., assignments are performed incorrectly, accidents will occur, detention will be assigned, etc.).

31. Limit the student's opportunity to engage in activities in which he/she will not follow directives from teachers and other school personnel (e.g., recess, industrial arts activities, field trips, etc.).

32. Do not allow the student to be unsupervised anywhere in the school environment.

46 Ignores consequences of his/her behavior

1. Make certain that consequences are delivered consistently for behavior demonstrated (e.g., appropriate behavior results in positive consequences and inappropriate behavior results in negative consequences).

2. Provide the student with many social and academic successes.

3. Structure the environment in such a way as to limit opportunities for inappropriate behavior (e.g., keep the student engaged in activities, have the student seated near the teacher, maintain visibility to and from the student, etc.).

4. Prevent the student from becoming overstimulated by an activity (e.g., monitor or supervise student behavior to limit overexcitement in physical activities, games, parties, etc.).

5. Provide the student with natural consequences for inappropriate behavior (e.g., for disturbing others during group activities, the student should have to leave the activity).

6. Provide the student with a clearly identified list of consequences for inappropriate behavior.

7. Teach the student problem-solving skills: (a) identify the problem, (b) identify goals and objectives, (c) develop strategies, (d) develop a plan of action, and (e) carry out the plan.

8. Clarify for the student that it is his/her behavior which determines consequences (e.g., positive or negative).

9. Provide a learning experience which emphasizes the cause-and-effect relationship between behavior and the inevitability of some form of consequence (e.g., both negative and positive behaviors and consequences).

10. Point out the consequences of other students' behavior as they occur (e.g., take the opportunity to point out that consequences occur for all behavior and for all persons).

11. Call on the student when he/she can answer successfully.

12. Supervise the student closely in situations in which he/she is likely to act impulsively (e.g., maintain close physical proximity, maintain eye contact, communicate frequently with the student, etc.).

13. Prevent peers from engaging in those behaviors which would cause the student to fail to consider or regard the consequences of his/her behavior (e.g., keep other students from upsetting the student).

14. Make the consequence of a behavior obvious by identifying the consequence as it occurs and discussing alternative behavior which would have prevented the particular consequence.

15. Avoid competition. Failure may cause the student to ignore consequences of his/her behavior.

16. Allow the student more decision-making opportunities relative to class activities and assignments.

17. Present tasks in the most attractive and interesting manner possible.

18. Give the student responsibilities in the classroom (e.g., teacher assistant, peer tutor, group leader, etc.).

19. Evaluate the appropriateness of the task in relation to the student's ability to perform the task successfully.

20. Show an interest in the student (e.g., acknowledge the student, ask the student's opinion, spend time working one-on-one with the student, etc.).

21. Intervene early when there is a problem in order to prevent more serious problems from occurring.

22. Inform others who will be working with the student (e.g., teachers, the principal, clerks, etc.) about the student's tendency to ignore consequences of his/her behaviors.

23. Make certain the student does not become involved in overstimulating activities.

24. Teach the student to "think" before acting (e.g., ask himself/herself: "What is happening?" "What am I doing?" "What should I do?" "What will be best for me?").

25. Evaluate the appropriateness of the task to determine: (a) if the task is too difficult and (b) if the length of time scheduled to complete the task is appropriate.

26. Communicate with parents (e.g., notes home, phone calls, etc.) in order to share information concerning the student's progress and so that they can reinforce the student at home for engaging in appropriate behaviors at school.

27. Write a contract with the student specifying what behavior is expected (e.g., acting in a deliberate and responsible manner) and what reinforcement will be made available when the terms of the contract have been met. (See Appendix for Behavioral Contract.)

28. Remove the student from the group or activity until he/she can demonstrate appropriate behavior and self-control.

29. Reinforce the student for demonstrating appropriate behavior based on the length of time the student can be successful. Gradually increase the length of time required for reinforcement as the student demonstrates success.

30. Reinforce those students in the classroom who engage in appropriate behavior.

31. Establish classroom rules:
1. Work on-task.
2. Work quietly.
3. Remain in your seat.
4. Finish task.
5. Meet task expectations.

Reiterate rules often and reinforce students for following rules.

32. Speak with the student to explain: (a) what the student is doing wrong (e.g., taking action before thinking about what he/she is doing) and (b) what the student should be doing (e.g., considering consequences, thinking about the correct response, considering other persons, etc.).

33. Reinforce the student for engaging in appropriate behavior: (a) give the student a tangible reward (e.g., classroom privileges, line leading, passing out materials, five minutes free time, etc.) or (b) give the student an intangible reward (e.g., praise, handshake, smile, etc.).

47 Fails to follow a routine

1. Reinforce the student for demonstrating the ability to follow a routine: (a) give the student a tangible reward (e.g., classroom privileges, line leading, passing out materials, five minutes free time, etc.) or (b) give the student an intangible reward (e.g., praise, handshake, smile, etc.).

2. Speak to the student to explain: (a) what he/she is doing wrong (e.g., failing to come to class on time, failing to follow the schedule of activities, etc.) and (b) what he/she should be doing (e.g., coming to class on time, following the schedule of activities, etc.).

3. Establish classroom rules (e.g., work on-task, work quietly, remain in your seat, finish task, meet task expectations). Reiterate rules often and reinforce students for following rules.

4. Reinforce those students in the classroom who demonstrate the ability to follow a routine.

5. Reinforce the student for demonstrating the ability to follow a routine based on the length of time the student can be successful. Gradually increase the length of time required for reinforcement as the student demonstrates success.

6. Write a contract with the student specifying what behavior is expected (e.g., following the schedule of activities) and what reinforcement will be made available when the terms of the contract have been met.

7. Communicate with parents (e.g., notes home, phone calls, etc.) in order to share information concerning the student's progress and so that they can reinforce the student at home for demonstrating the ability to follow a routine at school.

8. Evaluate the appropriateness of the routine to determine: (a) if the routine is oversimplified, (b) if the routine is too difficult, and (c) if the length of time scheduled to complete the routine is appropriate.

9. Identify a peer to act as a model for the student to imitate the ability to follow a routine.

10. Have the student question any directions, explanations, instructions he/she does not understand about the routine.

11. Have the student work near a peer in order to follow the same routine that the peer follows.

12. Make certain that the student's routine is consistent on a daily basis.

13. Provide the student with a schedule of daily events which identifies the daily activities and the times at which they occur.

14. Schedules of daily events should be attached to the student's desk and/or carried with the student at all times.

15. Post the class routine throughout the classroom (e.g., on the student's desk, chalkboard, bulletin board, etc.).

16. Limit interruptions in the student's routine by persons or events in the school (e.g., testing, special services, delays; cancellations of classes or activities such as art, music, P.E., etc.).

17. Provide the student with a limited routine to follow. Gradually increase the activities in the routine as the student experiences success.

18. Discuss any necessary changes in the student's routine well in advance of the occurrence of the changes.

19. Make certain the student is able to tell time in order to enhance his/her ability to follow a routine.

20. Teach the student to tell time in order to enhance his/her ability to follow a routine.

21. Have the student rely on a predetermined signal in order to enhance his/her ability to follow a routine (e.g., bells, lights, etc.).

22. Have the student use a timer to indicate when to change activities in his/her routine.

23. Determine an expected length of time for each individual activity in order to help the student follow his/her routine (i.e., make certain the student can finish an activity in an established length of time in order to help him/her stay within the time restrictions of the routine).

24. Reduce distracting stimuli which might cause the student to be unable to follow a routine (e.g., peers, physical activity, etc.).

25. Monitor the student's performance in activities or tasks to make certain the student begins, works on, and completes an assignment in order to be ready to move to the next activity in his/her routine.

26. Make certain that the teacher is a model for following a routine.

27. Maintain flexibility in following a routine when changes in the routine are required.

28. Discuss the student's routine with him/her at the beginning of each day and make certain that he/she knows the expectations.

29. Have a peer remind the student when to change activities according to his/her routine.

30. Have the student rely on environmental events to remind him/her when to change activities in his/her routine (e.g., other students changing activities, bells, etc.).

31. Remind the student when it is time to change activities in order to enhance his/her ability to follow a routine.

32. Make certain that the activities in the student's routine are on his/her ability level.

33. Provide the student with additional activities to engage in when he/she finishes an activity early, in order to maintain a routine.

34. Have a peer accompany the student to other locations in the building which are part of the student's routine.

35. Allow the student to contribute to the development of his/her routine in order to enhance his/her ability to follow the routine (e.g., have the student determine the order of activities).

36. Provide the student with an alternative routine to follow if he/she encounters difficulty in following his/her regular routine.

37. Be consistent when expecting the student to follow a routine. Do not allow the student to get out of following a routine one time and expect him/her to follow a routine the next time.

38. Do not leave a lot of unstructured time for the student.

48 Does not follow the rules of games

1. Reinforce the student for demonstrating appropriate behavior in games: (a) give the student a tangible reward (e.g., classroom privileges, line leading, passing out materials, five minutes free time, etc.) or (b) give the student an intangible reward (e.g., praise, handshake, smile, etc.).

2. Speak to the student to explain: (a) what he/she is doing wrong (e.g., failing to follow rules, cheating, etc.) and (b) what he/she should be doing (e.g., following rules, playing fairly, etc.).

3. Establish classroom rules (e.g., work on-task, work quietly, remain in your seat, finish task, meet task expectations). Reiterate rules often and reinforce students for following rules.

4. Reinforce those students in the classroom who follow the rules of games.

5. Reinforce the student for following the rules of games based on the length of time the student can be successful. Gradually increase the length of time required for reinforcement as the student demonstrates success.

6. Write a contract with the student specifying what behavior is expected (e.g., following the rules of games) and what reinforcement will be made available when the terms of the contract have been met.

7. Communicate with parents (e.g., notes home, phone calls, etc.) in order to share information concerning the student's appropriate behavior and so that they can reinforce the student at home for following the rules of games at school.

8. Evaluate the appropriateness of games to determine if the games are too difficult and if the length of time scheduled to complete the games is appropriate.

9. Identify a peer to act as a model for the student to imitate following rules of games.

10. Have the student question any directions, explanations, or instructions for games he/she does not understand.

11. Evaluate the expectations for participation in games in order to determine if the student can be successful in the interaction and for the expected length of time.

12. Allow the student to choose a group of peers with whom he/she feels comfortable.

13. Have the student engage in a game activity with one peer and gradually increase the size of the group as the student demonstrates success.

14. Determine the peers with whom the student would most prefer to interact in games and attempt to facilitate success.

15. Assign outgoing, nonthreatening peers to interact with the student in games.

16. Structure the environment so that the student has many opportunities to participate with peers in games.

17. Assign the student to interact with younger peers in games.

18. Assign the student to games in which he/she is likely to interact successfully with peers.

19. Conduct a sociometric activity with the class in order to determine those peers who would most prefer to interact with the student in games.

20. Make certain that the student demonstrates appropriate behavior in nonacademic situations prior to placing him/her with peers for games.

21. Make certain that the student understands that interacting with peers in group games is contingent upon following the rules.

22. Teach the student appropriate ways to interact with peers in group games (e.g., suggest activities, share materials, problem solve, take turns, follow game rules, etc.).

23. Supervise games closely in order that the peers with whom the student interacts do not stimulate inappropriate behavior.

24. Make certain that games are not so stimulating as to make successful interactions with peers difficult.

25. Assign older peers with desirable social skills to interact with the student in games.

26. Involve the student in extracurricular activities in order to encourage interaction with peers in games.

27. Reduce the emphasis on competition. Failure may stimulate inappropriate behavior in games.

28. Teach the student problem-solving skills in order that he/she may better deal with problems that may occur in interactions with peers in games (e.g., talking, walking away, calling upon an arbitrator, compromising, etc.).

29. Find the peer with whom the student is most likely to be able to successfully interact in games (e.g., a student with similar interests, background, classes, behavior patterns, nonacademic schedule, etc.).

30. Structure games according to the needs/ abilities of the student (e.g., establish rules, limit the stimulation of the activities, limit the length of the game, consider the time of day, etc.).

31. Limit opportunities for interaction in games on those occasions in which the student is not likely to be successful (e.g., the student has experienced academic or social failure prior to the scheduled game).

32. Select games designed to enhance appropriate interaction of the student and peers.

33. Through interviews with other students and observations, determine those characteristics of the student which interfere with following rules during games in order to determine skills or behaviors which the student needs to develop.

34. Have the student practice appropriate interactions with the teacher(s) in games.

35. Make certain beforehand that the student is able to successfully engage in the game (e.g., the student understands the rules, is familiar with the game, will be compatible with the other students playing the game, etc.).

36. Make certain that the student understands that failing to interact appropriately with peers during games may result in termination of the game and/or loss of future opportunities to engage in games.

37. Have the student interact with peers for short periods of time in order to enhance success. Gradually increase the length of time as the student demonstrates success.

38. Have the student study, practice, simulate, etc., the rules for group games before participating.

39. Establish a set of standard behavior rules for games (e.g., follow the rules of the game, take turns, make positive comments, work as a team member, be a good sport, etc.).

40. Remove the student from games if he/she is unable to demonstrate appropriate behavior.

41. Play the game with the student before he/she engages in the game with peers in order to model appropriate behavior, determine the student's ability to play the game, determine the student's ability to follow behavior rules, etc.

42. Have the student engage in games of short duration. Gradually increase the duration of games as the student demonstrates success.

43. Allow the student to choose the game which he/she will play with peers.

44. Teach the student necessary skills to successfully participate in particular games (e.g., volleyball, basketball, football, baseball, etc.).

49 Leaves seat without permission

1. Reinforce the student for staying in his/her seat: (a) give the student a tangible reward (e.g., classroom privileges, line leading, passing out materials, five minutes free time, etc.) or (b) give the student an intangible reward (e.g., praise, handshake, smile, etc.).

2. Speak with the student to explain: (a) what he/she is doing wrong (e.g., leaving seat without permission, etc.) and (b) what he/she should be doing (e.g., remaining in his/her seat, asking permission to leave seat, etc.).

3. Establish classroom rules (e.g., work on-task, work quietly, remain in your seat, finish task, meet task expectations). Reiterate rules often and reinforce students for following rules.

4. Reinforce those students in the classroom who stay in their seat, ask permission to leave their seat, etc.

5. Reinforce the student for staying in his/her seat based on the length of time he/she can be successful. Gradually increase the length of time required for reinforcement as the student demonstrates success.

6. Remove the student from the group or activity until he/she can stay in his/her seat.

7. Write a contract with the student specifying what behavior is expected (e.g., staying in his/ her seat) and what reinforcement will be made available when the terms of the contract have been met.

8. Communicate with the parents (e.g., notes home, phone calls, etc.) in order to share information concerning the student's appropriate behavior and so that they may reinforce the student at home for staying in his/her seat at school.

9. Evaluate the appropriateness of tasks to determine: (a) if the tasks are too easy, (b) if the tasks are too difficult, and (c) if the length of time scheduled for the tasks is appropriate.

10. Try various groupings in order to determine the situation in which the student is most comfortable.

11. Make the necessary adjustments in the environment to prevent the student from experiencing stress, frustration, anger, etc., as much as possible.

12. Interact frequently with the student to prevent the student from leaving his/her seat.

13. Maintain visibility to and from the student. The teacher should be able to see the student and the student should be able to see the teacher, making eye contact possible at all times.

14. Facilitate on-task behavior by providing a full schedule of daily events. Prevent lag time when the student is free to leave his/her seat. (See Appendix for Schedule of Daily Events.)

15. Reduce stimuli which would contribute to the student leaving his/her seat.

16. Interact frequently with the student in order to maintain his/her attention to the activity (e.g., ask the student questions, ask the student's opinions, stand close to the student, seat the student near the teacher's desk, etc.).

17. Give the student additional responsibilities (e.g., chores, errands, etc.) to keep him/her actively involved and give him/her a feeling of success or accomplishment.

18. Modify or eliminate situations at school which cause the student to experience stress or frustration.

19. Maintain supervision at all times and in all parts of the school environment.

20. Prevent the student from becoming overstimulated by an activity (i.e., monitor or supervise student behavior to limit overexcitement in physical activities, games, parties, etc.).

21. Provide the student with a predetermined signal when he/she begins to leave his/her seat.

22. Make certain that reinforcement is not inadvertently given for inappropriate behavior (e.g., attending to the student only when he/she leaves his/her seat).

23. Separate the student from the peer who stimulates the inappropriate behavior.

24. Provide the student with the most attractive and interesting activities possible.

25. Provide the student with a calm, quiet environment in which to work.

26. Provide the student with a quiet place in the environment where he/she may go when he/she becomes upset. This is not meant as punishment, but as a means of helping the student to be able to function more successfully in his/her environment.

27. Provide the student with frequent opportunities to participate, take a turn, etc., in order to keep him/her involved in an activity.

28. Avoid discussions of topics sensitive to the student (e.g., divorce, death, unemployment, alcoholism, etc.).

29. Identify a peer to act as a model for the student to imitate staying in his/her seat.

30. Have the student question any directions, explanations, instructions he/she does not understand.

31. Schedule short activities for the student to perform while seated. Gradually increase the length of the activities as the student demonstrates success at staying in his/her seat.

32. Give the student frequent opportunities to leave his/her seat for appropriate reasons (e.g., getting materials, running errands, assisting the teacher, etc.).

33. Seat the student near the teacher.

34. Make certain the student has all necessary materials at his/her desk in order to reduce the need to leave his/her seat.

35. Have the student chart the length of time he/she is able to remain in his/her seat.

36. Work the first few problems of an assignment with the student in order that he/she will know what is expected.

37. Make sure the student knows when it is acceptable to leave his/her seat (e.g., in an emergency).

1. Reinforce the student for working in a group situation: (a) give the student a tangible reward (e.g., classroom privileges, line leading, passing out materials, five minutes free time, etc.) or (b) give the student an intangible reward (e.g., praise, handshake, smile, etc.).

2. Speak with the student to explain: (a) what the student is doing wrong (e.g., failing to take part) and (b) what the student should be doing (e.g., talking, taking turns, playing, sharing, etc.).

3. Establish classroom rules:
1. Work on-task.
2. Remain in your seat.
3. Finish task.
4. Meet task expectations.
5. Raise your hand.
Reiterate rules often and reinforce students for following rules.

4. Reinforce other students in the classroom for working appropriately in a group situation.

5. Write a contract with the student specifying what behavior is expected (e.g., working appropriately with peers) and what reinforcement will be made available when the terms of the contract have been met. (See Appendix for Behavioral Contract.)

6. Communicate with parents (e.g., notes home, phone calls, etc.) in order to share information concerning the student's progress and so that they can reinforce the student at home for participating in group situations at school.

7. DO NOT FORCE the student to participate in group situations until he/she can be successful.

8. Assign a peer to sit/work directly with the student (e.g., in different settings such as art, music, P.E., on the bus; or different activities such as tutoring, group projects, running errands in the building, recess, etc.).

9. Reward or encourage other students for participation in group situations.

10. Give the student the responsibility of helping a peer in group situations.

11. Give the student responsibilities in group situations in order that others might view the student in a positive light.

12. Call on the student when he/she is most likely to be able to respond successfully (e.g., when discussing a topic in which the student is interested, when the teacher is certain the student knows the answer, etc.).

13. Try various groupings in order to determine the situation in which the student is most comfortable.

14. Have peers invite the student to participate in school or extracurricular activities.

15. Have the student lead a small group activity when he/she possesses mastery or an interest in the activity.

16. Allow the student to be present during group activities without requiring active participation. Require more involvement over time as the student becomes more active in group situations.

17. Reduce the emphasis on competition. Fear of failure may cause the student to be reluctant to participate in group situations.

18. Have the student work with one or two other group members. Gradually increase group size as the student becomes more comfortable.

19. Demonstrate respect for the student's opinions, responses, suggestions, etc.

20. Give the student the opportunity to pick a topic or activity for the group to work on together.

21. Give the student the opportunity to choose a group activity and the group members (e.g., along with the teacher decide what the activity will be, decide what individual group members will do, etc.).

22. Assign the student a role to perform in the group activity which he/she can perform successfully (e.g., secretary, researcher, group behavior monitor, etc.).

23. Make certain the student is productive and accurate in performing individual assignments before placing him/her in a group activity.

24. Go over group rules and expectations at the beginning of each group activity.

25. Make certain that the student can follow classroom rules and expectations independently before placing him/her in a group activity.

26. Help the student learn to be satisfied with his/her own best effort rather than some arbitrary measure of success. Success is measured individually according to ability level, and progress of any kind is a measure of success.

27. Group the student with peers who will be appropriate role models and are likely to facilitate the student's academic and behavioral successes.

28. Group the student with group members who are least likely to be threatening (e.g., younger students, students just learning a skill he/she has mastered, etc.).

29. Make certain the student understands instructions/directions for the group activity (e.g., give instructions in a variety of ways, make certain that the student understands his/her role, go over the rules for group behavior before the activity begins, etc.).

30. Make certain the student has all needed materials in order to perform his/her role in the group (e.g., paper, pencil, art supplies, reference materials, etc.).

31. Make certain the student has enough room to work successfully (e.g., distance from other students, room for all materials, etc.).

32. Make certain the academic and social demands of the group situation are within the student's ability level.

33. Remove the student from the group if his/her behavior is inappropriate.

34. Make certain the student is actively involved in the group situation (e.g., call on the student frequently, assign the student a responsibility such as teacher assistant, have him/her be the group leader, etc.).

35. Evaluate the appropriateness of the assigned task to determine: (a) if the task is too difficult and (b) if the length of time scheduled is appropriate.

36. Help the student get to know group members before requiring group participation (e.g., introduce the students to one another, allow the students unstructured free time together, etc.).

37. Reduce distracting stimuli which could interfere with the student's success in a group activity (e.g., provide enough room to move without physical contact, keep noise level at a minimum, keep movement in the environment to a minimum, etc.).

38. Schedule group activities in order that the teacher's time can be spent uninterrupted with the group.

39. Schedule group activities as part of the student's daily routine (i.e., group activities should occur on a regularly scheduled basis so the student will be prepared and know what to expect).

40. Place the student in those group activities he/she prefers. Gradually require the student to participate in less desirable activities.

41. Provide the student with alternative ways to perform a group assignment and allow the student to choose the most desirable (e.g., a written paragraph assignment may be accomplished by writing a note to a friend, writing about a recent experience, describing a favorite pastime, etc.).

42. Allow the student to participate in one group activity he/she prefers. Require the student to participate in more group activities as he/she experiences success.

43. Schedule group activities when the student is most likely to be successful (e.g., before recess rather than immediately after recess, after the first individual assignment of the day has been completed in order to establish productive behavior, etc.).

44. Program alternative individual activities if the student is unlikely to be successful (e.g., if the schedule has been changed, if holidays or special events have stimulated the student and make successful group interaction unlikely, etc.).

45. Allow the student to join the group after the activity has begun if he/she is unable to participate appropriately at the beginning of the group activity.

46. Position the student's desk or work area in such a way that he/she works near other students but is not visually distracted by them (e.g., turn the student's desk away from other students, etc.).

47. Allow the student to leave a group activity and return to independent work when he/she can no longer be successful in the group activity (e.g., as an alternative to disrupting the group, fighting, etc.).

48. Carefully consider the student's age and experience before expecting him/her to get along in a group.

49. Intervene early when there is a problem in order to prevent more serious problems from occurring.

50. Do not force the student to interact with people with whom he/she is not completely comfortable.

51. Teach the student acceptable ways to communicate displeasure, anger, frustration, etc.

52. Teach the student to "think" before acting (e.g., ask himself/herself: "What is happening?" "What am I doing?" "What should I do?" "What will be best for me?").

53. Encourage the student to use problem-solving skills: (a) identify the problem, (b) identify goals and objectives, (c) develop strategies, (d) develop a plan for action, (e) carry out the plan.

54. Make certain the student is allowed to voice an opinion in a situation in order to avoid becoming angry or upset.

55. Talk to the student about ways of handling situations successfully without conflict (e.g., walk away from the situation, change to another activity, ask for help, etc.).

51 Hops, skips, and jumps when moving from one place to another instead of walking

1. Reinforce the student for demonstrating appropriate behavior when walking, moving with a group, etc.: (a) give the student a tangible reward (e.g., classroom privileges, line leading, passing out materials, five minutes free time, etc.) or (b) give the student an intangible reward (e.g., praise, handshake, smile, etc.).

2. Speak to the student to explain: (a) what he/she is doing wrong (e.g., hopping, skipping, jumping, etc.) and (b) what he/she should be doing (e.g., walking).

3. Reinforce those students who demonstrate appropriate behavior when walking, moving with a group, etc.

4. Reinforce the student for walking appropriately alone or with a group based on the length of time he/she can be successful. Gradually increase the length of time required for reinforcement as the student demonstrates success.

5. Write a contract with the student specifying what behavior is expected (e.g., walking in the classroom, walking in the halls, etc.) and what reinforcement will be made available when the terms of the contract have been met.

6. Communicate with parents (e.g., notes home, phone calls, etc.) in order to share information concerning the student's appropriate behavior and so that they may reinforce the student at home for walking appropriately at school.

7. Evaluate the appropriateness of the expectation of walking appropriately to determine: (a) if the task is too easy, (b) if the task is too difficult, and (c) if the length of time scheduled to complete the task is appropriate.

8. Identify a peer to act as a model for the student to imitate appropriate walking in the classroom, hallways, etc.

9. Have the student question any directions, explanations, instructions he/she does not understand.

10. Reinforce the student for waiting appropriately in line (e.g., standing against the wall, talking quietly, standing near others without making physical contact, etc.).

11. Reinforce the student for walking at the same pace as other students when moving with a group.

12. Have the student walk with his/her arms crossed, arms against his/her side, hands in pockets, etc., if touching others is a problem.

13. Form a second line or group for those students who move at a slower pace.

14. Separate the student from the peer(s) who stimulates his/her inappropriate behavior when moving with a group.

15. Have the student walk alone, behind the group, beside the teacher, etc., when he/she displays inappropriate behavior when moving with a group.

16. Provide the student with a demonstration/model for moving appropriately with a group.

17. Have the student act as a line leader, line monitor, etc., when moving with a group.

18. Have the students walk in pairs when moving as a group.

19. Stop the line frequently in order to assure student success when moving with a group.

20. Provide the student with rules for moving appropriately with a group (e.g., walk in the halls, go directly from one area to another, talk quietly in the halls, walk on the right side of the hall, use the appropriate stairway). Reiterate rules often and reinforce the student for following rules.

52 Handles objects

1. Reinforce the student for sitting and working quietly in his/her seat: (a) give the student a tangible reward (e.g., classroom privileges, line leading, passing out materials, five minutes free time, etc.) or (b) give the student an intangible reward (e.g., praise, handshake, smile, etc.).

2. Speak to the student to explain: (a) what he/she is doing wrong (e.g., twirling pencil, playing with things in desk, spinning ruler on pencil, clicking ballpoint pen, repeatedly sharpening pencils, etc.) and (b) what he/she should be doing (e.g., sitting and working quietly in his/her chair).

3. Establish classroom rules (e.g., work on-task, work quietly, remain in your seat, finish task, meet task expectations). Reiterate rules often and reinforce students for following rules.

4. Reinforce those students in the classroom who work and sit appropriately in their seats.

5. Reinforce the student for working and sitting appropriately in his/her seat based on the length of time he/she can be successful. Gradually increase the length of time required for reinforcement as the student demonstrates success.

6. Write a contract with the student specifying what behavior is expected (e.g., working and sitting appropriately in his/her seat) and what reinforcement will be made available when the terms of the contract have been met.

7. Communicate with parents (e.g., notes home, phone calls, etc.) in order to share information concerning the student's appropriate behavior and so that they may reinforce the student at home for working and sitting appropriately in his/her seat at school.

8. Evaluate the appropriateness of tasks to determine: (a) if tasks are too easy, (b) if tasks are too difficult, and (c) if the length of time scheduled to complete tasks is appropriate.

9. Identify a peer to act as a model for the student to imitate appropriate ways in which to work and sit in his/her seat.

10. Have the student question any directions, explanations, instructions he/she does not understand.

11. Provide the student with a specific description of appropriate in-seat behavior (e.g., face forward, feet on floor, back straight, hands free of objects, etc.).

12. Implement logical consequences for students who fail to work and sit appropriately in their seats (e.g., the student would have to sit on the floor, stand next to his/her desk to work, sit in a chair without a desk, etc.).

13. Maintain consistency of expectations for having the student work and sit appropriately in his/her seat.

14. Make certain the student is aware of the natural consequences that may occur from failing to work and sit appropriately in his/her seat (e.g., tasks will not be completed, work will have to be made up during recreational time, etc.).

15. Place the student in a carrel in order to reduce distracting stimuli which may cause him/her to have difficulty working and sitting appropriately in his/her seat.

16. Seat the student next to a peer who works and sits appropriately in his/her seat.

17. Deliver a predetermined signal (e.g., hand signal, bell ringing, etc.) when the student fails to work or sit appropriately in his/her seat.

18. Model for the student appropriate ways in which to work and sit in a chair or at a desk.

19. Provide activities which are interesting to the student in order to keep him/her on-task and sitting appropriately in his/her seat.

20. Seat the student near the teacher.

21. Seat the student away from peers in order to reduce the likelihood that he/she will behave inappropriately in his/her seat.

22. Remove any materials the student uses to make noises while seated.

23. Use natural consequences when the student touches others as they walk by (e.g., move the student to another location in the room, have others walk away from the student, etc.).

24. Prevent unnecessary objects, toys, materials from being available to the student or kept in his/her desk.

25. Make certain the student has only those materials necessary for him/her at any given time.

26. Have the student sharpen pencils before activities begin.

53 Talks beyond what is expected or at inappropriate times

1. Reinforce the student for talking an appropriate length of time and at appropriate times in the classroom: (a) give the student a tangible reward (e.g., classroom privileges, line leading, passing out materials, five minutes free time, etc.) or (b) give the student an intangible reward (e.g., praise, handshake, smile, etc.).

2. Speak with the student to explain: (a) what he/she is doing wrong (e.g., talking more than is necessary or at inappropriate times), and (b) what he/she should be doing (e.g., keeping comments brief, waiting until it is appropriate to speak, thinking of comments which relate to the situation, etc.).

3. Establish classroom rules (e.g., work on-task, work quietly, remain in your seat, finish task, meet task expectations). Reiterate rules often and reinforce students for following rules.

4. Reinforce those students in the classroom who make their comments brief or speak at appropriate times.

5. Reinforce the student for making appropriate comments or speaking at the appropriate time based on the length of time he/she can be successful. Gradually increase the length of time required for reinforcement as the student demonstrates success.

6. Remove the student from the group or activity until he/she can demonstrate appropriate behavior and self-control.

7. Write a contract with the student specifying what behavior is expected (e.g., making short, appropriate comments and speaking at appropriate times) and what reinforcement will be made available when the terms of the contract have been met.

8. Communicate with the parents (e.g., notes home, phone calls, etc.) in order to share information concerning the student's appropriate behavior and so that they may reinforce the student at home for making appropriate comments at school.

9. Evaluate the appropriateness of the task to determine: (a) if the task is too easy, (b) if the task is too difficult, and (c) if the length of time scheduled for the task is appropriate.

10. Make certain that reinforcement is not inadvertently given for inappropriate behavior (e.g., talking beyond what is expected or at inappropriate times).

11. Give adequate opportunities to respond (i.e., enthusiastic students need many opportunities to contribute).

12. Have the student be the leader of a small group activity if he/she possesses mastery of skills or an interest in that area.

13. Provide the student with a predetermined signal if he/she begins to talk beyond what is expected or at inappropriate times.

14. Explain to the student that he/she may be trying too hard to fit in and he/she should relax and talk less and at appropriate times.

15. Structure the environment in such a way as to limit opportunities for inappropriate behaviors (e.g., keep the student engaged in activities, have the student seated near the teacher, etc.).

16. Give the student responsibilities in the classroom (e.g., running errands, opportunities to help the teacher, etc.).

17. Reduce activities which might threaten the student (e.g., announcing test score ranges or test scores aloud, making students read aloud in class, emphasizing the success of a particular student or students, etc.).

18. Provide the student with many social and academic successes.

19. Make the necessary adjustments in the environment to prevent the student from experiencing stress, frustration, or anger (e.g., reduce peer pressure, academic failure, teasing, etc.).

20. Maintain visibility to and from the student. The teacher should be able to see the student and the student should be able to see the teacher, making eye contact possible at all times.

21. Interact frequently with the student to reduce the need to talk beyond what is expected or at inappropriate times.

22. Assess the appropriateness of the social situation in relation to the student's ability to function successfully.

23. Try various groupings in order to determine the situation in which the student is most comfortable.

24. Reinforce the student for raising his/her hand in order to be recognized.

25. Call on the student when he/she is most likely to be able to respond correctly.

26. Teach the student to recognize when to speak, to know how much to say and to make appropriate comments (e.g., brief comments, comments within the context of the situation, comments that are a follow-up to what has just been said, etc.).

27. Have the student work in small groups in which he/she would have frequent opportunities to speak. Gradually increase the size of the group as the student learns to wait longer for his/her turn to speak.

28. Make certain that the student's feelings are considered when it is necessary to deal with his/her inappropriate comments (i.e., handle comments in such a way as to not diminish the student's enthusiasm for participation).

29. Encourage the student to model the behavior of peers who are successful.

30. Help the student improve concentration skills (e.g., listening to the speaker, taking notes, preparing comments in advance, making comments in the appropriate context, etc.).

31. Have the student question any directions, explanations, instructions he/she does not understand.

32. Deliver directions, explanations, and instructions in a clear and concise manner in order to reduce the student's need to ask questions.

33. Have the student practice waiting for short periods of time for his/her turn to speak. Gradually increase the length of time required for reinforcement as the student demonstrates success.

34. Explain to the student the reasons why talking beyond what is expected and at inappropriate times is unacceptable (e.g., is impolite, interrupts others, etc.).

35. Attempt to provide equal attention to all students in the classroom.

36. Make the student aware of the number of times he/she talks beyond what is expected and at inappropriate times.

54 Does not wait appropriately for assistance from instructor

1. Reinforce the student for waiting appropriately for assistance from an instructor: (a) give the student a tangible reward (e.g., classroom privileges, line leading, passing out materials, five minutes free time, etc.) or (b) give the student an intangible reward (e.g., praise, handshake, smile, etc.).

2. Speak to the student to explain: (a) what he/she is doing wrong (e.g., leaving his/her seat, talking to other students, etc.), and (b) what he/she should be doing (e.g., remaining in seat or assigned area, remaining quiet, etc.).

3. Establish classroom rules (e.g., remain seated or in an assigned area, remain quiet). Reiterate rules often and reinforce students for following rules.

4. Reinforce those students in the classroom who remain seated in assigned areas and remain quiet.

5. Reinforce the student for waiting appropriately for assistance from an instructor based on the length of time he/she can be successful. Gradually increase the length of time required for reinforcement as the student demonstrates success.

6. Write a contract with the student specifying what behavior is expected (e.g., remaining in seat or assigned area, remaining quiet, etc.) and what reinforcement will be made available when the terms of the contract have been met.

7. Identify a peer to act as a model for the student to imitate appropriate behavior (e.g., remaining in seat or assigned area, remaining quiet, etc.) when waiting for assistance from an instructor.

8. Have the student question any directions, explanations, instructions he/she does not understand.

9. Communicate with parents (e.g., notes home, phone calls, etc.) in order to share information concerning the student's progress and so that they can reinforce the student at home for waiting appropriately for assistance from an instructor at school.

10. Evaluate the appropriateness of the task to determine: (a) if the task is too easy, (b) if the task is too difficult, and (c) if the length of time scheduled to complete the task is appropriate.

11. Tell the student that you will assist him/her as soon as possible (e.g., "Stephen, I'll be with you shortly.") in order to increase the probability that the student will wait appropriately for assistance.

12. Identify a peer from whom the student may seek assistance.

13. Attempt to provide assistance immediately. Gradually increase the length of time the student must wait for assistance when the teacher is helping another student, instructing, etc.

14. Encourage the student to go to the next problem, go to another part of the assignment, begin a new assignment, etc., when waiting for assistance from an instructor.

15. Establish alternative activities for the student to perform when waiting for assistance from an instructor (e.g., check work already completed, color, look at a magazine, organize work area, begin another task, etc.).

16. Position yourself in order that visibility to and from the student may be maintained until assistance can be provided.

17. Maintain verbal communication with the student until assistance can be provided (e.g., "Thank you for waiting quietly. I'll be there shortly.").

55 Does not adjust behavior to expectations of different situations

1. Reinforce the student for changing his/her behavior from one situation to another without difficulty: (a) give the student a tangible reward (e.g., classroom privileges, line leading, passing out materials, five minutes free time, etc.) or (b) give the student an intangible reward (e.g., praise, handshake, smile, etc.).

2. Speak to the student to explain: (a) what he/she is doing wrong (e.g., failing to stop one activity and begin another) and (b) what he/she should be doing (e.g., changing from one activity to another).

3. Establish classroom rules (e.g., work on-task, work quietly, remain in your seat, finish task, meet task expectations). Reiterate rules often and reinforce students for following rules.

4. Reinforce those students in the classroom who change their behavior from one situation to another without difficulty.

5. Reinforce the student for demonstrating acceptable behavior based on the length of time he/she can be successful. Gradually increase the length of time required for reinforcement as the student demonstrates success.

6. Write a contract with the student specifying what behavior is expected (e.g., putting materials away and getting ready for another activity) and what reinforcement will be made available when the terms of the contract have been met.

7. Communicate with parents (e.g., notes home, phone calls, etc.) in order to share information concerning the student's progress and so that they may reinforce the student at home for demonstrating acceptable behavior at school.

8. Evaluate the appropriateness of the task to determine: (a) if the task is too easy, (b) if the task is too difficult, and (c) if the length of time scheduled to complete the task is appropriate.

9. Have the student question any directions, explanations, instructions he/she does not understand.

10. Assign a peer to work with the student to provide an appropriate model.

11. Explain to the student that he/she should be satisfied with his/her best effort rather than insisting on perfection.

12. Prevent the student from becoming overstimulated by an activity. Supervise student behavior in order to limit overexcitement in physical activities, games, parties, etc.

13. Have the student time his/her activities in order to monitor his/her own behavior and accept time limits.

14. Convince the student that work not completed in one sitting can be completed later. Provide the student ample time to complete earlier assignments in order to guarantee closure.

15. Provide the student with more than enough time to finish an activity and decrease the amount over time as the student demonstrates success.

16. Structure time limits in order that the student knows exactly how long he/she has to work and when he/she must be finished.

17. Allow a transition period between activities in order that the student can make adjustments in his/her behavior.

18. Employ a signal technique (e.g., turning the lights off and on) to warn that the end of an activity is near.

19. Establish definite time limits and provide the student with this information before the activity begins.

20. Assign the student shorter activities and gradually increase the length of the activities as the student demonstrates success.

21. Maintain consistency in daily routine.

22. Maintain consistency of expectations and keep expectations within the ability level of the student.

23. Allow the student to finish the activity unless it will be disruptive to the schedule.

24. Schedule activities so that the student has more than enough time to finish the activity if he/she works consistently.

25. Provide the student with a list of materials needed for each activity (e.g., pencil, paper, textbook, workbook, etc.).

26. Present instructions/directions prior to handing out necessary materials.

27. Collect the student's materials (e.g., pencil, paper, textbook, workbook, etc.) when it is time to change from one situation to another.

28. Provide the student with clearly stated expectations for all situations.

29. Prevent the student from becoming so stimulated by an event or activity that he/she cannot control his/her behavior.

30. Establish rules that are to be followed in various parts of the school building (e.g., lunchroom, music room, art room, gymnasium, library, playground, etc.).

31. Identify the expectations of different environments and help the student develop the skills to be successful in those environments.

32. In conjunction with other school personnel, develop as much consistency across the various environments as possible (e.g., rules, criteria for success, behavioral expectations, consequences, etc.).

33. Reduce the student's involvement in activities which prove too stimulating for him/her.

34. Have the student engage in relaxing transitional activities designed to reduce the effects of stimulating activities (e.g., put head on desk, listen to the teacher read a story, put head phones on and listen to relaxing music, etc.).

35. Provide the student with more than enough time to adapt or modify his/her behavior to different situations (e.g., have the student stop recess activities five minutes prior to coming into the building).

36. Communicate clearly to the student when it is time to begin an activity.

37. Communicate clearly to the student when it is time to stop an activity.

38. Provide the student with a schedule of daily events in order that he/she will know which activity comes next and can prepare for it. (See Appendix for Schedule of Daily Events.)

39. Reduce the emphasis on competition (e.g., academic or social). Fear of failure may cause the student to fail to adapt or modify his/her behavior to different situations.

40. Have the student begin an activity in a private place (e.g., carrel, "office," quiet study area, etc.) in order to reduce his/her difficulty in adapting or modifying his/her behavior to different situations.

41. Allow the student the option of performing the activity at another time (e.g., earlier in the day, later in the day, on another day, etc.).

42. Do not allow the student to begin a new activity until he/she has gained self-control.

43. Evaluate the appropriateness of the situation in relation to the student's ability to successfully adapt or modify his/her behavior.

1. Identify a peer to act as a model for the student to imitate appropriate ways to sit in his/her seat.

2. Have the student question any directions, explanations, and instructions not understood.

3. Have desks and/or chairs that can be fastened to the floor or which are designed to prevent tipping.

4. Provide the student with a specific description of appropriate in-seat behavior (e.g., facing forward, feet on floor, back straight, etc.).

5. Implement logical consequences for students who fail to sit appropriately in their seats (e.g., the student will have to sit on the floor, stand next to his/her desk to work, sit in a chair without a desk, etc.).

6. Maintain consistency of expectations for having the student sit appropriately in his/her seat.

7. Make certain the student is aware of the natural consequences that may occur from sitting inappropriately in his/her seat (e.g., injury, damaging property, hurting others, etc.).

8. Place the student in a carrel in order to reduce distracting stimuli which may cause the student to sit inappropriately in his/her seat.

9. Seat the student next to a peer who sits appropriately in his/her seat.

10. Deliver a predetermined signal (e.g., give a hand signal, ring a bell, etc.) when the student begins to sit inappropriately in his/her seat.

11. Model for the student appropriate ways in which to sit in a chair or at a desk.

12. Provide activities which are interesting to the student in order to keep the student on-task and sitting appropriately in his/her seat.

13. Seat the student near the teacher.

14. Seat the student away from peers in order to reduce the likelihood that the student will sit inappropriately in his/her seat.

15. Evaluate the necessity of having the student to sit facing forward, feet on floor, back straight, etc.

16. Make certain that the chair or desk the student is assigned to use is appropriate and/or comfortable for him/her (e.g., the desk is not too high, the chair is not too big, etc.).

17. Remove any materials with which the student makes noises while seated.

18. Use natural consequences when the student touches others as they walk by (e.g., move the student to another location in the room, have others walk away from the student, etc.).

19. Intervene early when there is a problem in order to prevent more serious problems from occurring.

20. Teach the student to "think" before acting (e.g., ask himself/herself: "What is happening?" "What am I doing?" "What should I do?" "What will be best for me?").

21. Evaluate the appropriateness of the task to determine: (a) if the task is too easy, (b) if the task is too difficult, and (c) if the length of time scheduled to complete the task is appropriate.

22. Communicate with parents (e.g., notes home, phone calls, etc.) in order to share information concerning the student's progress and so that they can reinforce the student at home for sitting appropriately in his/her seat at school.

23. Write a contract with the student specifying what behavior is expected (e.g., sitting appropriately in his/her seat) and what reinforcement will be made available when the terms of the contract have been met. (See Appendix for Behavioral Contract.)

24. Reinforce the student for sitting appropriately in his/her seat based on the length of time the student can be successful. Gradually increase the length of time required for reinforcement as the student demonstrates success.

25. Reinforce those students in the classroom who sit appropriately in their seats.

26. Establish classroom rules:
1. Work on-task.
2. Work quietly.
3. Remain in your seat.
4. Finish task.
5. Meet task expectations.
6. Raise your hand.

Reiterate rules often and reinforce students for following rules.

27. Speak to the student to explain: (a) what the student is doing wrong (e.g., tipping chair) and (b) what the student should be doing (e.g., sitting appropriately in his/her chair).

28. Reinforce the student for sitting appropriately in his/her seat: (a) give the student a tangible reward (e.g., classroom privileges, line leading, passing out materials, five minutes free time, etc.) or (b) give the student an intangible reward (e.g., praise, handshake, smile, etc.).

1. Evaluate the visual and auditory stimuli in the classroom in order to determine the level of stimuli the student can respond to appropriately.

2. Reduce visual and auditory stimuli to a level at which the student can successfully function. Gradually allow visual and auditory stimuli to increase as the student demonstrates that he/she can successfully tolerate the increased levels.

3. Seat the student so that he/she experiences the least amount of visual and auditory stimuli.

4. Provide the student with a quiet place in which to work where visual and auditory stimuli are reduced. This is used to reduce distracting stimuli and not as a form of punishment.

5. Place the student away from those peers who create the most visual and auditory stimulation in the classroom.

6. Provide the student with a carrel or divider at his/her desk to reduce visual and auditory stimuli.

7. Make certain that all visual and auditory stimuli in the classroom are reduced as much as possible for all learners.

8. Provide the student with the opportunity to move to a quiet place in the classroom any time that visual and auditory stimuli interfere with his/ her ability to function successfully.

9. Provide the student with earphones to wear if auditory stimuli interfere with his/her ability to function. Gradually remove the earphones as the student can more successfully function in the presence of auditory stimuli.

10. Allow the student to close the door or windows in order to reduce visual and auditory stimuli from outside of the classroom.

11. Remove the student from an activity in the classroom if he/she is unable to demonstrate self-control in the presence of visual and auditory stimuli involved with the activity.

12. Require the student to be productive in the presence of visual and auditory stimuli for short periods of time. Gradually increase the length of time the student is required to be productive as he/she becomes more successful.

13. Provide the student with shorter tasks that do not require extended attention in order for the student to be successful. Gradually increase the length of the tasks as the student demonstrates he/she can be successful in the presence of visual and auditory stimuli.

14. Have the student engage in small group activities (e.g., free time, math, reading, etc.) in order to reduce the level of visual and auditory stimuli in the group. Gradually increase group size as the student can function successfully in the presence of visual and auditory stimuli.

15. Teach the student appropriate ways to respond to visual and auditory stimuli in the classroom (e.g., moving to another part of the room, asking others to be quiet, leaving the group, etc.).

16. Model for the student appropriate behavior in the presence of visual and auditory stimuli in the classroom (e.g., continuing to work, asking for quiet, moving to a quieter part of the classroom, etc.).

17. Make the necessary adjustments in the environment in order to prevent the student from experiencing stress, frustration, anger, etc.

18. Provide a consistent routine for the student in order to enhance stability.

19. Allow flexibility in meeting academic demands when the student becomes overexcited (e.g., allow more time, modify assignments, provide help with assignments, etc.).

20. Teach the student to recognize signs of becoming overexcited in order that he/she may deal with it appropriately.

21. Make certain the student does not become involved in overstimulating activities.

22. Provide a pleasant/calm atmosphere which will lessen the possibility of the student becoming overexcited.

23. Post classroom rules in various locations in the classroom in order to enhance the student's ability to remember the rules.

24. Avoid discussion or prevent stimuli in the environment which remind the student of unpleasant experiences/sensitive topics (e.g., divorce, death, unemployment, alcoholism, etc.).

25. Deliver directions in a supportive rather than a threatening manner (e.g., "Please put materials away so we can go to lunch." rather than "You had better put your materials away or we won't go to lunch!").

26. Intervene early when there is a problem in order to prevent more serious problems from occurring.

27. Provide the student with a predetermined signal when he/she begins to display inappropriate behavior.

28. Teach the student to "think" before acting (e.g., ask himself/herself: "What is happening?" "What am I doing?" "What should I do?" "What will be best for me?").

29. Have the student question any directions, explanations, and instructions not understood.

30. Identify a peer to act as a model for the student to imitate demonstrating self-control in the presence of visual and auditory stimuli in the classroom.

31. Communicate with parents (e.g., notes home, phone calls, etc.) in order to share information concerning the student's progress and so that they can reinforce the student at home for demonstrating self-control in the presence of visual and auditory stimuli in the classroom.

32. Write a contract with the student specifying what behavior is expected (e.g., maintaining self-control in the presence of visual and auditory stimuli in the classroom) and what reinforcement will be made available when the terms of the contract have been met. (See Appendix for Behavioral Contract.)

33. Reinforce the student for demonstrating self-control in the presence of visual and auditory stimuli in the classroom based on the length of time the student can be successful. Gradually increase the length of time required for reinforcement as the student demonstrates success.

34. Reinforce those students in the classroom who demonstrate self-control in the presence of visual and auditory stimuli in the classroom.

35. Establish classroom rules:
1. Work on-task.
2. Work quietly.
3. Remain in your seat.
4. Finish task.
5. Meet task expectations.

Reiterate rules often and reinforce students for following rules.

36. Speak to the student to explain: (a) what the student is doing wrong (e.g., becoming easily angered or upset) and (b) what he/she should be doing (e.g., following rules, considering others, controlling impulsive behavior, etc.).

37. Reinforce the student for demonstrating self-control in the presence of visual and auditory stimuli in the classroom: (a) give the student a tangible reward (e.g., classroom privileges, line leading, passing out materials, five minutes free time, etc.) or (b) give the student an intangible reward (e.g., praise, handshake, smile, etc.).

58 Demonstrates in appropriate behavior when moving with a group

1. Reinforce the student for waiting appropriately in line (e.g., standing against the wall, talking quietly, standing near others without making physical contact, etc.).

2. Reinforce the student for walking at the same pace as other students when moving with a group.

3. Have the student walk with arms crossed, arms against his/her side, hands in pockets, etc., if touching others is a problem.

4. Form a second line or group for those students who move at a slower pace.

5. Separate the student from the peer(s) who stimulates his/her inappropriate behavior when moving with a group.

6. Have the student walk alone, behind the group, beside the teacher, etc., when he/she displays inappropriate behavior when moving with a group.

7. Provide the student with a demonstration of the appropriate way to move with a group.

8. Have the student act as a line leader, line monitor, etc., when moving with a group.

9. Have the students walk in pairs when moving as a group.

10. Stop the line frequently in order to assure student success when moving with a group.

11. Provide the student with rules for moving appropriately with a group:
   1. Walk in the halls.
   2. Go directly from one area to another.
   3. Talk quietly in the halls.
   4. Walk on the right side of the hall.
   5. Use the appropriate stairway.
Reiterate rules often and reinforce the student for following rules.

12. Intervene early when there is a problem in order to prevent future problems from occurring.

13. Before leaving the classroom, remind the student of the rules for walking in a group (e.g., walk behind the person in front of you, keep hands to yourself, walk quietly, etc.).

14. Have the student question any directions, explanations, and instructions not understood.

15. Identify a peer to act as a model for the student to imitate appropriate movement with a group.

16. Evaluate the appropriateness of the expectation of moving with a group to determine: (a) if the task is too difficult and (b) if the length of time scheduled to complete the task is appropriate.

17. Communicate with parents (e.g., notes home, phone calls, etc.) in order to share information concerning the student's progress and so that they can reinforce the student at home for moving appropriately with a group at school.

18. Write a contract with the student specifying what behavior is expected (e.g., walking in the halls) and what reinforcement will be made available when the terms of the contract have been met. (See Appendix for Behavioral Contract.)

19. Reinforce the student for moving appropriately with a group based on the length of time the student can be successful. Gradually increase the length of time required for reinforcement as the student demonstrates success.

20. Reinforce those students who demonstrate appropriate behavior when moving with a group.

21. Speak to the student to explain: (a) what the student is doing wrong (e.g., running, pushing peers, etc.) and (b) what the student should be doing (e.g., walking without touching peers).

22. Reinforce the student for demonstrating appropriate behavior when moving with a group: (a) give the student a tangible reward (e.g., classroom privileges, line leading, passing out materials, etc.) or (b) give the student an intangible reward (e.g., praise, handshake, smile, etc.).

1. Try various groupings in order to determine the situation in which the student is most comfortable.

2. Make the necessary adjustments in the environment to prevent the student from experiencing stress, frustration, anger, etc., as much as possible.

3. Interact frequently with the student to prevent excessive or unnecessary body movements.

4. Maintain visibility to and from the student. The teacher should be able to see the student and the student should be able to see the teacher, making eye contact possible at all times.

5. Facilitate on-task behavior by providing a full schedule of daily events. Prevent lag time when the student is free to engage in excessive and unnecessary body movements. (See Appendix for Schedule of Daily Events.)

6. Reduce stimuli which would contribute to unnecessary or excessive behavior.

7. Interact frequently with the student in order to maintain his/her attention to the activity (e.g., ask the student questions, ask the student's opinion, stand close to the student, seat the student near the teacher's desk, etc.).

8. Give the student additional responsibilities (e.g., chores, errands, etc.) to keep him/her actively involved and give him/her a feeling of success or accomplishment.

9. Modify or eliminate situations at school which cause the student to experience stress or frustration.

10. Maintain supervision at all times and in all parts of the school environment.

11. Prevent the student from becoming overly stimulated by an activity (i.e., monitor or supervise student behavior to limit overexcitement in physical activities, games, parties, etc.).

12. Provide the student with a predetermined signal when he/she exhibits inappropriate behavior.

13. Make certain that reinforcement is not inadvertently given for inappropriate behavior (e.g., attending to the student only when he/she engages in excessive/unnecessary body movements).

14. Separate the student from the peer who stimulates the inappropriate behavior.

15. Provide the student with the most attractive and interesting activities possible.

16. Provide the student with a calm, quiet environment in which to work.

17. Provide the student with a quiet place in the environment to go when he/she becomes upset. This is not meant as punishment, but as a means of helping the student be able to function more successfully in the environment.

18. Provide the student with frequent opportunities to participate, take turns, etc., in order to keep him/her involved in the activity.

19. Avoid discussion of topics sensitive to the student (e.g., divorce, death, unemployment, alcoholism, etc.).

20. Identify a peer to act as a model for the student to imitate staying in his/her seat.

21. Have the student question any directions, explanations, and instructions not understood.

22. Schedule short activities for the student to perform while seated. Gradually increase the length of the activities as the student demonstrates success at staying in his/her seat.

23. Give the student frequent opportunities to leave his/her seat for appropriate reasons (e.g., getting materials, running errands, assisting the teacher, etc.).

24. Seat the student near the teacher.

25. Make certain the student has all necessary materials in order to reduce the need to leave his/her seat.

26. Have the student chart the length of time he/she is able to remain in his/her seat.

27. Work the first few problems of an assignment with the student in order that he/she will know what is expected.

28. Carefully consider the student's age before expecting him/her to sit quietly for a period of time.

29. Intervene early when there is a problem in order to prevent more serious problems from occurring.

30. Make certain the student does not become involved in activities which may be overstimulating.

31. Do not leave a lot of unstructured time for the student.

32. Evaluate the appropriateness of the task to determine: (a) if the task is too difficult and (b) if the length of time required to complete the task is appropriate.

33. Communicate with parents (e.g., notes home, phone calls, etc.) in order to share information concerning the student's progress and so that they can reinforce the student at home for demonstrating physical self-control at school.

34. Remove the student from the group or activity until he/she can demonstrate appropriate behavior and self-control.

35. Write a contract with the student specifying what behavior is expected (e.g., demonstrating physical self-control) and what reinforcement will be made available when the terms of the contract have been met. (See Appendix for Behavioral Contract.)

36. Reinforce the student for demonstrating appropriate behavior based on the length of time the student can be successful. Gradually increase the length of time required for reinforcement as the student demonstrates success.

37. Reinforce those students in the classroom who demonstrate physical self-control.

38. Establish classroom rules:
1. Work on-task.
2. Work quietly.
3. Remain in your seat.
4. Finish task.
5. Meet task expectations.
Reiterate rules often and reinforce students for following rules.

39. Speak with the student to explain: (a) what the student is doing wrong (e.g., moving in seat, moving about the room, running, etc.) and (b) what the student should be doing (e.g., practicing self-control, following rules, etc.).

40. Reinforce the student for demonstrating physical self-control: (a) give the student a tangible reward (e.g., classroom privileges, line leading, passing out materials, five minutes free time, etc.) or (b) give the student an intangible reward (e.g., praise, handshake, smile, etc.).

1. Reinforce the student for demonstrating appropriate behavior: (a) give the student a tangible reward (e.g., classroom privileges, line leading, passing out materials, five minutes free time, etc.) or (b) give the student an intangible reward (e.g., praise, handshake, smile, etc.

2. Speak with the student to explain: (a) what he/she is doing wrong (e.g., chewing on pencil, nail biting, twirling objects, etc.) and (b) what he/she should be doing (e.g., practicing self-control, working on-task, performing responsibilities, etc.).

3. Establish classroom rules (e.g., work on-task, work quietly, remain in your seat, finish task, meet task expectations). Reiterate rules often and reinforce students for following rules.

4. Reinforce those students in the classroom who demonstrate appropriate behavior.

5. Reinforce the student for demonstrating appropriate behavior (academic or social) based on the length of time he/she can be successful. Gradually increase the length of time required for reinforcement as the student demonstrates success.

6. Remove the student from the group or activity when he/she engages in nervous habits.

7. Write a contract with the student specifying what behavior is expected (e.g., demonstrating appropriate behavior) and what reinforcement will be made available when the terms of the contract have been met.

8. Communicate with the parents (e.g., notes home, phone calls, etc.) in order to share information concerning the student's progress and so that they may reinforce the student at home for demonstrating appropriate behavior at school.

9. Evaluate the appropriateness of the task to determine: (a) if the task is too easy, (b) if the task is too difficult, and (c) if the length of time scheduled for the task is appropriate.

10. Provide the student with a predetermined signal when he/she engages in nervous habits.

11. Reduce situations which may contribute to nervous behavior (e.g., testing situations, timed activities, competition, etc.).

12. Prevent the student from becoming overly stimulated by an activity.

13. Try various groupings in order to determine the situation in which the student is most comfortable.

14. Provide the student with as many social and academic successes as possible.

15. Make the necessary adjustments in the environment to prevent the student from experiencing stress, frustration, anger, etc.

16. Assign a peer tutor to work directly with the student in order to prevent stress, frustration, anxiety, etc.

17. Interact frequently with the student in order to maintain his/her involvement in class assignments.

18. Allow the student additional time in which to complete class assignments or homework.

19. Interact frequently with the student to reduce nervous behavior.

20. Remove from the environment any object which may be used by the student to engage in nervous habits (e.g., pencils, pens, rubberbands, paperclips, etc.).

21. Reduce the emphasis on competition and perfection.

22. Reduce stimuli which may cause the student to engage in nervous habits (e.g., noise, movement, etc.).

23. Prevent situations in which peers contribute to the student's nervous behaviors.

24. Provide the student with another activity designed to result in productive behavior (e.g., coloring, cutting, using a calculator, working with a peer, etc.).

25. Structure the environment in order that time does not allow the student the opportunity to engage in nervous habits.

26. Avoid discussion of topics that are sensitive to the student (e.g., divorce, death, unemployment, alcoholism, etc.).

27. Provide the student with a high-interest activity which he/she prefers.

28. Provide a calm/pleasant atmosphere.

29. Encourage the student to practice self-control activities designed to allow him/her to gain composure before continuing an activity (e.g., placing hands on desk, sitting with feet on the floor, making eye contact with the instructor, etc.).

V. Supplemental Interventions

61 Has difficulty with short-term or long-term memory

1. Make certain the student's hearing has been recently checked.

2. Have the student question any directions, explanations, and instructions he/she does not understand.

3. Have the student act as a classroom messenger. Give the student a verbal message to deliver to another teacher, secretary, administrator, etc. Increase the length of the messages as the student demonstrates success.

4. Review the schedule of the morning and afternoon activities with the student and have him/her repeat the sequence. Increase the length of the sequence as the student is successful.

5. Have the student engage in concentration game activities with a limited number of symbols. Gradually increase the number of symbols as the student demonstrates success.

6. Reinforce the student for remembering to have such materials as pens, pencils, paper, textbooks, notebooks, etc.

7. At the end of the school day, have the student recall three activities in which he/she was engaged during the day. Gradually increase the number of activities the student is required to recall as the student demonstrates success.

8. After a field trip or special event, have the student sequence the activities which occurred.

9. After reading a short story, have the student identify the main characters, sequence the events, and report the outcome of the story.

10. Have the student deliver the schedule of daily events to other students.

11. Use multiple modalities (e.g., auditory, visual, tactile, etc.) when presenting directions, explanations, and instructional content.

12. Assign a peer tutor to engage in short-term memory activities with the student (e.g., concentration games, following directions, etc.).

13. Record a message on tape. Have the student write the message after he/she has heard it. Increase the length of the message as the student demonstrates success.

14. Involve the student in activities in order to enhance short-term memory skills (e.g., carry messages from one location to another; act as group leader, teacher assistant, etc.).

15. Have the student practice short-term memory skills by engaging in activities which are purposeful (e.g., delivering messages, being in charge of room clean-up, acting as custodian's helper, operating equipment, etc.).

16. Informally assess the student's auditory and visual short-term memory skills in order to determine which is the stronger. Utilize the results when presenting directions, explanations, and instructional content.

17. Have the student practice repetition of in-formation in order to increase short-term memory skills (e.g., repeating names, telephone numbers, dates of events, etc.).

18. Teach the student how to organize information into smaller units (e.g., break the number sequence 132563 into units of 13, 25, 63).

19. Use sentence dictation to develop the student's short-term memory skills (e.g., begin with sentences of three words and increase the length of the sentences as the student demonstrates success).

20. Show the student an object or a picture of an object for a few seconds. Ask the student to recall specific attributes of the object (e.g., color, size, shape, etc.).

21. Deliver directions, explanations, and instructional content in a clear manner and at an appropriate pace.

22. Have the student practice taking notes for specific information the student needs to remember.

23. Teach the student to recognize key words and phrases related to information in order to increase short-term or long-term memory skills.

24. Make certain the student is attending to the source of information (e.g., eye contact is being made, hands are free of materials, student is looking at assignment, etc.).

25. Reduce distracting stimuli when information is being presented, the student is studying, etc.

26. Stop at various points during the presentation of information to check the student's comprehension.

27. Give the student one task to perform at a time. Introduce the next task only when the student has successfully completed the previous task.

28. Have the student memorize the first sentence or line of poems, songs, etc. Require more to be memorized as the student experiences success.

29. Teach the student information-gathering skills (e.g., listen carefully, write down important points, ask for clarification, wait until all information is received before beginning, etc.).

30. Have the student repeat/paraphrase directions, explanations, and instructions.

31. Reduce the emphasis on competition. Competitive activities may cause the student to hurry and begin without listening carefully.

32. Provide the student with environmental cues and prompts designed to enhance success in the classroom (e.g., posted rules, schedule of daily events, steps for performing tasks, etc.). (See Appendix for Schedule of Daily Events.)

33. Provide the student with written lists of things to do, materials needed, etc.

34. Maintain consistency in sequential activities in order to increase the likelihood of student success (e.g., the student has math every day at one o'clock, recess at two o'clock, etc.).

35. Break the sequence into units and have the student learn one unit at a time.

36. Establish a regular routine for the student to follow in performing activities, assignments, etc. (e.g., listen to the person speaking to you, wait until directions are completed, make certain you have all necessary materials, etc.).

37. Teach the student to use associative cues or mnemonic devices to remember sequences.

38. Actively involve the student in learning to remember sequences by having the student physically perform sequential activities (e.g., operating equipment, following recipes, solving math problems, etc.).

39. Have the student be responsible for helping a peer remember sequences.

40. Use concrete examples and experiences in sharing information with the student.

41. Teach the student to recognize main points, important facts, etc.

42. Teach the student to rely on resources in the environment to recall information (e.g., notes, textbooks, pictures, etc.).

43. When the student is required to recall information, provide auditory cues to help the student remember the information (e.g., key words, a brief oral description to cue the student, etc.).

44. Assess the meaningfulness of the material to the student. Remembering is more likely to occur when the material is meaningful and the student can relate it to real experiences.

45. Relate the information being presented to the student's previous experiences.

46. Give the student specific categories and have the student name as many items as possible within that category (e.g., objects, persons, places, etc.).

47. Give the student a series of words or pictures and have the student name the category to which they belong (e.g., objects, persons, places, etc.).

48. Describe objects, persons, places, etc., and have the student name the items described.

49. Help the student employ memory aids in order to recall words (e.g., a name might be linked to another word; for example, "Mr. Green is a very colorful person.").

50. Give the student a series of words describing objects, persons, places, etc., and have the student identify the opposite of each word.

51. Encourage the student to play word games such as *Hangman, Scrabble,* and *Password.*

52. Have the student complete "fill-in-the-blank" sentences with appropriate words (e.g., objects, persons, places, etc.).

53. Have the student outline, highlight, underline, or summarize information which should be remembered.

54. Make certain the student has adequate opportunities for repetition of information through different experiences in order to enhance memory.

55. Label objects, persons, places, etc., in the environment in order to help the student be able to recall their names.

56. Make certain the student receives information from a variety of sources (e.g., texts, discussions, films, slide presentations, etc.) in order to enhance memory/recall.

57. Teach the student listening skills (e.g., stop working, look at the person delivering questions and directions, have necessary note-taking materials, etc.).

58. Teach the student direction-following skills (e.g., stop doing other things, listen carefully, write down important points, wait until all directions are given, question any directions not understood, etc.).

59. Have the student tape record directions, explanations, instructions, lectures, etc., in order that the student may replay the information as needed.

60. Highlight or underline important information the student reads (e.g., directions, reading assignments, math word problems, etc.).

61. Tell the student what to listen for when being given directions, receiving information, etc.

62. Have the student repeat to himself/herself information just heard in order to help remember the information.

63. Make certain the student is not required to learn more information than he/she is capable of at any one time.

64. Evaluate the appropriateness of the memory activities to determine: (a) if the task is too difficult and (b) if the length of time scheduled to complete the task is appropriate.

65. Write a contract with the student specifying what behavior is expected (e.g., following one-step directions, two-step directions, etc.) and what reinforcement will be made available when the terms of the contract have been met. (See Appendix for Behavioral Contract.)

66. Reinforce the student for demonstrating short-term or long-term memory skills based on the length of time the student can be successful. Gradually increase the length of time required for reinforcement as the student demonstrates success.

67. Reinforce the student for demonstrating short-term or long-term memory skills: (a) give the student a tangible reward (e.g., classroom privileges, line leading, passing out materials, five minutes free time, etc.) or (b) give the student an intangible reward (e.g., praise, handshake, smile, etc.).

62 Does not respond appropriately to environmental cues

1. Identify a peer to act as a model for the student to imitate appropriate responses to environmental cues.

2. Have the student question any environmental cues not understood.

3. Establish environmental cues that the student is expected to follow (e.g., bells, rules, point cards, reminders, etc.).

4. Provide supportive information to assist the student in responding appropriately to environmental cues (e.g., "When the bell rings, it is time for lunch.").

5. Provide repeated practice in responding appropriately to environmental cues.

6. Make the student responsible for identifying environmental cues for peers (e.g., bells, rules, reminders, etc.).

7. Provide the student with universal environmental cues (e.g., symbols for male and female, arrows, exit signs, danger symbols, etc.).

8. Pair environmental cues with verbal explanations and immediate reinforcement for appropriate responses.

9. Prepare the student in advance of the delivery of environmental cues in order to increase successful responding.

10. Make certain the same environmental cues are used throughout all locations in and outside of the building.

11. Match the environmental cues to the student's ability to respond (e.g., visual cues are used for students who cannot hear, symbols or auditory cues are used for students who cannot read, etc.).

12. Model appropriate responses to environmental cues for the student to imitate.

13. Have the student master appropriate responses to one environmental cue at a time, prioritizing environmental cues in order of importance for mastery, before introducing additional cues.

14. In order to increase success in learning environmental cues, have the student observe and imitate the responses of peers to environmental cues (e.g., as the student is learning to respond appropriately to doors identified as *In* and *Out*, the student can imitate the behavior of peers who use the appropriate doors to enter and leave areas of the educational environment).

15. Reinforce the student for asking the meaning of environmental cues not understood (e.g., bells, signs, etc.).

16. Provide the student with simulation activities in the classroom in order to teach successful responses to environmental cues (e.g., responses to words, symbols, directions, etc.).

17. Assign a peer to accompany the student as the student moves throughout the building, to act as a model in teaching appropriate responses to environmental cues.

18. Stop at various points throughout the day (e.g., when the lunch bell rings, when walking by restroom signs, etc.) to point out the different cues to the students.

19. Provide the student with verbal reminders or prompts when he/she misses an environmental cue.

20. Review, on a daily basis, the environmental cues that are important to the student (e.g., bells, signs, etc.).

21. When delivering directions, explanations, and information, be certain to use vocabulary that is within the student's level of comprehension.

22. Evaluate the appropriateness of the environmental cues the student is expected to follow in order to determine: (a) if the cue is too difficult and (b) if the length of time required to respond to the cue is appropriate.

23. Communicate with parents (e.g., notes home, phone calls, etc.) in order to share information concerning the student's progress and so that they can reinforce the student at home for responding appropriately to environmental cues at school.

24. Write a contract with the student specifying what behavior is expected (e.g., responding appropriately to bells, rules, point cards, reminders, etc.) and what reinforcement will be made available when the terms of the contract have been met. (See Appendix for Behavioral Contract.)

25. Reinforce those students in the classroom who respond appropriately to environmental cues.

26. Reinforce the student for responding appropriately to environmental cues based on the number of environmental cues the student can successfully follow. Gradually increase the number of environmental cues required for reinforcement as the student demonstrates success.

27. Speak to the student to explain: (a) what the student is doing wrong (e.g., failing to respond appropriately to bells, signs indicating restroom directions, etc.) and (b) what the student should be doing (e.g., responding appropriately to bells, restroom signs, etc.).

28. Reinforce the student for responding appropriately to environmental cues: (a) give the student a tangible reward (e.g., classroom privileges, line leading, passing out materials, five minutes free time, etc.) or (b) give the student an intangible reward (e.g., praise, handshake, smile, etc.).

63 Demonstrates difficulty with auditory memory

1. Make certain the student's hearing has been recently checked.

2. Draw the student's attention to key aspects of auditory communications as they occur (e.g., repeat important points, call the student by name, tell the student which information is particularly important, etc.).

3. Provide the student with more than one source of directions, explanations, instructions, etc., before requiring him/her to remember.

4. When the student is required to recall information, provide auditory cues to help the student remember information previously presented (e.g., say, "Remember yesterday when I said . . ." etc.).

5. Provide visual information to support information the student receives auditorily.

6. Teach the student to learn sequences and lists of information in segments (e.g., telephone numbers are learned as 314, then 874, then 1710).

7. Have the student follow verbal one-, two-, and three-step directions.

8. Provide the student with verbal directions, rules, lists, etc. Reinforce the student for being able to recall the information presented in verbal form.

9. Write stories, directions, etc., so the student may listen as he/she reads along.

10. Tell the student what to listen for before delivering auditory information.

11. Send the student on errands to deliver verbal messages to other teachers in the building.

12. Be certain that auditory information is presented slowly enough for the student to know what is being communicated.

13. Use pictures, diagrams, the chalkboard, and gestures when delivering information.

14. While reading a story to the student, stop on occasion to ask questions about the plot, main characters, events in the story, etc.

15. Have the student pretend to be a waiter/waitress. Have the student recall what a customer orders from him/her.

16. Have the student paraphrase directions, explanations, and instructions soon after hearing them.

17. Use as much visual information as possible when teaching (e.g., chalkboard, projections, pictures, etc.).

18. Have the student tape record directions, explanations, and instructions in order that he/she may replay needed information.

19. Use simple, concise sentences to convey information to the student.

20. Have the student recall names of friends, days of the week, months of the year, addresses, telephone numbers, etc.

21. After listening to a tape, story, record, etc., have the student recall characters, main events, sequence of events, etc.

22. Reduce distracting stimuli (e.g., noise and motion) around the student (e.g., place the student on the front row, provide a carrel or quiet place away from distractions, etc.). This is to be used as a means of reducing distracting stimuli and not as a form of punishment.

23. Use multiple modalities (e.g., auditory, visual, tactile, etc.) when presenting directions, explanations, and instructional content. Determine which modality is stronger and utilize the results.

24. Make certain the student is attending to the source of information (e.g., eye contact is being made, hands are free of materials, student is looking at the assignment, etc.).

25. Stop at various points during a presentation of information to check the student's comprehension.

26. Make certain the student has adequate opportunities for repetition of information through different experiences in order to enhance memory.

27. Provide visual information (e.g., written directions or instructions, etc.) to support information the student receives auditorily.

28. Make certain that all directions, questions, explanations, and instructions are delivered in the most clear and concise manner and at an appropriate pace for the student.

29. When delivering directions, explanations, and information, be certain to use vocabulary that is written at the student's level of comprehension.

30. Evaluate the appropriateness of the task to determine: (a) if the task is too difficult (e.g., too much information to remember) or (b) if the length of time required for the student to remember is inappropriate (e.g., presentation of information was too brief or time lapse between presentation of material and request for recall was too long).

31. Reinforce the student for remembering information received auditorily: (a) give the student a tangible reward (e.g., special privileges, line leading, passing out materials, five minutes free time, etc.) or (b) give the student an intangible reward (e.g., praise, handshake, smile, etc.).

1. Draw the student's attention to key aspects of visual images (e.g., by highlighting, outlining, drawing arrows, etc.).

2. Provide the student with more than one exposure to the visual information prior to requiring him/her to remember it.

3. Reduce visual distractions by isolating the information that is presented to the student (e.g., cover other information on the page, expose only a portion of a picture at a time, etc.).

4. When the student is required to recall information, provide the student with visual cues to help the student remember the information previously presented (e.g., using key words printed on the chalkboard, exposing part or all of a picture, etc.).

5. When the student is required to recall information, provide the student with auditory cues to help the student remember the information previously presented (e.g., say key words, give brief oral description to cue the student, etc.).

6. When the student is required to recall information, remind him/her of the situation in which the material was originally presented (e.g., say, "Remember yesterday when we talked about . . . ," "Remember when we were outside and we looked at the . . . ," etc.).

7. Teach the student to learn sequences and lists of information in segments (e.g., telephone numbers are learned as 314, then 874, then 1710, etc.).

8. Cut pictures from a cartoon strip. Let the student look at the pictures in sequence, then mix them up and let the student put them back in order.

9. Have the student play concentration games (e.g., matching numbers, words, symbols, etc., by turning them over and remembering where they were located).

10. Have the student read and follow one-, two-, and three-step directions.

11. Provide the student with written directions, rules, lists, etc.. Reinforce the student for being able to recall the information given in written form.

12. Tape record stories, directions, etc., so the student may listen to the information while reading along.

13. Require the student to recall days of the week, months of the year, birth dates, addresses, telephone numbers, etc., after seeing this information in written form.

14. Teach the student to recognize common visual symbols (e.g., a red octagon means stop, golden arches symbolize McDonald's fast food restaurant, a skull and crossed bones represents poison, etc.).

15. Use multiple modalities (e.g., auditory, visual, tactile, etc.) when presenting directions, explanations, and instructional content.

16. Reduce the amount of information on a page if it is causing visual distractions for the student (e.g., less print to read, fewer problems, isolate information that is presented to the student, etc.).

17. Provide auditory information (e.g., verbal directions or instructions, etc.) to support information the student receives visually.

18. Identify the student's most efficient learning mode and use it consistently to increase the probability of understanding (e.g., if the student has difficulty understanding written information or directions, present the information verbally).

19. Highlight or underline important information the student reads (e.g., directions, reading assignments, math word problems, etc.).

20. Make it pleasant and positive for the student to ask questions about things not understood. Reinforce the student by assisting, congratulating, praising, etc.

21. Evaluate the appropriateness of the task to determine if: (a) the task is too difficult (e.g., too much information to remember) or (b) the length of time required for the student to remember is inappropriate (e.g., the presentation of information was too brief, time lapse between presentation of material and request for recall was too long, etc.).

22. Reinforce the student for remembering information received visually: (a) give the student a tangible reward (e.g., classroom privileges, line leading, five minutes free time, etc.) or (b) give the student an intangible reward (e.g., praise, handshake, smile, etc.).

23. Present directions following the outline of: (1) What, (2) How, (3) Materials, and (4) When.

24. Have the student take notes when directions are being given following the "What, How, Materials, and When" format. (See Appendix for Assignment Form.)

25. While concepts are presented, have the student listen and take notes for "Who, What, Where, When, How, and Why." (See Appendix for Outline Form.)

26. Present concepts following the outline of: (1) Who, (2) What, (3) Where, (4) When, (5) How, and (6) Why.

65 Has limited note-taking skills

1. Evaluate the appropriateness of note taking to determine: (a) if the task is too difficult and (b) if the length of time scheduled to complete the task is appropriate.

2. Have the student question any directions, explanations, instructions he/she does not understand.

3. Teach the student to take notes in an early grade (i.e., third grade).

4. Teach the student to use the Outline Form (e.g., Who, What, Where, When, How, Why). The student should be required to practice this technique with attention given to note-taking skill development. (See Appendix for Outline Form.)

5. Teach the student to use the Mapping Form (e.g., Who, What, Where, When, How, Why). The student should be required to practice this technique with attention given to note-taking skill development. (See Appendix for Mapping Form.)

6. Teach the student to use the Double-Column Form (e.g., Who, What, Where, When, How, Why). The student should be required to practice this technique with attention given to note-taking skill development. (See Appendix for Double-Column Form.)

7. Teach the student to listen and look for key words (e.g., *Christopher Columbus, Spain, New World,* etc.).

8. Teach the student to listen and look for action words (e.g., *sailed, discovered, founded,* etc.).

9. Teach the student to listen and look for direction words (e.g., *circle, underline, choose, list,* etc.).

10. The teacher should practice pausing periodically during the lecture to allow students to fill in gaps and think about concepts presented.

11. Teach the student that it is acceptable to write notes in incomplete sentences.

12. Teach the student, when taking notes, to write the key words and main ideas that answer Who, What, Where, When, How, and Why. Students should then be given time periodically to go back to fill in connecting details (e.g., The student writes, "Christopher Columbus - Spain -New World - 1492," and is given time to go back to fill in "sailed from - to discover - during the year," resulting in a complete statement: "Christopher Columbus sailed from Spain to discover the New World during the year 1492.").

13. Teach the student to divide note-taking paper in the middle, writing main ideas and key words on the left side of the paper, filling in details and connecting points on the right side of the paper. These details and connecting points may be filled in after the lecture or during a pause.

14. Teach the student to learn and use abbreviations for words frequently used in order to take notes more effectively. Give the student the list of Selected Abbreviations and Symbols. (See Appendix.)

15. The teacher should give students several minutes at the end of a lecture to individually review their notes and ask questions to clarify points.

16. Assign the student a peer to work with to review notes at the end of each lecture. This teaches the student to clarify points and increases retention of material.

17. The teacher should require the student to review the previous day's notes for a short period of time before the new lecture.

18. Require the student to review lecture notes the first five minutes of each homework session (e.g., read notes silently, read notes orally, cover notes with a cover sheet and review from memory, etc.).

19. Have the student keep his/her notes organized in a folder for each subject or activity.

20. Teach the student to associate a known word or symbol with new information. This "association key" will serve to stimulate the student's memory.

21. The teacher should practice using several modalities when delivering a lecture (e.g., oral, written, overheads, etc.).

22. While delivering instructions, directions, lectures, etc., point out to the student that information should be written in the form of notes.

23. Check the student's notes before he/she begins an assignment in order to determine if they are correct and adequate for the assignment.

24. Provide the student with an outline or questions to be completed during teacher delivery of instructions, directions, lectures, etc.

25. Provide the student with samples of notes taken from actual instructions, directions, lectures, etc., given in the classroom in order that he/she may learn what information is necessary when taking notes.

26. Provide a standard format for lecture note taking (e.g., have paper and pencil or pen ready, listen for main ideas or important information, write a shortened form of main ideas or important information, ask to have any main ideas or important information repeated when necessary, etc.).

27. Make certain the student is in the best location in the classroom to receive information for note taking (e.g., near the board, teacher, or other source of information).

28. Make certain you can easily provide supervision of the student's note taking.

29. Make certain that instructions, directions, lectures, etc., are presented clearly and loudly enough for the student to hear.

30. Summarize the main points of instructions, directions, lectures, etc., for the student.

31. Make certain to maintain visibility to and from the student when delivering instructions, directions, lectures, etc., in order to enhance the likelihood of successful note taking.

32. Match the rate of delivery of instructions, directions, lectures, etc., to the student's ability to take notes.

33. Provide instructions, directions, lectures, etc., in sequential steps in order to enhance student note taking.

34. Provide delivery of information in short segments for the student to take notes. Gradually increase the length of delivery as the student experiences success in note taking.

35. Make certain that the vocabulary used in delivering instructions, directions, lectures, etc., is appropriate for the student's ability level.

36. Place the student next to a peer in order that the student can copy notes taken by the peer.

37. Make certain the student has all necessary materials for note taking (e.g., paper, pencil, pen, etc.).

38. Make certain the student has adequate surface space on which to write when taking notes (e.g., uncluttered desk top).

39. Reduce distracting stimuli that would interfere with the student's note taking (e.g., other students talking, outdoor activities, movement in the classroom, hallway noise, etc.).

40. Present the information in the most interesting manner possible.

41. As an alternative to note taking, have the student tape record instructions, directions, lectures, etc.

42. Make certain the student uses any necessary aids in order to facilitate note taking (e.g., eyeglasses, hearing aid, etc.).

1. Make certain the student's hearing has been recently checked.

2. Have the student question any directions, explanations, and instructions he/she does not understand.

3. Have the student act as a classroom messenger. Give the student a verbal message to deliver to another teacher, secretary, administrator, etc. Increase the length of the messages as the student demonstrates success.

4. Review the schedule of the morning and afternoon activities with the student and have him/her repeat the sequence. Increase the length of the sequence as the student is successful.

5. Have the student engage in concentration game activities with a limited number of symbols. Gradually increase the number of symbols as the student demonstrates success.

6. Reinforce the student for remembering to have such materials as pens, pencils, paper, textbooks, notebooks, etc.

7. At the end of the school day, have the student recall three activities in which he/she was engaged during the day. Gradually increase the number of activities the student is required to recall as the student demonstrates success.

8. After a field trip or special event, have the student sequence the activities which occurred.

9. After reading a short story, have the student identify the main characters, sequence the events, and report the outcome of the story.

10. Have the student deliver the schedule of daily events to other students.

11. Use multiple modalities (e.g., auditory, visual, tactile, etc.) when presenting directions, explanations, and instructional content.

12. Assign a peer tutor to engage in short-term memory activities with the student (e.g., concentration games, following directions, etc.).

13. Record a message on tape. Have the student write the message after he/she has heard it. Increase the length of the message as the student demonstrates success.

14. Involve the student in activities in order to enhance short-term memory skills (e.g., carry messages from one location to another; act as group leader, teacher assistant, etc.).

15. Have the student practice short-term memory skills by engaging in activities which are purposeful (e.g., delivering messages, being in charge of room clean-up, acting as custodian's helper, operating equipment, etc.).

16. Informally assess the student's auditory and visual short-term memory skills in order to determine which is the stronger. Utilize the results when presenting directions, explanations, and instructional content.

17. Have the student practice repetition of information in order to increase short-term memory skills (e.g., repeating names, telephone numbers, dates of events, etc.).

18. Teach the student how to organize information into smaller units (e.g., break the number sequence 132563 into units of 13, 25, 63).

19. Use sentence dictation to develop the student's short-term memory skills (e.g., begin with sentences of three words and increase the length of the sentences as the student demonstrates success).

20. Show the student an object or a picture of an object for a few seconds. Ask the student to recall specific attributes of the object (e.g., color, size, shape, etc.).

21. Deliver directions, explanations, and instructional content in a clear manner and at an appropriate pace.

22. Have the student practice taking notes for specific information the student needs to remember.

23. Teach the student to recognize key words and phrases related to information in order to increase short-term or long-term memory skills.

24. Make certain the student is attending to the source of information (e.g., eye contact is being made, hands are free of materials, student is looking at assignment, etc.).

25. Reduce distracting stimuli when information is being presented, the student is studying, etc.

26. Stop at various points during the presentation of information to check the student's comprehension.

27. Give the student one task to perform at a time. Introduce the next task only when the student has successfully completed the previous task.

28. Have the student memorize the first sentence or line of poems, songs, etc. Require more to be memorized as the student experiences success.

29. Teach the student information-gathering skills (e.g., listen carefully, write down important points, ask for clarification, wait until all information is received before beginning, etc.).

30. Have the student repeat/paraphrase directions, explanations, and instructions.

31. Reduce the emphasis on competition. Competitive activities may cause the student to hurry and begin without listening carefully.

32. Provide the student with environmental cues and prompts designed to enhance success in the classroom (e.g., posted rules, schedule of daily events, steps for performing tasks, etc.). (See Appendix for Schedule of Daily Events.)

33. Provide the student with written lists of things to do, materials needed, etc.

34. Maintain consistency in sequential activities in order to increase the likelihood of student success (e.g., the student has math every day at one o'clock, recess at two o'clock, etc.).

35. Break the sequence into units and have the student learn one unit at a time.

36. Establish a regular routine for the student to follow in performing activities, assignments, etc. (e.g., listen to the person speaking to you, wait until directions are completed, make certain you have all necessary materials, etc.).

37. Teach the student to use associative cues or mnemonic devices to remember sequences.

38. Actively involve the student in learning to remember sequences by having the student physically perform sequential activities (e.g., operating equipment, following recipes, solving math problems, etc.).

39. Have the student be responsible for helping a peer remember sequences.

40. Use concrete examples and experiences in sharing information with the student.

41. Teach the student to recognize main points, important facts, etc.

42. Teach the student to rely on resources in the environment to recall information (e.g., notes, textbooks, pictures, etc.).

43. When the student is required to recall information, provide auditory cues to help the student remember the information (e.g., key words, a brief oral description to cue the student, etc.).

44. Assess the meaningfulness of the material to the student. Remembering is more likely to occur when the material is meaningful and the student can relate it to real experiences.

45. Relate the information being presented to the student's previous experiences.

46. Give the student specific categories and have the student name as many items as possible within that category (e.g., objects, persons, places, etc.).

47. Give the student a series of words or pictures and have the student name the category to which they belong (e.g., objects, persons, places, etc.).

48. Describe objects, persons, places, etc., and have the student name the items described.

49. Help the student employ memory aids in order to recall words (e.g., a name might be linked to another word; for example, "Mr. Green is a very colorful person.").

50. Give the student a series of words describing objects, persons, places, etc., and have the student identify the opposite of each word.

51. Encourage the student to play word games such as *Hangman, Scrabble,* and *Password.*

52. Have the student complete "fill-in-the-blank" sentences with appropriate words (e.g., objects, persons, places, etc.).

53. Have the student outline, highlight, underline, or summarize information which should be remembered.

54. Make certain the student has adequate opportunities for repetition of information through different experiences in order to enhance memory.

55. Label objects, persons, places, etc., in the environment in order to help the student be able to recall their names.

56. Make certain the student receives information from a variety of sources (e.g., texts, discussions, films, slide presentations, etc.) in order to enhance memory/recall.

57. Teach the student listening skills (e.g., stop working, look at the person delivering questions and directions, have necessary note-taking materials, etc.).

58. Teach the student direction-following skills (e.g., stop doing other things, listen carefully, write down important points, wait until all directions are given, question any directions not understood, etc.).

59. Have the student tape record directions, explanations, instructions, lectures, etc., in order that the student may replay the information as needed.

60. Highlight or underline important information the student reads (e.g., directions, reading assignments, math word problems, etc.).

61. Tell the student what to listen for when being given directions, receiving information, etc.

62. Have the student repeat to himself/herself information just heard in order to help remember the information.

63. Make certain the student is not required to learn more information than he/she is capable of at any one time.

64. Evaluate the appropriateness of the memory activities to determine: (a) if the task is too difficult and (b) if the length of time scheduled to complete the task is appropriate.

65. Write a contract with the student specifying what behavior is expected (e.g., following one- step directions, two-step directions, etc.) and what reinforcement will be made available when the terms of the contract have been met. (See Appendix for Behavioral Contract.)

66. Reinforce the student for demonstrating short-term or long-term memory skills based on the length of time the student can be successful. Gradually increase the length of time required for reinforcement as the student demonstrates success.

67. Reinforce the student for demonstrating short-term or long-term memory skills: (a) give the student a tangible reward (e.g., classroom privileges, line leading, passing out materials, five minutes free time, etc.) or (b) give the student an intangible reward (e.g., praise, handshake, smile, etc.).

67 Requires repeated drill and practice to learn what other students master easily

1. Reduce the emphasis on competition. Competitive activities may cause the student to hurry and make mistakes.

2. Give the student fewer concepts to learn at any one time, spending more time on each concept until the student learns it correctly.

3. Have a peer spend time each day engaged in drill activities with the student.

4. Have the student use new concepts frequently throughout the day.

5. Have the student highlight or underline key words, phrases and sentences from reading assignments, newspapers, magazines, etc.

6. Develop crossword puzzles which contain only the student's spelling words and have him/her complete them.

7. Write sentences, passages, paragraphs, etc., for the student to read which reinforce new concepts.

8. Have the student act as a peer tutor to teach concepts just learned to another student.

9. Have the student review new concepts each day for a short period of time rather than two or three times per week for longer periods of time.

10. Use wall charts to introduce new concepts with visual images, such as pictures for the student to associate with previously learned concepts.

11. Initiate a "learn a concept a day" program with the student and incorporate the concept into the assigned activities for the day.

12. Require the student to use resources (e.g., encyclopedia, dictionary, etc.) to provide information to help him/her be successful when performing tasks.

13. Allow the student to use devices to help him/her successfully perform tasks (e.g., calculator, multiplication tables, abacus, dictionary, etc.).

14. Provide the student with times throughout the day when he/she can engage in drill activities with the teacher, an aide, a peer, etc.

15. Provide the student with opportunities for drill activities in the most interesting manner possible (e.g., working with the computer, using a calculator, playing educational games, watching a film, listening to a tape, etc.).

16. Give the student a list of key words, phrases, or main points to learn for each new concept introduced.

17. Underline, circle, or highlight important information from any material the student is to learn (e.g., science, math, geography, etc.).

18. Provide the student with the information he/she needs to learn in the most direct manner possible (e.g., a list of facts, a summary of important points, an outline of important events, etc.).

19. Tape record important information the student can listen to as often as necessary.

20. Obtain computer software which provides repeated drill of general concepts and facts.

21. Obtain computer software which has the capability of programming the student's individual spelling words, facts, etc., for repeated drill and practice.

22. Encourage the student to review new concepts each evening for a short period of time.

23. Use concrete examples in teaching the student new information and concepts.

24. Break the sequence into units and have the student learn one unit at a time.

25. Make certain the student has adequate opportunities for repetition of information through different experiences in order to enhance his/her memory.

26. Make certain the student receives information from a variety of sources (e.g., texts, discussions, films, etc.) in order to enhance the student's memory/recall.

27. When a student is required to recall information, remind him/her of the situation in which the material was originally presented (e.g., "Remember when we talked about . . ." etc.).

28. Have the student listen and take notes for the "Who, What, Where, When, How, and Why" while concepts are presented. (See Appendix for Outline Form.)

29. Present concepts following the outline of: (1) Who, (2) What, (3) Where, (4) When, (5) How, and (6) Why.

30. Have the student prepare for tests using the "Who, What, Where, When, How, and Why" system. (See Appendix for Outline Form.)

31. Develop tests and quizzes for the student using the "Who, What, Where, When, How, and Why" approach.

68 Does not demonstrate an understanding of spatial relationships

1. Introduce each spatial concept individually before pairing the concepts. Avoid introducing spatial relationships such as near-far at the same time.

2. Provide repeated physical demonstrations of spatial relationships.

3. Have the student physically perform spatial relationships (e.g., have the student stand near the teacher, far from the teacher, over a table, under a table, etc.).

4. Provide the student with a variety of pictures representing spatial concepts. Have the student match the concepts which form relationships.

5. Emphasize spatial relationships which have particular meaning to the student (e.g., students who live "near" school walk and students who live "far" from school ride the bus).

6. Call attention to spatial relationships which occur naturally in the environment (e.g., call attention to a bird flying over a tree, a squirrel running under a bush, etc.).

7. To teach the student relationships of left and right, place paper bands labeled left and right around the student's wrists. Remove the paper bands when the student can successfully identify left and right.

8. Give the student a series of spatial relationship directions to follow (e.g., crawl under the table, stand near the closet, put the chalk below the clock, etc.).

9. Include spatial relationships in directions given to the student (e.g., "Write your name on the dotted line." "Keep your feet under your desk." etc.).

10. Have the student practice performing spatial relationship concepts with peers (e.g., *Simon Says, Follow the Leader*, following directions, etc.).

11. When introducing initial spatial concepts, rely on tangible objects rather than the spoken and printed word (i.e., use a concrete medium rather than abstract symbols).

12. For more abstract concepts such as left and right, north, south, east, and west, have the student follow simple map directions. Begin with a map of the building and progress to a map of the community, state, nation, etc., with more complex directions to follow.

13. Identify areas and objects in the classroom with cards indicating spatial concepts (e.g., a light fixture labeled above; a rug labeled under; walls labeled north, south, east, west, etc.).

14. Review, on a daily basis, those spatial relationships which have been previously introduced.

15. Use concrete examples and experiences in teaching concepts and sharing information with the student.

16. Review, on a daily basis, those skills, concepts, tasks, etc., which have been previously introduced.

17. Have the student question any directions, explanations, instructions he/she does not understand.

18. Evaluate the appropriateness of the task to determine: (a) if the task is too difficult and (b) if the length of time scheduled to complete the task is appropriate.

69 Does not demonstrate an understanding of directionality

1. Make certain to use the terms right and left as part of the directions you give to the student (e.g., refer to the windows on the left side of the room, the chalkboard on the right side of the room, etc.).

2. Identify directions in the classroom with signs (e.g., on the ceiling put "UP" on the floor put "DOWN" etc.).

3. Have the student practice following directions on paper. Instruct the student to make a mark or picture on the right, left, middle, top and bottom parts of the paper according to the directions given.

4. Avoid the problem of mirror images by standing next to the student when giving right and left directions.

5. Design an obstacle course using materials in the room. Students can step into the box, crawl over the desk, walk under the coat rack, stand on the table, etc.

6. Use concrete examples when teaching concepts of up-down, high-low, above-below, etc. Use books, balls, regular classroom materials, etc., when trying to convey these concepts.

7. Hang directional signs in the room (e.g., "turn left," "games under cabinet," etc.).

8. Play *Simon Says* for directions (e.g., "Raise your left hand." "Walk behind the chair." etc.).

9. Conduct scavenger hunts. Have the student look for a pencil in the desk, a book under the table, a glass on the chair, etc.

10. Have the student sort left and right gloves, shoes, paper hand and foot cut-outs, etc.

11. Teach north, south, east, and west using the classroom, playground, school building, etc.

12. Label strips of paper left and right and attach them to the student's wrists.

13. Have the student practice walking forward and backward, moving toy cars and trucks forward and backward, etc.

14. Have the student identify objects which move up and down (e.g., airplanes, teeter-totter, etc.).

15. Point out doors which are labeled push and pull and activities which require pushing and pulling (e.g., opening drawers, opening doors, etc.).

16. Have the student find things that represent the concept of in and out (e.g., we pour milk in a glass and pour it out, we walk in a room and walk out, etc.).

17. Identify objects which represent over and under (e.g., a bridge is over water, people sleep under covers, birds fly over our heads, rugs are under our feet, etc.).

18. Teach the concept of above and below with examples in the classroom (e.g., the ceiling is above our heads and the floor below our feet, etc.).

19. Teach the concept of before and after with examples from the student's daily routine (e.g., we wake up before we eat breakfast, we go to school after we eat breakfast, we eat lunch after we have morning recess, etc.).

20. Emphasize activities which require the action of off and on (e.g., we turn lights on for light and off when we do not need them, we turn the stove on to heat things and off when things are hot, we put clothes on to go to school, leaves fall off a tree in the fall, etc.).

21. Use concrete examples and experiences in teaching directionality (e.g., east-west signs on the wall, left-right armbands, etc.).

22. Review on a daily basis the concepts of directionality.

1. Make certain the student has had his/her vision checked recently.

2. Give the student the opportunity to find objects which are the same or different in size, shape, color, etc.

3. Have the student sort objects according to size, shape, color, etc.

4. Have the student use play equipment such as a ladder, the jungle gym, blocks, the teeter-totter, a balance beam, etc., to become more aware of body position in space.

5. Have the student complete partially drawn figures, words, numbers, etc.

6. Have the student use paper pictures from magazines, catalogs, etc., to assemble features and body parts.

7. Have the student build an object according to a pattern (e.g., Tinker Toys, blocks, etc.).

8. Have the student engage in sequencing activities (e.g., put numbers in order, place pictures in correct order, etc.).

9. Have the student pick out specific objects from pictures around the classroom, in the environment while on the playground, etc.

10. Have the student perform a variety of activities such as tracing, cutting, coloring, pasting, etc.

11. Have the student complete jigsaw puzzles (e.g., beginning with simple self-made puzzles and progressing to more complex puzzles).

12. Develop a variety of activities for the student using a pegboard.

13. Provide the student with a variety of classifying activities (e.g., from simple classifying of types of clothes, cars, etc., to more complex classifying of the items that would be located at certain stores, etc.).

14. Have the student find specific shapes in the room (e.g., the door is a rectangle, the clock is a circle, etc.).

15. Provide the student with simple designs to be reproduced with blocks, sticks, paper, etc.

16. Provide the student with dot-to-dot worksheets following specific patterns, etc.

17. Have the student identify objects by looking at the outline of objects on a cardboard silhouette, etc.

18. Reduce visual stimuli on a worksheet or in a book by covering all of the page except the activity on which the student is working.

19. Provide the student with a variety of exercises in which he/she must identify the missing body parts, common objects, etc.

20. Provide the student with a variety of visual recall tasks (e.g., the student writes numbers, shapes, and words he/she was shown for a specific time, etc.).

21. Use a variety of colored tiles to make a pattern. Have the student duplicate the pattern while looking at the model, then complete the design from memory without using the model.

22. Place on a tray several items, such as a pencil, a flower, a penny, and a piece of gum. Allow the student to study the items, then take the items away and have the student identify what was on the tray.

23. Have the student practice tracing outlines of pictures. Worksheets with dotted lines of pictures, letters, numbers, etc., can be used to develop eye-hand coordination.

24. Play a matching game like *Concentration* in which hidden pictures, numbers, or shapes, are turned over one at a time and the student must remember where the matching picture is located.

25. Using pictures from magazines, remove an important part of the picture and ask the student to identify the missing part.

26. Read directions orally to the student before he/she is asked to do a workbook page. Work the first problem with the student so he/she understands what is expected.

27. Reduce the amount of information on a page for the student (e.g., less print, fewer problems, etc.).

28. Provide math problems on graph paper so the numbers are in columns in the ones, tens, and hundreds places.

29. Have writing paper color-coded so the student knows where to start and stop on the page.

30. Highlight or underline important words, phrases, etc., in the student's assignments.

31. Allow the student to use a typewriter to facilitate skills and reinforce word recognition.

32. Provide the student with shorter tasks, but more of them. Increase the length of tasks as the student demonstrates success.

33. Reduce distracting stimuli on or near the student's desk (e.g., materials on the desk, things inside the desk, etc.).

34. Provide the student with a quiet place to work (e.g., carrel, "office," etc.). This is used as a means of reducing distracting stimuli and not as a form of punishment.

35. Identify the student's most efficient learning mode and use it consistently to increase the probability of understanding (e.g., if the student has difficulty understanding written information or directions, present it verbally).

71   Has difficulty classifying

1. Make certain the student understands that all objects, people, ideas, actions, etc., can be grouped based on how they are alike. Provide the student with concrete examples.

2. Give the student pairs of objects and have the student name all the ways in which they are alike and then the ways in which they are different. Proceed from simple things which can be seen and touched to more abstract ideas which cannot be seen or touched.

3. Name a category or group and ask the student to identify as many things as possible which belong in the group. Begin with large categories (e.g., living things) and move to more specific categories (e.g., things which are green).

4. Explain that each new word which is learned is an example of some category. When defining a word, it should first be put into a category (e.g., a hammer is a kind of tool, anger is a kind of emotion, etc.).

5. Present a series of objects and have the student create a category into which they fit.

6. Present a series of objects or words and have the student tell which ones do not belong in the same category as the others.

7. Give the student a list of words or pictures and have him/her identify the categories to which they belong. (Love and hate are both emotions. Love fits into the specific category of good feelings, and hate fits into the specific category of bad or unhappy feelings.)

8. Explain that words can be categorized according to many different attributes, such as size, function, texture, etc.

9. Ask the student to help make lists of some categories which fit inside larger categories (e.g., flowers, trees, and bushes are all categories which can be included in the plant category).

10. Play a game such as "I'm thinking of an object" in which an object is described and the student must guess the item based on questions asked.

11. Suggest that parents ask for the student's help when grocery shopping by having him/her make a list of items needed in a particular food group (e.g., dairy products, meats, etc.).

12. Have the student cut out pictures for a notebook of favorite foods, television shows, or other categories, and then group the pictures in appropriate arrangement.

13. Give the student specific categories and have him/her name as many items as possible within the categories (e.g., objects, persons, places, etc.).

14. Give the student a word and have the student list as many words that he/she can think of which have similar meanings (synonyms).

15. Make the subject matter meaningful to the student (e.g., explain the purpose of an assignment, relate the subject matter to the student's environment, etc.).

16. Stop at various points during the presentation of information to check the student's comprehension.

17. Use pictures, diagrams, the chalkboard, and gestures when delivering information.

1. Make certain the student's vision has been checked recently.

2. Make certain that all directions, explanations, and instructions are delivered in the most clear and concise manner.

3. Teach the student direction-following skills (e.g., stop doing other things; listen to what is being said; do not begin until all information is delivered; question any directions, explanations, and instructions you do not understand).

4. Teach the student to rely on environmental cues when moving about the school and related areas (e.g., look for signs, room numbers, familiar surroundings, etc.).

5. Make certain the student knows how to ask questions, ask for directions, etc.

6. Teach the student a basic survival/directional word vocabulary (e.g., ladies, gentlemen, push, pull, left, right, etc.).

7. Have a peer accompany the student to locations in the building until the student develops familiarity with his/her surroundings.

8. Have the student practice finding various locations in the building before or after school or during classes when few other students are in the halls.

9. Have the student practice finding locations in the building by following verbal directions, written directions, directions from teachers or other students, etc.

10. Have the student follow a schedule of daily events as he/she moves from place to place in the school. (See Appendix for Schedule of Daily Events.)

11. Pair the student with a classmate who has a similar class schedule in order to have a peer who can direct the student if he/she gets lost or confused.

12. Have the student learn to use a floor plan to find specific rooms, hallways, and areas while following his/her daily class or work schedule.

13. Make certain the student has designated instructors or peers who act as a source of information within the school.

14. Have the student verbally repeat/paraphrase instructions and information given so that the instructor can provide a means of clarification and redirection of the given information.

15. Make certain the student has been provided with an adequate orientation to all areas of the school environment he/she will be using.

16. Have the student practice problem-solving skills if he/she should become lost or confused in the school environment (e.g., ask directions, return to where you started, look for familiar surroundings, read signs, etc.).

17. Make certain the school environment is conducive to finding locations the student uses (e.g., posting signs, posting directions, color-coding pods and similar areas, etc.).

18. Before leaving the classroom have the student review directions to locate certain points throughout the building (e.g., have the student repeat directions back to you, have the student look at a map, etc.).

19. When giving the student directions to certain points throughout the building, use concrete cues such as the drinking fountain, restroom, lunchroom, etc. (e.g., "go to the room that is just past the lunchroom," "the bathroom is on the left side of the drinking fountain,"etc.).

20. When delivering directions, explanations, and information, be sure to use vocabulary that is within the student's level of comprehension.

21. Make certain the student is attending when directions are being given (e.g., eye contact is being made, hands are free of materials, etc.).

22. Reduce or remove those stimuli from the environment which are distracting to the student and interfering with his/her ability to listen successfully.

23. Have the student act as a peer tutor to teach another student a concept he/she has mastered. This can serve as reinforcement for the student.

24. Make certain the student has mastery of concepts at one level before introducing a new skill level.

25. Call on the student when he/she is most likely to be able to respond successfully.

26. Provide the student with shorter tasks, but more of them, throughout the day (e.g., 4 assignments of 5 problems each rather than one assignment of 20 problems).

27. Review, on a daily basis, those skills, concepts, tasks, etc., which have been previously introduced.

28. Give the student one task to perform at a time. Introduce the next task only when the student has successfully completed the previous task.

29. Stop at various points during the presentation of information to check the student's comprehension.

30. Make certain the student is attending to the source of information (e.g., eye contact is being made, hands are free of materials, student is looking at the assignment, etc.).

31. Provide the student with environmental cues and prompts designed to enhance his/her success in the classroom (e.g., posted rules, schedule of daily events, steps for performing a task, etc.).

32. Reduce the amount of information on a page if it causes visual distractions for the student (e.g., have less print to read, have fewer problems, isolate information that is presented to the student).

33. Assign the student shorter tasks and gradually increase the length of tasks as the student demonstrates success.

34. Identify the student's most efficient learning mode and use it consistently to increase the probability of understanding (e.g., if the student fails to understand directions or information verbally, present it in written form; if the student has difficulty understanding written information or directions, present it verbally.).

35. Make certain that verbal directions are delivered in a nonthreatening and supportive manner (e.g., positive voice, facial expressions and language such as "Will you please . . ." or "You need . . ." rather than "You better . . ." or "If you don't . . .").

36. Use pictures, diagrams, the chalkboard, and gestures when delivering information.

37. When delivering directions, explanations, and information, be certain to use vocabulary that is within the student's level of comprehension.

38. Deliver information to the student on a one-to-one basis or employ a peer tutor.

1. Explain that the student should be satisfied with his/her best effort rather than insist on perfection.

2. Have the student time activities in order to monitor his/her own behavior and accept time limits.

3. Convince the student that work not completed in one sitting can be completed later. Provide the student ample time to complete earlier assignments in order to guarantee closure.

4. Provide the student with more than enough time to finish an activity and decrease the amount of time as the student demonstrates success.

5. Structure time limits in order that the student knows exactly how long he/she has to work and when work must be finished.

6. Allow a transition period between activities in order that the student can make adjustments in his/her behavior.

7. Employ a signal technique (e.g., turning lights off and on) to warn that the end of an activity is near.

8. Establish definite time limits and provide the student with this information before an activity begins.

9. Assign the student shorter activities and gradually increase the length of the activities as the student demonstrates success.

10. Maintain consistency in the daily routine.

11. Maintain consistency of expectations and keep expectations within the ability level of the student.

12. Allow the student to finish the activity unless it will be disruptive to the schedule.

13. Provide the student with a list of materials needed for each activity (e.g., pencil, paper, textbook, workbook, etc.).

14. Present instructions/directions prior to handing out necessary materials.

15. Collect the student's materials (e.g., pencil, paper, textbook, workbook, etc.) when it is time to change from one activity to another.

16. Provide the student with clearly stated expectations for all situations.

17. Provide adequate transition time for the student to finish an activity and get ready for the next activity.

18. Prevent the student from becoming so stimulated by an event or activity that the student cannot control his/her behavior.

19. Identify expectations of different environments and help the student develop the skills to be successful in those environments.

20. In conjunction with other school personnel, develop as much consistency across all school environments as possible (e.g., rules, criteria for success, behavioral expectations, consequences, etc.).

21. Have the student engage in relaxing transitional activities designed to reduce the effects of stimulating activities (e.g., put head on desk, listen to the teacher read a story, put headphones on and listen to relaxing music, etc.).

22. Provide the student with a schedule of daily events in order that the student knows exactly what is expected for the day. (See Appendix for Schedule of Daily Events.)

23. Provide the student with verbal reminders or prompts when he/she perseverates.

24. Reduce distraction stimuli (noise and motion) around the student (e.g, place the student on the front row, provide a carrel or quiet place away from distractions, etc.). This is used as a means of reducing stimuli and not as a form of punishment.

25. Provide the student with increased opportunity for help or assistance on academic tasks (e.g., peer tutoring, directions for work sent home, frequent interactions, etc.).

26. Assign a peer to provide an appropriate model for changing from one activity to another.

27. Have the student question any directions, explanations, instructions he/she does not understand.

28. Evaluate the appropriateness of the task to determine: (a) if the task is too easy, (b) if the task is too difficult, and (c) if the length of time scheduled to complete the task is appropriate.

29. Write a contract with the student specifying what behavior is expected (e.g., put materials away and get ready for another activity) and what reinforcement will be made available when the terms of the contract have been met.

30. Reinforce the student for demonstrating acceptable behavior based on the length of time the student can be successful. Gradually increase the length of time required for reinforcement as the student demonstrates success.

31. Reinforce those students in the classroom who change from one activity to another without difficulty.

32. Establish classroom rules (e.g., work on-task, work quietly, remain in your seat, finish task, meet task expectations). Reiterate the rules often and reinforce students for following the rules.

33. Speak to the student to explain: (a) what he/she is doing wrong (e.g., failing to stop one activity and begin another) and (b) what he/she should be doing (e.g., changing from one activity to another).

34. Reinforce the student for changing from one activity to another without difficulty: (a) give the student a tangible reward (e.g., classroom privileges, line leading, passing out materials, five minutes free time, etc.) or (b) give the student an intangible reward (e.g., praise, handshake, smile, etc.).

1. Give the student responsibilities that require logical thinking (e.g., assign the student to water plants and provide a watering can and a glass, telling the student to use the most appropriate container, etc.).

2. Each day provide the student with problem-solving situations which require logical thinking (e.g., "A stranger takes you by the arm in a department store. What do you do?" "You see smoke coming out of a neighbor's house and no one is home. What do you do?" etc.).

3. Make certain the student experiences the consequences of his/her behavior (e.g., appropriate behavior results in positive consequences while inappropriate behavior results in negative consequences).

4. Provide the student with a list of questions involving logic, which he/she answers orally (e.g., "Why do we post wet paint signs?" "Why do we have Stop signs at intersections?" "Why do we wear seat belts?" etc.).

5. When something is broken, lost, etc., have the student identify what could have been done to prevent the situation. When materials are properly organized, maintained, and serviceable, have the student discuss the value of such practices.

6. Have the student read stories involving a moral (e.g., "The Tortoise and the Hare," "The Boy Who Cried Wolf," etc.) and explain the reason for the outcome of the story.

7. Have the student read short stories without endings. Require the student to develop logical endings for the stories.

8. Give the student situations/pictures and have him/her explain what variables are related (e.g., "Snow is falling, and the wind is blowing. Is the temperature hot or cold? What should you wear outdoors?").

9. Have the student sequence cartoon strips, after they have been cut apart and rearranged, and explain the logic of the sequence created.

10. Give the student fill-in-the-blank statements requiring an appropriate response from multiple-choice possibilities (e.g., The boy's dog was dirty so the boy decided to give his dog a ___ (dog biscuit, bath, toy).).

11. Show the student pictures of dangerous situations and have him/her explain why it is dangerous (e.g., a child running into the street from between parked cars, a child riding a bicycle without using his/her hands, etc.).

12. Use cause-and-effect relationships as they apply to nature and people. Discuss what led up to a specific situation in a story or a picture, what could happen next, etc.

13. Make certain that the student can verbalize the reason for real-life outcomes of behavior (e.g., why the student had to leave the class line on the way to recess, why he/she earned the privilege of being line leader, etc.).

14. Have the student make up rules. Have the student explain why each is necessary.

15. Have the student identify appropriate consequences for rules (e.g., consequences for following rules and consequences for not following rules). Have the student explain the choice of consequences he/she identified.

16. Have the student answer such questions as "Why do we have rules?" "Why do you have to be a certain age before you can drive a car?" etc.

17. Have the student answer analogy situations (e.g., a garage is to a car as a house is to a _____).

18. Set aside time each day for a problem-solving game, analogies, decision-making activities, assigned responsibilities, etc.

19. Make certain the student is attending to the source of information (e.g., eye contact is being made, hands are free of materials, student is looking at the assignment, etc.).

20. Have the student questions any directions, explanations, and instructions he/she does not understand.

21. Reinforce those students in the classroom who demonstrate logical thinking (e.g., making appropriate decisions, solving problems, making references, etc.).

22. Reinforce the student for appropriate decision-making: (a) give the student a tangible reward (e.g., classroom privileges, line leading, passing out materials, five minutes free time, etc.) or (b) give the student an intangible reward (e.g., smile, handshake, etc.).

75 Does not follow directives form teachers or other school personnel

1. Structure the environment in such a way that the student remains active and involved in appropriate behavior.

2. Maintain visibility to and from the student. The teacher should be able to see the student and the student should be able to see the teacher, making eye contact possible at all times.

3. Give the student preferred responsibilities.

4. Present the tasks in the most interesting and attractive manner possible.

5. Maintain maximum supervision of the student and gradually decrease supervision as the student becomes successful at following directives.

6. Have the student maintain a chart representing the amount of time spent following teacher directives or rules, with reinforcement given for increasing appropriate behavior.

7. Be mobile in order to frequently be near the student.

8. Provide the student with many social and academic successes.

9. Provide the student with positive feedback that indicates he/she is successful.

10. Post rules in various places, including on the student's desk.

11. Make certain the student receives the information necessary to perform activities (e.g., written information, verbal directions, reminders, etc.).

12. Teach the student direction-following skills: (a) listen carefully, (b) ask questions, (c) use environmental cues, (d) rely on examples, and (e) wait until all directions are given before beginning, etc.

13. Maintain the most positive, professional relationship with the student (i.e., an adversary relationship is likely to result in failure to follow directions).

14. Be a consistent authority figure (e.g., be consistent in relationship with student).

15. Provide the student with optional courses of action in order to prevent total refusal to obey directives from teachers and other school personnel.

16. Intervene early to prevent the student's behavior from leading to contagion for other students.

17. Deliver directions in a step-by-step sequence.

18. Have a peer act as a model for following teacher directives.

19. Interact with the student frequently to determine if directives are being followed.

20. Maintain consistency in rules, routine, and general expectations of conduct and procedure.

21. Allow natural consequences to occur as a result of not following directives from teachers and other school personnel (e.g., assignments are performed incorrectly, accidents will occur, detention will be assigned, etc.).

22. Limit the student's opportunity to engage in activities in which he/she will not follow directives from teachers and other school personnel (e.g., recess, industrial arts activities, field trips, etc.).

23. Do not allow the student to be unsupervised anywhere in the school environment.

24. Along with a directive, provide an incentive statement (e.g., "When you finish your math, you may go outside." "You may have free time after you finish your work.").

25. In order to determine if the student heard a direction, have the student repeat it.

26. Deliver directions in a supportive rather than a threatening manner (e.g., "Please finish your work." rather than "You had better finish your work or else!").

27. Teach the student to respect others and their belongings by respecting the student's belongings.

28. Teach the student to "think" before acting (e.g., ask himself/herself: "What is happening?" "What am I doing?" "What should I do?" "What will be best for me").

29. Make certain the student is allowed to voice an opinion in a situation in order to avoid becoming angry or upset.

30. Evaluate the appropriateness of the task to determine: (a) if the task is too difficult, or (b) if the length of time scheduled to complete the task is appropriate.

31. Communicate with parents (e.g., notes home, phone calls, etc.) in order to share information concerning the student's progress and so that they can reinforce the student at home for following directives from teachers and other school personnel.

32. Write a contract with the student specifying what behavior is expected (e.g., following teacher directives) and what reinforcement will be made available when the terms of the contract have been met. (See Appendix for Behavioral Contract.)

33. Remove the student from the group or activity until he/she can demonstrate appropriate behavior and self-control.

34. Reinforce the student for following the directives of teachers and other school personnel based on the length of time the student can be successful). Gradually increase the amount of time required for reinforcement as the student demonstrates success.

35. Reinforce those students in the classroom who follow directives from teachers and other school personnel.

36. Establish classroom rules:
1. Work on-task.
2. Work quietly.
3. Remain in your seat.
4. Finish task.
5. Meet task expectations.
6. Raise your hand.

Reiterate rules often and reinforce students for following rules.

37. Speak with the student to explain: (a) what the student is doing wrong (e.g., failing to follow directions or observe rules) and (b) what the student should be doing (e.g., following established guidelines or expectations).

38. Reinforce the student for following directives from teachers or other school personnel: (a) give the student a tangible reward (e.g., classroom privileges, line leading, passing out materials, five minutes free time, etc.) or (b) give the student an intangible reward (e.g., praise, handshake, smile, etc.).

1. Provide clearly stated verbal directions (e.g., make the directions as simple and concrete as possible).

2. Help the student be successful with multi-step directions (e.g., give verbal reminders, etc.), gradually reducing the amount of assistance given.

3. Provide verbal cues or signals to help the student recall steps.

4. Identify a peer to act as a model for the student to imitate following multi-step verbal directions.

5. Assign a peer to work with the student to help him/her follow multi-step verbal directions.

6. Carefully consider the student's age and ability before expecting him/her to follow multi-step directions.

7. Present directions following the outline of: (1) What, (2) How, (3) Materials, and (4) When.

8. Have the student take notes when directions are being given following the "What, How, Materials, and When" format. (See Appendix for Assignment Form.)

9. Have the student practice following one-step directions. When he/she is successful, add a second step and have the student practice two-step directions until he/she is successful. Continue this process as the student develops the skills necessary to follow multi-step directions.

10. Provide multi-step directions in written form as well as verbal form for the student.

11. Deliver multi-step directions to the student one step at a time. Gradually combine steps when giving directions as the student demonstrates success.

12. Have the student make notes for multi-step directions, which he/she can then follow by reading the written form.

13. Reduce multi-step verbal directions to fewer steps, gradually increasing expectations.

14. Communicate clearly to the student when it is time to listen to directions.

15. Make certain the student has all the materials necessary to perform all steps of the directions.

16. Make certain the student is attending to the teacher (e.g., making eye contact, looking at chalkboard, etc.) before giving multi-step directions.

17. Provide the student with a written copy of the multi-step directions.

18. Tape record multi-step directions for the student to listen to individually and repeat as necessary.

19. Maintain consistency in the format in which verbal directions are given.

20. Have a peer help the student with any steps of the directions that he/she does not understand.

21. Seat the student close to the source of the verbal directions.

22. Work through the steps of the verbal directions as they are delivered in order to make certain the student follows the directions accurately.

23. Reduce distracting stimuli in order to increase the student's ability to follow verbal directions (e.g., place the student in the front row, provide a carrel or "office" space away from distractions, etc.). This is used as a means of reducing distracting stimuli and not as a form of punishment.

24. Interact frequently with the student in order to help him/her follow multi-step verbal directions.

25. Provide alternatives for the traditional format of presenting verbal directions (e.g., tape record directions, summarize directions, directions given by peers, etc.).

26. Have the student practice following multi-step verbal directions for nonacademic tasks (e.g., recipes, games, etc.).

27. Have the student repeat or paraphrase multi-step verbal directions.

1. Make sure the reading level is appropriate for the student.

2. Make sure directions are completely understood by the student (e.g., have the student paraphrase the directions).

3. Require the student to read all multiple- choice answers before responding.

4. On true-false items, have the student underline key words before responding.

5. On true-false items, teach the student that, in order for an item to be true, the whole statement must be true.

6. On matching items, teach the student to read all choices prior to responding.

7. On matching items, teach the student to respond to known items first, marking off used responses.

8. Teach the student to pace himself/herself on timed tests.

9. For standardized bubble-format tests, require the student to use a place marker on the response sheet.

10. Teach the student mnemonic devices to remember information.

11. Require the student to list important points prior to the test as a pretest.

12. For spelling tests, have the student write spelling words five times each while saying them aloud.

13. For spelling tests, have the student take a pretest one day prior to the test.

14. Teach the student not to spend too much time on any one item on timed tests.

15. Teach the student to proofread all items on a test.

16. On essay tests, have the student include Who, What, Where, When, How, and Why in the answer.

17. Give the student a practice test in class.

18. Have the student study with a peer.

19. Allow the student to take the test in another place in the building (e.g., resource room, counselor's office, etc.).

20. Allow the student additional time to take the test.

21. Provide the student with sample questions from the test.

22. Make certain the student knows what topic/ areas will be covered by the test.

23. Provide a review session in which test topics and typical questions are covered.

24. Require the student to check all answers on tests for accuracy.

25. Allow the student to take the test orally (i.e., read the test to the student with the student responding orally).

26. For standardized tests, give the student sample test questions in order that he/she may become comfortable with the format.

27. Have the student study for tests according to the Who, What, Where, When, How, and Why format; then test according to that same information.

28. Provide time for the student to study for tests at school rather than home.

29. Provide the student with multiple opportunities to master what will be covered by the test (e.g., listening to presentations in class; reading assigned materials; studying with a friend; playing games over the test material, such as *Jeopardy*; etc.).

1.   Evaluate the appropriateness of the task to determine: (a) if the task is too difficult and (b) if the length of time scheduled for the task is appropriate.

2.   Assign a peer to help the student with class assignments.

3.   Assess the degree of task difficulty in comparison with the student's ability to perform the task.

4.   Assign the student shorter tasks (e.g., modify a 20-problem math activity to 4 activities of 5 problems each, to be done at various times during the day). Gradually increase the length of the task over time.

5.   Present tasks in the most attractive and interesting manner possible.

6.   Reduce distracting stimuli (e.g., place the student in the front row, provide a carrel or quiet place away from distractions). This is used as a means of reducing stimuli and not as a form of punishment.

7.   Interact frequently with the student in order to maintain involvement with class assignments (e.g., ask the student questions, ask the student's opinion, stand close to the student, seat the student near the teacher's desk, etc.).

8.   Allow the student additional time to complete class assignments.

9.   Supervise the student during class assignments in order to maintain on-task behavior.

10.   Deliver directions orally in order to increase the probability of the student's understanding of class assignments.

11.   Make certain the student understands the natural consequences of failing to complete assignments (e.g., students who do not finish their work will not get to do more desirable activities).

12.   Repeat directions in order to increase the probability of understanding.

13.   Encourage the student to ask for clarification of directions for classroom assignments.

14.   Follow a less desirable task with a highly desirable task, making the completion of the first necessary to perform the second.

15.   Give directions in a variety of ways to increase the probability of understanding (e.g., if the student fails to understand verbal directions, present them in written form).

16.   Provide the student with step-by-step written directions for class assignments.

17.   Allow the student to perform alternative assignments. Gradually introduce more components of the regular assignments until those assignments are routinely performed.

18.   Maintain consistency of expectations while keeping expectations within the ability level of the student.

19.   Allow the student the option of performing the assignment at another time (e.g., earlier in the day, later in the day, on another day, or later at home).

20.   Provide the student with a selection of assignments and require him/her to choose a minimum number from the total amount (e.g., present the student with 10 academic tasks from which he/she must finish 6 that day).

21.   Maintain mobility in order to be frequently near the student to provide cues and prompts to assist the student in performing classroom assignments.

22.   Communicate with parents (e.g., notes home, phone calls, etc.) in order to share information concerning the student's progress and so that they may reinforce the student at home for completing assignments at school.

23. Modify the task assignment in order that the student will be able to complete the assignment during class time (e.g., individualize spelling lists by matching lists to the student's ability level).

24. Teach the student basic study skills (e.g., finding key words and phrases; underlining or highlighting important facts; identifying "Who, What, Where, When, How, and Why"; etc.).

25. Teach direction-following skills (e.g., key words in directions; use of sequential words in directions in order to perform steps such as *first, then, next*; etc.).

26. Have the student take notes when directions are being given following the "What, How, Materials, and When" format. (See Appendix for Assignment Form.)

27. Present assignments following the outline of: (1) What, (2) How, (3) Materials, and (4) When.

28. Maintain consistency in the daily routine.

29. Work a few problems with the student on an assignment in order to serve as a model and help the student begin a task.

30. Reinforce the student for beginning, staying on, and completing assignments.

31. Identify a peer to act as a model for the student to imitate appropriate completion of assignments.

32. Have the student question any directions, explanations, instructions he/she does not understand.

33. Assess the quality and clarity of directions, explanations, and instructions given to the student.

34. Structure the environment in such a way as to provide the student with increased opportunity for help or assistance (e.g., seat the student close to the teacher's desk, seat the student near a peer who can provide assistance, etc.).

35. Communicate clearly to the student the length of time he/she has to complete the assignment.

36. Communicate clearly to the student when the assignment should be completed.

37. Have the student time his/her assignments in order to monitor his/her own behavior and accept time limits.

38. Structure time units in order that the student knows exactly how long he/she has to work and when he/she must be finished.

39. Provide the student with more than enough time to finish an activity and decrease the amount of time as the student demonstrates success.

40. Have the student repeat the directions orally to the teacher.

41. Provide the student with a Schedule of Daily Events in order that he/she knows exactly what and how much there is to do in a day. (See Appendix.)

42. Prevent the student from becoming over-stimulated by an activity (e.g., frustrated, angry, etc.).

43. Specify exactly what is to be done for the completion of the task (e.g., indicate definite starting and stopping points, indicate a minimum requirement, etc.).

44. Require the student to begin each assignment within a specified period of time (e.g., three minutes, five minutes, etc.).

45. Provide the student with shorter tasks given more frequently.

46. Provide clearly stated directions in written or verbal form (i.e., make the directions as simple and concrete as possible).

47. Interact frequently with the student in order to help him/her follow directions for the assignments.

48. Provide alternatives for the traditional format of directions (e.g., tape record directions, summarize directions, directions given by peers, etc.).

49. Practice direction-following skills on nonacademic tasks.

50. Reduce directions to steps (e.g., give the student each additional step after completion of the previous step).

51. Make certain the student achieves success when following directions.

52. Reduce the emphasis on early completion. Hurrying to complete assignments may cause the student to fail to follow directions.

53. Establish assignment rules (e.g., listen to directions, wait until all directions have been given, ask questions about anything you do not understand, begin an assignment only when you are certain about what you are supposed to do, make certain you have all necessary materials, etc.).

54. Allow the student access to pencils, pens, etc., only after directions have been given.

55. Make certain that the student is attending to the teacher when directions are given (e.g., making eye contact, hands free of writing materials, looking at assignment, etc.).

56. Maintain visibility to and from the student in order to make certain the student is attending. The teacher should be able to see the student and the student should be able to see the teacher, making eye contact possible at all times.

57. Present one assignment at a time. As each assignment is completed, deliver reinforcement along with the presentation of the next assignment.

58. Have the student use a timer in order to complete tasks within a given period of time.

59. Provide the student with the opportunity to perform assignments/activities in a variety of ways (e.g., on tape, with a calculator, orally, etc.).

60. Have the student explain to the teacher what he/she should do in order to perform the assignments.

61. Make certain that the reading demands of the assignment are within the ability level of the student.

62. Read directions, explanations, and instructions to the student when necessary.

63. Use a sight word vocabulary approach in order to teach the student key words and phrases when reading directions and instructions (e.g., key words such as *circle, underline, match*, etc.).

64. Shorten the length of assignments in order that the student can complete his/her assignments in the same length of time as other students.

65. Provide the student with additional time to complete assignments if necessary, in order for the student to be successful.

66. When testing, make certain the student's knowledge of content is being assessed rather than the student's ability to read directions, instructions, and information.

67. Maintain mobility in order to be frequently near the student and to provide reading assistance.

68. Have the student practice timed drills consisting of reading directions, explanations, information, etc., in order to reduce reading time.

69. Keep written directions as concise and concrete as possible.

70. Provide the student with a copy of written directions at his/her desk rather than on the chalkboard, posted in the classroom, etc.

71. Seat the student close to the source of written information (e.g., chalkboard, projector, etc.).

72. Make certain that the print is large enough to increase the student's likelihood of success.

73. Gradually increase the degree of difficulty or complexity of written directions, explanations, instructions, information, etc., as the student becomes more successful.

74. Modify or rewrite the reading level of material presented to the student.

75. Reduce the emphasis on competition. Competitive activities may make it difficult for the student to finish assignments because of frustration with reading difficulties.

76. Reinforce the student for attempting and completing assignments based on the amount of work he/she can successfully complete. Gradually increase the amount of work required for reinforcement as the student demonstrates success.

77. Provide the student a quiet place (e.g., carrel, study booth, etc.) where he/she may go to engage in reading activities.

78. Write a contract with the student specifying what behavior is expected (e.g., attempting and completing class assignments) and what reinforcement will be made available when the terms of the contract have been met.

79. Communicate with parents (e.g., notes home, phone calls, etc.) in order to share information concerning the student's progress and so that they may reinforce the student at home for finishing assignments at school.

80. Reinforce the student for finishing assignments within a length of time which is reasonable for him/her. Gradually reduce the length of time the student has to complete assignments as he/she demonstrates success.

81. Tape record directions, explanations, and instructions in order to enhance the student's success.

82. Have a peer read directions, explanations, and instructions to the student in order to enhance the student's success.

83. Require the student to verbally repeat directions, explanations, and instructions he/she has read.

79 Performs classroom tests or quizzes at a failing level

1. Evaluate the appropriateness of the task to determine: (a) if the task is too difficult and (b) if the length of time scheduled for the task is appropriate.

2. Have the student question anything he/she does not understand while taking tests or quizzes.

3. Make certain that the tests or quizzes measure knowledge of content and not related skills, such as reading or writing.

4. Teach the student test-taking strategies (e.g., answer questions you are sure of first, learn to summarize, recheck each answer, etc.). (See Appendix for Test-Taking Skills.)

5. Give shorter tests or quizzes, but give them more frequently. Increase the length of tests or quizzes over time as the student demonstrates success.

6. Have tests or quizzes read to the student.

7. Have the student answer tests or quizzes orally.

8. Have the tests or quizzes tape recorded and allow the student to listen to questions as often as necessary.

9. Allow the student to take tests or quizzes in a quiet place in order to reduce distractions (e.g., study carrel, library, resource room, etc.).

10. Have the student take tests or quizzes in the resource room where the resource teacher can clarify questions, offer explanations, etc.

11. Provide the student with opportunities for review before taking tests or quizzes.

12. Have the student maintain a performance record for each subject in which he/she is experiencing difficulty.

13. Teach and encourage the student to practice basic study skills (e.g., reading for the main point, taking notes, summarizing, highlighting, studying in an appropriate environment, using time wisely, etc.) before taking tests or quizzes.

14. Assess student performance in a variety of ways (e.g., have the student give verbal explanations, simulations, physical demonstrations of a skill, etc.).

15. Arrange a time for the student to study with a peer tutor before taking tests or quizzes.

16. Provide a variety of opportunities for the student to learn the information covered by tests or quizzes (e.g., films, visitors, community resources, etc.).

17. Allow the student to respond to alternative test or quiz questions (e.g., more generalized questions which represent global understanding).

18. Provide the opportunity for the student to study daily assignments with a peer.

19. Have the student take a sample test or quiz before the actual test.

20. Remove the threat of public knowledge of failure (e.g., test or quiz results are not read aloud or posted, test ranges are not made public, etc.).

21. Provide parents with information on test and quiz content (e.g., the material that will be covered by the test or quiz, the format, the types of questions, etc.).

22. Modify instruction to include more concrete examples in order to enhance student learning.

23. Monitor student performance in order to detect errors and determine where learning problems exist.

24. Reduce the emphasis on competition. Students who compete academically and fail may cease to try to succeed and do far less than they are capable of achieving.

25. Only give tests and quizzes when the student is certain to succeed (e.g., after he/she has learned the information).

26. Make certain that the test questions are worded exactly as the information was given in either verbal or written form.

27. Prior to the test, provide the student with all information that will be on the test (e.g., "You will need to know . . ." and list those items).

28. Provide the student with a set of prepared notes that summarize the material to be tested.

29. Have the student listen and take notes for the "Who, What, Where, When, How, and Why" while concepts are presented. (See Appendix for Outline Form.)

30. Present concepts following the outline of: (1) Who, (2) What, (3) Where, (4) When, (5) How, and (6) Why.

31. Have the student prepare for tests using the "Who, What, Where, When, How, and Why" system. (See Appendix for Outline Form.)

32. Develop tests and quizzes for the student using the "Who, What, Where, When, How, and Why" approach.

33. Teach the student skills to use when taking tests. (See Appendix for Test-Taking Skills.)

34. Review with the student the "Additional Suggestions" located in the Appendix under Test-Taking Skills.

35. Teach the student skills for studying for tests/quizzes. (See Appendix for Studying for a Test.)

36. Review with the student the "Additional Suggestions" located in the Appendix under Studying for a Test.

37. Teach the student skills to use when taking notes. (See Appendix for Note Taking.)

38. Speak with the student to explain: (a) what he/she is doing wrong (e.g., not attending in class, not using study time, etc.) and (b) what he/she should be doing (e.g., attending during class, asking questions, using study time, etc.).

39. Write a contract with the student specifying what behavior is expected (e.g., improved test or quiz scores) and what reinforcement will be made available when the terms of the contract have been met.

40. Communicate with the parents (e.g., notes home, phone calls, etc.) in order to share information concerning the student's progress and so that they may reinforce the student at home for improved test or quiz scores.

80 Has difficulty retrieving or recalling concepts, persons, places, etc.

1. Have the student act as a classroom messenger. Give the student a verbal message to deliver to another teacher, secretary, administrator, etc. Increase the length of messages as the student is successful.

2. At the end of the school day, have the student recall three activities in which he/she participated during the day. Gradually increase the number of activities the student is required to recall as he/she demonstrates success.

3. After a field trip or special event, have the student recall the activities which occurred.

4. After reading a short story, have the student recall the main characters, sequence the events, and recall the outcome of the story.

5. Help the student employ memory aids or mnemonic devices in order to recall words (e.g., a name might be linked to another word; for example, "Mr. Green is a very colorful person.").

6. Encourage the student to play word games such as *Hangman, Concentration, Password*, etc.

7. Have the student compete against himself/herself by timing how fast he/she can name a series of pictured objects. The student tries to increase his/her speed each time.

8. Have the student take notes from classes, presentations, lectures, etc., to help him/her facilitate recall.

9. Have the student make notes, lists, etc., of things he/she needs to be able to recall. The student carries these reminders with him/her.

10. Have the student tape record important information he/she should remember.

11. Have the student outline, highlight, underline, or summarize information he/she should remember.

12. Make certain the student has adequate opportunities for repetition of information through different experiences in order to enhance his/her memory.

13. When the student is required to recall information, remind him/her of the situation in which the material was originally presented (e.g., "Remember yesterday when we talked about . . ." "Remember when we were outside and I told you about the . . ." etc.).

14. Have the student practice repetition of information in order to increase accurate memory skills (e.g., repeating names, telephone numbers, dates of events, etc.).

15. Show the student an object or a picture of an object for a few seconds. Ask the student to recall specific attributes of the object (e.g., color, size, shape, etc.).

16. Teach the student to recognize key words and phrases related to information in order to increase his/her memory skills.

17. Make certain the student receives information from a variety of sources (e.g., texts, discussions, films, slide presentations, etc.) in order to enhance the student's memory/recall.

18. Provide the student with verbal cues to stimulate recall of material previously presented (e.g., key words, a brief oral description, etc.).

19. Teach concepts through associative learning (e.g., build new concepts based on previous learning).

20. Encourage the student to use semantic mapping techniques in order to stimulate visual memory.

21. Provide opportunities for overlearning material presented, in order for the student to be able to recall the information.

22. Have the student use a Schedule of Daily Events to recall assignments to be reviewed. (See Appendix.)

23. Evaluate the appropriateness of the information to be recalled to determine: (a) if the task is too difficult and (b) if the length of time scheduled to complete the task is appropriate.

24. Use multiple modalities (e.g., auditory, visual, tactile, etc.) when presenting instructional content.

25. Have a peer tutor engage in memory activities with the student (e.g., concentration games, flash cards, math facts, etc.).

26. Teach the student how to organize information into smaller units (e.g., break a number sequence into small units - 132563 into 13, 25, 63).

27. Stop at various points during the presentation of information to check the student's comprehension.

28. Use concrete examples and experiences in sharing information with the student.

29. Have the student memorize the first sentence or line of a poem or song. Progressively have the student memorize the remainder as he/she experiences success.

30. Assess the meaningfulness of the material to the student. Remembering is more likely to occur when the material is meaningful and the student can relate it to real experiences.

31. Have the student listen and take notes for the "Who, What, Where, When, How, and Why" while concepts are presented. (See Appendix for Outline Form.)

32. Present concepts following the outline of: (1) Who, (2) What, (3) Where, (4) When, (5) How, and (6) Why.

33. Have the student prepare for tests using the "Who, What, Where, When, How, and Why" system. (See Appendix for Outline Form.)

34. Develop tests and quizzes for the student using the "Who, What, Where, When, How, and Why" approach.

81 Fails to generalize knowledge from one situation to another

1. Make certain the student understands that all objects, people, ideas, actions, etc., can be grouped based on how they are alike. Provide the student with concrete examples (e.g., dogs, cats, cows, and horses are all mammals).

2. Give the student pairs of objects, and have the student name the ways in which they are alike and the ways they are different. Proceed from simple things which can be seen and touched to more abstract ideas which cannot be seen or touched.

3. Name a category or group and ask the student to identify as many things as possible which belong in the group. Begin with large categories (e.g., living things) and move to more specific categories (e.g., living things which are green).

4. Ask the student to help in making lists of some categories which fit inside larger categories (e.g., flowers, trees, and bushes are all categories which can be included in the plant category).

5. Identify related concepts and explain to the student how we can generalize from one to another (e.g., numbers to money, fuel to energy, words to sentences, etc.).

6. Have the student play analogy games involving multiple-choice possibilities (e.g., food is to a person as gasoline is to ___ [a skateboard, an automobile, a house].).

7. Deliver instructions by using examples of relationships (e.g., rely on what has already been learned, use examples from the student's environment, etc.).

8. Call attention to situations in the classroom which generalize to more global situations (e.g., being on time for class is the same as being on time for work; schoolwork not done during work time has to be made up before school, after school, or during recreational time, just as responsibilities at places of employment have to be completed at night or on weekends if not completed on the job; etc.).

9. Require the student to explain outcomes, consequences, etc. (e.g., when the student earns a reward or privilege, make certain he/she can explain that the reward was the result of hard work and accomplishment, etc.).

10. Have the student respond to statements that begin with "What if" (e.g., "What if it rained for 40 days and 40 nights?" "What if there were no rules and laws?" etc.).

11. Be certain to relate what the student has learned in one setting or situation to other situations (e.g., vocabulary words learned should be pointed out in reading selections, math word problems, story writing, etc.).

12. Have the student write letters, fill out applications, etc., in order to see the generalization of handwriting, spelling, grammar, sentence structure, etc., to real-life situations.

13. Provide the student with situations in which he/she can generalize skills learned in mathematics to simulations of the use of money (e.g., making change, financing a car, computing interest earned from savings, etc.).

14. Make certain that the student is provided with an explanation of "why" he/she is learning particular information or skills (e.g., we learn to spell, read, and write in order to be able to communicate; we learn to solve math problems in order to be able to make purchases, use a checking account, measure, and cook; etc.).

15. Have the student develop a series of responses representing his/her ability to generalize from common situations in the environment (e.g., "We should drive no more than 55 miles per hour on our highways because . . ." Appropriate responses concern safety, conservation of fuel, care of vehicle, fines for speeding.).

16. As soon as the student learns a skill, make certain that he/she applies it to a real-life situation (e.g., when the student learns to count by fives, have him/her practice adding nickels).

17. Use a variety of instructional approaches to help the student generalize knowledge gained to real-life situations (e.g., after studying the judicial system, provide a simulated courtroom trial, etc.).

18. Use multiple modalities (e.g., auditory, visual, tactile, etc.) when presenting instructional material that requires the student to generalize knowledge. Determine which modality is stronger and utilize the results.

19. Use concrete examples and experiences when teaching concepts and sharing information with the student.

20. When the student is required to generalize knowledge from one situation to another, provide him/her with visual and/or auditory cues to help in remembering the information previously presented (e.g., provide key words, expose part of a picture, etc.).

21. Use pictures, diagrams, the chalkboard, and gestures when delivering information.

22. When delivering explanations and information, be certain to use vocabulary that is within the student's level of comprehension.

23. Use daily drill activities to help the student memorize math facts, sight words, etc.

1. Have the student take notes relative to important information he/she should remember.

2. Have the student tape record important information he/she should remember.

3. If the student has difficulty remembering information in written form, and if the student has difficulty remembering information he/she sees, present the information auditorily.

4. Have the student repeat/paraphrase important information he/she should remember.

5. Have the student outline, highlight, underline, or summarize information he/she should remember.

6. Use concrete examples and experiences in sharing information with the student.

7. Teach the student to recognize main points, important facts, etc.

8. Make certain the student has adequate opportunities for repetition of information through different experiences in order to enhance his/her memory.

9. Make certain information is presented to the student in the most clear and concise manner possible.

10. Reduce distracting stimuli when the student is attempting to remember important information.

11. Teach the student to rely on resources in the environment to recall information (e.g., notes, textbooks, pictures, etc.).

12. When the student is required to recall information, provide him/her with auditory cues to help him/her remember the information (e.g., key words, a brief oral description to cue the student, etc.).

13. Relate the information being presented to the student's previous experiences.

14. When the student is required to recall information, remind him/her of the situation in which the material was originally presented (e.g., key words, a brief oral description to cue the student, etc.).

15. Assess the meaningfulness of the material to the student. Remembering is more likely to occur when the material is meaningful and the student can relate it to real experiences.

16. Have the student make notes, lists, etc., of things he/she needs to remember. The student carries these reminders with him/her.

17. Have the student follow a regular routine of daily events to establish consistency in his/her behavior pattern.

18. Teach the student to use mnemonic devices to recall information (e.g., to spell geography: George Ellen's Old Grandmother Rode A Pony Home Yesterday.).

19. Teach the student study techniques, such as SQ3R, to recall information.

20. Provide the student with verbal cues to stimulate recall of material.

21. Provide the student with a multi-sensory approach while learning new material in order to increase the likelihood that learning through several modalities will result in improved retention and recall.

22. Use techniques such as semantic mapping, color-coding and highlighting to stress important concepts to be recalled.

23. Have the student practice verbal repetition of information learned in order to increase accurate memory skills (e.g., phone numbers, dates of events, etc.).

24. Teach the student to use associative cues or mnemonic devices to remember information.

25. Provide the student with multiple opportunities to practice or use information immediately after it has been learned in order to increase retention of the information.

26. Have the student act as a peer tutor to another student in order to cement mastering of information learned and to prevent forgetting.

27. Have the student outline, highlight, underline or summarize information he/she should remember.

28. Review new information periodically during the week.

29. Teach the student how to organize information into smaller units (e.g., break a number sequence into smaller units - 132563 into 13, 25, 63).

30. Have the student listen and take notes for the "Who, What, Where, When, How, and Why" while concepts are presented. (See Appendix for Outline Form.)

31. Present concepts following the outline of: (1) Who, (2) What, (3) Where, (4) When, (5) How, and (6) Why.

32. Have the student prepare for tests using the "Who, What, Where, When, How, and Why" system. (See Appendix for Outline Form.)

83 Requires slow, sequential, substantially broken-down presentation of concepts

1. Evaluate the level of difficulty of the information to which the student is expected to listen (e.g., information communicated on the student's ability level).

2. Have the student question any directions, explanations, instructions he/she does not understand.

3. Have the student repeat or paraphrase what is said to him/her to determine what was heard.

4. Give the student short directions, explanations, or presentations of concepts. Gradually increase the length of the directions, explanations, or presentations of concepts as the student demonstrates success.

5. Maintain consistency in the delivery of verbal instructions.

6. Make certain the student is attending to the source of information (e.g., making eye contact, hands free of writing materials, looking at the assignment, etc.).

7. Provide the student with written directions and instructions to supplement verbal directions and instructions.

8. Emphasize or repeat word endings, key words, etc.

9. Speak clearly and concisely when delivering directions, explanations, and instructions.

10. Place the student near the source of information.

11. Reduce distracting stimuli (e.g., noise and motion in the classroom) in order to enhance the student's ability to listen successfully.

12. Stop at key points when delivering directions, explanations, and instructions in order to determine student comprehension.

13. Deliver directions, explanations, and instructions at an appropriate pace for the student.

14. Identify a list of word endings, key words, etc., that the student will practice listening for when someone is speaking.

15. Deliver oral questions and directions that involve only one concept or step. Gradually increase the number of concepts or steps as the student demonstrates success.

16. Move the student away from other students who may interfere with his/her ability to attend to directions, explanations, and instructions.

17. Teach the student listening skills (e.g., listen carefully, write down important points, ask for clarification, wait until all directions are received before beginning, etc.).

18. Use demonstrations along with the presentation of information.

19. Scan all materials for new words. Use simple terms when possible. Teach new vocabulary and provide practice through application.

20. Reduce abstractions by giving concrete examples and firsthand experiences.

21. Refer to previously presented, related information when presenting a new concept.

22. Prepare or obtain simplified manuals with definitions of technical vocabulary, simple vocabulary and sentence structure, step-by-step instructions, and diagrams or pictures.

23. Begin with concepts that are known and then sequence with skills or concepts not already mastered or integrated. Relationships will be more obvious when progressing to new skills and concepts.

24. Highlight or underline the important facts in reading material.

25. Rewrite instructions at an appropriate reading level for the student.

26. Identify the student's most efficient learning mode and use it consistently for the presentation of concepts.

27. If the student has difficulty with the oral presentation of concepts, provide the student with a written copy of material covered.

28. If the student has difficulty with the written presentation of concepts, provide the student with an oral presentation of material.

29. Tape record the presentation of concepts to be learned in order that the student can listen to it as often as necessary.

30. Have a peer repeat the presentation of concepts when the student does not understand.

31. When the student masters small units of information, have the student act as a peer tutor to teach units of information to another student.

32. Provide the student with the information he/she needs to learn in the most direct manner possible (e.g., list of facts, a summary of important points, outline of important events, etc.).

33. Have the student listen and take notes for "Who, What, Where, When, How, and Why" while concepts are presented. (See Appendix for Outline Form.)

34. Have the student use semantic mapping techniques when taking notes from the presentation of concepts. (See Appendix for Mapping Form.)

35. Present concepts following the outline of: (1) Who, (2) What, (3) Where, (4) When, (5) How, and (6) Why.

36. Develop tests and quizzes for the student using the "Who, What, Where, When, How, and Why" approach.

84 Turns in incomplete or inaccurately finished assignments

1. Speak with the student to explain: (a) what he/she is doing wrong (e.g., turning in work which is incomplete) and (b) what he/she should be doing (e.g., taking time to check for completeness of assignments).

2. Assess the appropriateness of the assignment for the student.

3. Provide the student with structure for all academic activities (e.g., specific directions, routine format for tasks, time units, etc.).

4. Interact frequently with the student to monitor his/her task performance.

5. Have the student question any directions, explanations, instructions he/she does not understand.

6. Assign a peer to accompany the student to specified activities in order to make certain the student has the necessary materials.

7. Provide the student with a list of necessary materials for each activity of the day.

8. Provide the student with verbal reminders of materials required for each activity.

9. Make certain that all educators who work with the student maintain consistent expectations of assignment completion.

10. Provide the student with assignment "forms" to enhance the completeness of assignments (e.g., provide blank number equations for word problems which the student fills in, etc.).

11. Provide the student with an organizational system for approaching assignments (e.g., name on paper, numbers listed on left column, etc.).

12. Provide the student with evaluative feedback for assignments completed (i.e., identify what the student did successfully, what errors were made, and what should be done to correct the errors).

13. Minimize the steps needed in order to complete the assignments accurately.

14. Maintain consistency in assignment format and expectations so as not to confuse the student.

15. It is not necessary to grade every assignment performed by the student. Assignments may be used to evaluate student ability or knowledge and provide feedback. Grades may not need to be assigned until mastery/minimal accuracy has been attained.

16. Have the student respond to tasks orally.

17. Have the student perform assignments, in which he/she might experience difficulty, in the resource room where the resource teacher can answer questions.

18. Provide the student with opportunities for review prior to grading assignments.

19. Arrange a time for the student to study with a peer tutor before completing a graded assignment.

20. Evaluate the appropriateness of the task to determine: (a) if the task is too difficult and (b) if the length of time scheduled to complete the task is appropriate.

21. Assign a peer to work with the student in order to provide an acceptable model for the student to imitate.

22. Assign the student shorter tasks while increasing quality expectations.

23. Provide the student with clearly stated criteria for acceptable work.

24. Work the first few problems of an assignment with the student in order to make certain that he/she knows what to do, how to perform the assignment, etc.

25. Modify academic tasks (e.g., format, requirements, length, etc.).

26. Provide the student with clearly stated step-by-step directions for homework in order that someone at home may be able to provide assistance.

27. Make certain that homework assignments relate to concepts already taught rather than introducing a new concept.

28. Work through the steps of written directions as they are delivered in order to make certain the student follows the directions accurately.

29. Identify a peer to act as a model for the student to imitate turning in complete homework assignment.

30. Meet with parents to instruct them in appropriate ways to help the student with homework.

31. Identify a peer to act as a model for the student to imitate the appropriate following of written directions.

32. Teach the student the skills of following written directions: (e.g., read carefully, write down important points, ask for clarification, wait until all directions are received before beginning, etc.).

33. Give directions in a variety of ways to increase the probability of understanding (e.g., if the student fails to understand written directions, present them in verbal form).

34. Assign a peer to help the student with assignments.

35. Allow the student additional time to turn in assignments.

36. Repeat directions in order to increase the student's probability of understanding.

37. Provide the student with written directions for doing assignments.

38. Maintain consistency of expectations while keeping the expectations within the ability level of the student.

39. Maintain consistency in assigning homework (i.e., assign the same amount of homework each day).

40. Teach the student to prioritize assignments (e.g., according to importance, length, etc.).

41. Provide adequate time for completion of activities.

42. Establish a level of minimum accuracy which will be accepted as a level of mastery.

43. Deliver reinforcement for any and all measures of improvement.

44. Mastery should not be expected too soon after introducing new information, skills, etc.

45. Provide the student with self-checking materials, requiring correction before turning in assignments.

46. Should the student consistently fail to complete assignments with minimal accuracy, evaluate the appropriateness of tasks assigned.

47. If the student has difficulty completing homework assignments with minimal accuracy, provide a time during the day when he/she can receive assistance at school.

48. Make certain the assignments measure knowledge of content and not related skills such as reading or writing.

49. Have assignments read to the student.

50. Have the student read/review his/her schoolwork with the teacher in order that the student can become more aware of the quality of his/her work.

51. Provide the student with samples of work which may serve as models for acceptable quality (e.g., the student is to match the quality of the sample before turning in the assignment).

52. Provide the student with additional time to perform schoolwork in order to achieve quality.

53. Teach the student procedures for doing quality work (e.g., listen to directions, make certain directions are understood, work at an acceptable pace, check for errors, correct for neatness, copy the work over, etc.).

54. Recognize quality (e.g., display student's work, congratulate the student, etc.).

55. Conduct a preliminary evaluation of the work, requiring the student to make necessary corrections before final grading.

56. Provide the student with quality materials to perform the assignment (e.g., pencil with eraser, paper, dictionary, handwriting sample, etc.).

57. Provide the student with shorter assignments given more frequently. Increase the length of the assignments as the student demonstrates success.

58. Structure the environment in such a way as to provide the student with increased opportunity for help or assistance on academic or homework tasks (e.g., peer tutors, seat the student near the teacher or aide, etc.).

59. Provide the student with clearly stated written directions for homework in order that someone at home may be able to provide assistance.

85 Has difficulty taking class notes

1. Evaluate the appropriateness of note taking to determine: (a) if the task is too difficult and (b) if the length of time scheduled to complete the task is appropriate.

2. Teach the student note-taking skills (e.g., copy main ideas from the board, identify main ideas from lectures, condense statements into a few key words, etc.).

3. Provide a standard format for note taking of directions and explanations (e.g., have paper and pencil or pen ready, listen for the steps in directions or explanations, write a shortened form of directions or explanations, ask to have any steps repeated when necessary, etc.).

4. Identify a peer to act as a model for the student to imitate appropriate note taking during class when necessary.

5. Have the student question any directions, explanations, instructions he/she does not understand.

6. Establish classroom rules (e.g., take notes when necessary, work on-task, work quietly, remain in your seat, finish task, meet task expectations). Reiterate rules often and reinforce students for following rules.

7. Reinforce the student for taking notes during class when necessary based on the length of time he/she can be successful. Gradually increase the length of time required for reinforcement as the student demonstrates success.

8. Write a contract with the student specifying what behavior is expected (e.g., taking notes) and what reinforcement will be made available when the terms of the contract have been met.

9. Provide a standard format for note taking of lectures (e.g., have paper and pencil or pen ready, listen for main ideas of important information, write a shortened form of main ideas or important information, ask to have any main ideas or important information repeated when necessary, etc.).

10. While delivering instructions, directions, lectures, etc., point out to the student that information should be written in the form of notes.

11. Have the student practice legible manuscript or cursive handwriting during simulated and actual note-taking activities.

12. Have the student keep his/her notes organized in a folder for each subject or activity.

13. Check the student's notes before he/she begins an assignment in order to determine if they are correct and adequate for the assignment.

14. Provide the student with an outline or questions to be completed during teacher delivery of instructions, directions, lectures, etc.

15. Provide the student with samples of notes taken from actual instructions, directions, lectures, etc., given in the classroom in order that he/she may learn what information is necessary for note taking.

16. Make certain the student is in the best location in the classroom to receive information for note taking (e.g., near the board, teacher, or other source of information).

17. Make certain you can easily provide supervision of the student's note taking.

18. Make certain to maintain visibility to and from the student when delivering instructions, directions, lectures, etc., in order to enhance the likelihood of successful note taking.

19. Make certain that the instructions, directions, lectures, etc., are presented clearly and loudly enough for the student to hear.

20. Match the rate of delivery of instructions, directions, lectures, etc., to the student's ability to take notes.

21. Provide the student with both verbal and written instructions.

22. Provide instructions, directions, lectures, etc., in sequential steps in order to enhance student note taking.

23. Provide delivery of information in short segments for the student to take notes. Gradually increase the length of delivery as the student experiences success in note taking.

24. Make certain that the vocabulary used in delivering instructions, directions, lectures, etc., is appropriate for the student's ability level.

25. Place the student next to a peer in order that the student can copy notes taken by the peer.

26. Make certain the student has all necessary materials for note taking (e.g., paper, pencil, pen, etc.).

27. Make certain the student uses any necessary aids in order to facilitate note taking (e.g., eyeglasses, hearing aid, etc.).

28. Make certain the student has adequate surface space on which to write when taking notes (e.g., uncluttered desk top).

29. Reduce distracting stimuli that would interfere with the student's note taking (e.g., other students talking, outdoor activities, movement in the classroom, hallway noise, etc.).

30. Present the information in the most interesting manner possible.

31. Summarize the main points of instructions, directions, concepts, etc., for the student.

32. Identify the most successful note-taking style for the student. Encourage use of this approach for all note-taking activities. This will be more successful if all teachers the student comes in contact with allow this identified approach.

33. Provide the student with a limited outline of notes, and have the student add to the outline during class lecture.

34. Have the student listen and take notes for the "Who, What, Where, When, How, and Why" while concepts are presented. (See Appendix for Outline Form.)

35. Present concepts following the outline of:
(1) Who, (2) What, (3) Where, (4) When, (5) How, and (6) Why.

36. Have the student prepare for tests using the "Who, What, Where, When, How, and Why" system. (See Appendix for Outline Form.)

1. Present the task in the most interesting and attractive manner possible.

2. Maintain mobility in order to provide assistance to the student.

3. Structure time units in order that the student knows exactly how long he/she has to work and when the work must be finished.

4. Provide the student with more than enough time to finish an activity, and decrease the amount of time as the student demonstrates success.

5. Give directions in a variety of ways in order to increase the probability of understanding (e.g., if the student fails to understand verbal directions, present them in written form).

6. Have the student repeat the directions orally to the teacher.

7. Give a signal (e.g., clapping hands, turning lights off and on, etc.) before giving verbal directions.

8. Provide the student with a predetermined signal when he/she is not beginning a task (e.g., verbal cue, hand signal, etc.).

9. Tell the student that directions will only be given once.

10. Rewrite directions at a lower reading level.

11. Deliver verbal directions in a more basic way.

12. Help the student with the first few items on a task and gradually reduce the amount of help over time.

13. Follow a less desirable task with a highly desirable task, making the completion of the first necessary to perform the second.

14. Provide the student with shorter tasks given more frequently.

15. Provide the student with a schedule of daily events in order that he/she knows exactly what and how much there is to do in a day. (See Appendix for Schedule of Events.)

16. Prevent the student from becoming overstimulated by an activity (e.g., frustrated, angry, etc.).

17. Specify exactly what is to be done for the completion of a task (e.g., definite starting and stopping points, a minimum requirement, etc.).

18. Require the student to begin each assignment within a specified period of time (e.g., three minutes, five minutes, etc.).

19. Provide the student with a selection of assignments, requiring him/her to choose a minimum number from the total (e.g., present the student with 10 academic tasks from which 6 must be finished that day).

20. Start with a single problem and add more problems to the task over time.

21. Reduce the emphasis on competition (e.g., academic or social). Fear of failure may cause the student to refuse to attempt new assignments/ tasks.

22. Provide the student with self-checking materials in order that he/she may check work privately, thus reducing the fear of public failure.

23. Have the student attempt the new assignment/task in a private place (e.g., carrel, "office," quiet study area, etc.).

24. Have the student practice a new skill (e.g., jumping rope, dribbling a basketball, etc.) alone, with a peer or the teacher before the entire group attempts the activity.

25. Provide the student with the opportunity to perform the assignment/task in a variety of ways (e.g., on tape, with a calculator, orally, etc.).

26. Allow the student to perform a new assignment/task in a variety of places in the building (e.g., resource room, library, learning center, etc.).

27. Provide the student with a sample of the assignment/task which has been partially completed by a peer or teacher (e.g., book report, project, etc.).

28. Do not require the student to complete the assignment/task in one sitting.

29. Allow the student the option of performing the assignment/task at another time (e.g., earlier in the day, later, on another day, etc.).

30. Deliver directions/instructions before handing out materials.

31. Make certain that the student has all the materials needed in order to perform the assignment/task.

32. Have the student paraphrase to the teacher what should be done in order to perform the assignment/task.

33. Explain to the student that work not done during work time will have to be made up at other times (e.g., at recess, before school, after school, during lunch time, etc.).

34. Teach the student direction-following skills: (a) listen carefully, (b) ask questions, (c) use environmental cues, (d) rely on examples provided, and (e) wait until directions are given before beginning.

35. Provide the student with optional courses of action to prevent total refusal to obey teacher directives.

36. Allow the student to perform alternative versions of a new assignment. Gradually introduce more components of the regular assignments until those can be performed successfully.

37. Have the student act as a peer tutor to teach another student a concept he/she has mastered. This can serve as reinforcement for the student.

38. Provide practice in new assignments or tasks by using a computer software program that gives the student immediate feedback.

39. Make certain the student has mastery of concepts at each level before introducing a new skill level.

40. Have the student time activities in order to monitor his/her own behavior and accept time limits.

41. Communicate clearly to the student when it is time to begin.

42. Have the student maintain a record (e.g., chart or graph) of his/her performance in attempting new assignments/tasks.

43. Reduce distracting stimuli (e.g., place the student on the front row, provide a carrel or "office" space away from distractions, etc.). This is used as a means of reducing distracting stimuli and not as a form of punishment.

44. Structure the environment in such a way as to provide the student with increased opportunities for help or assistance.

45. Assign a peer or volunteer to help the student begin a task.

46. Assess the quality and clarity of directions, explanations, and instructions given to the student.

47. Have the student question any directions, explanations, and instructions not understood.

48. Evaluate the appropriateness of the task to determine: (a) if the task is too difficult and (b) if the length of time scheduled to complete the task is appropriate.

49. Communicate with parents (e.g., notes home, phone calls, etc.) in order to share information concerning the student's progress and so that they can reinforce the student at home for attempting a new assignment/task at school.

50. Write a contract with the student specifying what behavior is expected (e.g., attempting a new assignment/task) and what reinforcement will be made available when the terms of the contract have been met. (See Appendix for Behavioral Contract.)

51. Reinforce the student for attempting a new assignment/task within the length of time he/she can be successful. Gradually decrease the amount of time to begin the task in order to be reinforced as the student demonstrates success.

52. Reinforce those students in the classroom who attempt a new assignment/task.

53. Speak with the student to explain: (a) what the student is doing wrong (e.g., not attempting a new task) and (b) what the student should be doing (e.g., asking for assistance or clarification, following directions, starting on time, etc.).

54. Reinforce the student for attempting a new assignment/task: (a) give the student a tangible reward (e.g., classroom privileges, line leading, passing out materials, five minutes free time, etc.) or (b) give the student an intangible reward (e.g., praise, handshake, smile, etc.).

87 Does not turn in homework assignments

1. Reinforce the student for turning in homework. Gradually increase the number of times required for reinforcement as the student demonstrates success.

2. Write a contract with the student specifying what behavior is expected (e.g., turning in homework) and what reinforcement will be made available when the terms of the contract have been met. (See Appendix for Behavioral Contract.)

3. Communicate with the parents (e.g., notes home, phone calls, etc.) in order to share information concerning the student's progress and so that they can reinforce the student at home for turning in homework at school.

4. Evaluate the appropriateness of the homework assignment to determine: (a) if the task is too difficult and (b) if the length of time scheduled to complete the task is appropriate.

5. Identify a peer to act as a model for the student to imitate turning in homework assignments.

6. Have the student keep a chart or graph of the number of homework assignments turned in to the teacher.

7. Have the student question any directions, explanations, and instructions not understood.

8. Assess the appropriateness of assigning the student homework if his/her ability or circumstances at home make it impossible to complete and return the assignments.

9. Meet with parents to instruct them in appropriate ways to help the student with homework.

10. Assign a peer to help the student with homework.

11. Present the tasks in the most attractive and interesting manner possible.

12. Allow the student additional time to turn in homework assignments.

13. Deliver directions orally in order to increase the probability of the student's understanding of homework assignments.

14. Chart homework assignments completed.

15. Repeat directions in order to increase the student's probability of understanding.

16. Allow the student to perform a highly desirable task when homework has been turned in.

17. Give directions in a variety of ways in order to increase the probability of understanding (e.g., if the student fails to understand verbal directions, present them in written form).

18. Provide the student with written directions for doing homework assignments.

19. Allow natural consequences to occur for failure to turn in homework assignments (e.g., students who do not finish their homework do not get to engage in more desirable activities).

20. Encourage the parents to provide the student with a quiet, comfortable place and adequate time to do homework.

21. Introduce the student to other resource persons who may be of help in doing homework (e.g., other teachers, the librarian, etc.).

22. Allow the student to perform alternative homework assignments. Gradually introduce more components of the regular homework assignment until the assignments are routinely performed and returned to school.

23. Take proactive steps to deal with student refusal to perform a homework assignment in order that the rest of the group will not be exposed to contagion (e.g., refrain from arguing with the student, place the student in a carrel or other quiet place to work, remove the student from the group or classroom, etc.).

24. Reinforce those students who complete their assignments at school during the time provided.

25. Maintain consistency of expectations and keep the expectations within the ability level of the student.

26. Work a few problems with the student on homework assignments in order to serve as a model and start the student on a task.

27. Make certain that homework is designed to provide drill activities rather than introduce new information.

28. Develop a contract with the student and his/her parents requiring that homework be done before more desirable activities take place at home (e.g., playing, watching television, going out for the evening, etc.).

29. Should the student fail to take necessary materials home, provide a set of these materials to be kept at home and send directions for homework with the student.

30. Assign small amounts of homework initially, gradually increasing the amount as the student demonstrates success (e.g., one or two problems may be sufficient to begin the homework process).

31. Find a tutor (e.g., peer, volunteer, etc.) to work with the student at home.

32. Maintain consistency in assigning homework (i.e., assign the same amount of homework each day).

33. Provide time at school for homework completion when the student cannot be successful in performing assignments at home.

34. Provide the student with a book bag, backpack, etc., to take homework assignments and materials to and from home.

35. Send homework assignments and materials directly to the home with someone other than the student (e.g., brother or sister, neighbor, bus driver, etc.).

36. Schedule the student's time at school in order that homework will not be absolutely necessary if he/she takes advantage of the school time provided to complete assignments.

37. Create a learning center at school, open the last hour of each school day, where professional educators are available to help with homework.

38. Do not use homework as a punishment (i.e., homework should not be assigned as a consequence for inappropriate behavior at school).

39. Arrange with the student's parents to pick up homework each day if the student has difficulty "remembering" to take it home.

40. Set up a homework system for the student (e.g., two days a week work with drill flash cards, three days a week work on book work sent home, etc.). This will add some variety to homework.

41. Specify exactly what is to be done for the completion of the homework task (e.g., indicate definite starting and stopping points, indicate the minimum requirements, etc.).

42. Make certain the student has mastered the concepts presented at school. All homework should be a form of practice for what has been learned at school.

43. Reinforce those students in the classroom who turn in their homework assignments.

44. Establish homework assignment rules:
1. Work on-task.
2. Finish task.
3. Meet task expectations.
4. Turn in task.

Reiterate rules often and reinforce students for following rules.

45. Speak to the student to explain: (a) what the student is doing wrong (e.g., not turning in homework assignments) and (b) what the student should be doing (e.g., completing homework assignments and returning them to school).

46. Reinforce the student for turning in homework assignments: (a) give the student a tangible reward (e.g., classroom privileges, line leading, passing out materials, five minutes free time, etc.) or (b) give the student an intangible reward (e.g., praise, handshake, smile, etc.).

88 Is unable to work appropriately with peers in a tutoring situation

1. Reinforce the student for working appropriately with peers in a tutoring situation: (a) give the student a tangible reward (e.g., classroom privileges, line leading, passing out materials, five minutes free time, etc.) or (b) give the student an intangible reward (e.g., praise, handshake, smile, etc.).

2. Speak to the student to explain: (a) what he/she is doing wrong (e.g., not attending to the tutor, arguing with peers, etc.) and (b) what he/she should be doing (e.g., attending to the tutor, doing his/her own work, etc.).

3. Establish tutoring rules:
   1. Work on-task.
   2. Work quietly.
   3. Remain in your seat.
   4. Finish task.
   5. Meet task expectations.
Reiterate rules often and reinforce students for following rules.

4. Reinforce those student in the classroom who work appropriately with peers in a tutoring situation.

5. Reinforce the student for working appropriately with peers in a tutoring situation based on the length of time he/she can be successful. Gradually increase the length of time required for reinforcement as the student demonstrates success.

6. Write a contract with the student specifying what behavior is expected (e.g., attending to the tutor, taking turns, sharing materials, etc.) and what reinforcement will be made available when the terms of the contract have been met.

7. Communicate with parents (e.g., notes home, phone calls, etc.) in order to share information concerning the student's progress and so that they can reinforce the student at home for working appropriately with peers in a tutoring situation at school.

8. Evaluate the appropriateness of the tutoring situation in order to determine: (a) if the task is too easy, (b) if the task is too difficult, and (c) if the length of time scheduled to complete the task is appropriate.

9. Identify a peer to act as a model for the student to imitate working appropriately with peers in a tutoring situation.

10. Have the student question any directions, explanations, and instructions he/she does not understand.

11. Make certain that the student and peer tutor are compatible (e.g., the student accepts his/her role in the tutoring situation, the student and peer tutor are accepting of one another, the peer tutor has skills and knowledge to share, etc.).

12. Be certain that the opportunity to work with a peer tutor is contingent upon appropriate behavior prior to and during the tutoring situation.

13. Make certain that the students being tutored together are on the same ability level.

14. Teach the student appropriate behavior for peer tutoring situations (e.g., follow directions, work quietly, etc.).

15. Supervise tutoring situations closely in order to make certain that the student's behavior is appropriate, the task is appropriate, he/she is learning from the situation, etc.

16. Make certain the tutoring activity involves practice, drill, or repetition of information or skills previously presented.

17. Determine the peer(s) the student would most prefer to interact with in tutoring situations and attempt to group these students together for peer tutoring.

18. Assign an outgoing, nonthreatening peer to act as a peer tutor.

19. Structure the environment so that the student has many opportunities for success in the tutoring situation.

20. Assign the student to tutoring situations in which he/she is likely to interact successfully with peers being tutored.

21. Conduct a sociometric activity with the class in order to determine the peer(s) who would most prefer to interact with the student in tutoring situations.

22. Make certain that the student demonstrates appropriate behavior in tutoring situations prior to pairing him/her with a peer.

23. Make certain the student understands that interacting with a peer(s) in tutoring situations is contingent upon appropriate behavior.

24. Supervise tutoring situations closely in order that the peer(s) with whom the student works does not stimulate inappropriate behavior.

25. Make certain that the tutoring situation is not so overstimulating as to make successful interactions with another peer difficult.

26. Reduce the emphasis on competition. Fear of failure may stimulate inappropriate behavior in tutoring situations.

27. Teach the student problem-solving skills in order that he/she may better deal with problems that occur in interactions with another peer(s) in tutoring situations (e.g., talking, walking away, calling upon an arbitrator, compromising, etc.).

28. Find a peer with whom the student is most likely to be able to successfully interact in tutoring situations (e.g., a student with similar interests, background, ability, behavior patterns, etc.).

29. Through interviews with other students and observation, determine those characteristics of the student which interfere with successful interactions during tutoring situations in order to determine skills or behaviors the student needs to develop for successful interactions.

30. Structure the activities of the tutoring situation according to the needs/abilities of the student (e.g., establish rules, limit the stimulation of the activity, limit the length of the activity, consider the time of day, etc.).

31. Limit opportunities for interaction in tutoring situations on those occasions when the student is not likely to be successful (e.g., the student has experienced academic or social failure prior to the scheduled tutoring activity).

32. Select nonacademic activities designed to enhance appropriate interaction of the student and a peer(s) (e.g., board games, model building, coloring, etc.).

33. Have the student work with the teacher to practice appropriate interactions in tutoring situations.

34. Make certain the student is able to successfully engage in the tutoring activity (e.g., the student understands the rules, the student is familiar with the activity, the student will be compatible with the other students engaged in the free-time activity, etc.).

35. Make certain the student understands that failing to interact appropriately with a peer(s) during tutoring activities may result in removal from the activity and/or loss of participation in future activities.

36. Have the student engage in the tutoring situation with peers for short periods of time and gradually increase the length of time as the student demonstrates success.

37. Provide an appropriate location for the tutoring situation (e.g., quiet corner of the classroom, near the teacher's desk, etc.).

38. Intervene early when there is a problem in order to prevent a more serious problem from occurring.

39. Do not force the student to work in a tutoring situation with a peer with whom he/she is not completely comfortable.

40. Provide the student with a predetermined signal when he/she begins to display inappropriate behaviors in a tutoring situation with peers.

41. Allow the student to attempt something new in private before doing so in a tutoring situation with peers.

89 Does not take notes during class when necessary

1. Reinforce the student for taking notes during class when necessary: (a) give the student a tangible reward (e.g., classroom privileges, line leading, passing out materials, five minutes free time, etc.) or (b) give the student an intangible reward (e.g., praise, handshake, smile, etc.).

2. Speak to the student to explain: (a) what he/she is doing wrong (e.g., failing to take notes) and (b) what he/she should be doing (e.g., taking notes).

3. Establish classroom rules (e.g., take notes when necessary, work on-task, work quietly, remain in your seat, finish task, meet task expectations). Reiterate rules often and reinforce students for following rules.

4. Reinforce those students in the classroom who take notes during class when necessary.

5. Reinforce the student for taking notes during class when necessary based on the length of time he/she can be successful. Gradually increase the length of time required for reinforcement as the student demonstrates success.

6. Write a contract with the student specifying what behavior is expected (e.g., taking notes) and what reinforcement will be made available when the terms of the contract have been met.

7. Communicate with parents (e.g., notes home, phone calls, etc.) in order to share information concerning the student's progress and so that they may reinforce the student at home for taking notes during class when necessary.

8. Evaluate the appropriateness of note taking to determine: (a) if the task is too difficult and (b) if the length of time scheduled to complete the task is appropriate.

9. Identify a peer to act as a model for the student to imitate appropriate note taking during class when necessary.

10. Have the student question any directions, explanations, instructions he/she does not understand.

11. Teach the student note-taking skills (e.g., copy main ideas from the board, identify main ideas from lectures, condense statements into a few key words, etc.).

12. Provide a standard format for note taking of directions or explanations (e.g., have paper and pencil or pen ready, listen for the steps in directions or explanations, write a shortened form of directions or explanations, ask to have any steps repeated when necessary, etc.).

13. Provide a standard format for lecture note taking (e.g., have paper and pencil or pen ready, listen for main ideas or important information, write a shortened form of main ideas or important information, ask to have any main ideas or important information repeated when necessary, etc.).

14. While delivering instructions, directions, lectures, etc., point out to the student that information should be written in the form of notes.

15. Have the student practice legible manuscript or cursive handwriting during simulated and actual note-taking activities.

16. Have the student keep his/her notes organized in a folder for each subject or activity.

17. Check the student's notes before he/she begins an assignment in order to determine if they are correct and adequate for the assignment.

18. Provide the student with an outline or questions to be completed during teacher delivery of instructions, directions, lectures, etc.

19. Provide the student with samples of notes taken from actual instructions, directions, lectures, etc., given in the classroom in order that he/she may learn what information is necessary for note taking.

20. Make certain the student is in the best location in the classroom to receive information for note taking (e.g., near the board, teacher, or other source of information).

21. Make certain the teacher can easily provide supervision of the student's note taking.

22. Make certain to maintain visibility to and from the student when delivering instructions, directions, lectures, etc., in order to enhance the likelihood of successful note taking.

23. Make certain that instructions, directions, lectures, etc., are presented clearly and loudly enough for the student to hear.

24. Match the rate of delivery of instructions, directions, lectures, etc., to the student's ability to take notes.

25. Provide the student with both verbal and written instructions.

26. Provide instructions, directions, lectures, etc., in sequential steps in order to enhance student note taking.

27. Provide delivery of information in short segments for the student to take notes. Gradually increase the length of delivery as the student experiences success in note taking.

28. Make certain that the vocabulary used in delivering instructions, directions, lectures, etc., is appropriate for the student's ability level.

29. Make certain the student has all necessary materials for note taking (e.g., paper, pencil, pen, etc.).

30. Make certain the student uses any necessary aids in order to facilitate note taking (e.g., eyeglasses, hearing aid, etc.).

31. Place the student next to a peer in order that the student can copy notes taken by the peer.

32. Make certain the student has adequate surface space on which to write when taking notes (e.g., uncluttered desk top).

33. Reduce distracting stimuli that would interfere with the student's note taking (e.g., other students talking, outdoor activities, movement in the classroom, hallway noise, etc.).

34. Present the information in the most interesting manner possible.

35. As an alternative to note taking, have the student tape record instructions, directions, lectures, etc.

36. Summarize the main points of instructions, directions, lectures, etc., for the student.

37. Have the student listen and take notes for the "Who, What, Where, When, How and Why" while concepts are presented. (See Appendix for Outline Form.)

38. Present concepts following the outline of: (1) Who, (2) What, (3) Where, (4) When, (5) How, and (6) Why.

39. Have the student prepare for tests using the "Who, What, Where, When, How and Why" method. The teacher should then test this same information. (See Appendix for Outline Form.)

40. Present directions following the outline of: (1) What, (2) How, (3) Materials, and (4) When. (See Appendix for Assignment Form.)

41. Have the student take notes when directions are being given following the "What, How, Materials, and When" format. (See Appendix for Assignment Form.)

90 Does not follow the rules of the classroom

1. Structure the environment in such a way that the student remains active and involved while demonstrating acceptable behavior.

2. Maintain visibility to and from the student. The teacher should be able to see the student and the student should be able to see the teacher, making eye contact possible at all times.

3. Give the student preferred responsibilities.

4. Present tasks in the most interesting and attractive manner possible.

5. Have the student maintain a chart representing the amount of time spent following classroom rules, with reinforcement for increasing acceptable behavior.

6. Practice mobility to be frequently near the student.

7. Provide the student with many social and academic successes.

8. Provide the student with positive feedback that indicates he/she is successful.

9. Post rules in various places, including on the student's desk.

10. Make certain the student receives the information necessary to perform activities (e.g., written information, verbal directions, reminders, etc.).

11. Teach the student direction-following skills.

12. Maintain a positive and professional relationship with the student (e.g., an adversary relationship is likely to result in failure to follow directions).

13. Be a consistent authority figure (e.g., be consistent in relationships with students).

14. Provide the student with optional courses of action in order to prevent total refusal to obey teacher directives.

15. Intervene early to prevent the student's behavior from leading to contagion of other students.

16. Have the student question any directions, explanations, and instructions not understood.

17. Require the student to verbalize the classroom rules at designated times throughout the day (e.g., before school, during recess, at lunch, at the end of the day, etc.).

18. Deliver directions in a step-by-step sequence.

19. Have a peer act as a model for following the rules of the classroom.

20. Interact with the student frequently to determine if directives are being followed.

21. Maintain consistency in rules, routine, and general expectations of conduct and procedure.

22. Provide the student with a list of rules and/or behavior expectations.

23. Help the student identify specific rules he/she has difficulty following and make these areas goals for behavior improvement.

24. Separate the student from the peer(s) who stimulates his/her inappropriate behavior.

25. Make certain that rules and behavior expectations are consistent throughout the school and classrooms.

26. Along with a directive, provide an incentive statement (e.g., "When you finish your math, you may go outside to play." "You may have free time after you finish your work.").

27. Intervene early when there is a problem in order to prevent more serious problems from occurring.

28. Before beginning a new activity, make sure the student knows the classroom rules.

29. Teach the student to "think" before acting (e.g., ask himself/herself: "What is happening?" "What am I doing?" "What should I do?" "What will be best for me?").

30. Evaluate the appropriateness of the assigned task to determine: (a) if the task is too difficult, and (b) if the length of time scheduled to complete the task is appropriate.

31. Communicate with parents (e.g., notes home, phone calls, etc.) in order to share information concerning the student's progress and so that they can reinforce the student at home for following the rules of the classroom.

32. Write a contract with the student specifying what behavior is expected (e.g., following classroom rules) and what reinforcement will be made available when the terms of the contract have been met. (See Appendix for Behavioral Contract.)

33. Remove the student from the group or activity until he/she can demonstrate acceptable behavior and self-control.

34. Reinforce the student for following the rules of the classroom based on the length of time the student can be successful. Gradually increase the length of time required for reinforcement as the student demonstrates success.

35. Reinforce those students who follow the rules of the classroom.

36. Establish classroom rules:
1. Work on-task.
2. Work quietly.
3. Remain in your seat.
4. Finish task.
5. Meet task expectations.
6. Raise your hand.
Reiterate rules often and reinforce students for following rules.

37. Speak with the student to explain: (a) what the student is doing wrong (e.g., failing to follow classroom rules) and (b) what the student should be doing (e.g., following the rules of the classroom).

38. Reinforce the student for following the rules of the classroom: (a) give the student a tangible reward (e.g., classroom privileges, line leading, passing out materials, five minutes free time, etc.) or (b) give the student an intangible reward (e.g., praise, handshake, smile, etc.).

1. Communicate with parents, agencies, or appropriate parties in order to inform them of the problem, determine the cause of the problem, and consider possible solutions to the problem.

2. Record or chart attendance with the student.

3. Begin the day or class with a success-oriented activity which is likely to be enjoyable for the student.

4. Give the student a preferred responsibility to be performed at the beginning of each day or each class (e.g., feeding the classroom pet, helping to get the classroom ready for the day, etc.).

5. Reinforce the student for getting on the bus or leaving home on time.

6. Assess the degree of task difficulty in comparison with the student's ability to perform the task.

7. Provide the student with as many high-interest activities as possible.

8. Involve the student in extracurricular activities.

9. Provide the student with many social and academic successes.

10. Provide the student with academic activities presented in the most attractive and interesting manner possible.

11. Require the student's attendance to be documented by his/her teachers (e.g., have teachers sign an attendance card).

12. Interact with the student in a positive manner frequently throughout the day.

13. Collect anecdotal information on the student's absent behavior. If a trend can be determined, remove the student from the situation, modify the situation, or help the student develop the skills to be more successful in the situation.

14. Have the parent bring the student to school.

15. Have a responsible peer walk to school/class with the student.

16. Establish a time for the student to leave his/her home in the morning.

17. Require that time spent away from class/school be made up at recess, during lunch, or after school.

18. Have the student document personal attendance at the end of each school day (e.g., have the student maintain a record of attendance in the library, office, etc., and fill in the data at the end of each day).

19. Make certain the student is appropriately placed in those classes in which he/she is enrolled (e.g., the class is not too difficult).

20. Reduce the emphasis on competition. Repeated failure may cause the student to remove himself/herself from the competition by not attending school or class.

21. Help the student develop friendships which may encourage his/her attendance in school/class.

22. Maintain open communication with the student's family in order to make certain that the student is leaving for school at the designated time.

23. Do not force the student to interact with others or do things that make him/her uncomfortable and would cause the student to not want to come to school.

24. Make certain the student and parents are aware of the laws involving attendance in school.

25. Evaluate the appropriateness of the task to determine: (a) if the task is too difficult and (b) if the length of time scheduled to complete the task is appropriate.

26. Communicate with the parents (e.g., notes home, phone calls, etc.) in order to share information concerning the student's progress and so that they can reinforce the student at home for coming to school and class.

27. Write a contract with the student specifying what behavior is expected (e.g., being in attendance) and what reinforcement will be made available when the terms of the contract have been met. (See Appendix for Behavioral Contract.)

28. Speak with the student to explain: (a) what the student is doing wrong (e.g., being absent from school/class) and (b) what the student should be doing (e.g., being in attendance).

29. Establish classroom rules:
1. Work on-task.
2. Work quietly.
3. Remain in your seat.
4. Finish task.
5. Meet task expectations.

Reiterate rules often and reinforce students for following rules.

30. Reinforce those students who come to school/class.

31. Reinforce the student for coming to school/class: (a) give the student a tangible reward (e.g., classroom privileges, line leading, passing out materials, five minutes free time, etc.) or (b) give the student an intangible reward (e.g., praise, handshake, smile, etc.).

1. Provide the student with a schedule of daily events in order that he/she will know which activities to attend and at what times. (See Appendix for Schedule of Daily Events.)

2. Make certain that the student's daily schedule follows an established routine.

3. Limit the number of interruptions in the student's schedule.

4. Make certain the student has adequate time to get to an activity.

5. Make certain that the student knows how to get from one activity to another.

6. Use a timer to help the student get to activities at specified times.

7. Give the student a specific responsibility to be performed at the beginning of each activity or class in order to encourage the student to be on time.

8. Provide the student with verbal cues when it is time to change activities (e.g., "It is time for the red group to have reading." "Now it is time for the red group to put away materials and move to the next activity." etc.).

9. Determine why the student is not arriving at activities at the specified times.

10. Ask the student the reason for not arriving at activities at the specified times. The student may have the most accurate perception as to why he/she is not arriving at activities at the specified times.

11. Help the student understand that it is permissible to leave work unfinished and return to it at a later time.

12. Determine if there are aspects of activities that the student dislikes. Remove, reduce, or modify the unpleasant aspects of activities in order to encourage the student to be on time for and participate in activities.

13. Make the student responsible for time missed (i.e., if the student misses five minutes of an activity, the time must be made up during recess, lunch, or other desired activities).

14. Have a peer accompany the student to activities.

15. Make certain that the student is successful in school-related activities. The student will be more likely to be on time for activities in which he/she experiences success.

16. Make the student a leader of the activity or group.

17. Make certain that other students do not make it unpleasant for the student to attend activities.

18. Make certain the student has all necessary materials for activities.

19. Record or chart promptness with the student.

20. Begin activities with a task that is highly reinforcing to the student.

21. Give the student a preferred responsibility to be performed at the beginning of each activity.

22. Assess the appropriateness of the degree of difficulty of the task in comparison with the student's ability to perform the task successfully.

23. Provide the student with as many high- interest activities as possible.

24. Provide the student with many social and academic successes.

25. Provide the student with academic activities presented in the most attractive manner possible.

26. Give the student a schedule of daily events to be signed by each teacher in order to document promptness. (See Appendix for Schedule of Daily Events.)

27. Collect anecdotal information on the student's behavior. If a trend can be determined, remove the student from the situation and/or help the student to be prompt.

28. Have the student document personal attendance at the end of each activity.

29. Make certain the student is appropriately placed according to ability level in those classes in which he/she is enrolled.

30. Reduce the emphasis on competition. Repeated failure may cause the student to avoid being on time for activities which are competitive.

31. Involve the student in extracurricular activities.

32. Interact with the student in a positive manner throughout the day.

33. Give the student a special responsibility for each morning (e.g., feeding the student classroom pet, helping to get the classroom ready for the day, etc.).

34. Maintain open communication with the student's family in order to make certain that the student is leaving for school at the designated time.

35. Do not force the student to interact with others or do things that make him/her uncomfortable and would cause the student to want to be late.

36. Begin each day with a fun activity which will cause the student to want to be on time for class.

37. Identify a peer to act as a model for the student to imitate arriving at an activity at the specified time.

38. Evaluate the appropriateness of the task to determine: (a) if the task is too difficult and (b) if the length of time scheduled to complete the task is appropriate.

39. Communicate with parents (e.g., notes home, phone calls, etc.) in order to share information concerning the student's progress and so that they can reinforce the student at home for coming to activities at the specified times at school.

40. Write a contract with the student specifying what behavior is expected (e.g., coming to school on time) and what reinforcement will be made available when the terms of the contract have been met. (See Appendix for Behavioral Contract.)

41. Reinforce the student for coming to an activity within a given period of time. Gradually reduce the length of time the student has to come to an activity as the student becomes more successful at being punctual.

42. Reinforce those students in the classroom who come to an activity at the specified time.

43. Establish classroom rules:
1. Come to class on time.
2. Work on-task.
3. Work quietly.
4. Remain in your seat.
5. Finish task.
6. Meet task expectations.

Reiterate rules often and reinforce students for following rules.

44. Speak to the student to explain: (a) what the student is doing wrong (e.g., coming late to an activity) and (b) what the student should be doing (e.g., coming to an activity at the specified time).

45. Reinforce the student for coming to an activity at the specified time: (a) give the student a tangible reward (e.g., classroom privileges, line leading, passing out materials, five minutes free time, etc.) or (b) give the student an intangible reward (e.g., praise, handshake, smile, etc.).

1. Establish general rules for the classroom (e.g., be in attendance, be on time, be productive, be accurate, follow classroom rules). Reiterate rules often and reinforce students for following rules.

2. Identify a peer to serve as a model for the student in checking his/her work for accuracy.

3. Maintain mobility throughout the classroom to monitor the student checking his/her work for accuracy.

4. Provide the student with self-checking materials to check his/her work for accuracy.

5. Offer the student assistance frequently throughout the day in checking his/her work for accuracy.

6. Make certain that the student is assigned short enough tasks in order that he/she can complete assignments in time to check for accuracy. Gradually increase the length of the assignments as the student demonstrates success.

7. Allow the student additional time to complete assignments and check his/her work for accuracy.

8. Provide the student with step-by-step written directions for performing assignments. Make certain that the last directive is to check work for accuracy.

9. Require that work not checked for accuracy must be checked at another time (e.g., break time, recreational time, after school, etc.).

10. Reinforce those students in the classroom who check their work for accuracy.

11. Reinforce the student for checking his/her work for accuracy: (a) give the student a tangible reward (e.g., classroom privileges, line leading, passing out materials, five minutes free time, etc.) or (b) give the student an intangible reward (e.g., praise, handshake, smile, etc.).

12. Speak with the student to explain: (a) what he/she is doing wrong (e.g., not checking work for accuracy) and (b) what he/she should be doing (e.g., checking work for accuracy).

13. Check a few problems with the student to serve as a model for checking his/her work for accuracy.

14. Reinforce the student for checking work for accuracy based on the number of times he/she can be successful. Gradually increase the number of times required for reinforcement as the student demonstrates success.

15. Write a contract with the student specifying what behavior is expected (e.g., checking work for accuracy) and what reinforcement will be made available when the terms of the contract have been met.

16. Evaluate the appropriateness of the task to determine: (a) if the task is too difficult and (b) if the length of time scheduled to complete the task is appropriate.

17. Have the student question any directions, explanations, and instructions he/she does not understand.

18. Assess the quality and clarity of directions, explanations, and instructions given to the student.

19. Structure the environment in such a way as to provide the student with increased opportunity for checking his/her work for accuracy.

20. Have the student maintain a record (e.g., chart or graph) of his/her performance in checking work for accuracy.

21. Communicate clearly to the student when it is time to check his/her work for accuracy.

22. Reinforce the student for beginning, working on, and completing assignments; and checking work for accuracy.

23. Give the student a list of specific strategies for checking the accuracy of completed work. Some specific strategies are: (1) Check math problems with the inverse operation. (2) Check language assignments for capitalization, punctuation, and neatness. (3) Use the dictionary to check spelling in written work. (4) Check spelling quizzes for careless errors. (5) Check written paragraphs using the "Who, What, Where, When, How, and Why" format. (6) Check tests and quizzes for careless errors and omitted or incomplete answers.

24. Provide the student with clearly stated written directions for homework in order that someone at home may be able to provide assistance in checking work for accuracy.

25. Provide time at school for checking homework for accuracy if homework has not been checked. (The student's failure to check homework for accuracy may be the result of variables in the home over which he/she has no control.)

26. Identify resource personnel from whom the student may receive additional assistance in checking work for accuracy (e.g., librarian, special education teacher, paraprofessional, etc.).

27. Deliver reinforcement for any and all measures of improvement in checking work for accuracy.

28. Provide the student with opportunities for checking work for accuracy prior to grading assignments.

29. Monitor student performance in order to detect errors and determine where learning problems exist.

30. Allow/require the student to make corrections after assignments have been checked the first time.

31. Provide the student with evaluative feedback for assignments completed (i.e., identify what the student did successfully, what errors were made, and what should be done to correct the errors).

32. Allow the student to put an assignment away and return to it at a later time to check for accuracy.

33. Assign a peer or volunteer to help the student check work for accuracy.

1. Speak to the student to explain: (a) what he/she is doing wrong (e.g., failing to bring necessary materials for specified activities) and (b) what he/she should be doing (e.g., having necessary materials for specified activities).

2. Establish classroom rules (e.g., have necessary materials, work on-task, work quietly, remain in your seat, finish task, and meet task expectations). Reiterate rules often and reinforce students for following rules.

3. Reinforce the student for being organized/prepared for specified activities based on the number of times he/she can be successful. Gradually increase the number of times required for reinforcement as the student demonstrates success.

4. Write a contract with the student specifying what behavior is expected (e.g., having necessary materials for specified activities) and what reinforcement will be made available when the terms of the contract have been met.

5. Evaluate the appropriateness of the task to determine: (a) if the task is too difficult and (b) if the length of time scheduled to complete the task is appropriate.

6. Identify a peer to act as a model for the student to imitate being organized/prepared for specified activities.

7. Have the student question any directions, explanations, instructions he/she does not understand.

8. Assign a peer to accompany the student to specified activities in order to make certain the student has the necessary materials.

9. Provide the student with a list of necessary materials for each activity of the day.

10. Provide the student with verbal reminders of necessary materials required for each activity.

11. Provide time at the beginning of each day for the student to organize his/her materials.

12. Provide time at various points throughout the day for the student to organize his/her materials (e.g., before school, during recess, at lunch, at the end of the day, etc.).

13. Provide storage space for materials the student is not using at any particular time.

14. Act as a model for being organized/prepared for specified activities.

15. Make certain that work not completed because necessary materials were not brought to the specified activity must be completed during recreational or break time.

16. Have the student chart the number of times he/she is organized/prepared for specified activities.

17. Remind the student at the end of the day when materials are required for specified activities for the next day (e.g., by a note sent home, verbal reminder, etc.).

18. Have the student establish a routine to follow before coming to class (e.g., check which activity is next, determine what materials are necessary, collect materials, etc.).

19. Have the student leave necessary materials at specified activity areas.

20. Provide the student with a container in which to carry necessary materials for specified activities (e.g., backpack, book bag, briefcase, etc.).

21. Provide adequate transition time between activities for the student to organize his/her materials.

22. Establish a routine to be followed for organization and appropriate use of work materials. Provide the routine for the student in written form or verbally reiterate often.

23. Provide adequate time for the completion of activities.

24. Assess the quality and clarity of directions, explanations, and instructions given to the student.

25. Provide the student with structure for all academic activities (e.g., specific directions, routine format for tasks, time units, etc.).

26. Minimize materials needed for specified activities.

27. Provide an organizer for materials inside the student's desk.

28. Provide the student with an organizational checklist (e.g., routine activities, materials needed, and steps to follow).

29. Make certain that all personal property is labeled with the student's name.

30. Teach the student how to conserve rather than waste materials (e.g., amount of glue, paper, tape, etc., to use; putting lids, caps, tops on such materials as markers, pens, bottles, jars, cans, etc.).

31. Teach the student to maintain care of personal property and school materials (e.g., keep property with him/her, know where property is at all times, secure property in lockers, leave valuable property at home, etc.).

32. Provide the student with an appropriate place to store/secure personal property (e.g., desk, locker, closet, etc.) and require that the student store all property when not in use.

33. Limit the student's freedom to take property from school if he/she is unable to remember to return such items.

34. Make certain that failure to have necessary materials results in loss of opportunity to participate in activities or a failing grade for that day's activity.

35. Provide the student with more work space (e.g., a larger desk or table at which to work).

36. Reduce the number of materials for which the student is responsible. Increase the number as the student demonstrates appropriate use of property.

37. Require that lost or damaged property be replaced by the student. If the student cannot replace the property, restitution can be made by working at school.

38. Make certain that the student is not inadvertently reinforced for losing materials. Provide the student with used materials, copies of the materials, etc., rather than new materials if he/she fails to care for the materials in an appropriate manner.

39. Reduce distracting stimuli (e.g., place the student in the front row, provide a carrel or quiet place away from distractions, etc.). This is used as a means of reducing distracting stimuli and not as a form of punishment.

40. Interact frequently with the student in order to prompt organizational skills and appropriate use of materials.

41. Assign the student organizational responsibilities in the classroom (e.g., organizing equipment, software, materials, etc.).

42. Limit the student's use of materials (i.e., provide the student with only those materials necessary at any given time).

43. Act as a model for organization and appropriate use of work materials (e.g., putting materials away before getting others out, having a place for all materials, maintaining an organized desk area, following a schedule for the day, etc.).

44. Have the student maintain an assignment notebook which indicates those materials needed for each activity.

45. Provide the student with a Schedule of Daily Events in order that he/she knows exactly what and how much there is to do in a day. (See Appendix for Schedule of Daily Events.)

46. Supervise the student while he/she is performing schoolwork in order to monitor quality.

47. Allow natural consequences to occur as the result of the student's inability to organize or use materials appropriately (e.g., work not done during work time must be made up during recreational time, materials not maintained will be lost or not serviceable, etc.).

48. Assist the student in beginning each task in order to reduce impulsive behavior.

49. Provide a color-coded organizational system (e.g., notebook, folders, etc.).

50. Teach the student to prioritize assignments (e.g., according to importance, length, etc.).

51. Provide adequate time for completion of activities.

52. Develop monthly calendars to keep track of important events, due dates, assignments, etc.

53. Have the student use an assignment form in order to be sure all materials needed are listed. (See Appendix for Assignment Form.)

54. Require the student to use the daily Assignment Sheet with both teacher and parent signatures. (See Appendix for Assignment Sheet.)

55. Have a peer remind the student of the necessary materials required for specified activities.

56. Provide the student with enough materials to satisfy his/her immediate needs (e.g., one of everything). Gradually reduce the number of materials over time, requiring the student to bring materials as he/she becomes more successful at doing so.

95 Does not demonstrate appropriate use of school-related materials

1. Provide time at the beginning of each day to help the student organize his/her school-related materials.

2. Provide time at various points throughout the day to help the student organize school-related materials (e.g., before school, during recess, during lunch, at the end of the day, etc.).

3. Provide the student with adequate work space (e.g., larger desk or table at which to work).

4. Provide storage space for school-related materials the student is not using at any particular time.

5. Reduce distracting stimuli (e.g., place the student on the front row, provide a carrel or quiet place away from distractions, etc.). This is used as a means of reducing distracting stimuli and not as a form of punishment.

6. Interact frequently with the student in order to prompt organizational skills and appropriate use of school-related materials.

7. Assign the student organizational responsibilities in the classroom (e.g., equipment, software materials, etc.).

8. Limit the student's use of school-related materials (e.g., provide the student with only those school-related materials necessary at any given time).

9. Act as a model for organization and appropriate use of school-related materials (e.g., putting materials away before getting other materials out, having a place for all materials, maintaining an organized desk area, following a schedule for the day, etc.).

10. Provide adequate transition time between activities for the student to organize himself/herself.

11. Establish a routine to be followed for organization and appropriate use of school-related materials.

12. Provide adequate time for the completion of activities.

13. Require the student to organize his/her work area at regular intervals. (It is recommended that this be done at least three times per day or more often if necessary.)

14. Supervise the student while he/she is performing schoolwork in order to monitor quality.

15. Allow natural consequences to occur as the result of the student's inability to organize or use school-related materials appropriately (e.g., materials not maintained appropriately will be lost or not serviceable).

16. Assess the quality and clarity of directions, explanations, and instructions given to the student.

17. Assist the student in beginning each task in order to reduce impulsive behavior.

18. Provide the student with structure for all academic activities (e.g., specific directions, routine format for tasks, time units, etc.).

19. Give the student a checklist of school-related materials necessary for each activity.

20. Minimize school-related materials necessary for each activity.

21. Provide an organizer inside the student's desk for school-related materials.

22. Provide the student with an organizational checklist (e.g., routine activities and steps to follow).

23. Teach the student appropriate care of school-related materials (e.g., sharpening pencils, keeping books free of marks and tears, etc.).

24. Make certain that all of the student's school-related materials are labeled with his/her name.

25. Point out to the student that loaning his/her school-related materials to other students does not reduce personal responsibility for the materials.

26. Teach the student to conserve rather than waste school-related materials (e.g., amount of glue, paper, tape, etc., to use; putting lids, caps, and tops on materials such as markers, pens, bottles, jars, cans, etc.).

27. Teach the student appropriate ways to deal with anger and frustration rather than destroying school-related materials.

28. Teach the student to maintain school-related materials (e.g., keep materials with him/her, know where materials are at all times, secure materials in his/her locker, etc.).

29. Provide the student with an appropriate place to store/secure materials (e.g., desk, locker, closet, etc.) and require him/her to store all materials when not in use.

30. Explain to the student that failure to care for school-related materials will result in the loss of freedom to maintain materials.

31. Provide reminders (e.g., a list of school-related materials) to help the student maintain and care for school-related materials.

32. Limit the student's freedom to take school-related materials from school if he/she is unable to return such items.

33. Provide the student with verbal reminders of school-related materials needed for each activity.

34. Limit the student's opportunity to use school-related materials if the student is unable to care for personal property.

35. Make certain that failure to have necessary school-related materials results in loss of opportunity to participate in activities or a failing grade for that day's activity.

36. Reduce the number of school-related materials for which the student is responsible. Increase the number as the student demonstrates appropriate care of materials.

37. Teach the student safety rules in the handling of school-related materials (e.g., pencils, scissors, compass; biology, industrial arts, and home economics materials; etc.).

38. Teach the student appropriate use of school-related materials (e.g., scissors, pencils, compass, rulers; biology, industrial arts, and home economics materials; etc.).

39. Do not give the student additional materials if he/she is not able to take care of what he/she has.

40. Have the student earn the things he/she needs (e.g., pencils, paper, etc.). If the student has earned something, he/she may be more willing to take care of it.

41. Have the student question any directions, explanations, and instructions not understood.

42. Identify a peer to act as a model for the student to imitate appropriate use of school-related materials.

43. Evaluate the appropriateness of the task to determine: (a) if the task is too difficult and (b) if the length of time scheduled to complete the task is appropriate.

44. Communicate with parents (e.g., notes home, phone calls, etc.) in order to share information concerning the student's progress and so that they can reinforce the student at home for using school-related materials appropriately at school.

45. Write a contract with the student specifying what behavior is expected (e.g., appropriate use of school-related materials) and what reinforcement will be made available when the terms of the contract have been met. (See Appendix for Behavioral Contract.)

46. Reinforce those students in the classroom who use school-related materials appropriately.

47. Reinforce the student for using school-related materials appropriately based on the length of time the student can be successful. Gradually increase the length of time required for reinforcement as the student demonstrates success.

48. Establish classroom rules:
1. Work on-task.
2. Remain in your seat.
3. Finish task.
4. Meet task expectations.
5. Raise your hand.

Reiterate rules often and reinforce students for following rules.

49. Speak to the student to explain: (a) what the student is doing wrong (e.g., failing to use school-related materials appropriately) and (b) what the student should be doing (e.g., using school-related materials as directed).

50. Reinforce the student for demonstrating appropriate use of school-related materials: (a) give the student a tangible reward (e.g., classroom privileges, line leading, passing out materials, five minutes free time, etc.) or (b) give the student an intangible reward (e.g., praise, handshake, smile, etc.).

1. Make certain the student's hearing has been checked recently.

2. Evaluate the level of difficulty of the information to which the student is expected to listen (e.g., /ch/ and /sh/ sounds, similar consonant sounds, rhyming words, etc.).

3. Have the student repeat or paraphrase what is said to him/her in order to determine what was heard.

4. Make certain the student is attending to the source of information (e.g., making eye contact, hands free of writing materials, looking at assignments, etc.).

5. Emphasize or repeat /ch/ or /sh/ sounds, similar vowel sounds, similar consonant sounds, rhyming words, etc.

6. Speak clearly and concisely when communicating with the student.

7. Place the student in the location most appropriate for him/her to hear what is being said.

8. Reduce distracting stimuli (e.g., noise and motion in the classroom) in order to enhance the student's ability to listen successfully.

9. Stop at key points when delivering directions, explanations, and instructions in order to determine student comprehension.

10. Identify a list of /ch/ and /sh/ sounds, similar vowel sounds, similar consonant sounds, rhyming words, etc., that the student will practice listening for when someone else is speaking.

11. Stand directly in front of the student when delivering information.

12. Use pictures of similar words (e.g., if the student has trouble differentiating /ch/ and /sh/ sounds, use pictures of /ch/ and /sh/ words such as "chips" and "ship") in order to help the student recognize the difference.

13. Play a game in which the student tries to imitate the sounds made by the teacher or other students (e.g., *Simon Says*).

14. Give the student simple words and ask him/her to rhyme them orally with as many other words as possible.

15. Have the student keep a notebook with pictures of words that rhyme.

16. Use fill-in-the-blank sentences and have the student pick the correct word from a group of similar words (e.g., I _____ (wonder, wander) what's in the box.).

17. Have the student make up poems and tongue twisters using /ch/ and /sh/ sounds, similar vowel sounds, similar consonant sounds, and rhyming words.

18. Present pairs of words and have the student tell if the words rhyme.

19. Explain and demonstrate how similar sounds are made (e.g., where the tongue is placed, how the mouth is shaped, etc.).

20. Encourage the student to watch the lips of the person speaking to him/her.

21. Have the student listen to a series of directions and act out the ones that make sense (e.g., bake your head, rake your bread, shake your head).

22. Identify the speech sounds the student has difficulty differentiating. Spend time each day having the student listen to what is said and have him/her use the words.

23. Make certain the student is attending to the source of information (e.g., eye contact is being made, hands are free of materials, the student is looking at the assignment, etc.).

24. Teach the student listening skills (e.g., stop working, look at the person delivering questions and directions, have necessary note-taking materials, etc.).

1.   Make certain the student's hearing has recently been checked.

2.   Be sure that the student can hear the difference between the target sound the way it should be made and the way it sounds when incorrectly produced.

3.   Have the student raise a hand or clap hands when he/she hears the target sound produced during a series of isolated sound productions (e.g., ssss, shshsh, rrrr, mmmm, rrrr, t, k, rrrr, zzzz, w, nnnn, rrrr, etc.).

4.   Use a puppet to produce the target sound correctly and incorrectly. The student earns a sticker for correctly distinguishing a set number of correct/incorrect productions the puppet makes.

5.   Have the student stand up each time he/she hears the target sound produced accurately as contrasted with inaccurate productions (e.g., ssss, ththth, ssss, ssss, ththth, etc.).

6.   Have the student show *thumbs up* each time the target sound is produced accurately when pictures are labeled and *thumbs down* if the target sound is produced inaccurately.

7.   Use pictures of similar sounding words (e.g., if the student says /sh/ for /ch/, use pictures of /sh/ and /ch/ words such as ships and chips). As the teacher says the words, the student points to the appropriate picture, then the student takes a turn saying the words as the teacher points.

8.   Have the student tally the number of correct productions of the targeted sound when the teacher or a peer reads a list of words.

9.   Tape record a spontaneous monologue given by the student, and then have him/her listen and tally error and/or correct productions. The teacher should also listen to the tape recording, and the teacher and the student should compare their analyses of the productions.

10.   Have the student read simple passages and tape record them. Then have the student listen and mark error and/or correct productions.

11.   Have the student read a list of words and rate his/her production after each word.

12.   Play a game such as *Simon Says* in which the student tries to imitate correct productions of targeted words.

13.   Use a schematic drawing as a visual aid to show the student how the mouth looks during production of the target sound.

14.   Make cards with the target sound and cards with vowels. Have the student combine a target sounds card with a vowel card to make a syllable that he/she can produce (e.g., ra, re, ro, and ar, er, or).

15.   Use a board game that requires the student to label pictures containing the target sound. The student needs to produce the target sound correctly before he/she can move on the game board. (This activity can be simplified or expanded based on the level of expertise of the student.)

16.   Have the student cut out pictures of items depicting words containing the target sound. Display them where they can be practiced each day.

17.   Provide the student with a list of words containing the target sound. Have the student practice the words daily. As the student masters the word list, add more words. (Using words from the student's everyday vocabulary, reading lists, spelling lists, etc., will facilitate transfer of correct production of the target sound into everyday speech.)

18.   Have the student use old phonics "fun" sheets to practice his/her sound orally. These are good for home practice also.

19.   Have the student keep a notebook of difficult words encountered each day. These can be practiced by the student with teacher or peer assistance.

20.   Have the student keep a list of all words he/she can think of which contain sounds he/she has difficulty producing accurately.

21. Have the student use a carrier phrase combined with a word containing the target sound (e.g., "I like ___." "I see a ___.").

22. Have the student make up sentences using words containing the target sound.

23. During oral reading, underline words containing the target sound and reinforce the student for correct productions.

24. Involve parents by asking them to rate their child's speech for a specific length of time (e.g., during dinner count "no errors," "a few errors," or "many errors").

25. Present a list of topics from which the student may select, and then have the student give a spontaneous speech for a specific length of time. Count errors and suggest ways to improve.

26. Provide the student with verbal reminders or prompts when he/she requires help imitating speech sounds.

27. Make certain the student is attending to the source of information (e.g., eye contact is being made, hands are free of materials, etc.).

28. Tell the student what to listen for when requiring him/her to imitate speech sounds.

29. Reinforce the student for correct productions of the target sound: (a) give the student a tangible reward (e.g., classroom privileges, line leading, passing out materials, five minutes free time, etc.) or (b) give the student an intangible reward (e.g., praise, handshake, smile, etc.).

30. Speak to the student to explain what he/she needs to do differently (e.g., make the sound like you do). The teacher should be careful to use the <u>sound</u> that is being targeted and not the letter name (e.g., "ssss" not "es").

31. Evaluate the appropriateness of requiring the student to accurately produce certain sounds (e.g., developmentally, certain sounds may not be produced accurately until the age of 8 or 9).

1. Make certain the student's hearing has recently been checked.

2. Be sure that the student can hear the difference between the sound as it should be made (target sound) and the way he/she is producing it incorrectly (error sound).

3. Be sure that the student can hear the difference between words as they should be made and the way the words sound when incorrectly produced (e.g., sounds inserted or omitted).

4. Have the student raise a hand or clap hands when he/she hears the target sound produced during a series of isolated sound productions (e.g., ssss, shshsh, rrrr, mmmm, rrrr, t, k, rrrr, zzzz, w, nnnn, rrrr, etc.).

5. Use a puppet to produce the target and error sounds. The student earns a sticker for correctly distinguishing a set number of correct/incorrect productions the puppet makes.

6. Use a puppet to produce targeted words correctly and incorrectly. The student earns a sticker for correctly distinguishing a set number of correct/incorrect productions the puppet makes.

7. Have the student stand up each time he/she hears the target sound produced accurately in contrast to the error sound (e.g., w, rrrr, rrrr, w, w, w, rrrr, rrrr, etc.).

8. Have the student stand up each time he/she hears targeted words produced accurately when contrasted with inaccurate productions (e.g., play, pay, pay, play, etc.).

9. Have the student show *thumbs up* each time the target sound is produced accurately when a picture is labeled and *thumbs down* if the target sound is produced inaccurately.

10. Using pictures of similar sounding words, say each word and have the student point to the appropriate picture (e.g., *run* and *one*, or *bat* and *back*).

11. Have the student tally the number of correct productions of the target sound when the teacher or a peer reads a list of words.

12. Have the student read simple passages and tape record them. Then have him/her listen and mark error and/or correct productions.

13. Tape record a spontaneous monologue given by the student, then have him/her listen and tally error and/or correct productions. The teacher should also listen to the tape recording, and the teacher and the student should compare their analyses of the productions.

14. Have the student read a list of words and rate his/her production of the target sound or target word after each.

15. Identify a peer who correctly produces the target sound or word to act as a model for the student.

16. Play a game such as *Simon Says* in which the student tries to imitate the target sound or words when produced by the teacher or peers.

17. Use a schematic drawing as a visual aid to show the student how the mouth looks during production of the target sound.

18. Make cards with the target sound and cards with vowels. Have the student combine a target sound card with a vowel card to make a syllable that he/she can produce (e.g., ra, re, ro, and ar, er, or).

19. Use a board game that requires the student to label pictures containing the target sound or words. The student needs to produce the target sound or words correctly before he/she can move on the game board. (This activity can be simplified or expanded based on the level of expertise of the student.)

20. Have the student cut out pictures of items containing the target sound or words and display them where they can be practiced each day.

21. Provide the student with a list of words containing the target sound. (The student will probably be able to produce the target sound more easily at the beginning or end of a word than in the middle.) Have the student practice the words daily. As the student masters the word list, add more words. (Using words from the student's everyday vocabulary, reading lists, spelling lists, etc., will facilitate transfer of correct production of the target sound into everyday speech.)

22. Provide the student with a list of the targeted words. Have the student practice the words daily. As the student masters the word list, add more words. (Using words from the student's everyday vocabulary, reading lists, spelling lists, etc., will facilitate transfer of correct production of the target sound into everyday speech.)

23. Have the student use old phonics "fun" sheets to practice his/her sound orally. These are good for home practice also.

24. Have the student keep a notebook of difficult words encountered each day. These can be practiced by the student with teacher or peer assistance.

25. Have the student use a carrier phrase combined with a word containing the target sound (e.g., "I like ___." "I see ___.").

26. Have the student keep a list of all the words he/she can think of which contain sounds that are difficult to produce accurately.

27. Have the student make up sentences using the target sound or words.

28. During oral reading, underline targeted sounds or words and reinforce the student for correct production.

29. Involve parents by asking them to rate their child's speech for a specific length of time (e.g., during dinner count "no errors," "a few errors," or "many errors").

30. Present a list of topics from which the student may select, and then have the student give a spontaneous speech for a specific length of time. Count errors and suggest ways to improve.

31. Reinforce the student for correct productions of the target sound: (a) give the student a tangible reward (e.g., classroom privileges, line leading, passing out materials, five minutes free time, etc.) or (b) give the student an intangible reward (e.g., praise, handshake, smile, etc.).

32. Speak to the student to explain what he/she needs to do differently (e.g., use the /r/ sound instead of the /w/ sound). The teacher should be careful to use the sound that is being targeted and not the letter name (e.g., "rrrr" not "ar").

33. Evaluate the appropriateness of requiring the student to accurately produce certain sounds (e.g., developmentally, certain sounds may not be produced accurately until the age of 8 or 9).

99 Distorts or mispronounces words or sounds when speaking (not attributed to dialect or accent)

1. Make certain the student's hearing has recently been checked.

2. Be sure that the student can hear the difference between words as they should be made and the way the words sound when incorrectly produced (sounds distorted).

3. Have the student raise a hand or clap hands when he/she hears the target sound produced during a series of isolated sound productions (e.g., ssss, shshsh, rrrr, mmmm, rrrr, t, k, rrrr, zzz, w, nnnn, rrrr, etc.).

4. Use a puppet to produce targeted words correctly and incorrectly. The student earns a sticker for correctly distinguishing a set number of correct/incorrect productions the puppet makes.

5. Have the student stand up each time he/she hears targeted words produced accurately as contrasted with inaccurate productions (e.g., shoup, soup, soup, shoup, soup, etc.).

6. Have the student show *thumbs up* each time targeted words are produced accurately when pictures are labeled and *thumbs down* if targeted words are produced inaccurately.

7. Using pictures of similar sounding words, say each word and have the student point to the appropriate picture (e.g., *run* and *one*, or *bat* and *back*).

8. Have the student tally the number of correct productions of targeted words when the teacher or a peer reads a list of words.

9. Have the student read simple passages and tape record them. Then have the student listen and mark error and/or correct productions.

10. Tape record a spontaneous monologue given by the student, then have him/her listen and tally error and/or correct productions. The teacher should also listen to the tape recording, and the teacher and the student should compare their analyses of the productions.

11. Have the student read a list of words and rate his/her production after each word.

12. Identify a peer who correctly produces targeted words to act as a model for the student.

13. Play a game such as *Simon Says* in which the student tries to imitate the targeted words when produced by the teacher or peers.

14. Using pictures of similar sounding words, have the student say each word as the teacher points to a picture (e.g., *run* and *one*, or *bat* and *back*).

15. Use a schematic drawing as a visual aid to show the student how the mouth looks during production of the target sound.

16. Make cards with the target sound and cards with vowels. Have the student combine a target sound card with a vowel card to make a syllable that he/she can produce (e.g., ra, re, ro, and ar, er, or).

17. Use a board game that requires the student to label pictures of the targeted words. The student needs to produce the targeted words correctly before he/she can move on the game board. (This activity can be simplified or expanded based on the level of expertise of the student.)

18. Have the student cut out pictures of items depicting the targeted words and display them where they can be practiced each day.

19. Provide the student with a list of the targeted words. Have the student practice the words daily. As the student masters the word list, add more words. (Using words from the student's everyday vocabulary, reading lists, spelling lists, etc., will facilitate transfer of correct production of the target sound into everyday speech.)

20. Have the student use old phonics "fun" sheets to practice his/her sound orally. These are good for home practice also.

21. Have the student keep a notebook of difficult words encountered each day. These can be practiced by the student with teacher or peer assistance.

22. Have the student use a carrier phrase combined with a word containing the target sound (e.g., "I like ___." "I see a ___.").

23. Have the student keep a list of all the words he/she can think of which contain sounds the student can produce accurately.

24. Have the student make up sentences using targeted words.

25. During oral reading, underline targeted words and reinforce the student for correct productions.

26. Involve parents by asking them to rate their child's speech for a specific length of time (e.g., during dinner count "no errors," "a few errors," or "many errors").

27. Present a list of topics from which the student may select, and then have the student give a spontaneous speech for a specific length of time. Count errors and suggest ways to improve.

28. Reinforce the student for correct production of the target sound or words: (a) give the student a tangible reward (e.g., classroom privileges, line leading, passing out materials, five minutes free time, etc.) or (b) give the student an intangible reward (e.g., praise, handshake, smile, etc.).

29. Speak to the student to explain what he/she needs to do differently (e.g., make sounds more precisely). The teacher should be careful to use the <u>sound</u> that is being targeted and not the letter name (e.g., "ssss" not "es").

30. Evaluate the appropriateness of requiring the student to accurately produce certain sounds (e.g., developmentally, certain sounds may not be produced accurately until the age of 8 or 9).

100 Does not use appropriate subject-verb agreement when speaking

1. Make certain the student's hearing has recently been checked.

2. Speak to the student to explain that he/she is using inappropriate subject-verb agreement and emphasize the importance of speaking in grammatically correct sentences.

3. Ascertain the type of grammatical model to which the student is exposed at home. Without placing negative connotations on his/her parent's grammatical style, explain the difference between standard and nonstandard grammar.

4. Evaluate the appropriateness of requiring the student to speak with subject-verb agreement (e.g., developmentally a child may not utilize appropriate subject-verb agreement until the age of 6 or 7).

5. Determine if the student's errors are the result of dialectical differences (the pattern of subject-verb agreement may not be atypical within his/her social group).

6. Reinforce the student for appropriate use of subject-verb agreement: (a) give the student a tangible reward (e.g., classroom privileges, line leading, passing out materials, five minutes free time, etc.) or (b) give the student an intangible reward (e.g., praise, handshake, smile, etc.).

7. Increase the student's awareness of the problem by tape recording the student when speaking with another student who exhibits appropriate subject-verb agreement. Play back the tape for the student to analyze and see if he/she can identify correct/incorrect subject-verb forms.

8. Identify a peer who uses appropriate subject/verb agreement to act as a model for the student.

9. Make sure the student understands that sentences express thoughts about a subject and what that subject is or does.

10. Make sure the student understands the concept of "subject" and "verb" by demonstrating through the use of objects, pictures, and/or written sentences (depending on the student's abilities).

11. Make sure the student understands the concept of plurality (e.g., have the student "point to a picture of a cat" and "point to a picture of cats").

12. Explain that certain forms of verbs go with certain subjects and that correct subject-verb agreement requires the appropriate match of subject and verb. Be certain that the student knows the various possibilities of subject-verb agreement and how to select the correct one.

13. Provide the student with correct examples of subject-verb agreement for those combinations he/she most commonly uses incorrectly.

14. Use a private signal (e.g., touching earlobe, raising index finger, etc.) to remind the student to use correct subject-verb agreement.

15. Make a list of those verbs the student most commonly uses incorrectly. This list will become the guide for learning activities in subject-verb agreement.

16. Routinely tape record the student's speech and point out errors in subject-verb agreement. With each successive taping, reinforce the student as his/her use of grammar improves.

17. After tape recording the student's speech, have him/her identify the errors involving subject-verb agreement and make appropriate corrections.

18. Have the student complete written worksheets in which he/she must choose the correct verb forms to go with specific subjects (e.g., "I ___ (saw, seen) a new car.").

19. Have the student complete written worksheets in which he/she must choose the correct subject forms to go with specific verbs (e.g., "(I, She) ___ eats.").

20. During the day, write down specific subject-verb errors produced by the student. Read the sentences to the student and have him/her make appropriate corrections orally.

21. Write down specific subject-verb errors made by the student during the day. Give the written sentences to the student and have him/her make appropriate corrections. (At first, mark the errors for the student to correct. As the student becomes more proficient with this task, have him/her find and correct the errors independently.)

22. When speaking privately with the student, restate subject-verb error with a rising inflection (e.g., "He <u>done</u> it?") to see if the student recognizes errors and spontaneously makes appropriate corrections.

23. Have the student verbally construct sentences with specific verb forms and subjects.

24. Give the student a series of sentences, both written and oral, and have him/her identify which are grammatically correct and incorrect.

25. Ask the parents to help encourage the student's correct use of grammar at home by praising him/her when correct subject-verb agreement is used.

26. Have the student identify a verb as a goal to master using correctly. As the student masters the correct use of the verb, he/she puts it on a list with a star and identifies another verb to master.

101 Does not carry on conversations with peers and adults

1. Encourage or reward others for interacting with the noninteracting student.

2. Give the student the responsibility of tutoring another student.

3. Ask the student to choose another student to work with on a specific assignment. (If the student has difficulty choosing someone, determine the student's preference by other means, such as a class survey.)

4. Be certain to greet or recognize the student as often as possible (e.g., hallways, cafeteria, welcome to class, acknowledge a job well done, etc.).

5. Request that the student be the leader of a small group activity if he/she possesses mastery of skills or has an interest in that area.

6. Have the student run errands which will require interactions with teachers, administrators, staff, etc. (e.g., delivering attendance reports to the office, taking messages to other teachers, etc.).

7. Interact with the student from a distance, gradually decreasing the distance until close proximity is achieved.

8. Plan for one-to-one teacher-student interactions at various times throughout the school day.

9. Try various groupings to determine the situation in which the student is most comfortable carrying on a conversation with peers and adults.

10. Provide the student with many social and academic successes.

11. Have the student deliver oral messages to other staff members in order to increase his/her opportunity to carry on conversations.

12. Have sharing time at school. Encourage the student to talk about anything that interests him/her.

13. Allow the student to show visitors and new students around the school.

14. Have the student play games which require conversing with others.

15. Determine an individual(s) in the school environment with whom the student would most want to converse (e.g., custodian, librarian, resource teacher, principal, older student, etc.). Allow the student to spend time with the individual(s) each day.

16. Identify another student who would be willing to spend time each day with the student.

17. Spend time each day talking with the student on an individual basis about his/her friends.

18. Pair the student with an outgoing student who engages in conversation with peers and adults on a frequent basis.

19. Teach the student conversational questions (e.g., "How are you?" "What have you been up to?" "How's it going?" etc.) to use when speaking to peers and adults.

20. Have the student engage in simulated conversational activities with feedback designed to teach conversational skills (e.g., greetings, questions, topics of conversation, etc.).

21. Provide the student with positive feedback which indicates he/she is successful, important, respected, etc.

22. Have the student work with a peer who is younger or smaller (e.g., choose a peer who is nonthreatening).

23. Recognize the student's attempts to communicate his/her needs (e.g., facial expressions, gestures, inactivity, self-depreciating comments, etc.).

24. Spend some time talking with the student on an individual basis about his/her interests.

25. Allow the student to be a member of a group without requiring active participation.

26. Assign a peer to sit/work with the student (e.g., in different settings or activities such as art, music, P.E., on the bus, tutoring, group projects, running errands in the building, recess, etc.) in order to increase the student's opportunity to engage in conversation.

27. Evaluate the appropriateness of expecting the student to carry on a conversation with peers and adults.

28. Identify a peer to act as a model for the student to imitate conversing with peers and adults.

29. Communicate with parents (e.g., notes home, phone calls, etc.) in order to share information concerning the student's progress and so that they may reinforce the student at home for conversing with peers and adults at school.

30. Reinforce those students in the classroom who converse with peers and adults.

31. Write a contract with the student specifying what behavior is expected (e.g., conversing with peers and adults) and what reinforcement will be made available when the terms of the contract have been met.

32. Reinforce the student for conversing with peers and adults based on the length of time he/she can be successful. Gradually increase the length of time required for reinforcement as the student demonstrates success.

33. Speak to the student to explain: (a) what he/she is doing wrong (e.g., failing to converse with peers and adults) and (b) what he/she should be doing (e.g., conversing with peers and adults).

34. Reinforce the student for conversing with peers and adults: (a) give the student a tangible reward (e.g., classroom privileges, line leading, passing out materials, five minutes free time, etc.) or (b) give the student an intangible reward (e.g., praise, handshake, smile, etc.).

1. Make certain the student's hearing has recently been checked.

2. Have the student label all the objects, persons, places, etc., in the environment that he/she can. Then have the student point to the items in the environment as you label the ones he/she was unable to name. The items the student is unable to label will comprise a foundation for new vocabulary to be learned. Activities to foster expansion of expressive vocabulary should focus on the items the student pointed to but could not label.

3. Have the student divide cards that label objects, persons, places, etc., in the environment into difference categories (e.g., function, color, size, use, composition, etc.). Point out the similarities and differences between items as they change categories (e.g., a ball and an apple may be red, round, and smooth; but you can only eat the apple, etc.).

4. Explain to the student how to classify new words as to category, function, antonym and synonym, etc., so the student will have a way of "filing" the words to memory.

5. In addition to labeling the objects, persons, places, etc., have the student provide verbs that could be used with each (e.g., "book" - read, browse through, skim, etc.).

6. In addition to identifying objects, persons, actions, etc., have the student provide places where each could be seen (e.g., "actor" - TV, theater, stage, etc.).

7. In addition to labeling objects, have the student state the uses of each (e.g., "knife" - cut, spread, slice, etc.).

8. Have the student provide as many adjectives as possible to go with a given noun. Then have the student choose one of the adjectives and produce as many nouns as possible to go with it.

9. Have the student provide as many adverbs as possible to go with a given verb. Then have the student choose one of the adverbs and produce as many verbs as possible to go with it.

10. Have the student list all the vocabulary he/she can think of that goes with a specific word (e.g.,

"space" - astronaut, lunar rover, rocket, shuttle, launch, etc.).

11. Give the student a picture of a specific location (e.g., grocery store) and have the student name as many objects, actions, persons, etc., as he/she can think of that can be found there.

12. Reinforce those students in the classroom who use an expanded speaking vocabulary.

13. Identify a peer who demonstrates comprehension and use of an expanded vocabulary to work with the student to improve comprehension of vocabulary and act as a model to expand the student's speaking vocabulary.

14. Use "hands-on" activities to teach vocabulary by constructing objects and/or organizing manipulatives.

15. Teach the student to use context clues and known vocabulary to determine the meaning of unknown vocabulary.

16. Explain to the student how to use context clues to determine the meanings of words he/she hears or sees (e.g., listening to or looking at the surrounding words and determining what type of word would be appropriate).

17. Explain to the student where he/she can go to find word meanings in the classroom library (e.g., dictionary, thesaurus, encyclopedia, etc.).

18. Have the student maintain a vocabulary notebook with definitions of words whose meanings he/she does not know.

19. Prepare a list of new words which the student will encounter while reading a given assignment. Help the student (or have a peer help the student) look up each word and practice saying it and using it in a sentence before reading the given assignment.

20. Select relevant and appropriate reading material and have the student underline each unfamiliar word. Make a list of these words and review their meanings with the student until he/she can use them when speaking.

21. Use a multi-sensory approach to enhance retention when teaching new vocabulary (e.g., the scent of fragrant flowers or freshly baked spice cake in the room will enhance retention of the vocabulary word "aroma").

22. Use visual aids whenever possible when introducing new vocabulary.

23. Use a large, old purse, box, bag, etc., with objects inside. Have the student reach into the container and try to determine what the item is based on the way if feels before he/she is allowed to see it.

24. Take advantage of unusual or unique situations to teach new vocabulary. Typically, a student will retain information learned in a novel situation better than that learned during the regular routine. The uniqueness of the situation will also enhance the student's memory skills when you provide a reminder to help the student recall the vocabulary (e.g., "Remember yesterday during the fire drill when we talked about ___.").

25. Make up or use games to teach comprehension and expression of new vocabulary. (Research has shown that novel situations help students to learn new information.)

26. To reinforce new vocabulary, write the new word on an envelope and put pictures inside that do and do not go with it (e.g., "arctic" - polar bears, snow, parrots, palm trees, etc.). Have the student remove the inappropriate vocabulary and explain why it doesn't belong.

27. Have the student paste a picture from a magazine on one side of a piece of paper and list all of the vocabulary that could be associated with it on the other side (including verbs). Have the student dictate or write a story about the picture using the vocabulary.

28. Refer to previously presented information that is related to the topic when presenting new vocabulary.

29. Teach new vocabulary within the context of known information (e.g., category, associations, etc.).

30. Have the student act out verbs and label actions performed by classmates.

31. Have the student demonstrate and identify different verbs of the same class (e.g., walk, creep, slither, saunter, march, etc.).

32. Have the students apply new vocabulary to personal experiences in written and oral work.

33. Include new vocabulary in daily conversation as often as possible.

34. Have the student engage in role-play to foster use of new vocabulary (e.g., set up an imaginary restaurant and have the student and peers play the various roles of customers, waiter/waitress, cook, etc., varying the time of day and the occasion).

35. Tape record the student's spontaneous speech, noting the specific words used, then have the student make a list of other words (synonyms) which could be substituted for these words.

36. Give the student a list of words and ask him/her to tell the opposite of each word.

37. Have the student make up sentences or stories using new words he/she has learned.

38. Name a category and have the student identify things within the category. Introduce new words which belong in the same group.

39. Give the student a series of words or pictures and have him/her name the category in which they belong (e.g., objects, persons, places, etc.).

40. Describe objects, persons, places, etc., and have the student name the items described.

41. Discuss with parents the ways in which they can help the student develop an expanded speaking vocabulary (e.g., encouraging the student to read the newspaper, novels, magazines, or other materials for enjoyment). Emphasize to parents that they can set a good example by reading with the student.

42. Send home new vocabulary words and encourage parents to use them in activities and general conversation.

43. Give the student a "word of the day" which is to be incorporated into conversations. Reinforce the student each time he/she uses the word.

44. During conversation, repeat phrases used by the student, revising the vocabulary to include additional words (e.g., if the student says, "The TV show was good." repeat by saying, "I'm glad the TV show was so entertaining.").

45. Use new words in a sentence completion activity. Have the student explain how the use of different words changes the meaning of the sentence (e.g., I like Jerry because he is ___ (sincere, humorous, competitive).).

46. Point out words that have a variety of meanings and use them appropriately in different contexts.

47. Have the student provide associations for given words (e.g., "circus" - clown, elephant, trapeze, tent, lion-tamer, etc.).

48. Review on a daily basis new vocabulary words and their meanings. Have the student use the words daily.

49. Review on a daily basis previously learned vocabulary words and their meanings. Have the student incorporate previously learned vocabulary words into daily conversation and activities.

50. Have the student maintain a notebook of all new vocabulary words to call upon for daily conversation and activities.

51. Use pictures to help the student understand the meanings of new vocabulary words.

52. Make certain the student is not expected to learn more vocabulary words and meanings than he/she is capable of comprehending.

53. Make certain the student has mastery of vocabulary words at each level before introducing new words.

54. Provide the student with fewer weekly vocabulary words and gradually increase the number of vocabulary words from week to week as the student demonstrates success.

55. Reinforce the student for expanding his/her vocabulary: (a) give the student a tangible reward (e.g., classroom privileges, line leading, passing out materials, five minutes free time, etc.) or (b) give the student an intangible reward (e.g., praise, handshake, smile, etc.).

56. Ascertain the type of language model the student has at home. Without placing negative connotations on the language model in his/her home, explain the difference between language which is rich in meaning and that which includes a limited repertoire of vocabulary.

57. Explain the importance of expanding one's vocabulary (i.e., comprehension and communication are based on the knowledge and use of appropriate/accurate vocabulary).

1. Make certain the student's hearing has recently been checked.

2. Explain that changes must be made in a verb to indicate when an event happened (e.g., past, present, future).

3. Ascertain the type of grammatical model to which the student is exposed at home. Without placing negative connotations on the parent's grammatical style, explain the difference between standard and nonstandard grammar.

4. Determine if the student's errors are the result of dialectical differences (i.e., the pattern of verb tense usage may not be atypical within his/her social group).

5. Reinforce the student for using verb tenses correctly: (a) give the student a tangible reward (e.g., classroom privileges, line leading, passing out materials, five minutes free time, etc.) or (b) give the student an intangible reward (e.g., praise, handshake, smile, etc.).

6. Reinforce those students in the classroom who use verb tenses correctly.

7. Increase the student's awareness of the problem by tape recording the student while he/she is speaking with another student who uses verb tenses correctly. Play the tape back for the student to see if he/she can identify correct/incorrect verb tensing.

8. Identify a peer who uses verb tenses appropriately to act as a model for the student.

9. Make sure the student understands the concept of verb tenses by demonstrating what "is happening," what "already happened" and what "will happen" through the use of objects, pictures, and/or written sentences (depending on the student's abilities).

10. Determine whether the student understands the concept of time, which influences comprehension of verb tensing (e.g., Can he/she answer questions using "yesterday," "today," "tomorrow," "before," "later," etc.? Does he/she use such vocabulary when speaking even though the verb tense is incorrect?).

11. Determine whether the student has appropriate sequencing skills. The concept of sequencing influences comprehension of verb tensing (e.g., Can the student answer questions using "first," "next," "then," etc.? Does he/she use such vocabulary when speaking even though verb tenses are incorrect?).

12. Use a private signal (e.g., hand over shoulder/past tense, pointing forward/future tense, etc.) to remind the student to use correct verb tense.

13. Make a list of those verb tenses the student most commonly uses incorrectly. This list will become the guide for identifying the verb tenses which the student should practice each day.

14. Tape record the student's speech to point out errors in verb tenses. With each successive taping, reinforce the student as his/her use of verb tenses improves.

15. After tape recording the student's speech, have him/her identify the errors involving verb tenses and make appropriate corrections.

16. Have the student complete worksheets in which he/she supplies the correct verb tenses to go with the sentences (e.g., "Yesterday I _____ to school.).

17. Have the student make corrections for incorrect verb tenses on written worksheets.

18. During the day, write down specific verb tense errors produced by the student. Read the sentences to the student and have him/her make appropriate corrections orally.

19. Write down specific verb tense errors made by the student during the day. Give the written sentences to the student and have him/her make appropriate corrections. (At first, mark the errors for him/her to correct. As the student becomes more proficient with this task, have him/her find and correct the errors independently.).

20. Have the student make up sentences with given verbs in the past, present, and future tenses.

21. Give the student a sentence and have him/her change it from present to past, past to present, future to past, etc.

22. Copy a simple paragraph which is in the present tense. Highlight the verbs and have the student change all the verbs to past and/or future tense. This activity could be completed orally or in written form.

23. Have the student assist in correcting other students' written work, looking for errors in verb tenses.

24. When speaking privately with the student, restate his/her verb tense error with a rising inflection (e.g., "Yesterday he plays?") to see if the student recognizes errors and spontaneously makes appropriate corrections.

25. Give the student a series of sentences, both written and oral, and have him/her identify the ones which demonstrate appropriate verb tensing. Have him/her make appropriate modifications for those sentences which demonstrate inappropriate verb tensing.

26. Ask the parents to encourage the student's correct use of verb tenses at home by praising him/her when appropriate verb tenses are used.

27. Have a peer practice verb tenses with the student. Each tense should be used in a sentence rather than only conjugating the verbs.

28. Make the conjugation of verbs a daily activity.

29. Have the student identify a verb as a goal to master using correctly. As the student masters the correct use of the verb, he/she puts it on a list with a star and identifies another verb to master.

30. Videotape the student and his/her classmates performing various actions. Play back the tape with the sound turned off and have the student narrate what is happening in present tense, what happened in past tense, and/or what will happen in future tense. (This activity could be modified by using a prerecorded videotape.)

31. Make headings entitled "Yesterday," "Today," and "Tomorrow," under which the class can list activities they "were doing," "are doing," or "will do." The following day, change the "today" heading to "yesterday" and the "tomorrow" heading to "today." Emphasize appropriate verb tenses throughout this activity.

32. Have the student list activities he/she did when little, activities the student can do now, and things he/she will be able to do when grown up. Emphasize appropriate verb tenses throughout this activity.

33. While the class is engaged in various activities, describe your observations using present tense. Have students do likewise. Expand this activity to include past and future tenses by asking appropriate questions (e.g., "What just happened?" "What were you doing?" "What will you do next?").

1. Make certain the student's hearing has recently been checked.

2. During conversations, calmly delay your verbal responses by one to two seconds.

3. Use a tape recorder so the student may listen to and evaluate his/her own speech.

4. Have the student identify a good speaker and give the reasons that make that person a good speaker.

5. Develop a list of the attributes which are likely to help a person become a good speaker and have the student practice each characteristic.

6. During oral reading, underline or highlight words which are difficult for the student to say and provide reinforcement when he/she says them fluently.

7. Have the student keep a list of times and/or situations in which speech is difficult (e.g., times when he/she is nervous, embarrassed, etc.). Discuss the reasons for this and seek solutions to the difficulty experienced.

8. Have the student practice techniques for relaxing (e.g., deep breathing, tensing and relaxing muscles, etc.) which can be employed when he/she starts to speak dysfluently.

9. Have the student identify the specific words or phrases with which he/she becomes dysfluent and practice those particular words or phrases.

10. Encourage the student to maintain eye contact during all speaking situations. If the student is noticeably more fluent when eye contact is averted, attempt to increase eye contact on a gradual basis.

11. Have the student speak in unison with you while you are modeling slow, easy speech.

12. Reinforce the student's moments of relative fluency and emphasize that these occurred during moments when he/she was speaking slowly and easily.

13. Empathize with the student and explain that he/she is not more or less valuable as a person because of stuttering. Emphasize the student's positive attributes.

14. Empathize with feelings of anger which the student may be experiencing due to speaking dysfluently.

15. When the student is speaking fluently, try to extend the positive experience by allowing him/her ample opportunity to continue speaking.

16. Reinforce the student each time he/she answers a question or makes a spontaneous comment in class.

17. If the student is speaking too rapidly, remind him/her to slow down. Develop a private signal (e.g., raising one finger, touching earlobe, etc.) to avoid calling too much attention to the student's speech in front of the whole class.

18. Try to give the student your undivided attention so he/she will not feel a need to hurry or compete with others for attention.

19. If the student is more dysfluent when involved in another activity at the same time he/she is talking, encourage the student to stop the other activity.

20. If the student is highly excited, wait until he/she is calmer before requiring any verbal explanations or interactions. A high level of excitement often precipitates an anxiety level that interferes with fluency.

21. During moments of nonfluency, use nonverbal activities to relax the student.

22. Do not interrupt or finish the student's sentences even if you think you can anticipate what the student is going to say. This can be extremely frustrating and may decrease the student's willingness to engage in future communicative interactions.

23. Help the student learn to identify periods of dysfluency and periods of slow, easy speech.

24. Help the student learn to identify situations in which he/she is more fluent or less fluent. Determine the aspects of the fluent situations that seem to enhance fluency and try to transfer those features to the less fluent situations.

25. When the student is dysfluent during conversation, explain that this happens to everyone at times.

26. Have the student make a list of his/her strong points or the things done well in order to improve the student's overall level of confidence.

27. Point out to the student that he/she is capable of fluent speech and is in control of speech in many situations.

28. Model slow, easy speech for the student and encourage the student to speak at a similar rate. Practice with the student for a short time each day until he/she is able to match the rate.

29. Provide the student with a list of sentences and encourage him/her to read these at a slow rate.

30. Prepare simple oral reading passages in written form in which phrases are separated by large spaces (indicating "pause"). Have the student practice reading the passages aloud.

31. Use a private cue (e.g., raise a finger, touch earlobe, etc.) to encourage the student to answer questions at a slow rate of speech.

32. Use a private cue (e.g., raise a finger, touch earlobe, etc.) to encourage the student to use a slow speaking rate during classroom activities.

33. Reduce the emphasis on competition. Competitive activities may increase the student's anxiety and cause him/her to speak more dysfluently.

34. As the student is able to speak fluently in more situations, increase those experiences as long as the student continues to be successful (e.g., delivering messages to the office, speaking with the counselor, etc.).

35. Provide the student with as many social and academic successes as possible.

36. Do not require the student to speak in front of other students if he/she is uncomfortable doing so. Have the student speak to the teacher or another student privately if the student would be more comfortable doing so.

37. Meet with the student's parents to determine the level of dysfluency at home, parental reactions to the dysfluency, and successful strategies the parents might have employed when dealing with the dysfluent speech.

38. Determine whether or not the student avoids certain situations because of his/her perception of increased dysfluency. Discuss with the student aspects of those situations that seem to cause increased anxiety. Examine possible modifications that could be implemented in the classroom to increase frustration tolerance (e.g., if speaking in front of the whole class causes stress, reduce the number of listeners and gradually increase the group size as the student's frustration tolerance increases).

39. Identify a peer to act as a model for appropriate speech. Pair the students to sit together, perform assignments together, etc.

40. Provide the student with an appropriate model of slow, easy speech. Lengthen the pauses between words, phrases, and sentences.

41. Evaluate the appropriateness of requiring the student to speak without dysfluency (e.g., developmentally, young children experience normal dysfluency in their speech and all persons are occasionally dysfluent).

42. Familiarize yourself and the student with the terms fluency, dysfluency, stuttering, easy speech, etc. Keep these words as neutral as possible, without negative connotations.

43. Reinforce the student for speaking fluently: (a) give the student a tangible reward (e.g., classroom privileges, line leading, passing out materials, five minutes free time, etc.) or (b) give the student an intangible reward (e.g., praise, handshake, smile, etc.).

105 Does not complete statements or thoughts when speaking

1. Make certain the student's hearing has recently been checked.

2. Allow the student to speak without being interrupted or hurried.

3. Reduce the emphasis on competition. Competitive activities may cause the student to hurry and fail to speak in complete sentences.

4. Have the student keep a list of times and/or situations in which he/she is nervous, anxious, etc., and has more trouble than usual with speech. Help the student identify ways to feel more successful in those situations.

5. Make a list of the attributes which are likely to help a person become a good speaker (e.g., takes his/her time, thinks of what to say before starting, etc.).

6. List the qualities a good speaker possesses (e.g., rate, diction, volume, vocabulary, etc.) and have the student evaluate himself/herself on each characteristic. Set a goal for improvement in only one or two areas at a time.

7. Have the student identify a good speaker and give the reasons that make that person a good speaker.

8. Have a peer who speaks in complete sentences act as a model for the student. Assign the students to work together, perform assignments together, etc.

9. When the student has difficulty during a conversation, remind him/her that this occasionally happens to everyone.

10. Increase the student's awareness of the problem by tape recording the student while he/she is speaking with another student who uses complete sentences. Play back the tape for the student to see if he/she can identify incomplete sentences and nondescript terminology. Have the student make appropriate modifications.

11. Demonstrate acceptable and unacceptable speech (including incomplete thoughts and nondescriptive terminology such as "thing" or "stuff,"

etc.) and have the student critique each example making suggestions for improvement.

12. Make sure the student understands the concept of a "complete" sentence by pointing out the "subject/verb/object" components through the use of objects, pictures, and/or written sentences (depending on the student's abilities).

13. Make certain the student understands that a complete sentence has to express a complete thought about a subject and what that subject is or does, and that use of specific vs. nondescriptive vocabulary is important to clarify the message.

14. Teach the concept of verb and noun phrases as soon as possible so the student has a means of checking to see if a sentence is complete.

15. Use a private signal (e.g., touching earlobe, raising index finger, etc.) to remind the student to speak in complete sentences and use specific terminology.

16. Routinely tape record the student's speech and point out incomplete statements and nondescript terminology. With each successive taping, reinforce the student as his/her use of complete sentences and specific vocabulary improves.

17. Give the student a series of complete and incomplete sentences, both written and oral, and ask him/her to identify which are correct and incorrect and make appropriate modifications.

18. Have the student correct a series of phrases by making each a complete sentence.

19. Have the student complete worksheets in which he/she must replace nondescriptive or inaccurate vocabulary with specific and appropriate terminology (e.g., "The thing tastes good." could be changed to "The cake (meal, soda, etc.) tastes good." or "He used the digger to make the hole." could be changed to "He used the shovel (backhoe, spade, etc.) to make the hole.").

20. Give the student a subject and have him/her make up as many complete sentences about it as possible, emphasizing the use of specific vocabulary.

21. Make groups of cards containing subjects, verbs, adjectives, etc. Have the student combine the cards in various ways to construct complete sentences.

22. Give the student several short sentences and have him/her combine them in order to produce one longer sentence (e.g., "The dog is big." "The dog is brown." "The dog is mine." becomes "The big, brown dog is mine.").

23. Give the student a list of transition words (e.g., therefore, although, because, etc.) and have him/her make up sentences using each word.

24. Give the student a group of related words (e.g., baseball, fans, glove, strikeout, etc.) and have him/her write a paragraph including each word.

25. Provide the student with sentence starters (e.g., Go ___. Run ___. Today I ___. Anyone can ___. etc.) and have him/her make up complete sentences.

26. Provide the student with a topic (e.g., rules to follow when riding your bike) and have him/her make up complete sentences about it.

27. Give the student a factual statement (e.g., Some animals are dangerous.) and have him/her provide several complete sentences relating to that topic.

28. Have the student give process statements to sequence an activity (e.g., how to make a peanut butter and jelly sandwich). Have the student focus on making each statement a complete thought with specific vs. nondescriptive vocabulary.

29. Give the student scrambled words and have him/her put them in the correct order to form a complete sentence.

30. Choose a topic for a paragraph or story and alternate making up sentences with the student in order to provide a model of the components of a complete sentence.

31. Ask the parents to encourage the student's use of complete sentences and thoughts at home by praising him/her when these are used.

32. Have a number of students build a sentence together (e.g., The first one starts with a word such as "I." The next student adds the second word such as "like." This process continues as long as possible to create one long, complete sentence. Do not accept nondescriptive terminology.).

33. Ask questions which stimulate language. Avoid those which can be answered by yes/no or a nod of the head (e.g., "What did you do at recess?" instead of "Did you play on the slide?" or "Tell me about your vacation." instead of "Did you stay home over the holidays?").

34. Make a list of the student's most common incomplete statements and uses of nondescriptive terminology. Spend time with the student practicing how to make these statements or thoughts complete and making appropriate replacements for nondescriptive vocabulary.

35. Have the student role-play various situations in which good speech is important (e.g., during a job interview).

36. When speaking privately with the student, restate his/her incomplete sentences and/or nondescriptive vocabulary with a rising inflection to indicate the need for more information (e.g., "You saw the <u>stuff</u> in the sky" or "Your brown dog . . .?") to see if the student recognizes the problem and spontaneously makes appropriate corrections.

37. Have the student describe himself/herself and/or classmates in complete sentences with emphasis on specific vocabulary to differentiate one student from another.

38. Videotape the student and classmates performing various actions. Play back the tape with the sound turned off and have the student narrate observations in complete sentences with descriptive vocabulary. (This activity could be modified by using a prerecorded videotape.)

39. Using a book without words, have the student tell the story using descriptive vocabulary and complete sentences. Tape record the story and play it back for the student to listen for complete/incomplete sentences and specific/non-descriptive terminology and make appropriate corrections.

40. After a field trip or special event, have the student retell the activities which occurred with an emphasis on using descriptive vocabulary and complete sentences.

41. After reading a short story, have the student recall the main characters, sequence the events, and retell the outcome of the story.

42. Give the student a series of words or pictures and have him/her name as many items as possible within that category (e.g., objects, persons, places, things that are hot, etc.).

43. Give the student specific categories and have him/her name as many items as possible within that category (e.g., things that are cold, objects, persons, places, etc.).

44. Describe objects, persons, places, etc., and have the student name the items described.

45. Help the student employ memory aids in order to recall words (e.g., a name might be linked to another word; for example, "Mr. Green" is a very colorful person).

46. Give the student a series of words describing objects, persons, places, etc., and have him/her identify the opposite of each word.

47. Have the student complete "fill-in-the-blank" sentences with appropriate words (e.g., objects, persons, places, etc.).

48. Give the student a series of words (e.g., objects, persons, places, etc.) and have the student list all the words he/she can think of with similar meanings (synonyms).

49. Encourage the student to use an appropriate synonym when experiencing difficulty retrieving the "exact" word he/she wants to say.

50. Have the student complete associations (e.g., knife, fork, and ___; men, women, and ___; etc.).

51. When the student is required to recall information, remind him/her of the situation in which the material was originally presented (e.g., "Remember yesterday when we talked about . . ." "Remember when we were outside and I told you about the . . ." etc.).

52. Encourage the student to use gestures when necessary to clarify his/her message. Gestures may also facilitate recall of vocabulary the student is having difficulty retrieving.

53. Have the student compete against himself/herself by timing how fast he/she can name a series of pictured objects. Each time, the student tries to increase speed.

54. Have the student make notes, lists, etc., of vocabulary that is needed to be recalled and have the student carry these reminders for reference.

55. Show the student an object or a picture of an object for a few seconds. Ask the student to recall specific attributes of the object (e.g., color, size, shape, etc.).

56. Teach the student to recognize key words and phrases related to information in order to increase his/her recall.

57. Label objects, persons, places, etc., in the environment in order to help the student be able to recall names.

58. Make certain the student receives information from a variety of sources (e.g., textbooks, like presentations, discussions, etc.) in order to enhance memory/recall.

59. Ask the student leading questions to facilitate the process of speaking in complete sentences and using specific vocabulary.

60. Provide the student with the first sound of a word he/she is having difficulty retrieving in order to facilitate recall.

61. Encourage verbal output. Increase the student's opportunities to communicate verbally in order to provide him/her with necessary practice.

62. Focus on completeness of the student's thought and not the grammatical accuracy of the statement. Reinforce complete thoughts that include specific vocabulary.

63. When the student uses incomplete sentences or nondescriptive terminology, provide the student with models of expansion and specific vocabulary using his/her statements as a foundation.

64. When the student is required to recall information, provide visual and/or auditory cues to help him/her remember the information (e.g., mention key words, expose part of a picture, etc.).

65. Call on the student when he/she is most likely to be able to respond successfully.

66. Provide frequent interactions and encouragement to support the student's confidence (e.g., make statements such as "You're doing great." "Keep up the good work." "I really am proud of you." etc.).

67. Provide the student with an appropriate model to imitate speaking in complete sentences or thoughts (e.g., speak clearly, slowly, concisely, and in complete sentences, statements, and thoughts).

68. Reinforce the students in the classroom who use complete sentences or thoughts when speaking.

69. Reinforce the student for using complete sentences or thoughts when speaking: (a) give the student a tangible reward (e.g., classroom privileges, line leading, passing out materials, five minutes free time, etc.) or (b) give the student an intangible reward (e.g., praise, handshake, smile, etc.).

70. Speak to the student to explain that he/she is using incomplete sentences or thoughts when speaking and explain the importance of speaking in complete sentences and choosing specific words to express ideas.

1. Get a list of words and phrases from the student's reading material which he/she does not recognize. Have the student practice using phonic skills, context clues, picture clues, etc., using these words.

2. Have the student identify words and phrases that he/she does not recognize. Make these words the student's word list to be learned.

3. Emphasize that the student learn a root word sight vocabulary in order to be able to add various prefixes and suffixes to develop word attack skills.

4. Reinforce the student each time he/she makes an attempt to sound out a word. Gradually increase the number of attempts required for reinforcement.

5. Use a peer tutor to review word attack skills utilizing games and activities previously learned.

6. Make certain the student uses a sight vocabulary to support weaknesses in phonic skills.

7. Make certain the student develops an awareness of hearing word sounds (e.g., say, "Listen to these words, each of them begins with a /bl/ sound: blue, black, block, blast.").

8. Make certain the student develops an awareness of seeing letter combinations that make the sounds (e.g., have the student circle all of the words in a reading passage that begin with the /bl/ sound).

9. Provide practice in reading /bl/ words, /pl/ words, /pr/ words, etc., by presenting a high-interest paragraph or story that contains these words.

10. Demonstrate skills in decoding words (e.g., using contractions from conversation, write the abbreviated form of the word and the two complete words to show how to recognize the contraction).

11. Encourage the student to try several sounds in order to arrive at the correct answer (e.g., omit letters from a word used in context and give several choices to be filled in).

12. Write paragraphs and short stories requiring word attack skills the student is currently learning. These passages should be of high interest to the student using his/her name, family members, friends, pets, and interesting experiences.

13. Have the student dictate stories which are then written for him/her to read. Require the student to place an emphasis on word attack skills.

14. Have the student read high-interest signs, advertisements, notices, etc., from newspapers, magazines, movie promotions, etc., placing emphasis on word attack skills.

15. Make certain the student is practicing word attack skills which are directly related to high-interest reading activities (e.g., adventures, romance, mystery, athletics, etc.).

16. Encourage the student to scan the newspapers, magazines, etc., and underline words he/she can identify using word attack skills (e.g., phonics, context clues, picture clues, etc.).

17. Require the student to verbally explain context clues in sentences to identify words not known.

18. Have the student use related pictures to help identify words in sentences not known.

19. Teach the student the most common prefixes and suffixes to add to root words he/she can identify.

20. When the student has difficulty with word attack skills, remind him/her that this can happen to everyone and not be upset. Everyone has areas where they are weak and areas of strength as well, but we must keep trying.

21. Have the student act as a peer tutor to teach another student a concept he/she has mastered. This can serve as a reinforcement for the student.

22. Avoid subjecting the student to uncomfortable reading situations (e.g., reading aloud in a group, identifying that the student's reading group is the lowest level, etc.).

23. Tape record difficult reading material for the student to listen to as he/she reads along.

24. Use reading material with pictures and predictable reading, in order to help the student master word attack skills.

25. Have the student read aloud to the teacher each day in order to provide evaluative feedback.

26. Introduce new words and their meanings to the student before he/she reads new materials. These may be entered in a "vocabulary" notebook kept by the student.

27. First teach the foundation for reading and writing in a sequential, systematic method with much positive reinforcement.

28. Teach the student individual consonant and vowel sounds.

29. Allow the student to use the chalkboard so that teaching and learning become active. The student hears, writes, and sees the sounds in isolation and then they "slide together" to make words.

30. The student should practice vocabulary words from required reading material by writing them while saying the sounds.

31. Teach the student pronunciation rules (e.g., vowel sounds, blends, etc.).

32. Start with simple words and sounds where the student achieves 95%-100% accuracy. Do not move on to more difficult words until practice, drill, and review of preceding lessons produces accuracy.

33. Use D'Nealian handwriting when teaching sounds by hearing, writing, and saying. This eliminates many potential reversal problems.

34. Have the student memorize word meanings and practice spotting the most common prefixes and suffixes. Using a sheet of paper with a window cut in it, target the base word.

35. Play alphabet bingo with the student using phonics instead of letter names.

1. Make certain the student's vision has recently been checked.

2. Make certain the student is reading material on his/her level. If not, modify or adjust reading material to the student's ability level.

3. Reinforce the student for demonstrating comprehension of reading material: (a) give the student a tangible reward (e.g., classroom privileges, line leading, passing out materials, five minutes free time, etc.) or (b) give the student an intangible reward (e.g., praise, handshake, smile, etc.).

4. Reduce distracting stimuli in order to increase the student's ability to concentrate on what he/she is reading (e.g., place the student on the front row, provide a carrel or "office" space away from distractions, etc.). This should be used as a means of reducing distracting stimuli and not as a form of punishment.

5. Teach the student to use context clues to identify the meaning of words and phrases not known.

6. Prerecord the student's reading material and have him/her listen to the recording while simultaneously reading the material.

7. Have the student read ahead on a subject to be discussed in class so that he/she is familiar with new vocabulary and concepts that will be used during instructional periods.

8. Outline reading material for the student using words and phrases on his/her ability level.

9. Arrange a peer who demonstrates good comprehension skills to read with the student and help him/her with the meanings of words not understood.

10. Have the student take notes while reading in order to increase comprehension.

11. Teach the student to draw from personal learning experiences to enhance comprehension of reading material. Provide a variety of learning experiences at school in order to expand the student's background of knowledge.

12. Maintain mobility in the classroom in order to frequently be near the student to provide reading assistance.

13. Have the student verbally paraphrase material just read in order to assess his/her comprehension.

14. Teach the student to identify main points in material in order to enhance his/her comprehension.

15. Underline or highlight important points before the student reads the material silently.

16. Have the student outline, underline, or highlight important points in reading material.

17. Provide the student with written direction-following activities that target concrete experiences (e.g., following a recipe, following directions to put a model together, etc.) in order to enhance comprehension.

18. Provide the student with written one-step, two-step, and three-step direction-following activities (e.g., sharpen your pencil, open your text to page 121, etc.).

19. Have the student read progressively longer segments of reading material in order to build comprehension skills (e.g., begin with a single paragraph and progress to several paragraphs, chapters, short stories, etc.).

20. Have the student read high-interest signs, advertisements, notices, etc., from newspapers, magazines, movie promotions, etc., placing an emphasis on comprehension skills.

21. Reduce the emphasis on competition. Competitive activities may make it difficult for the student to comprehend what he/she reads.

22. Use a sight word vocabulary approach in order to teach the student key words and phrases when reading directions and instructions (e.g., key words such as *circle, underline, match*, etc.).

23. Have the student list new or difficult words in categories such as people, food, animals, things that are hot, etc.

24. Have the student maintain a vocabulary notebook with definitions of words whose meanings are not known.

25. When the student encounters a new word or one whose meaning is not understood, have the student practice making up sentences in which the word can be used in the correct context.

26. Make certain the student learns dictionary skills in order to find the meanings of words independently.

27. Have the student identify words he/she does not comprehend. Finding the definitions of these words can then become the dictionary assignment.

28. Have the student identify one word each day that is not understood and require him/her to use that word throughout the day in various situations.

29. Have the student match vocabulary words with pictures representing the words.

30. Introduce new words and their meanings to the student before reading new material.

31. Make certain the student learns the meanings of all commonly used prefixes and suffixes.

32. Write notes and letters to the student to provide reading material which he/she will want to read for comprehension. Students may be encouraged to write notes and letters to classmates at a time set aside each day, once a week, etc.

33. Give the student time to read a selection more than once, emphasizing accuracy not speed.

34. Have the student supply missing words in sentences provided by classmates and/or the teacher in order to enhance comprehension skills.

35. Cut out pictures from magazines and newspapers and have the student match captions to them. This activity could be varied by having one student write a caption while another student determines if it is appropriate.

36. Have the student read a short paragraph which contains one or more errors which make comprehension difficult. See if the student recognizes the errors. If not, encourage the student to stop frequently while reading to ask himself/herself, "Does this make sense?"

37. Determine whether or not the student can make inferences, predictions, determine cause-effect, etc., in everyday experiences. Teach these skills in contexts that are meaningful to the student in order to enhance the ability to employ these concepts when reading.

38. Have the student read a story. Provide statements reflecting the main points of the story out of sequence. Have the student arrange the statements in the correct order to demonstrate comprehension.

39. Have the student prepare "test" questions based on information that has been read in order to enhance the ability to focus on key elements of the reading material.

40. Include frequent written assignments on topics which are of interest to the student in order to reinforce the correlation between writing and reading ability.

41. Reduce the amount of material the student reads at one time (e.g., reduce reading material to single sentences on a page, a single paragraph, etc.). Gradually increase the amount of material as the student experiences success.

42. Avoid subjecting the student to uncomfortable reading situations (e.g., reading aloud in a group, reading with time limits, etc.).

43. Stop the student at various points throughout a reading selection to check for comprehension.

44. Reduce the amount of information on a page if it is causing visual distractions for the student (e.g., less print to read, fewer pictures, etc.).

45. Highlight or underline important information the student should pay close attention to when reading.

46. Make it pleasant and positive for the student to ask questions about things not understood.

47. Have the student use a highlighter pen to highlight the facts requested by the teacher.

48. Allow the student to work with a peer and teacher. The first student would dictate a short paragraph to be typed by the teacher and would also compose a comprehension question. The second student, after listening to the process, would read the story orally and point out the answer. Then student roles could be reversed.

49. Present directions following the outline of: (1) What, (2) How, (3) Materials, and (4) When.

50. Have the student take notes when directions are being given following the "What, How, Materials, and When" format. (See Appendix for Assignment Form.)

51. While concepts are presented, have the student listen and take notes for "Who, What, Where, When, How, and Why." (See Appendix for Outline Form.)

52. Present concepts following the outline of: (1) Who, (2) What, (3) Where, (4) When, (5) How, and (6) Why.

1. Make certain the student's hearing has been checked recently.

2. Each day have the student practice those sound-symbol relationships he/she does not know.

3. Have the student read and write friends' first names which include the sound-symbol relationships that he/she does not recognize.

4. Have the student say the sounds that consonants make as he/she points to them (e.g., d makes the /d/ sound, etc.).

5. Present the alphabet to the student on flash cards and have him/her make the sounds as the letters are flashed (e.g., d makes the /d/ sound, etc.). This is an appropriate activity for a peer tutor to conduct with the student each day.

6. Identify a sound the student does not know. Have the student circle all the words containing that sound in a paragraph or a page of a book.

7. Put each letter of the alphabet on an individual card. Have the student collect all the letters for which he/she knows the sound. The goal is to "own" all the letters of the alphabet.

8. Provide the student with sounds (e.g., /d/, /b/, /p/, etc.) and have him/her write or otherwise identify the letters that make the sounds.

9. Start by teaching the student sounds in the student's first name only. When the student has mastered the sounds in his/her first name, go on to the last name, parents' names, etc.

10. Take every opportunity throughout the day to emphasize a designated sound for that day (e.g., identify the sound when speaking, writing, reading, etc.).

11. Identify a letter for the day. Have the student listen for the sound made by that letter and identify the sound-symbol relationship each time the sound is heard.

12. Assign the student a sound-symbol relationship. Have the student use a highlight marker to identify each word in a passage in which the sound-symbol relationship appears.

13. Use a Language Master to pair the sounds of letters with the symbols of letters.

14. Make certain the student is not required to learn more information than he/she is capable of at any one time.

15. Have the student act as a peer tutor to teach another student a concept he/she has mastered. This can serve as reinforcement for the student.

16. Review on a daily basis those skills previously introduced.

17. Use both auditory and visual cues to help the student master sound-symbol relationships (i.e., the letter "a" a picture of an apple, and the sound the letter "a" makes).

18. Teach intensive phonics as a foundation for reading, spelling, and handwriting.

19. Practice, drill, and review every day.

20. Have the student make the sounds of letters as he/she writes words containing the letters (e.g., /d/ /a/ /d/).

21. Provide the student with a desktop chart (Phonovisual Company, Maryland, is excellent) of sounds. The student should be instructed to point to and say the sound the teacher says.

22. Have the student make sentences with words that begin with only one target letter sound (e.g., Tongue twisters tease Tootsie's tonsils.).

1. Set up a system of motivators, either tangible (e.g., extra computer time, free time, etc.) or intangible (e.g., smile, handshake, praise, etc.) to encourage the student to be more successful in reading.

2. Get a list of words and phrases from the student's reading material which he/she does not recognize. Have the student practice phonic skills using these words.

3. Have the student identify words and phrases that he/she does not recognize. Make these words the student's word list to be learned.

4. Emphasize that the student learn a root word sight vocabulary in order to be able to add various prefixes and suffixes to develop word attack skills.

5. Reinforce the student each time he/she makes an attempt to sound out a word. Gradually increase the number of attempts required for reinforcement.

6. Use a peer tutor to review phonic concepts previously instructed by utilizing games and activities.

7. Teach the student to use context clues to identify words and phrases he/she does not know.

8. Make certain the student uses a sight vocabulary to support weaknesses in phonic skills.

9. Make certain the student develops an awareness of hearing word sounds (e.g., say, "Listen to these words. Each of them begins with a /bl/ sound: blue, black, block, blast.").

10. Make certain the student develops an awareness of seeing letter combinations that produce sounds (e.g., have the student circle all of the words in a reading passage that begin with the /bl/ sound).

11. Provide practice in reading /bl/ words, /pl/ words, /pr/ words, etc., by presenting a high-interest paragraph or story that contains these words.

12. Demonstrate skills in decoding words (e.g., using contractions from conversation, write the abbreviated form of the word and the two complete words to show how to recognize the contraction, etc.).

13. Encourage the student to try several sounds in order to arrive at a correct answer (e.g., omit letters from a word used in context and give several choices to be filled in).

14. Encourage the student to scan newspapers, magazines, etc., and underline learned phonic elements.

15. Develop a list of phonic sounds the student needs to master. Remove sounds from the list as the student demonstrates mastery of phonic skills.

16. Write paragraphs and short stories requiring phonic skills the student is currently learning. These passages should be of high interest to the student using his/her name, family members, friends, pets, and interesting experiences.

17. Have the student dictate stories which are then written for him/her to read, placing an emphasis on reading skills.

18. Have the student read high-interest signs, advertisements, notices, etc., from newspapers, magazines, movie promotions, etc., placing an emphasis on phonic skills.

19. Make certain the student is practicing phonic skills which are directly related to high-interest reading activities (e.g., adventures, romance, mystery, athletics, etc.).

20. Have the student make a list of phonic skills that have been mastered (e.g., words he/she can identify by sounding out). The student continues to add to the list as he/she identifies more and more words.

21. Make certain the student knows all beginning sounds before expecting him/her to blend sounds into words.

22. Tape record difficult reading material for the student to listen to as he/she reads along.

23. Make certain that the reading demands of all subjects and assignments are within the ability level of the student. If they are not, modify or adjust the reading material to the student's ability level.

24. Make certain that the student's knowledge of a particular skill is being assessed rather than the student's ability to read directions, instructions, etc. Reading directions to the student may increase success.

25. Provide the student with verbal reminders or prompts when he/she is unsure of sounds that letters make when blended together.

26. Reduce the amount of information on a page if it is causing visual distractions for the student (e.g., less print to read, fewer pictures to look at, etc.).

27. Avoid subjecting the student to uncomfortable reading situations (e.g., reading aloud in a group, identifying that the student's reading group is the lowest level, etc.).

28. Determine if the student has instant recall of all consonant and vowel sounds and combinations.

29. Practice active learning at the chalkboard by having students hear, write, and read words.

30. Practice, drill, and review every day.

31. Have students say sounds as they write them.

32. Allow students to write a story, paragraph, or sentence using phonetic shorthand. This narrowing of sounds helps the student to identify the sounds with letters used to construct words.

110 Does not discriminate between similar letters and words

1. Make certain the student's hearing has been checked recently.

2. Each day have the student practice those letters and words he/she cannot discriminate.

3. Take every opportunity throughout the day to emphasize a designated letter or word the student cannot discriminate (e.g., identify the sound when speaking, writing, reading, etc.).

4. Use highlight markers (e.g., pink and yellow) to have the student mark the letters and words in a passage he/she does not discriminate (e.g., all m's marked with the pink marker and all n's marked with the yellow marker).

5. Make a list of words the student cannot discriminate. Have the student and a peer work together with flash cards to develop the student's ability to recognize the differences in the letters and words.

6. Tape record stories and paragraphs the student can listen to while reading along.

7. Have the student read aloud to the teacher each day in order to provide evaluative feedback relative to his/her ability to discriminate letters and words.

8. Verbally correct the student as often as possible when he/she does not discriminate between letters and words in order that he/she hears the correct version of the reading material.

9. Have the student write those letters and words he/she has trouble discriminating in order that he/she has a greater opportunity to conceptualize the correct version.

10. Teach the student to use context clues in reading. These skills will be particularly helpful when he/she is unable to discriminate between letters and words.

11. Make certain the student looks closely at word endings as well as beginnings in order to discriminate similar words (e.g., cap and cat).

12. Identify a letter or word each day which the student has difficulty discriminating. Have the student underline or highlight that letter or word each time he/she reads it that day.

13. Make certain the student has an alphabet strip at his/her desk in order that he/she has a reference when reading or performing assignments.

14. Reduce the emphasis on competition. Competitive activities may cause the student to hurry and not discriminate between similar letters and words.

15. Make certain that the reading demands of all subjects and assignments are within the ability level of the student. If they are not, modify or adjust the reading material to the student's ability level.

16. Make certain that the student's knowledge of a particular skill is being assessed rather than the student's ability to read directions, instructions, etc.

17. Have the student cut letters out of magazines or newspapers and glue the letters to make words, sentences, etc.

1. Set up a system of reinforcers, either tangible (e.g., computer time, helper for the day, etc.) or intangible (e.g., praise, handshake, smile, etc.) to encourage the student to learn the letters of the alphabet.

2. Make certain the student has an alphabet strip at his/her desk in order to have a reference.

3. Each day have the student print those letters of the alphabet he/she does not know.

4. Have a peer work with the student on one letter of the alphabet each day (e.g., tracing the letter, printing the letter, recognizing the letter in words in a paragraph, etc.).

5. Have the student read and write friends' first names which include letters the student does not recognize.

6. Introduce letters to the student as partners (e.g., Aa, Bb, Cc, Dd, etc.).

7. Have the student say the letters of the alphabet in sequence. Repeat by rote several times a day.

8. Present the alphabet to the student on flash cards. This is an appropriate activity for a peer tutor to conduct with the student each day.

9. Identify a letter the student does not know. Have the student find the letter in all the words in a paragraph or on a page of a book.

10. Put each letter of the alphabet on an individual card. Have the student collect and keep the letters he/she knows with the goal to "own" all the letters of the alphabet.

11. Start by teaching the names of letters in the student's first name only. When the student has mastered the letters in his/her first name, go on to the last name, parents' names, etc.

12. Give the student a word which begins with each letter of the alphabet (e.g., apple, bad, cat, etc.). Go over several of the words each day, stressing the alphabet letters being learned.

13. Take every opportunity throughout the day to emphasize a designated letter for that day (e.g., identify the letter when speaking, writing, reading, etc.).

14. Use daily drills to help the student memorize the alphabet.

15. Avoid subjecting the student to uncomfortable reading situations (e.g., reading aloud in a group, identifying that the student's reading group is the lowest level, etc.).

112 Understands what is read to him/her but not what he/she reads silently

1. Make certain the student is reading material on his/her level.

2. Modify or adjust reading material to the student's ability level.

3. Outline reading material the student reads silently using words and phrases on his/her reading level.

4. Tape record difficult reading material for the student to listen to as he/she reads along.

5. Use lower grade-level texts as alternative reading material in subject areas.

6. Make a list of main points from the student's reading material, written on the student's reading level.

7. Reduce distracting stimuli in order to increase the student's ability to concentrate on what he/she is reading (e.g., place the student in the front row, provide a carrel or "office" space away from distractions, etc.). This is used as a means of reducing distracting stimuli and not as a form of punishment.

8. Provide the student a quiet place (e.g., carrel, study booth, etc.) where he/she may go to engage in reading activities.

9. Have the student verbally paraphrase material he/she has just read in order to assess his/her comprehension.

10. Teach the student to identify main points in material he/she has read in order to assess his/her comprehension.

11. Have the student outline, underline, or highlight important points in reading material.

12. Have the student tape record what he/she reads in order to enhance comprehension by listening to the material read.

13. Have the student take notes while he/she is reading in order to increase comprehension.

14. Have the student read progressively longer segments of reading material in order to build comprehension skills (e.g., begin with a single paragraph and progress to several paragraphs, short stories, chapters, etc.).

15. Teach the student to use context clues to identify words and phrases he/she does not know.

16. Write paragraphs and short stories requiring reading skills the student is currently developing. These passages should be of high interest to the student using his/her name, family members, friends, pets, and interesting experiences.

17. Have the student read high-interest signs, advertisements, notices, etc., from newspapers, magazines, movie promotions, etc., placing emphasis on comprehension skills.

18. Make certain the student is practicing comprehension skills which are directly related to high-interest reading activities (e.g., adventures, romance, mystery, athletics, etc.).

19. Underline or highlight important points before the student reads the assigned material silently.

20. Write notes and letters to the student to provide reading material which he/she will want to read for comprehension. Students may be encouraged to write each other notes and letters at a time set aside each day, once a week, etc.

21. Give the student time to read a selection more than once, emphasizing comprehension not speed.

22. Use a sight word vocabulary approach in order to teach the student key words and phrases when reading directions and instructions (e.g., key words such as *circle, underline, match*, etc.).

23. Teach the student to think about the reading selection and predict what will happen next, prior to completing the selection.

24. Teach the student to look for key words (e.g., *Christopher Columbus, Spain, New World,* etc.).

25. Teach the student to look for action words (e.g., *sailed, discovered, founded,* etc.).

26. Teach the student to look for direction words (e.g., *circle, underline, choose, list,* etc.).

27. Teach the student when reading to look for key words and main ideas that answer "Who, What, Where, When, How, and Why" (e.g., "Christopher Columbus sailed from Spain to discover the New World during the year 1492.").

28. Make available for the student a learning center where a variety of information is available in content areas (e.g., the library may have a selection of films, slides, videotapes, taped lectures, etc.).

29. Have the student practice reading and following written directions in order to enhance comprehension (e.g., following a recipe, following directions to put together a model, etc.).

30. Have the student practice comprehension skills which are directly related to high-interest reading activities (e.g., adventures, romance, mystery, sports, etc.).

31. Teach the student meanings of abbreviations in order to assist in comprehending material read. (See Appendix for Selected Abbreviations and Symbols.)

32. Have the student outline reading material using the Outline Form. (See Appendix.)

33. Have the student read independently each day to practice reading skills.

34. Give the student high-interest reading material requiring him/her to answer the questions "Who, What, Where, When, How and Why" (e.g, comic books, adventure stories, etc.).

35. Teach new vocabulary words prior to having the student read the material.

36. Pair the student with a peer to summarize material read in order to answer the questions "Who, What, Where, When, How and Why."

37. Have the student answer in writing the questions "Who, What, Where, When, How and Why" using the Flash Card Study Aid. (See Appendix.)

38. When reading orally with the student, pause at various points to discuss material read up to that point. Have the student predict what will happen next before proceeding.

39. After reading a selection, have the student complete a semantic map answering the questions "Who, What, Where, When, How, and Why." (See Appendix for Mapping Form.)

40. Prior to reading a selection, familiarize the student with the general content of the story (e.g., if the selection is about elephants, brainstorm and discuss elephants to develop a point of reference).

1. Make certain the student's hearing has recently been checked.

2. Make certain the student is reading material on his/her level. If not, modify or adjust reading material to the student's ability level.

3. Reinforce the student for demonstrating comprehension of reading material: (a) give the student a tangible reward (e.g., classroom privileges, line leading, passing out materials, five minutes free time, etc.) or (b) give the student an intangible reward (e.g., praise, handshake, smile, etc.).

4. Reduce distracting stimuli in order to increase the student's ability to concentrate on what he/she is reading (e.g., place the student on the front row, provide a carrel or "office" space away from distractions, etc.). This should be used as a means of reducing distracting stimuli and not as a form of punishment.

5. Teach the student to use context clues to identify the meanings of words and phrases not known.

6. Prerecord the student's reading material and have him/her listen to the recording while simultaneously reading the material.

7. Have the student read ahead on a subject to be discussed in class so that he/she is familiar with new vocabulary and concepts that will be used during instructional periods.

8. Outline reading material for the student using words and phrases on his/her ability level.

9. Arrange for a peer who demonstrates good comprehension skills to read with the student and help him/her with the meanings of words not understood.

10. Maintain mobility in the classroom in order to frequently be near the student to provide reading assistance.

11. Teach the student to draw from personal learning experiences to enhance comprehension of reading material. Provide a variety of learning experiences at school in order to expand the student's background of knowledge.

12. Have the student verbally paraphrase material just read in order to assess his/her comprehension.

13. Teach the student to identify main points in material in order to enhance his/her comprehension.

14. Underline or highlight important points before the student reads the material silently.

15. Have the student outline, underline, or highlight important points in reading material.

16. Have the student take notes while reading in order to increase comprehension.

17. Provide the student with written direction-following activities that target concrete experiences (e.g., following a recipe, following directions to put a model together, etc.) in order to enhance comprehension.

18. Provide the student with written one-, two-, and three-step direction-following activities (e.g., sharpen your pencil, open your text to page 121, etc.).

19. Have the student read progressively longer segments of reading material in order to build comprehension skills (e.g., begin with a single paragraph and progress to several paragraphs, chapters, short stories, etc.).

20. Have the student read high-interest signs, advertisements, notices, etc., from newspapers, magazines, movie promotions, etc., placing an emphasis on comprehension skills.

21. Reduce the emphasis on competition. Competitive activities may make it difficult for the student to comprehend what he/she reads.

22. Use a sight word vocabulary approach in order to teach the student key words and phrases when reading directions and instructions (e.g., key words such as *circle, underline, match,* etc.).

23. Have the student list new or difficult words in categories such as *people, food, animals, things that are hot,* etc.

24. Have the student maintain a vocabulary notebook with definitions of words whose meanings are not known.

25. When the student encounters a new word or one whose meaning is not understood, have the student practice making up sentences in which the word can be used in the correct context.

26. Make certain the student learns dictionary skills in order to find the meanings of words independently.

27. Have the student identify words he/she does not comprehend. Finding the definitions of these words can then become the dictionary assignment.

28. Have the student identify one word each day that is not understood and require him/her to use that word throughout the day in various situations.

29. Have the student match vocabulary words with pictures representing the words.

30. Introduce new words and their meanings to the student before reading new material.

31. Make certain the student learns the meanings of all commonly used prefixes and suffixes.

32. Write notes and letters to the student to provide reading material which he/she will want to read for comprehension. Students may be encouraged to write notes and letters to classmates at a time set aside each day, once a week, etc.

33. Give the student time to read a selection more than once, emphasizing accuracy not speed.

34. Have the student supply missing words in sentences provided by classmates and/or the teacher in order to enhance comprehension skills.

35. Cut out pictures from magazines and newspapers and have the student match captions to them. This activity could be varied by having one student write the caption while another student determines if it is appropriate.

36. Have the student read a short paragraph which contains one or more errors which make comprehension difficult. See if the student recognizes the errors. If not, encourage the student to stop frequently while reading to ask himself/herself, "Does this make sense?"

37. Determine whether or not the student can make inferences, make predictions, determine cause-effect, etc., in everyday experiences. Teach these skills in contexts that are meaningful to the student in order to enhance the ability to employ these concepts when reading.

38. Have the student read a story. Provide statements reflecting the main points of the story out of sequence. Have the student arrange the statements in the correct order to demonstrate comprehension.

39. Have the student prepare "test" questions based on information that has been read in order to enhance the ability to focus on key elements of the reading material.

40. Frequently give assignments on topics which are of interest to the student in order to reinforce the correlation between writing and reading ability.

41. Reduce the amount of material the student reads at one time (e.g., reduce reading material to single sentences on a page, a single paragraph, etc.). Gradually increase the amount of material as the student experiences success.

42. Avoid subjecting the student to uncomfortable reading situations (e.g., reading aloud in a group, reading with time limits, etc.).

43. Stop the student at various points throughout a reading selection to check for comprehension.

44. Reduce the amount of information on a page if it is causing visual distractions for the student (e.g., less print to read, fewer pictures, etc.).

45. Highlight or underline important information the student should pay close attention to when reading.

46. Make it pleasant and positive for the student to ask questions about things not understood.

47. Have the student use a highlighter pen to highlight the facts requested by the teacher.

48. Allow the student to work with a peer and teacher. The first student will dictate a short paragraph to be typed by the teacher and will also compose a comprehension question. The second student, after listening to the process, will read the story orally and point out the answer. Then student roles can be reversed.

49. Find the central word or phrase around which the story is constructed. Check for pinpoint words that relate back to the central word/phrase and determine the number of times they are used and how this helps to develop the story.

1. Make certain the student is reading material on his/her ability level.

2. Modify or adjust reading materials to the student's ability level.

3. Set up a system of motivators, either tangible (e.g., extra computer time, helper for the day, etc.) or intangible (e.g., smile, handshake, praise, etc.) to encourage the student to be more successful in reading.

4. Tape record reading material for the student to listen to as he/she reads along.

5. Provide the student with a quiet place (e.g., carrel, study booth, "office," etc.) where he/she may go to engage in reading activities.

6. Write paragraphs and short stories for the student. These passages should be of high interest to the student using his/her name, family members, friends, pets, and interesting experiences.

7. Have the student dictate stories which are then written for him/her to read.

8. Have the student read high-interest signs, advertisements, notices, etc., from newspapers, magazines, movie promotions, etc.

9. Provide the student with many high-interest reading materials (e.g., comic books, magazines relating to sports or fashion, etc.).

10. Conduct a survey of the student's interests in order to provide reading material in that area.

11. Read, or have someone read, high-interest material to the student in order to promote his/her interest in reading.

12. Develop a library in the classroom that is appealing to the student (e.g., tent, bean bag chair, carpeted area, etc.).

13. Make reading materials easily accessible to the student in the classroom.

14. Provide the student with high-interest reading material that is also short in length in order that the student can finish reading the material without difficulty.

15. Encourage interest in reading by having students share interesting things they have read. This should be informal sharing in a group and not necessarily a "book report."

16. Have the student write to the author of material he/she reads in order to encourage an interest in reading more by the same author.

17. Encourage the student to read material with many illustrations and a limited amount of print. Gradually decrease the number of pictures.

18. Encourage parents to make reading material available to the student at home and to ensure that it is on the student's interest and reading level.

19. Encourage parents to read to their child at home and to have their child read to them. Encourage parents to read for their own enjoyment to serve as a model for their child.

20. Have the student read lower grade-level stories to younger children in order to enhance his/her feelings of confidence relative to reading.

21. Include predictable reading books in the class library. Predictability can make books more appealing to beginning readers and build confidence as well.

22. Avoid subjecting the student to uncomfortable reading situations (e.g., reading aloud in a group, identifying that the student's reading group is the lowest level, etc.).

23. Write periodic letters or notes to the student and encourage him/her to write back.

24. Set aside a fixed or random time (e.g., a half-hour daily, an hour a week, etc.) for a "Read-In." Everyone, teacher included, chooses a book that he/she likes and reads it for pleasure.

25. Expose the student to materials with large print. Large print can appear less intimidating to the student who does not choose to read.

26. Provide assistance in helping the student find reading material according to his/her interests and reading level. The student may not be comfortable or able to find books by himself/herself in the library.

27. Offer memberships in paperback book clubs to the student.

28. To encourage reading, make certain that the student knows he/she is not reading for assessment purposes but for enjoyment.

29. Make visiting the library an enjoyable weekly experience.

30. Encourage interesting reading by highlighting an author a month. The teacher should share information about an author, read books by the author and have additional titles by the author available for independent reading.

31. Pair the class with a lower grade-level class on a weekly basis in order for each student to read to a younger child.

32. Find a book series by an author that the student finds enjoyable. Make these books available for the student to read.

33. Read excerpts of your favorite children's books to entice the student to read the same book.

34. While teaching a unit in a content area, bring in related fiction or nonfiction books to share with your students to spark interest in reading.

1. Make certain the student is reading material on his/her level.

2. Set up a system of reinforcers, either tangible (e.g., extra computer time, helper for the day, etc.) or intangible (e.g., smile, handshake, praise, etc.) to encourage the student to be more successful in reading.

3. Modify or adjust reading materials to the student's ability level.

4. Outline reading material for the student using words and phrases on his/her reading level.

5. Use a sight word vocabulary approach to teach the student key words and phrases when reading directions and instructions (e.g., key words such as *circle, underline, match,* etc.).

6. Use a lower grade-level text as alternative reading material in subject areas.

7. Make a list of main points from the student's reading material, written on the student's reading level.

8. Reduce distracting stimuli in order to increase the student's ability to concentrate on what he/she is reading (e.g., place the student on the front row, provide a carrel or "office" space away from distractions). This is used as a means of reducing distracting stimuli and not as a form of punishment.

9. Provide the student with a quiet place (e.g., carrel, study booth, etc.) where he/she may go to engage in reading activities.

10. Have the student verbally paraphrase material that has just been read in order to assess comprehension.

11. Have the student outline, underline, or highlight important points in reading material.

12. Have the student read high-interest signs, advertisements, notices, etc., from newspapers, magazines, movie promotions, etc., placing an emphasis on comprehension skills.

13. Have the student tape record what he/she reads in order to enhance comprehension by listening to the recording.

14. Write paragraphs and short stories requiring skills the student is currently developing. These paragraphs should be of high interest to the student using his/her name, family members, friends, pets, and interesting experiences.

15. Have the student dictate stories which are then written for him/her to read, placing an emphasis on comprehension skills.

16. Reduce the emphasis on competition. Competitive activities may make it difficult for the student to comprehend what he/she reads.

17. Have the student list new or difficult words in categories such as people, food, animals, etc.

18. Have the student match objects or pictures with sounds produced by that object (e.g., telephone, vacuum cleaner, etc.).

19. Have the student maintain a vocabulary notebook with definitions of words whose meanings he/she does not know.

20. When the student encounters a new word or one whose meaning is not known, have the student practice making up sentences in which the word can be used in the correct context.

21. Have the student identify a word each day which he/she does not understand, and require the student to use that word throughout the day in various situations.

22. Have the student identify words he/she does not comprehend. Finding the definitions of these words can then become the student's dictionary assignment.

23. Have the student match vocabulary words with pictures representing the words.

24. Make certain the student learns dictionary skills in order to be able to independently find meanings of words.

25. Have the student develop a picture dictionary of pictures representing those words which are difficult for him/her to recognize.

26. Introduce new words and their meanings to the student before he/she reads new material.

27. Make certain the student learns the meanings of all commonly used prefixes and suffixes.

28. Identify a peer the student can rely upon to help with the meanings of words not understood.

29. Provide the student with a variety of visual teaching materials to support word comprehension (e.g., filmstrips, pictures, charts, etc.).

30. Teach the student to use context clues to identify words not understood.

31. Label objects and activities in the classroom to help the student associate words with tangible aspects of the environment.

32. Have the student make a list of new words that have been learned. The student can add words to the list at his/her own pace.

33. Teach the student to read for the main point in sentences, paragraphs, etc.

34. Reinforce the student for asking the meanings of words not understood.

35. Reinforce the student for looking up the definitions of words not understood.

36. Make it pleasant and positive for the student to ask the meanings or look up words not understood. Reinforce the student by assisting, congratulating, praising, etc.

37. Make certain the student is developing a sight word vocabulary of the most commonly used words in his/her reading material.

38. Make certain the student underlines or circles words not understood. These words will become the student's vocabulary assignment for the week.

39. Before reading, tell the student what he/she should find in the story (e.g., who are the main characters, what are the main events, etc.).

40. Make certain the student is not required to learn more information than he/she is capable of at any one time.

41. Give the student time to read a selection more than once, emphasizing comprehension rather than speed.

42. Use reading series material with high interest (e.g., adventures, romances, mysteries, athletics, etc.) and low vocabulary.

43. Write notes and letters to the student to provide reading material which he/she would want to read for comprehension. Students may be encouraged to write each other notes and letters at a time set aside each day, week, etc.

44. Make certain that the reading demands of all subjects and assignments are within the ability level of the student. If not, modify or adjust the reading material to the student's ability level.

45. Make certain that the student's knowledge of a particular skill is being assessed rather than the student's ability to read directions, instructions, etc. Reading directions, instructions, etc., to the student can increase success.

46. Reduce the amount of information on a page if it is causing visual distractions for the student (e.g., less print to read, fewer pictures, etc.).

47. Avoid subjecting the student to uncomfortable reading situations (e.g., reading aloud in a group, identifying that the student's reading group is the lowest level, etc.).

48. Anticipate new vocabulary words and teach them in advance of reading a selection.

49. Prepare a written list of vocabulary words. Orally present a sentence with a "blank" and have students determine which vocabulary word should be used.

50. In daily classroom conversation, make certain to use the current vocabulary word being studied by the student.

116　Has difficulty applying decoding skills when reading

1. Teach the student a root word sight vocabulary in order to be able to add various prefixes and suffixes to develop word attack skills.

2. Obtain a list of words and phrases from the student's reading material which he/she does not recognize. Have the student practice phonics skills, context clues, structural analysis, etc., using these words.

3. Use a peer tutor to review word attack skills by utilizing games and activities.

4. Write paragraphs and short stories requiring decoding skills the student is currently learning. These passages should be of high interest to the student using his/her name, family members, friends, pets and interesting activities.

5. Have the student dictate stories which are then written for him/her to read, placing an emphasis on decoding skills.

6. Encourage the student to scan newspapers, magazines, etc., and underline words he/she can identify using decoding skills.

7. Teach the student the most common prefixes and suffixes to add to root words he/she can identify.

8. Teach the student to use context clues to identify words and phrases he/she does not know.

9. Develop a list of phonics sounds the student needs to master. Remove sounds from the list as the student demonstrates mastery of phonics skills.

10. Reinforce the student for using decoding skills when attempting to decode a word.

11. Have the student read high-interest signs, advertisements, notices, etc., from newspapers, magazines, movie promotions, etc., placing an emphasis on decoding skills.

12. Make certain the student develops an awareness of seeing letter combinations that stand for a sound, prefix or suffix (e.g., have the student highlight all words in a reading passage that contain the suffix *-ed*).

13. Encourage the student to look for known sight words within a word to be decoded (e.g., for the word *interesting*, have the student identify the sight word *interest* to help decode the word).

14. Teach the student to be aware of word sounds and parts (e.g., read words with the /bl/ sound: blue, black, block, etc.).

15. Provide practice in reading a targeted group of words (e.g., words ending with *-ing*, etc.) by presenting a high-interest paragraph or story that contains these words.

16. Demonstrate skills in decoding words by modeling decoding words on the chalkboard or overhead (e.g., for the word *unassuming*, model decoding the word parts: *un-, -ing*, plus the root, to correctly read the word).

17. Encourage the student to try several sounds in order to arrive at the correct answer.

18. Have the student make a list of phonics skills he/she has mastered. The student continues to add to the list as he/she masters more and more skills.

19. Have the student identify syllables as he/she reads them in order to help him/her recognize word parts.

20. Encourage the student to learn additional basic sight words to assist him/her in reading.

21. Reduce the emphasis on competition. Competitive activities may cause the student to rush and not apply decoding skills accurately.

22. Provide the student with a list of common prefixes and suffixes to be posted on his/her desk to use as a reference when decoding words.

1. Set up a system of reinforcers which are either tangible (e.g., computer time, helper for the day, etc.) or intangible (e.g., smile, praise, handshake, etc.) to encourage the student to be more successful in reading.

2. Create a list of words and phrases from the student's reading material which he/she does not recognize (e.g., have the science teacher identify the words the student would not recognize in the following week's assignment). These words and phrases will become the student's reading word list for the following week.

3. Have the student identify words and phrases that he/she does not recognize. Make these words the student's list of words to be learned.

4. Modify or adjust reading materials to the student's ability level.

5. Outline reading material for the student using words and phrases on his/her reading level.

6. Teach the student to use context clues to identify words and phrases he/she does not know.

7. Emphasize that the student learn a root word sight vocabulary in order to be able to add various prefixes and suffixes to develop word attack skills.

8. Tape record difficult reading material for the student to listen to as he/she reads along.

9. Use a highlight marker to identify key words and phrases for the student. These words and phrases become the student's sight word vocabulary.

10. Teach the student to use related learning experiences in his/her classes (e.g., filmstrips, movies, tape recordings, demonstrations, discussions, videotapes, lectures, etc.). Encourage teachers to provide a variety of learning experiences for the student.

11. Arrange for a peer tutor to study with the student for quizzes, tests, etc.

12. Use a sight word vocabulary approach in order to teach the student key words and phrases when reading directions and instructions (e.g., key words such as *circle, underline, match,* etc.).

13. Maintain mobility in order to be frequently near the student to provide reading assistance.

14. Use lower grade-level texts as alternative reading materials in subject areas.

15. Have lectures tape recorded in order to provide an additional source of information for the student.

16. Make a list of main points from the student's reading material, written on the student's reading level.

17. Make available for the student a learning center area where a variety of information is available in content areas (e.g., the library may have a section with films, slides, videotapes, taped lectures, etc., on such subjects as Pilgrims, the Civil War, the judicial system, etc.).

18. Encourage classroom teachers to include more alternative learning experiences in their classrooms (e.g., lectures, demonstrations, guest speakers, field trips, discussions, films, filmstrips, slides, videotapes, etc.).

19. Write paragraphs and short stories requiring skills the student is currently developing. These passages should be of high interest to the student using his/her name, family members, friends, pets, and interesting experiences.

20. Have the student dictate stories which are then written for him/her to read, placing an emphasis on reading skills.

21. Have the student read high-interest signs, advertisements, notices, etc., from newspapers, movie promotions, magazines, etc., placing an emphasis on reading skills.

22. Use reading series material with high interest (e.g., adventures, romances, mysteries, athletics, etc.) and low vocabulary.

23. Make certain the student is practicing reading skills which are directly related to high-interest reading activities (e.g., adventures, romances, mysteries, athletics, etc.).

24. When the student has difficulty with reading words on grade level, remind him/her that this can happen to everyone and not to be upset. Everyone has areas where they are weak and areas of strength as well, and it is important to keep trying.

25. Make certain that the reading demands of all subjects and assignments are within the ability level of the student. If not, modify or adjust the reading material to the student's ability level. A lower grade-level text may be an alternative.

26. Make certain that the student's knowledge of a particular skill is being assessed rather than the student's ability to read directions, instructions, etc. Reading directions to the student can increase success.

27. Have the student read aloud to the teacher each day in order to provide evaluative feedback.

28. Teach the student individual consonant and vowel sounds.

29. Reduce the amount of material the student reads at one time (e.g., reduce reading material to single sentences on a page, a single paragraph, etc.). Gradually increase the amount of material as the student experiences success.

30. Provide the student with increased opportunities for help or assistance on academic tasks (e.g., peer tutoring, directions for work sent home, frequent interactions, etc.).

31. Allow students to use the chalkboard so that teaching and learning become active. The student hears, writes, and sees the sounds in isolation.

32. Have the student practice vocabulary words from required reading material by writing them while saying the sounds.

33. Start with simple words and sounds where the student achieves 95%-100% accuracy. Do not move on to more difficult words until practice, drill, and review of preceding lessons produces accuracy.

34. Use D'Nealian handwriting when teaching sounds by hearing, writing, and saying. This eliminates many potential reversal problems.

118　Does not summarize/retell important concepts after reading a selection

1. Teach the student to recognize main points, important facts, etc., by answering "Who, What, Where, When, How, and Why." (See Appendix for the Outline Form.)

2. Make certain the student is reading material on his/her level.

3. Modify or adjust reading material to the student's ability level.

4. Read shorter selections with the student, discussing the story in a one-on-one situation. Gradually increase the length of selections as the student demonstrates success.

5. Tape record reading material for the student to listen to as he/she reads along. Have the student stop at various points to retell/summarize the selection.

6. After reading a short story, have the student identify the main characters, sequence the events, and report the outcome of the story.

7. Relate the information being read to the student's previous experiences.

8. Assess the meaningfulness of the material being read to the student. Comprehension is more likely to occur when the material is meaningful and the student can relate to real experiences.

9. Have the student verbally paraphrase material he/she has read in order to assess his/her comprehension.

10. Prior to reading a selection, prepare an outline for the student to refer to and add details to while reading the selection.

11. Make a list of main points from the student's reading material. Have the student discuss each main point after reading the selection.

12. Teach the student to identify main points in material he/she has read in order to assess his/her comprehension.

13. Have the student outline, underline or highlight important points in reading material.

14. Have the student take notes while he/she is reading in order to increase comprehension.

15. Underline or highlight important points **before** the student reads the selection.

16. Give the student sufficient time to read a selection, emphasizing comprehension not speed.

17. Teach the student to think about the selection and predict what will happen next, prior to completing the selection.

18. Teach the student to look for key concepts when reading a selection.

19. Teach the student when reading a selection to look for key words and main ideas that answer "Who, What, Where, When, How, and Why."

20. Have the student read independently each day to practice reading skills.

21. Teach new vocabulary words prior to having the student read the material.

22. Have the student answer in writing the questions "Who, What, Where, When, How, and Why" using a Flash Card Study Aid. (See Appendix.)

23. After reading a selection, have the student complete a semantic map answering the questions "Who, What, Where, When, How, and Why." (See Appendix for Mapping Form.)

24. Arrange for a peer tutor to read with the student to develop comprehension skills.

25. Prior to reading a selection, familiarize the student with the general context of the story. (e.g., if the selection is about elephants, brainstorm and discuss elephants to develop a point of reference).

26. When reading orally with the student, pause at various points to discuss material read up to that point. Have the student predict what will happen next before proceeding.

27. Have the student complete a Fiction Frame after reading a selection. (See Appendix.)

28. Require the student to read a selection more than once, emphasizing comprehension rather than speed.

29. Teach the student to look for story elements when reading a selection (e.g., setting, characters, plot, ending). (See Appendix for Fiction Frame.)

119 Reads words correctly in one context but not in another

1. Make certain the student is reading material on his/her level.

2. Highlight or underline those words the student most frequently fails to recognize in different contexts.

3. Use a lower grade-level text as alternative reading material in subject areas.

4. Write paragraphs and short stories using those words the student most frequently fails to recognize in different contexts. These paragraphs should be of high interest to the student using his/her name, family members, friends, pets, and interesting experiences.

5. Make a reading "window" for the student. The student moves the reading "window" across and down the page as he/she reads.

6. Have the student list those words he/she most frequently fails to recognize into categories such as people, food, animals, etc., in order to help the student recognize those words in different contexts.

7. Teach the student to use context clues to identify words he/she does not understand.

8. Identify words the student does not recognize in different contexts and put these words on flash cards. Have the student match these words to the same words in sentences, paragraphs, short stories, etc.

9. Have the student print/write those words he/she most frequently fails to recognize in different contexts.

10. Have the student maintain a list with definitions of those words he/she most frequently fails to recognize in different contexts.

11. Highlight or underline those words in reading material the student is unable to recognize. Have the student identify those words as he/she reads them.

12. Reduce distracting stimuli in order to increase the student's ability to concentrate on what he/she is reading (e.g., place the student on the front row, provide a carrel or "office" space away from distractions). This is used as a means of reducing distracting stimuli and not as a form of punishment.

13. Provide the student with a quiet place (e.g., carrel, study booth, etc.) where he/she may go to engage in reading activities.

14. Reduce the emphasis on competition. Competitive activities may cause the student to hurry and fail to recognize words in a particular context.

15. Provide the student with a dictionary and require him/her to find the definitions of those words he/she does not recognize.

16. Have the student read short sentences in order to make it easier to recognize words in different contexts. Longer sentences are presented as the student demonstrates success.

17. Provide the student with large print reading material in order to increase the likelihood of the student recognizing words in different contexts.

18. Use daily drill activities to help the student memorize vocabulary words.

19. Tape record difficult reading material for the student to listen to as he/she reads along.

20. Write notes and letters to the student to provide reading material which includes words the student frequently has difficulty with.

21. Have the student read aloud to the teacher each day in order to provide evaluative feedback.

22. Reduce the amount of information on a page if it is causing visual distractions for the student (e.g., less print to read, fewer pictures to look at, etc.)

23. Avoid subjecting the student to uncomfortable reading situations (e.g., reading aloud in a group, identifying that the student's reading group is the lowest level, etc.).

24. Require the student to read a selection each day which includes the vocabulary currently being studied.

120   Uses inappropriate spacing between words or sentences when writing

1. Make certain the student's vision has been recently checked.

2. Have the student sit in an appropriate sized chair with feet touching the floor, his/her back pressed against the back of the chair, shoulders slightly inclined, arms resting on the desk, and elbows just off the lower edge of the desk.

3. Check the student's paper position. A right-handed person writing in cursive should tilt the paper to the left so the lower left-hand corner points toward the midsection and as writing progresses, the paper should shift, not the writing arm.

4. Place dots between letters and have the student use fingers as a spacer between words.

5. Make certain the student is shifting his/her paper when writing.

6. Using appropriate spacing, print or write words or sentences. Have the student trace what was written.

7. Reduce the emphasis on competition. Competitive activities may cause the student to hurry and fail to use correct spacing when writing words and sentences.

8. Provide the student with samples of handwritten words and sentences he/she can use as a reference for correct spacing.

9. Have the student leave a finger space between each word he/she writes.

10. Draw vertical lines for the student to use to space letters and words, (e.g.,| | | |).

11. Teach the student to always look at the next word to determine if there is enough space before the margin.

12. Provide the student with graph paper, instructing him/her to write letters in each block, while skipping a block between words and sentences.

13. Recognize quality work (e.g., display student's work, congratulate the student, etc.).

14. Provide the student with quality materials to perform the assignment (e.g., pencil with eraser, paper, dictionary, handwriting sample, etc.). Be certain that the student has only these necessary materials on the desk.

15. Check the student's work at various points throughout an assignment to make certain the student is using appropriate spacing.

16. Give the student one handwriting task to perform at a time. Introduce the next task only when the student has successfully completed the previous task.

17. Assign the student shorter tasks and gradually increase the number over time as the student demonstrates success.

18. Have the student practice writing letters, words, and sentences by tracing over a series of dots.

19. Use vertical lines or graph paper to help the student space letters correctly.

20. Have the student engage in writing activities designed to cause the student to want to be successful in writing (e.g., writing a letter to a friend, rock star, famous athlete, etc.).

21. Have the student look at correctly written material to serve as a model.

22. Have the student perform a "practice page" before turning in the actual assignment.

23. Reinforce the student for each word and/or sentence that is appropriately spaced: (a) give the student a tangible reward (e.g., classroom privileges, line leading, five minutes free time, etc.) or (b) give the student an intangible reward (e.g., praise, handshake, smile, etc.).

1. Make certain the student's vision has been checked recently.

2. Use board activities (e.g., drawing lines, circles, etc.) to teach the student proper directionality for each letter or numeral.

3. Physically guide the student's hand, providing the feeling of directionality.

4. Place letters on transparencies and project them on the chalkboard or paper. Have the student trace the letters.

5. Have the student trace letters and numbers in magazines, newspapers, etc., which he/she typically reverses when writing.

6. When correcting papers with reversed letters, use direction arrows to remind the student of correct directionality.

7. Identify the letters and numbers the student reverses and have him/her practice making one or more of the letters correctly each day.

8. Make certain the student recognizes the correct form of the letters and numbers when he/she sees them (e.g., *b, d, 2, 5*, etc.).

9. Make certain the student checks all work for those letters and numbers he/she typically reverses. Reinforce the student for correcting any reversed letters and numbers.

10. Provide the student with visual cues to aid in making letters and numbers (e.g., arrows indicating strokes).

11. Provide the student with large letters and numbers to trace which he/she typically reverses.

12. Given letters and numbers on separate cards, have the student match the letters and numbers that are the same.

13. Have the student keep a card with the word *bed* at his/her desk to help remember the correct form of *b* and *d* in a word he/she knows.

14. Have the student keep a list of the most commonly used words which contain letters he/she reverses. This list can be used as a reference when the student is writing.

15. After identifying those letters and numbers the student reverses, have him/her highlight or underline those letters and numbers found in a magazine, newspaper, etc.

16. Point out the subtle differences between letters and numbers that the student reverses. Have the student scan five typewritten lines containing only the letters or numbers that are confusing (e.g., nnhnhhnn). Have the student circle the "n's" and the "h's" with different colors.

17. Cursive handwriting may prevent reversals and may be used by some students as an alternative to manuscript.

18. Make certain the student has a number line and alphabet strip on his/her desk to use as a reference to make the correct forms of letters and numbers.

19. Reduce the emphasis on competition. Competitive activities may cause the student to hurry and reverse numbers and letters when writing.

20. Recognize quality work (e.g., display the student's work, congratulate the student, etc.).

21. Have the student practice writing letters, words, and sentences by tracing over a series of dots.

22. Require the student to proofread all written work. Reinforce the student for each correction made.

23. Have the student engage in writing activities designed to cause the student to want to be successful in writing (e.g., writing a letter to a friend, rock star, famous athlete, etc.).

24. Make certain that the student's formation of letters is appropriate and consistently correct. In manuscript writing, all strokes progressing from top to bottom, left to right, use a forward circle (e.g., circling to the right) for letters that begin with a line (e.g., *b*), and the backward circle (e.g., circling to the left) for letters in which the circle is written before the line (e.g., *d*).

25. Reinforce the student for making letters and numbers correctly when writing: (a) give the student a tangible reward (e.g., classroom privileges, line leading, passing out materials, five minutes free time, etc.) or (b) give the student an intangible reward (e.g., smile, handshake, praise, etc.).

1. Make certain the student's vision has been checked recently.

2. Evaluate the appropriateness of the task to determine: (a) if the task is too difficult and (b) if the length of time scheduled to complete the task is appropriate.

3. Check the student's paper position. A right-handed person writing in cursive should tilt the paper to the left so the lower left-hand corner points toward the midsection and as writing progresses, the paper should shift, not the writing arm.

4. Check the student's pencil grasp. The pencil should be held between the thumb and first two fingers, holding the instrument one inch from its tip.

5. Make certain the student is shifting his/her paper as writing progresses.

6. Draw a margin on the right side of the student's paper as a reminder for him/her to write within a given space.

7. Place a ruler or construction paper on the baseline, making certain the student touches the line for each letter.

8. Use a ruled paper with a midline, explaining to the student that minimum letters (a, b, c, d, e, f, g, h, etc.) touch the midline.

9. Highlight lines on the paper for the student to use as a prompt.

10. Reinforce the student for each word or letter correctly spaced.

11. Have the student look at correctly written material to serve as a model for him/her to imitate.

12. Darken the lines on the paper in order that the student can more easily use them to write within the given space.

13. Allow the student to draw his/her own lines on paper for writing activities.

14. Allow the student to use a ruler as a guide or "bottom line."

15. Provide the student with a physical prompt by guiding his/her hand as he/she writes.

16. Have the student correct his/her own writing errors.

17. Have the student perform a "practice page" before turning in the actual assignment.

18. Have the student practice writing letters, words, and sentences by tracing over a series of dots.

19. Provide the student with extra large sheets of paper on which to write. Gradually reduce the size of the paper to standard size as the student demonstrates success.

20. Recognize quality work (e.g., display student's work, congratulate the student, etc.).

21. Provide the student with quality materials to perform the assignment (e.g., pencil with eraser, paper, dictionary, handwriting sample, etc.). Be certain that the student has only the necessary materials on the desk.

22. Check the student's work at various points throughout the assignment in order to make certain that the student is writing within a given space.

23. Give the student one handwriting task to perform at a time. Introduce the next task only when the student has successfully completed the previous task.

24. Assign the student shorter writing assignments and gradually increase the number over time as the student demonstrates success.

25. Use vertical lines or graph paper to help the student space letters correctly.

26. Have the student engage in writing activities designed to cause the student to want to be successful in writing (e.g., writing a letter to a friend, rock star, famous athlete, etc.).

27. Make a border so the student knows when he/she has written to the edge of the writing space.

123 Fails to form letters correctly when printing or writing

1. Make certain the student is instructed in each letter formation, giving the student oral as well as physical descriptions and demonstrations.

2. Provide the student with physical prompts by moving the student's hand, giving him/her a feeling of directionality.

3. Have the student practice tracing letters at his/her desk.

4. Have the student practice tracing letters on the chalkboard.

5. Use arrows to show the student directionality when tracing or using dot-to-dot to form letters.

6. Use color cues for lines (e.g., red for the top line, yellow for the middle line, green for the bottom line) to indicate where letters are to be made.

7. Draw simple shapes and lines for the student to practice forming on lined paper.

8. Highlight the base line or top line on the paper in order to help the student stay within the given spaces.

9. Make certain the student sits in an appropriate-sized chair with feet touching the floor, his/her back pressed against the back of the chair, shoulders slightly inclined, arms resting on the desk, and elbows just off the lower edge of the desk.

10. Check the student's writing position. A right-handed person writing in cursive should tilt the paper to the left so the lower left-hand corner points toward the midsection. As writing progresses, the paper should shift, not the writing arm.

11. Check the student's pencil grasp. The pencil should be held between the thumb and the first two fingers, one inch from its tip, with the top pointing toward the right shoulder (if right-handed).

12. Have the student practice tracing with reduced cues. Write the complete letter and have the student trace it. Gradually provide less of the letter for the student to trace (e.g., dashes, then dots) as he/she is successful.

13. Identify those letters the student does not form correctly. Have him/her practice the correct form of one or more of the letters each day.

14. To facilitate appropriate holding of a pencil, put colored tape on parts of the pencil to correspond to finger positions. Then put colored tape on the student's fingernails and have the student match colors.

15. Reduce the emphasis on competition. Competitive activities may cause the student to hurry and fail to form letters correctly.

16. Make certain the student has an alphabet strip attached to his/her desk in either printed or written form to serve as a model for correct letter formations.

17. Have a peer act as a model for the student, working daily on drill activities involving letter formation, ending and connecting strokes, spacing, and slant.

18. Have the student practice forming letters correctly by using writing activities which are most likely to cause the student to want to be successful (e.g., writing a letter to a friend, rock star, famous athlete; filling out a job application, contest form, etc.).

19. Recognize quality work (e.g., display the student's work, congratulate the student, etc.).

20. Provide the student with quality materials to perform the assignment (e.g., pencil with eraser, paper, handwriting sample, etc.). Be certain that the student has only those necessary materials on the desk.

21. Make certain the student is not required to learn more information than the student is capable of at any one time.

22. Make certain the student has mastery of handwriting concepts at each level before introducing a new skill level.

23. Check the student's handwriting work at various points throughout a handwriting activity to make certain that the student is forming letters correctly.

24. Have the student practice forming letters correctly by tracing over a series of dots.

25. Require the student to proofread all written work. Reinforce the student for each correction made.

26. Provide tactile stimulation for the child (e.g., sand, fur, clay, wood, etc.).

27. Use specific manipulatives (strings, toothpicks, etc.) to form letters for visual models.

28. Reinforce the student for making correct letters: (a) give the student a tangible reward (e.g., classroom privileges, line leading, passing out materials, five minutes free time, etc.) or (b) give the student an intangible reward (e.g., praise, handshake, smile, etc.).

124   Fails to use verb tenses correctly when writing

1. Provide the student with examples of verb tenses for those verbs most commonly used incorrectly, and have the student keep the examples for reference.

2. Make a list of those verbs the student most commonly uses incorrectly. This list of verb tenses will become the guide for learning activities using verb tenses.

3. Reinforce the student with praise for using verb tenses correctly when writing.

4. Write a contract with the student specifying what behavior is expected (e.g., using correct verb tenses) and what reinforcement will be made available when the terms of the contract have been met.

5. Identify a peer to act as a model for the student to imitate using correct verb tenses.

6. Make certain the student understands that changes must be made in a verb in order to indicate when an event happened (e.g., past, present, future).

7. Have the student complete written worksheets in which he/she must supply the correct verb tense to go in the sentence (e.g., "Yesterday I ___ to my house.").

8. Have the student pick out the correct verb tense on "fill-in-the-blank" worksheets (e.g., "Tomorrow she ___ (ate, eat, will eat) her supper.").

9. Give the student specific verb tenses and have him/her supply appropriate sentences to go with each (e.g., *played*: "John played at my house last night.").

10. Have the student listen to examples of incorrect verb tenses and then identify each error and correct it.

11. Give the student a series of sentences (both oral and written) and ask him/her to indicate if each is grammatically correct.

12. Have the student make up sentences with given verbs in past, present, and future tenses.

13. Present a series of sentences and ask the student to change the tense from past to present, present to future, etc.

14. Ask the parents to help encourage the student's correct use of verb tenses by praising him/her when grammar is appropriate.

15. Explain the importance of correctly written communication and what would happen if the verb tenses were used incorrectly (e.g., confusion as to when an event took place).

16. Make certain the student proofreads all written work and makes corrections in verb tenses. Reinforce the student for each correction.

17. Allow the student to assist in proofreading or grading other students' papers in order to increase awareness of correct verb tense usage.

18. Encourage the student to read written work aloud in order to find errors in verb tenses.

19. Read a series of sentences to the student and have him/her identify which ones are in the past, present, or future tense.

20. Make certain the student knows or has access to all tenses of most commonly used verbs (e.g., have the student keep a list at his/her desk of the most commonly used verbs with their tenses).

21. Have a peer practice verb tenses with the student. Each tense is used in a sentence rather than only conjugating verbs.

22. Make conjugating of verb tenses a daily activity.

23. Recognize quality work (e.g., display the student's work, congratulate the student, etc.).

24. Make certain the student is not required to learn more information than he/she is capable of at any one time.

25. Provide the student with quality materials to perform the assignment (e.g., pencil with eraser, paper, dictionary, handwriting sample, etc.). Be certain the student has only those necessary materials on his/her desk.

26. Make certain the student has mastery of writing concepts at each level before introducing a new skill level.

27. Give the student a choice of answers on worksheets (e.g., "fill-in-the-blank," etc.). This increases the student's opportunity for recognizing the correct answer.

28. Check the student's work at various points throughout the assignment to make certain the student is using appropriate verb tenses.

29. Have the student engage in writing activities designed to cause him/her to want to be successful in writing (e.g., writing a letter to a friend, rock star, famous athlete, etc.).

30. Reinforce those students in the classroom who use correct verb tenses when writing.

31. Reinforce the student for using appropriate verb tenses when writing: (a) give the student a tangible reward (e.g., classroom privileges, line leading, passing out materials, five minutes free time, etc.) or (b) give the student an intangible reward (e.g., praise, handshake, smile, etc.).

125   Uses inappropriate letter size when writing

1. Check the student's posture. Have the student sit in an appropriately sized chair with feet touching the floor, his/her back pressed against the back of the chair, shoulders slightly inclined, arms resting comfortably on the desk, and elbows just off the edge of the desk.

2. Check the student's paper position. A right-handed person writing in cursive should tilt the paper to the left so the lower left-hand corner points toward the midsection and as writing progresses the paper should shift, not the writing arm.

3. Check the student's pencil grasp. The pencil should be between the thumb and first two fingers, holding the instrument one inch from its tip.

4. Use paper that has a midline and a descender space.

5. Have the student identify maximum (b, d, f, h, k, l, d), intermediate (t), and minimum (a, c, e, g, I, j, m, n, o, p, q, r, s, u, v, w, x, y, z) letters in order to help him/her locate the correct placement of each group.

6. Make certain the student is shifting his/her paper as writing progresses.

7. Evaluate writing alignment by drawing a horizontal line across the tops of the letters that are to be of the same size.

8. Highlight lines on the paper as a reminder for the student to make correct letter size.

9. Have a peer act as a model for the student to imitate making letters the appropriate size when writing.

10. Be certain the student has samples of letters of the appropriate size for activities requiring writing.

11. Provide the student with an alphabet strip at his/her desk with letters of the same size as those to be used.

12. Write letters on the student's paper and have him/her trace them.

13. Write letters on the student's paper in a broken line and have the student connect the lines.

14. Darken the lines on the student's paper which are used for correct letter size.

15. Have the student correct his/her mistakes in letter size.

16. Draw boxes to indicate the size of specific letters in relationship to the lines on the paper.

17. Using examples written on grid paper, have the student copy the examples beneath them.

18. Using tracing paper, have the student trace over specific letters or words.

19. Using a series of dots, have the student trace words or sentences.

20. Using an original story by the student, prepare a transparency to use on an overhead projector. Project the story onto a paper on the wall that the student will trace. This is particularly appropriate for those students who tend to write too small.

21. Provide the student with clearly stated criteria for acceptable work (e.g., neatness, etc.).

22. Recognize quality work (e.g., display the student's work, congratulate the student, etc.).

23. Provide the student with quality materials to perform the assignment (e.g., pencil with eraser, paper, dictionary, handwriting sample, etc.). Be certain that the student has only those necessary materials on the desk.

24. Make certain the student has mastery of handwriting concepts at each level before introducing a new skill level.

25. Check the student's work at various points throughout the assignment to make certain that the student is making letters the appropriate size.

26. Make certain the student has a number line and alphabet strip on the desk to use as a reference for correct form of letters and numbers in order to reduce errors.

27. Use vertical lines or graph paper to help the student space letters correctly.

28. Provide the student with a different size pencil or pencil grip.

29. Evaluate the appropriateness of the task to determine: (a) if the task is too difficult and (b) if the length of time scheduled to complete the task is appropriate.

30. Reinforce the student for using appropriate letter size when writing: (a) give the student a tangible reward (e.g., classroom privileges, line leading, passing out materials, five minutes free time, etc.), or (b) give the student an intangible reward (e.g., praise, handshake, smile, etc.).

31. Make certain the student's vision has been recently checked.

126 Fails to use capitalization correctly when writing

1. Make certain the student knows how to write all the capital letters of the alphabet.

2. Highlight or underline all the capitalized letters in a passage or paragraph, and have the student explain why each is capitalized.

3. Have the student engage in writing activities which will cause him/her to do as well as possible in capitalization and other writing skills (e.g., writing letters to a friend, rock star, famous athlete, etc.).

4. Emphasize one rule of capitalization until the student masters that rule, before moving on to another rule (e.g., proper names, cities, states, streets, etc.).

5. Provide the student with lists of words and have him/her indicate which should be capitalized (e.g., *water, new york, mississippi,* etc.).

6. Have the student practice writing words which are always capitalized (e.g., countries, bodies of water, nationalities, languages, capitals, days of the week, months of the year, etc.).

7. After checking the student's work, require him/her to make all necessary corrections in capitalization.

8. Make certain the student proofreads his/her work for correct capitalization. Reinforce the student for each correction made in capitalization.

9. Give the student a series of sentences representing all the capitalization rules. Have the student identify the rules for each capitalization. Remove each sentence from the assignment when the student can explain the rules for the capitalization in the sentence.

10. Make certain the student has a list of rules for capitalization at his/her desk to use as a reference.

11. Recognize quality work (e.g., display the student's work, congratulate the student, etc.).

12. Provide the student with quality materials to perform the assignment (e.g., pencil with eraser, paper, dictionary, handwriting sample, etc.). Be certain that the student has only the necessary materials on his/her desk.

13. Make certain the student is not required to learn more information than he/she is capable of at any one time.

14. Provide practice in capitalization by using a computer software program that gives the student immediate feedback.

15. Make certain the student has mastery of capitalization at each level before introducing a new skill level.

16. Check the student's work at various points throughout an assignment to make certain the student is capitalizing where needed.

17. Make a notebook of rules for capitalization to be used to proofread work.

18. Display a capitalization rules chart in the front of the classroom.

19. Have the student find proper names, cities, states, etc., on a newspaper page and underline them.

20. Make certain the student receives instruction in the rules of capitalization (e.g., first word of a sentence; the pronoun *I*; proper names; cities; states; streets; months; days of the week; dates; holidays; titles of movies, books, newspapers and magazines; etc.).

21. Write a contract with the student specifying what behavior is expected (e.g., using capitalization correctly) and what reinforcement will be made available when the terms of the contract have been met.

22. Reduce emphasis on competition. Competitive activities may cause the student to hurry and make mistakes in capitalization.

23. Reinforce the student for capitalizing correctly: (a) give the student a tangible reward (e.g., classroom privileges, line leading, five minutes free time, etc.) or (b) give the student an intangible reward (e.g., praise, handshake, smile, etc.).

1. Give the student sentences to complete requiring specific punctuation he/she is learning to use (e.g., periods, commas, question marks, etc.).

2. Have the student practice using one form of punctuation at a time before going on to another (e.g., period, question mark, etc.).

3. Highlight or underline punctuation in passages from the student's reading assignment. Have the student explain why each form of punctuation is used.

4. Require the student to proofread all written work for correct punctuation. Reinforce the student for each correction made on punctuation.

5. Have the student keep a list of basic rules of punctuation at his/her desk to use as a reference when writing (e.g., use a period at the end of a sentence, etc.).

6. Write a contract with the student specifying what behavior is expected (e.g., using punctuation correctly) and what reinforcement will be made available when the terms of the contract have been met.

7. Make certain the student receives instruction in the rules of punctuation (e.g., a period belongs at the end of a sentence, a question mark is used when a question is asked, etc.).

8. Make certain the student knows what all punctuation marks look like and their uses.

9. Have the student engage in writing activities which will cause him/her to do as well as possible on punctuation and other writing skills (e.g., writing letters to a friend, rock star, famous athlete, etc.).

10. After checking the student's work, require him/her to make all necessary corrections in punctuation.

11. Recognize quality work (e.g., display the student's work, congratulate the student, etc.).

12. Give the student a series of sentences representing all the punctuation rules. Have the student identify the rules for each punctuation. Remove a sentence from the assignment when the student can explain the rules for punctuation in the sentence.

13. Provide the student with quality materials to perform the assignment (e.g., pencil with eraser, paper, dictionary, handwriting sample, etc.). Be certain that the student has only the necessary materials on his/her desk.

14. Make certain the student is not required to learn more information than he/she is capable of at any one time.

15. Provide practice in punctuation by using a computer program that gives the student immediate feedback.

16. Make certain the student has mastery of punctuation at each level before introducing a new skill level.

17. Check the student's work at various points throughout an assignment to make certain the student is using appropriate punctuation.

18. Give the student a set of three cards: one with a period, one with a question mark, and one with an exclamation point. As you read a sentence to the student have him/her hold up the appropriate punctuation card.

19. Give the student a list of sentences in which the punctuation has been omitted. Have the student supply the correct punctuation with colored pencils.

20. Make a notebook of punctuation rules to be used when the student proofreads work.

21. Use a newspaper to locate different types of punctuation. Have the student circle periods in red, commas in blue, etc.

22. Display a chart of punctuation rules in the front of the classroom.

23. Reduce the emphasis on competition. Competitive activities may cause the student to hurry and make errors in punctuation.

24. Reinforce the student for using correct punctuation when writing: (a) give the student a tangible reward (e.g., classroom privileges, line leading, five minutes free time, etc.) or (b) give the student an intangible reward (e.g., praise, handshake, smile, etc.).

128 Does not use appropriate subject-verb agreement when writing

1. Require the student to proofread his/her written work for subject-verb agreement. Reinforce the student for correcting all errors.

2. Have the student complete written worksheets on which he/she must supply the correct verb form to go with specific subjects (e.g., "He _____ the dishes.").

3. Have the student pick out the correct verb when given choices on "fill-in-the-blank" worksheets (e.g., "They _____ (have, has) a new dog.").

4. Give the student specific verb forms and have him/her supply appropriate subjects to go with each (e.g., "___ runs.").

5. Have the student make up sentences with given verbs and subjects.

6. Have the student help correct other students' written work by checking subject-verb agreement and correcting the assignment.

7. Give the student a series of sentences with both incorrect and correct usage of verbs and ask the student to identify which are correct and which are incorrect.

8. Have the student find examples of correct subject-verb agreement in his/her favorite books or magazines.

9. Identify the most common errors the student makes in subject-verb agreement. Have the student spend time each day writing one or more of these subject-verb combinations in correct form.

10. Identify and make a list of the correct forms of subject-verb combinations the student has difficulty writing and have the student keep the list at his/her desk for a reference.

11. Reduce the emphasis on competition. Competitive activities may cause the student to hurry and make errors in subject-verb agreement.

12. Make certain the student receives instruction in subject-verb agreement for those subject-verb combinations he/she commonly has difficulty writing correctly.

13. Correct the student each time he/she uses subject-verb agreement incorrectly when speaking.

14. Make certain the student knows that different forms of verbs go with subjects and that correct subject-verb agreement requires the appropriate verb form. Have the student practice matching verb forms to lists of subjects.

15. Have the student read the written work of peers in which subject-verb agreement is used correctly.

16. Highlight or underline subject-verb agreements in the student's reading in order to call attention to the appropriate combinations.

17. After checking the student's written work, make certain he/she makes all necessary corrections in subject-verb agreement.

18. Recognize quality work (e.g., display the student's work, congratulate the student, etc.).

19. Make certain the student is not required to learn more information than he/she is capable of at any one time.

20. Have the student act as a peer tutor to teach another student a concept the student has mastered. This can serve as reinforcement for the student.

21. Give the student a choice of answers on worksheets (e.g., "fill-in-the-blank"). This increases the student's opportunity for recognizing the correct answer.

22. Review, on a daily basis, those skills, concepts, tasks, etc., which have been previously introduced.

23. Provide the student with increased opportunity for help or assistance on academic tasks (e.g., peer tutoring, directions for work sent home, frequent interactions, etc.).

24. Show the student pictures of people, places, or things. Ask him/her to make a statement about each picture. Have the student identify the subject and verb of the oral sentence and tell whether or not they agree.

25. Play a game such as *Concentration* to match subject-verb agreement.

26. Speak to the student to explain that he/she is using inappropriate subject-verb agreement and emphasize the importance of writing grammatically correct sentences.

27. Ascertain the type of grammatical model to which the student is exposed at home. Without placing negative connotations on his/her parent's grammatical style, explain the difference between standard and nonstandard grammar.

28. Make sure the student understands the concept of "subject" and "verb" by demonstrating through the use of objects, pictures, and/or written sentences (depending on the student's abilities).

29. Make sure the student understands that sentences express thoughts about a subject and what that subject is or does.

30. Make sure the student understands the concept of plurality (e.g., have the student point to a picture of a cat and point to a picture of cats).

31. Explain that certain forms of verbs go with certain subjects and that correct subject-verb agreement requires the appropriate match of subject and verb. Be certain that the student knows the various possibilities of subject-verb agreement and how to select the correct one.

32. Make a list of those verbs the student most commonly uses incorrectly. This list will become the guide for learning activities in subject-verb agreement.

33. Give the student a series of sentences, both written and oral, and have him/her identify which are grammatically correct and incorrect.

34. Reinforce the student for using appropriate subject-verb agreement when writing: (a) give the student a tangible reward (e.g., classroom privileges, line leading, passing out materials, five minutes free time, etc.) or (b) give the student an intangible reward (e.g., praise, handshake, smile, etc.).

129 Does not compose complete sentences or express complete thoughts when writing

1. Require the student to proofread all written work and reinforce him/her for completing sentences or expressing complete thoughts.

2. Give the student a series of written phrases and have him/her indicate which ones express complete thoughts.

3. Have the student correct a series of phrases by making each a complete sentence.

4. After reading his/her written work, have the student explain why specific sentences do not express complete thoughts.

5. Give the student a subject and have him/her write as many complete sentences as possible.

6. Make groups of cards containing subjects, verbs, adjectives, etc. Have the student combine the cards in various ways to construct complete sentences.

7. Give the student several short sentences and have him/her combine them in order to make one longer, complete sentence (e.g., "The dog is big." "The dog is brown." "The dog is mine." becomes "The big, brown dog is mine.").

8. Give the student a list of transition words (e.g., *therefore, although, because,* etc.) and have him/her make sentences using each word.

9. Make certain the student understands that a complete sentence has to express a complete thought about a subject and what that subject is or does.

10. Have the student write a daily log, expressing his/her thoughts in complete sentences.

11. Have the student write letters to friends, relatives, etc., in order to practice writing complete sentences and thoughts.

12. Encourage the student to read written work aloud in order to identify incomplete sentences and thoughts.

13. Give the student a group of related words (e.g., *author, read, love, bestseller,* etc.) and have him/her make up a paragraph including all the words.

14. Provide the student with clearly stated criteria for acceptable work (e.g., neatness, complete sentences, etc.).

15. Recognize quality work (e.g., display the student's work, congratulate the student, etc.).

16. Check the student's written work at various points throughout the assignment to make certain the student is using complete sentences.

17. Provide the student with appropriate time limits for the completion of written assignments.

18. Play a game by providing students with a box labeled "Trash." Provide sentence strips with complete and incomplete sentences. Instruct students to "trash" incomplete sentences.

19. Provide exercises for making sentences out of nonsentence groups of words.

20. Read orally to the student to stimulate the student's thinking and writing processes.

21. Be certain to act as a model for the student to imitate writing in complete sentences or thoughts.

22. Have a peer act as a model for writing in complete sentences or thoughts. Assign the students to work together, perform assignments together, etc.

23. Have the student identify a person who he/she thinks is a good writer and tell why.

24. Identify the qualities a good writer possesses (e.g., writing in complete sentences or thoughts, using correct vocabulary, etc.) and have the student evaluate himself/herself on each characteristic. Set a goal for improvement in one or two areas at a time.

25. Reduce the emphasis on competition. Competitive activities may cause the student to hurry and fail to write in complete sentences.

26. Reinforce the students in the classroom who use complete sentences or thoughts when writing.

27. Reinforce the student for using complete sentences or thoughts when writing: (a) give the student a tangible reward (e.g., classroom privileges, line leading, passing out materials, five minutes free time, etc.) or (b) give the student an intangible reward (e.g., praise, handshake, smile, etc.).

1. Have the student practice organizational skills in writing activities by having him/her engage in writing activities designed to cause the student to want to be successful (e.g., writing a letter to a friend, rock star, famous athlete, etc.).

2. Have the student write an account of the previous week, past weekend, etc., with primary attention given to organization (e.g., sequencing events, developing a paragraph, using correct word order, etc.).

3. Require the student to proofread all written work. Reinforce all corrections in organization.

4. Have the student write a daily log, expressing his/her thoughts in complete sentences.

5. Have the student create stories about topics which are of interest. The student is more likely to try to be successful if he/she is writing about something of interest.

6. Have the student read his/her written work aloud to help identify errors in organization.

7. Make certain the student knows that paragraphs, essays, etc., need an introduction, a middle where information is contained, and a conclusion or ending.

8. Have the student arrange a series of statements on a topic in an appropriate order so that they make sense in a paragraph.

9. Teach outlining principles to the student so he/she understands the difference between main ideas and supporting details.

10. Help the student "brain storm" ideas about a topic and then show him/her how to put these ideas into outline form, combining some ideas and discarding others.

11. Give the student a group of related words (e.g., *author, read, love, bestseller*, etc.) and have him/her make up an appropriately organized paragraph including each word.

12. Provide the student with a paragraph in which one statement does not belong. Have the student find the inappropriate statement.

13. Have the student write step-by-step directions (e.g., steps in making a cake) so he/she can practice sequencing events.

14. Using a written essay that the student has not seen, cut the paragraphs apart and ask him/her to reconstruct the essay by putting the paragraphs in an appropriate order.

15. Reduce the emphasis on competition. Competitive activities may cause the student to hurry and fail to correctly organize writing activities.

16. Reduce distracting stimuli by placing the student in a study carrel or "office" when engaged in writing activities. This is used as a means of reducing distracting stimuli and not as a form of punishment.

17. Make certain the student is not interrupted or hurried when engaging in writing activities.

18. Have the student read sentences, paragraphs, stories, etc., written by peers who demonstrate good organizational skills in writing.

19. When correcting the student's organizational skills in writing, be certain to provide evaluative feedback which is designed to be instructional (e.g., help the student rewrite for better organization, rewrite passages for the student, etc.).

20. Have the student develop organizational skills in writing simple sentences. Gradually increase the required complexity of sentence structure and move on to paragraphs, short stories, etc., as the student demonstrates success.

21. Have the student develop an outline or "skeleton" of what he/she is going to write. From the outline the student can then practice organizational skills in writing.

22. Recognize quality work (e.g., display the student's work, congratulate the student, etc.).

23. Make certain the student is not required to learn more information than he/she is capable of at any one time.

24. Provide practice in organizing writing activities by using a computer software program that gives the student immediate feedback.

25. Make certain the student has mastery of writing concepts at each level before introducing a new skill level.

26. Check the student's work frequently to make certain that the student is organizing the writing activity appropriately.

27. Provide the student with appropriate time limits for the completion of assignments.

28. On a piece of paper, write five or six sentences about a story the student has read. Have the student cut the sentences apart and paste them together in the proper order.

29. Have the student write a paragraph describing the events of a daily comic strip such as *Peanuts*.

30. Reinforce the student for correctly organizing writing activities: (a) give the student a tangible reward (e.g., classroom privileges, line leading, passing out materials, etc.) or (b) give the student an intangible reward (e.g., praise, handshake, smile, etc.).

1. Have the student write current spelling words in different locations throughout the classroom as he/she is learning them (e.g., on the chalkboard, transparencies, a posted list at his/her desk, etc.).

2. Teach spelling rules integrated with the total language arts program (e.g., activities, methods, and materials related to the teaching of spelling, reading, and language as a whole rather than in parts).

3. Require the student to use a dictionary to find the correct spelling of any word he/she cannot spell correctly. The emphasis in this situation becomes spelling accurately rather than memorizing spelling words.

4. Have the student practice spelling rules in a meaningful manner which will cause him/her to want to be successful (e.g., writing a letter to a friend, rock star, famous athlete, etc.).

5. Make certain the student knows why he/she is learning spelling rules (e.g., provide the student with a concrete example of how each word can be used in his/her life).

6. Have the student identify a list of spelling words (e.g., 5, 10, or 15) each week which he/ she wants to learn to spell. Have the student learn to spell these words using the spelling rules.

7. Make certain the student has had adequate practice using the spelling rules in writing words, sentences, etc.

8. Make certain the student has adequate time to perform written assignments in order to increase the likelihood of using spelling rules.

9. Reduce distracting stimuli in the classroom when the student is working on spelling and related activities (e.g., place the student in a carrel or "office" space).

10. Make certain the student is not being required to learn too many spelling words at one time.

11. Make certain the student learns to use spelling rules to spell words correctly rather than simply memorizing the spelling of words for testing purposes (e.g., *i* before *e* except after *c*, etc.).

12. Have the student keep a dictionary of "most often misspelled words" at his/her desk, and require the student to check the spelling of all words he/she is not certain are spelled correctly.

13. Have the student practice one spelling rule consistently until that rule is mastered (e.g., *i* before *e* except after *c*, etc.). When one rule is mastered, a new one is introduced.

14. Require the student to proofread written assignments using spelling rules. Reinforce the student for each correction made when using spelling rules.

15. Develop a list of spelling rules. Have the student keep the list of spelling rules at his/her desk, and require the student to refer to the rules when writing words, sentences, etc.

16. Require the student to verbally explain how he/she spells words using spelling rules (e.g., *i* before *e* except after *c*, etc.).

17. Require the student to practice those basic spelling rules which he/she uses on a daily basis.

18. Recognize quality work (e.g., display the student's work, congratulate the student, etc.).

19. Make certain the student is not required to learn more information than he/she is capable of at any one time.

20. Have the student act as a peer tutor to teach another student a spelling concept he/she has mastered. This can serve as reinforcement for the student.

21. Provide practice in spelling by using a computer software program that gives the student immediate feedback.

22. Make certain the student has mastery of spelling concepts at each level before introducing a new skill level.

23. Use daily drill activities to help the student memorize spelling rules.

24. Provide the student with self-checking materials, requiring correction before turning in assignments.

25. Have the student practice a new spelling skill with an aide, the teacher, a peer, etc., before the entire group attempts the activity or before performing for a grade.

26. Make certain the student has adequate opportunities for repetition of information through different experiences in order to enhance his/her memory.

27. Review, on a daily basis, those spelling skills which have been previously introduced.

28. Deliver information to the student on a one-to-one basis or employ a peer tutor.

29. Make up a rap using the spelling rule.

30. Print a spelling word and cut it apart letter-by-letter to make a puzzle word. Have the student scramble the letters and then arrange them in the correct order to spell the word.

31. Have the student type a list of spelling words.

32. Keep a salt box (or a sandbox) for the student to trace spelling words in.

33. Give the student a magazine or newspaper. Have him/her highlight words which follow spelling rules being studied.

34. Every day have the student practice using spelling rules in written words, sentences, etc.

35. Have a peer spend time each day with the student to practice the use of spelling rules when writing words, sentences, etc.

36. Reduce the emphasis on competition. Competitive activities may cause the student to hurry and make mistakes.

37. Reinforce the student for using spelling rules: (a) give the student a tangible reward (e.g., classroom privileges, line leading, passing out materials, five minutes free time, etc.) or (b) give the student an intangible reward (e.g., praise, handshake, smile, etc.).

132 Has difficulty spelling words that do not follow the spelling rules

1. Require the student to use a dictionary to find the spelling of any words he/she cannot spell correctly. The emphasis in this situation becomes spelling correctly rather than memorizing spelling words.

2. Have the student identify a list of spelling words (e.g., 5, 10, or 15) each week which he/she wants to learn to spell. These words become the student's spelling words for the week.

3. Make certain the student has had adequate time to perform written assignments in order that he/she will be more likely to spell words correctly.

4. Reduce distracting stimuli in the classroom when the student is working on spelling and related activities (e.g., place the student in a carrel or "office" space).

5. Have the student keep a dictionary of "most often misspelled words," and require the student to check the spelling of all words he/she is not certain are spelled correctly.

6. Require the student to proofread written assignments for spelling errors. Reinforce the student for each correction made.

7. Identify the most common words the student uses which do not follow spelling rules. Have the student learn to spell these words as a sight word vocabulary.

8. Develop a spelling list of words the student uses which do not follow the spelling rules. Add new words to the list as the student demonstrates mastery of any of the words.

9. Make certain the student does not have too many words to learn to spell at one time.

10. Make a list of the words the student most commonly misspells. Keep a copy of the list of correctly spelled words at his/her desk to use as a reference when writing.

11. Have the student use current spelling words in a meaningful manner which will cause him/her to want to be successful (e.g., writing a letter to a friend, rock star, famous athlete, etc.).

12. Make certain the student "hears" the sounds in the words misspelled. Have the student say the words aloud to determine if the student is aware of the letters or sound units in the words.

13. Recognize quality work (e.g., display the student's work, congratulate the student, etc.).

14. Make certain the student is not required to learn more information than he/she is capable of at any one time.

15. Have the student act as a peer tutor to teach another student a spelling concept the student has mastered. This can serve as reinforcement for the student.

16. Provide practice in spelling by using a computer software program that gives the student immediate feedback.

17. Make certain the student has mastery of spelling concepts at each level before introducing a new skill level.

18. Use daily drill activities to help the student memorize spelling words (e.g., flash cards, writing the spelling words three times, etc.).

19. Have the student practice a new skill or assignment alone, with an aide, the teacher, or a peer tutor before the entire group attempts the activity or before performing for a grade.

20. Review, on a daily basis, those spelling words which have been previously introduced.

21. Print a spelling word and cut it apart letter-by-letter to make a puzzle word. Have the student scramble the letters and then arrange them in the correct order to spell the word.

22. Have the student type the list of spelling words.

23. Have the student make a song or chant of spelling words (e.g., L-A-UGH, L-A-UGH).

24. Have the student write current spelling words in different locations throughout the classroom as he/she is learning them (e.g., on the chalkboard, transparencies, a posted list on his/her desk, etc.).

25. Have a peer spend time each day with the student to practice spelling words which do not use spelling rules.

26. Give the student fewer words to learn to spell at any one time, spending more time on each word until the student can spell it correctly.

27. Reinforce the student for spelling words that do not follow spelling rules: (a) give the student a tangible reward (e.g., classroom privileges, line leading, passing out materials, five minutes free time, etc.) or (b) give the student an intangible reward (e.g., praise, handshake, smile, etc.).

1. Have the student use current spelling words in sentences written each day.

2. Write sentences, paragraphs, etc., for the student to read which repeat the student's spelling words throughout the material.

3. Have the student write his/her spelling words in different locations throughout the classroom as he/she is learning them (e.g., on the chalkboard, transparencies, a posted list, etc.).

4. Have a list of the student's current spelling words taped on his/her desk with the requirement that they be practiced whenever the student has time. Reinforce the student for practicing the writing of the spelling words.

5. Teach spelling integrated with the total language arts program (e.g., activities, methods, and materials are related to the teaching of reading and language as a whole rather than in parts).

6. Require the student to use the dictionary to find the spelling of any word he/she cannot spell correctly. The emphasis in this situation becomes spelling accurately rather than memorizing spelling words.

7. Have the student use current spelling words in a meaningful manner which will cause him/ her to want to be successful (e.g., writing a letter to a friend, rock star, famous athlete, etc.).

8. Make certain the student knows why he/she is learning each spelling word (e.g., provide the student with a concrete example of how each word can be used in his/her life).

9. Have the student identify a list of words (e.g., 5, 10, 15) each week which he/she wants to learn to spell. If the student is interested in cars, identify words from automotive magazines, advertisements, etc.

10. Have a peer spend time each day engaged in drill activities with the student on spelling words.

11. Try various activities to help strengthen and reinforce the visual memory of the spelling words (e.g., flash cards, word lists on the chalkboard, a list on the student's desk, etc.).

12. Make certain the student has had adequate practice in writing the spelling words (e.g., drill activities, sentence activities, etc.).

13. Make certain the student has adequate time to perform written assignments.

14. Reduce distracting stimuli in the classroom when the student is working on spelling and related activities (e.g., place the student in a carrel or "office" space).

15. Have the student maintain a folder of all spelling words. Require the student to refer to the list when he/she is engaged in writing activities in order to check spelling.

16. Make certain the student learns to "use" spelling words rather than simply memorizing the spelling of the words for testing purposes (e.g., have the student use the words in writing activities each day).

17. Require the student to proofread all written work for spelling errors. Reinforce the student for correcting each spelling error.

18. Have the student keep a dictionary of "most often misspelled words," and require the student to check the spelling of all words he/she is not certain are spelled correctly.

19. Require the student to write spelling words frequently in order to increase the student's visual memory of the spelling words.

20. Make certain the student is not being required to learn too many spelling words at one time.

21. Recognize quality work (e.g., display the student's work, congratulate the student, etc.).

22. Make certain that the student's spelling words are those which he/she sees on a routine basis rather than infrequently, in order to assure correct spelling and use of the words.

23. Make certain the student is not required to learn more information than he/she is capable of at any one time.

24. Only give tests and quizzes when the student is certain to succeed (e.g., after you are sure the student has learned and retained the information).

25. Provide the student with self-checking materials, requiring correction before turning in assignments.

26. Give the student fewer words to learn to spell at any one time, spending more time on each word until the student can spell it correctly.

27. Reduce the emphasis on competition. Competitive activities may cause the student to hurry and make mistakes in spelling.

28. Reinforce the student for spelling words correctly in all contexts: (a) give the student a tangible reward (e.g., classroom privileges, line leading, passing out materials, five minutes free time, etc.) or (b) give the student an intangible reward (e.g., praise, handshake, smile, etc.).

1. Have the student highlight or underline spelling words in passages from reading assignments, newspapers, magazines, etc.

2. Develop crossword puzzles which contain only the student's spelling words and have him/her complete them.

3. Write sentences, passages, paragraphs, etc., for the student to read which repeat the student's spelling words throughout the material.

4. Have the student act as a peer tutor to teach spelling words to another student.

5. Have the student write spelling words in different locations throughout the classroom as he/she is learning them (e.g., on the chalkboard, transparencies, a posted list, the desk, etc.).

6. Have the student indicate when he/she has learned one of the spelling words. As the student demonstrates he/she can spell the word, it is removed from the current spelling list.

7. Have a list of the student's current spelling words taped on his/her desk with the requirement that they be practiced whenever the student has time. Reinforce the student for practicing the writing of the spelling words.

8. Have the student review spelling words each day for a short period of time rather than two or three times per week for longer periods of time.

9. Teach spelling integrated with the total language arts program (e.g., activities, methods, and materials are related to the teaching of reading and language as a whole rather than in parts).

10. Require the student to use a dictionary to find the spelling of any word he/she cannot spell correctly. The emphasis in this situation becomes spelling accurately rather than memorizing spelling words.

11. Have the student quiz others over spelling words (e.g., teacher, aide, peers, etc.).

12. Make certain that the student's spelling instruction is on a level where success can be met. Gradually increase the degree of difficulty as the student demonstrates success.

13. Initiate a "Learn to Spell a Word a Day" program with the student.

14. Use words for the student's spelling list which are commonly found in his/her daily surroundings (e.g., commercials, hazard signs, directions, lunch menu, etc.).

15. Evaluate the appropriateness of the task to determine: (a) if the task is too difficult and (b) if the length of time scheduled to complete the task is appropriate.

16. Have the student's current spelling words listed on the chalkboard at all times.

17. Have the student use current spelling words in a meaningful manner which will cause him/her to want to be successful (e.g., writing a letter to a friend, rock star, famous athlete, etc.).

18. Require the student to proofread all written work for spelling errors. Reinforce the student for correcting each spelling error.

19. Make certain the student knows why he/she is learning each spelling word (e.g., provide the student with a concrete example of how each word can be used in his/her life).

20. Have the student identify a list of spelling words (e.g., 5, 10, 15) each week which he/she wants to learn to spell. If the student is interested in cars, identify words from automotive magazines, advertisements, etc.

21. Recognize quality work (e.g., display the student's work, congratulate the student, etc.).

22. Make certain the student is not required to learn more information than he/she is capable of at any one time.

23. Provide practice in spelling by using computer software programs that give the student immediate feedback.

24. Have the student practice a new list of spelling words alone, with an aide, the teacher, or a peer before the entire group attempts the activity or before performing for a grade.

25. Have the student use current spelling words by writing sentences each day.

26. Have a peer spend time each day engaged in drill activities with the student on his/her spelling words.

27. Give the student fewer words to learn to spell at any one time, spending more time on each word until the student can spell it correctly.

28. Reduce the emphasis on competition. Competitive activities may cause the student to hurry and make mistakes in spelling.

29. Reinforce the student for learning to spell words correctly: (a) give the student a tangible reward (e.g., classroom privileges, line leading, passing out materials, five minutes free time, etc.) or (b) give the student an intangible reward (e.g., praise, handshake, smile, etc.).

135 Fails to correctly solve math problems requiring addition

1. Provide the student with a quiet place to work (e.g., "office," study carrel, etc.). This is used as a means of reducing distracting stimuli and not as a form of punishment.

2. Have the student solve addition problems by manipulating objects and by stating the process(es) used.

3. Discuss and provide the student with a list of words/phrases which indicate an addition operation in word problems (e.g., *together, altogether, sum, in all, both, gained, received, total, saved*, etc.).

4. Assign a peer to act as a model for the student and to demonstrate how to solve addition problems.

5. Provide the student with many concrete experiences to help him/help learn and remember math facts. Use popsicle sticks, tongue depressors, paper clips, buttons, fingers, etc., to form groupings to teach addition facts.

6. Have the student use a calculator to reinforce learning addition. Have the student solve several problems each day using a calculator.

7. Provide practice of addition facts using computer software programs that give immediate feedback to the student.

8. Use daily drill activities to help the student memorize addition facts (e.g., written problems, flash cards, etc.).

9. Have the student use a number line attached to his/her desk to solve addition problems.

10. Have the student use a calculator for drill activities of basic addition facts.

11. Find opportunities for the student to apply addition facts to real-life situations (e.g., getting change in the cafeteria, measuring the lengths of objects in industrial arts, etc.).

12. Have the student perform timed drills in addition to reinforce basic math facts. The student "competes" against his/her own best time.

13. Develop a math facts reference sheet for addition for the student to use at his/her desk when solving math problems.

14. Have the student independently solve half of his/her addition facts/problems each day, allow the use of a calculator as reinforcement to solve the rest of the problems.

15. Make certain the student understands number concepts and the relationship of number symbols to numbers of objects before requiring him/her to solve math problems requiring addition.

16. Make certain the student knows the concepts of *more than, less than, equal*, and *zero*. The use of tangible objects will facilitate the learning process.

17. Have the student make sets of objects and add the sets together to obtain a sum total.

18. Provide the student with opportunities for tutoring from peers or teacher. Allow the student to tutor others when he/she has mastered a concept.

19. Reinforce the student for attempting and completing work. Emphasize the number correct, then encourage him/her to see how many more he/she can correct without help. Have the student maintain his/her own "private" chart of math performance.

20. Provide the student with enjoyable math activities during free time in the classroom (e.g., computer games, math games, manipulatives, etc.).

21. Have the student check all math work. Reinforce the student for each error he/she corrects.

22. Allow the student to perform alternative assignments. Gradually introduce more components of the regular assignments until those assignments can be performed successfully by the student.

23. Make certain that the language used to communicate with the student about addition is consistent (e.g., "Add the numbers." "What is the total?" or "Find the sum.").

24. Make certain the student has mastery of math concepts at any level before introducing a new skill level.

25. Provide the student with shorter math tasks, but give more of them throughout the day (e.g., 4 assignments of 5 problems each rather than one assignment of 20 problems).

26. Work the first problem or two of the math assignment with the student in order to make certain that he/she understands the directions and the operation necessary to solve the problem.

27. Teach the student to use resources in the environment to help him/her solve math problems (e.g., counting figures, counting numbers of objects, using a calculator, etc.).

28. Have the student talk through the math problem as he/she solves it in order to identify errors the student is making.

29. Have the student add numbers of objects. Have him/her then pair number symbols with the numbers of objects while he/she solves simple addition problems. Gradually remove the objects as the student demonstrates success in solving simple addition problems.

136 Fails to correctly solve math problems requiring subtraction

1. Discuss words and phrases which usually indicate subtraction operations (e.g., *difference between, from, left, how many more or less, how much taller, how much farther,* etc.).

2. Assign a peer to act as a model for the student and to demonstrate how to solve subtraction problems.

3. Evaluate the appropriateness of the task to determine: (a) if the task is too difficult and (b) if the length of time scheduled for the task is appropriate.

4. Provide the student with many concrete experiences to help learn and remember math facts. Use popsicle sticks, paper clips, fingers, etc., to form groupings to teach subtraction facts.

5. Have the student use a calculator to reinforce the solving of math problems requiring subtraction. Have the student solve several problems each day using a calculator.

6. Provide practice of subtraction facts by using a computer with software programs that give immediate feedback for the student.

7. Use daily drill activities to help the student memorize subtraction facts (e.g., written problems, flash cards, etc.).

8. Have the student perform timed drills in subtraction to reinforce basic math facts. The student "competes" against his/her own best times.

9. Have the student use a number line attached to his/her desk to solve subtraction problems.

10. Have the student use a calculator for drill activities of basic subtraction facts.

11. Find opportunities for the student to apply subtraction facts to real-life situations (e.g., getting change in the cafeteria, measuring the lengths of objects in industrial arts, etc.).

12. Develop a reference sheet of subtraction math facts for the student to use at his/her desk when solving math problems.

13. Have the student independently solve half the assigned subtraction problems each day and use a calculator as reinforcement to solve the rest of the problems.

14. Make certain the student understands number concepts and the relationships of number symbols to numbers of objects before requiring him/her to solve math problems requiring subtraction.

15. Make certain the student knows the concepts of *more than, less than, equal,* and *zero.* The use of tangible objects will facilitate the learning process.

16. Provide the student with opportunities for tutoring from peers or a teacher. Allow the student to tutor others when he/she has mastered a concept.

17. Reinforce the student for attempting and completing work. Emphasize the number correct, then encourage the student to see how many more can be corrected without help. Have the student maintain his/her own "private" chart of math performance.

18. Call on the student when he/she is most likely to be able to respond successfully.

19. Provide the student with enjoyable math activities during free time in the classroom (e.g., computer games, math games, manipulatives, etc.).

20. Allow the student to perform alternative assignments. Gradually introduce more components of the regular assignments until those assignments can be performed successfully by the student.

21. Have the student check all math work. Reinforce the student for each error corrected.

22. Make certain that the language used to communicate with the student about subtraction is consistent (e.g., "Subtract the numbers. What is the difference?" etc.).

23. Make certain the student has mastery of math concepts at each level before introducing a new skill level.

24. Provide the student with shorter math tasks, but more of them throughout the day (e.g., 4 assignments of 5 problems rather than one assignment of 20 problems).

25. Work the first problem or two of the math assignment with the student in order to make certain that he/she understands the directions and the operation necessary to do the problems.

26. Teach the student to use resources in the environment to help solve math problems (e.g., counting figures, counting numbers of objects, using a calculator, etc.).

27. Have the student learn to subtract numbers of objects. Then have the student pair symbols with numbers of objects while solving the subtraction problems. In the last step, the student subtracts the number symbols without using objects.

28. Have the student talk through math problems while solving them in order to identify errors he/she is making.

29. Require the student to check subtraction problems by adding (i.e. the difference plus the subtrahend equals the minuend). Reinforce the student for each error corrected.

30. Make certain the student learns the concept of take away (e.g., "You have three toys and I take away two of them. How many do you have left?").

31. Require the student to use graph paper to make certain that columns are lined up appropriately.

32. Make certain the student knows why he/she is learning a math concept. Provide the student with concrete examples and opportunities to apply those concepts in real-life situations.

33. Make certain the student is not required to learn more information than the student is capable of at any one time.

34. Have the student act as a peer tutor to teach another student a concept he/she has mastered. This can serve as reinforcement for the student.

35. Provide the student with self-checking materials, requiring correction before turning in assignments.

36. Make certain that all directions, questions, explanations, and instructions are delivered in the most clear and concise manner and at an appropriate pace for the student.

37. Provide the student with increased opportunities for help or assistance on academic tasks (e.g., peer tutoring, directions for assignments sent home, frequent interactions, etc.).

38. Deliver information to the student on a one-to-one basis or use a peer tutor.

39. Have the student solve math problems by manipulating objects and stating the process(es) used.

40. Reduce the emphasis on competition. Competitive activities may cause the student to hurry and do subtraction problems incorrectly.

41. Provide the student with a quiet place to work (e.g., "office," carrel, etc.). This is used as a means of reducing distracting stimuli and not as a form of punishment.

42. Reinforce the student for correctly solving subtraction problems: (a) give the student a tangible reward (e.g., class privileges, line leading, passing out materials, five minutes free time, etc.) or (b) give the student an intangible reward (e.g., praise, handshake, smile, etc.).

137 Fails to correctly solve math problems requiring multiplication

1. Have the student solve math problems by manipulating objects and stating the process(es) involved.

2. Discuss words/phrases which usually indicate a multiplication operation (e.g., *area, each, times, product, double, triple, twice,* etc.).

3. Assign a peer to act as a model for the student and to demonstrate how to solve multiplication problems.

4. Evaluate the appropriateness of the task to determine: (a) if the task is too difficult and (b) if the length of time scheduled for the task is appropriate.

5. Provide the student with many concrete experiences to help the student learn and remember math facts. Use popsicle sticks, tongue depressors, paper clips, buttons, fingers, etc., to form groupings to teach multiplication facts.

6. Have the student use a calculator to reinforce learning multiplication facts. Have the student solve several multiplication problems each day using a calculator.

7. Provide practice of multiplication facts by using a computer with software programs that give immediate feedback to the student.

8. Use daily drill activities to help the student memorize multiplication facts (e.g., written problems, flash cards, etc.).

9. Have the student perform timed drills in multiplication to reinforce basic math facts. The student "competes" against his/her own best time.

10. Have the student use a calculator for drill activities of basic multiplication facts.

11. Develop a math facts reference sheet for multiplication for the student to use at his/her desk when solving math problems.

12. Have the student independently solve half of the assigned multiplication problems each day and use the calculator as reinforcement to complete the other half of the assignment.

13. Make certain the student understands number concepts and the relationship of number symbols to numbers of objects before requiring him/her to solve math problems requiring multiplication.

14. Provide the student with opportunities for tutoring from peers or a teacher. Allow the student to tutor others when he/she has mastered a concept.

15. Reinforce the student for attempting and completing work. Emphasize the number correct, then encourage the student to see how many more can be performed correctly without help. Have the student maintain a "private" chart of math performance.

16. Call on the student when he/she is most likely to be successful.

17. Provide the student with enjoyable math activities during free time in the classroom (e.g., computer games, math games, manipulatives, etc.).

18. Allow the student to perform alternative math assignments. Gradually introduce more components of the regular assignments until those assignments can be performed.

19. Have the student check all math work. Reinforce the student for each error corrected.

20. Provide the student with shorter tasks, but more of them throughout the day (e.g., 4 assignments of 5 problems each rather than one assignment of 20 problems).

21. Work the first problem or two of the math assignment with the student in order to make certain that he/she understands directions and the operation necessary to solve the problems.

22. Make certain the student has mastery of math concepts at each level before introducing a new skill level.

23. Teach the student to use resources in the environment to help solve math problems (e.g., counting figures, counting numbers of objects, using a calculator, etc.).

24. Have the student talk through the math problems as he/she solves them in order to identify errors made.

25. Make certain the student understands that multiplication is a short way of adding by giving examples of how much longer it takes to add than to multiply.

26. Practice skip counting with two's, three's, and five's.

27. Teach the student the identity element of one. Any number times one is always that number.

28. Have the student count by equal distances on a number line. Demonstrate that the equal distances represent skip counting or equal addition, which is the concept of multiplication.

29. Teach the student the zero element. Any number times zero will be zero.

30. Have the student practice the multiplication tables each day with a peer using flash cards.

31. Identify specific multiplication problems the student fails to correctly solve and target these problems for additional instruction and time to be spent in tutoring and drill activities.

32. Require the student to use graph paper to make certain columns are lined up appropriately.

33. Make certain the student knows why he/she is learning a math concept. Provide the student with concrete examples and opportunities to apply those concepts in real-life situations.

34. Make certain the student is not required to learn more information than the student is capable of at any one time.

35. Have the student act as a peer tutor to teach another student a concept the student has mastered. This can serve as reinforcement for the student.

36. Make certain the student has mastery of math concepts at each level before introducing a new skill level.

37. Provide the student with self-checking materials, requiring correction before turning in assignments.

38. Make certain that all directions, questions, explanations, and instructions are delivered in the most clear and concise manner and at an appropriate pace for the student.

39. Provide the student with increased opportunities for help or assistance on academic tasks (e.g., peer tutoring, directions for assignments sent home, frequent interactions, etc.).

40. Deliver information to the student on a one-to-one basis or employ a peer tutor.

41. Reduce the emphasis on competition. Competitive activities may cause the student to hurry and do multiplication problems incorrectly.

42. Provide the student with a quiet place to work (e.g., "office," study carrel, etc.). This is used as a means of reducing distracting stimuli and not as a form of punishment.

43. Reinforce the student for correctly solving multiplication problems: (a) give the student a tangible reward (e.g., classroom privileges, line leading, passing out materials, five minutes free time, etc.) or (b) give the student an intangible reward (e.g., praise, handshake, smile, etc.).

138   Fails to correctly solve math problems requiring division

1. Have the student solve math problems by manipulating objects and stating the process(es) used.

2. Discuss words and phrases which usually indicate a division operation (e.g., *into, share, each, average, quotient, half as many,* etc.).

3. Assign a peer to act as a model for the student and to demonstrate how to solve division problems.

4. Evaluate the appropriateness of the task to determine: (a) if the task is too difficult and (b) if the length of time scheduled for the task is appropriate.

5. Provide the student with many concrete experiences to help him/her learn and remember math facts. Use popsicle sticks, tongue depressors, paper clips, buttons, fingers, etc., to form groupings to teach division facts.

6. Have the student use a calculator to reinforce learning division. Have the student solve several problems each day using a calculator.

7. Provide practice of division facts by using a computer with software programs that give immediate feedback to the student.

8. Use daily drill activities to help the student memorize division facts (e.g., written problems, flash cards, etc.).

9. Have the student perform timed drill activities to reinforce basic math facts. The student "competes" against his/her own best time.

10. Have the student use a calculator for drill activities of basic division facts.

11. Find opportunities for the student to apply division facts to real-life situations (e.g., money, average length of time it takes to do a job, etc.).

12. Call on the student when he/she is most likely to be able to respond successfully.

13. Develop a math fact reference sheet for division for the student to use at his/her desk when solving math problems.

14. Have the student independently solve half of the assigned division problems each day and use a calculator as reinforcement to complete the other half of the problems.

15. Make certain the student understands number concepts and the relationship of number symbols to numbers of objects before requiring him/her to solve division problems.

16. Make certain the student knows the concepts of *more than, less than, equal,* and *zero.* The use of tangible objects will facilitate the learning process.

17. Give the student several objects (e.g., one inch cubes, connecting links, etc.) and have him/her divide them into groups.

18. Provide the student with opportunities for tutoring from peers or a teacher. Allow the student to tutor others when he/she has mastered a concept.

19. Reinforce the student for attempting and completing work. Emphasize the number correct, then encourage the student to see how many more he/she can correct without help. Have the student maintain a "private" chart of math performance.

20. Provide the student with enjoyable math activities during free time in the classroom (e.g., computer games, math games, manipulatives).

21. Allow the student to perform alternative versions of the assignments. Gradually introduce more components of the regular assignments until those assignments can be performed successfully.

22. Make certain that the language used to communicate with the student about division is consistent (e.g., "Divide the numbers." "What is the divisor?" "What is the dividend?" etc.).

23. Have the student check all math work. Reinforce the student for each error corrected.

24. Make certain the student has mastery of math concepts at each level before introducing a new skill level.

25. Provide the student with shorter math tasks, but more of them throughout the day (e.g., 4 assignments of 5 problems each rather than one assignment of 20 problems).

26. Work the first problem or two of the assignment with the student in order to make certain that he/she understands directions and the operation necessary to solve the problems.

27. Teach the student to use resources in the environment to help solve math problems (e.g., counting figures, counting numbers of objects, using a calculator, etc.).

28. Have the student learn to divide numbers of objects. Then the student pairs number symbols with numbers of objects while solving the division problem. In the last step, the student divides without using objects.

29. Have the student talk through the math problem as he/she solves it in order to identify errors the student is making.

30. Teach the student the identity element of one. Any number divided by one is always the number.

31. Have the student practice the division tables each day by using flash cards with a peer.

32. Identify specific division problems the student fails to correctly solve, and target problems for additional instruction and time to be spent in tutoring and drill activities.

33. Have the student list all the skills necessary to work a division problem (e.g., subtraction, multiplication, etc.).

34. Make certain that all directions, questions, explanations, and instructions are delivered in the most clear and concise manner and at an appropriate pace for the student.

35. Use practical applications of division. Have each student bring something that must be divided among the whole class.

36. Use task analysis on each problem to determine where the student is breaking down.

37. Make certain the student knows why he/she is learning a math concept. Provide the student with concrete examples and opportunities to apply those concepts in real-life situations.

38. Make certain the student is not required to learn more information than he/she is capable of at any one time.

39. Have the student act as a peer tutor to teach another student a concept he/she has mastered. This can serve as reinforcement for the student.

40. Have the student check all math work. Reinforce the student for each error corrected.

41. Provide the student with increased opportunities for help or assistance on academic tasks (e.g., peer tutoring, directions for assignments sent home, frequent interactions, etc.).

42. Deliver information to the student on a one-to-one basis or employ a peer tutor.

43. Reduce the emphasis on competition. Competitive activities may cause the student to hurry and do division problems incorrectly.

44. Provide the student with a quiet place to work (e.g., "office," study carrel, etc.). This is used as a means of reducing distracting stimuli and not as a form of punishment.

45. Reinforce the student for solving division problems: (a) give the student a tangible reward (e.g., classroom privileges, line leading, passing out materials, five minutes free time, etc.) or (b) give the student an intangible reward (e.g., praise, handshake, smile, etc.).

1. Beginning with the addition and subtraction facts, separate the basic facts into "sets," each to be memorized successively by the student.

2. Using the tracking technique to help the student learn math facts, present a few facts at a time. Gradually increase the number of facts the student must remember as he/she demonstrates success.

3. Provide the student with many concrete experiences to help him/her learn and remember math facts. Use popsicle sticks, tongue depressors, paper clips, buttons, etc., to form groupings to teach math facts.

4. Use fingers to teach the student to form addition and subtraction combinations. Have the student hold up fingers and add or subtract other fingers to find the correct answer.

5. Have the student use a calculator to reinforce learning of the math facts. Have the student solve several problems each day using a calculator.

6. Provide practice of math facts using computer software programs that provide immediate feedback to the student.

7. Use daily drill activities to help the student memorize math facts (e.g., written problems, flash cards, etc.).

8. Develop and post basic addition, subtraction, multiplication, and division charts, which the student can use in solving math problems.

9. Build upon math facts the student already knows, reinforcing facts the student has mastered. Add one new fact at a time as the student demonstrates success.

10. Have the student perform timed drills to reinforce basic math facts. The student "competes" against his/her own best time.

11. Have the student use a number line attached to his/her desk to add and subtract.

12. Choose one fact with which the student is unsuccessful and review it several times a day. Make that fact the student's "fact of the day."

13. Have the student complete a math facts worksheet and have him/her use a calculator to check and correct the problems.

14. Have a peer tutor work with the student each day on drill activities (e.g., flash cards).

15. Avoid going on to multiplication and division facts until addition and subtraction facts have been mastered.

16. Have the student use math fact records and tapes for math fact drill activities.

17. Use manipulative objects (e.g., pegboard, abacus, base ten blocks, etc.) to teach the student basic math facts while providing a visual image.

18. Have the student use a calculator for drill activities of basic math facts.

19. Find opportunities for the student to apply math facts to real-life situations (e.g., getting change in the cafeteria, measuring the lengths of objects in industrial arts, etc.).

20. Develop a math facts reference sheet for addition, subtraction, multiplication, or division for the student to use at his/her desk when solving math problems.

21. Have the student independently solve half of his/her math problems each day; allow the use of a calculator as reinforcement to complete the other half of the assignment.

22. Have the student reinforce multiplication facts by practicing skip counting by the number (e.g., 5's: 5, 10, 15, 20, 25, 30, etc.).

23. Have students complete a math fact quiz sheet for a daily drill as students arrive each morning.

24. If a student continues to have difficulty memorizing facts, allow him/her to keep a chart of facts at his/her desk for reference in related math problems.

25. Require the student to practice facts at home with flash cards, computer programs or games.

26. Play class games to reinforce math facts (e.g., *Bingo, Jeopardy,* teacher-made games, etc.).

27. Teach the student that once addition facts are mastered, subtraction facts are simply the inverse. The same concept holds true for multiplication and division.

28. Have the student play a math fact game with other students. Let each student take turns answering and checking facts.

29. Provide practice of math facts using a computer with software programs that provide game-like activities for reinforcement of facts.

140 Does not make use of columns when solving math problems

1. Identify a peer to act as a model for the student to demonstrate the use of columns when working math problems.

2. Use manipulative objects (e.g., base ten blocks, plastic links, etc.) to teach the student place value by providing a visual image.

3. Make certain the student has the prerequisite skills to learn place value (e.g., counting orally, understanding sets, writing numbers to 100, etc.).

4. Make certain the student knows the concepts and terminology necessary to learn place value (e.g., *set, column, middle, left, digit,* etc.).

5. Make certain the student understands that the collective value of ten *ones* is equal to one *ten* and that ten *tens* is equal to one *hundred*.

6. Provide the student with learning experiences in grouping tangible objects into groups of ones, tens, hundreds, etc.

7. Have the student practice labeling columns to represent ones, tens, hundreds, etc.

8. Have the student practice regrouping a number in different positions and determining its value (e.g., 372, 723, 237).

9. Make certain the student understands the zero concept in place value (e.g., there are no tens in the number "207," so a zero is put in the tens column).

10. Money concepts will help the student learn place value by association (e.g., $1.26 is the same as six pennies or six ones, two dimes or two tens, one dollar or one hundred).

11. Use vertical lines on graph paper to help the student visualize columns and put a single digit in each column.

12. Make certain the student understands that math problems of addition and multiplication move from right to left beginning with the ones column.

13. Provide the student with many opportunities to indicate the value of columns in multiple-digit numbers (e.g., 56= ( ) tens and ( ) ones; 329= ( ) hundreds, ( ) tens, and ( ) ones; etc.).

14. Teach the student the concept of filling each column and moving on to the next column from ones to tens, to hundreds, to thousands, etc.

15. Develop a marked column format (e.g. thousands | hundreds | tens | ones) on a master which can be copied for the student to use in solving all assigned math problems.

16. Require the student to check all his/her math assignments for accuracy. Reinforce the student for each correction made in the use of columns.

17. Have the student use a calculator to solve math problems involving the use of columns.

18. Provide the student with color-coded columns to help the student use columns accurately.

19. Provide the student with a masked window to help the student use columns accurately.

20. Have the student practice using columns when solving math problems by using a computer program which automatically chooses the correct column at input.

21. Provide the student with self-checking materials to reinforce the use of columns.

22. Have the student exchange 10 pennies for a dime and correlate that activity with grouping ten *ones* and placing a one in the *tens* column and a zero in the *ones* column.

1. Make certain that the student's inability to read is not the cause of his/her difficulty in solving math word problems.

2. Have the student read the math word problem first silently and then aloud and identify the mathematical operation required.

3. Provide word problems that require a one-step process, making certain that the sentences are short and concise.

4. Teach the student to look for "clue" or "key" words in word problems that indicate the mathematical operations.

5. Have the student orally analyze the steps that are required to solve word problems (e.g., "What is given?" "What is asked?" "What operation(s) is used?" etc.).

6. Represent the numerical amounts, in concrete forms, that are presented in the word problems (e.g., problems involving money can be represented by providing the student with the appropriate amount of real or play money).

7. Have the student write a number sentence after reading a math word problem. (This process will help the student see the numerical relationship prior to finding the answer.)

8. Have the student create word problems for number sentences. Place the number sentences on the chalkboard and have the student tell or write word problems that could be solved by the number sentence.

9. Have the student restate math word problems in his/her own words.

10. Ask the student to identify the primary question that must be answered to solve a given word problem. Continue this activity using more difficult word problems containing two or more questions. Make sure the student understands that questions are often implied rather than directly asked.

11. Have the student make up word problems. Direct the student to write problems involving specific operations. Other students in the classroom should be required to solve these problems. The student can also provide answers to his/her own problems.

12. Supplement textbook problems with teacher-made problems. These problems can deal with classroom experiences. Include students' names in the word problems to make them more realistic and meaningful to the student.

13. Use word problems that are of interest to the student and related to his/her experiences.

14. Make certain the student reads through the entire word problem before attempting to solve it.

15. Teach the student to break down each math word problem into specific steps.

16. Have the student make notes to "set the problem up" in written form as he/she reads the math word problem.

17. Have the student simulate situations which relate to math word problems (e.g., trading, selling, buying, etc.).

18. Have the student solve math word problems by manipulating objects and by stating the process(es) used.

19. Help the student recognize common patterns in math word problems (e.g., how many, add or subtract, etc.).

20. Discuss and provide the student with a list of words/phrases which usually indicate an addition operation (e.g., *together, altogether, sum, in all, both, gained, received, total, won, saved*, etc.).

21. Discuss words/phrases which usually indicate a subtraction operation (e.g., *difference between, from, left, how many (more, less), how much (taller, farther, heavier), withdrawal, spend, lost, remain, more*, etc.).

22. Discuss words/phrases which usually indicate a multiplication operation (e.g., *area, each, times, product, double, triple, twice,* etc.).

23. Discuss words/phrases which usually indicate a division operation (e.g., *into, share, each, average, monthly, daily, weekly, yearly, quotient, half as many,* etc.).

24. Teach the student to convert words into their numerical equivalents to solve word problems (e.g., two weeks = 14 days, one-third = 1/3, one year = 12 months, one quarter = 25 cents, one yard = 36 inches, etc.).

25. Teach the student relevant vocabulary often found in math word problems (e.g., dozen, amount, triple, twice, etc.).

26. Allow the student to use a calculator when solving word problems.

27. Require the student to read math word problems at least twice before beginning to solve the problem.

28. Have the student begin solving basic word problems which combine math problems and word problems such as:

> 7 apples
> and 3 apples
> equals 10 apples

Gradually change the problems to word problems as the student demonstrates success.

29. Before introducing complete word problems, present the student with phrases to be translated into numbers (e.g., 6 less than 10 equals 10 - 6).

30. Assign a peer to act as a model for the student and to demonstrate for the student how to solve math word problems.

31. Reduce the number of problems assigned to the student at one time (e.g., 5 problems instead of 10).

32. Demonstrate for the student how to solve math word problems by reading the problem and solving the problem on paper step-by-step.

33. Speak with the student to explain: (a) what the student is doing wrong (e.g., using the wrong operation, failing to read the problem carefully, etc.) and (b) what the student should be doing (e.g., using the appropriate operation, reading the problem carefully, etc.).

34. Evaluate the appropriateness of the task to determine: (a) if the task is too difficult and (b) if the length of time scheduled to complete the task is appropriate.

35. Correlate word problems with computation procedures just learned in the classroom (e.g., multiplication, operations with multiplication word problems, etc.).

36. Teach the student the meaning of mathematical terms (e.g., *sum, dividend,* etc.). Frequently review terms and their meanings.

37. Highlight or underline key words in math problems (e.g., the reference to the operation involved, etc.).

38. Provide the student with a checklist to follow in solving math word problems (e.g., what information is given, what question is asked, what operation(s) is used).

39. Make certain the student has a number line on his/her desk to use as a reference.

40. Make certain the student knows why he/she is learning to solve math word problems. Provide the student with concrete examples and opportunities to apply these concepts in real-life situations.

41. Have the student talk through math word problems as he/she is solving them in order to identify errors the student is making.

42. Develop a math reference sheet for the student to keep at his/her desk (e.g., steps used in doing subtraction, multiplication, addition, and division problems).

43. Have the student check his/her word problems using a calculator. The calculator can also be used to reinforce the learning of math facts.

44. Make certain the student knows the concepts of *more than, less than, equal to,* and *zero.* The use of tangible objects will facilitate the learning process.

45. Recognize quality work (e.g., display the student's work, congratulate the student, etc.).

46. Make certain the student is not required to learn more information than he/she is capable of at any one time.

47. Have the student act as a peer tutor to teach a peer a math concept the student has mastered. This can serve as reinforcement for the student.

48. Provide practice in solving math word problems by using a computer software program that gives the student immediate feedback.

49. Provide the student with a quiet place to work (e.g., "office" or study carrel, etc.). This is used as a means of reducing distracting stimuli and not as a form of punishment.

50. Make certain the student has mastery of math concepts at each level before introducing a new skill level.

51. Have the student manipulate objects (e.g., apples, oranges, toy cars, toy airplanes, etc.) as the teacher describes the operation.

52. Reduce the emphasis on competition. Competitive activities may cause the student to hurry and do math word problems incorrectly.

53. Have the student question any directions, explanations, or instructions he/she does not understand.

54. Reinforce the student for solving math word problems: (a) give the student a tangible reward (e.g., classroom privileges, line leading, passing out materials, five minutes free time, etc.) or (b) give the student an intangible reward (e.g., praise, handshake, smile, etc.).

142   Fails to change from one math operation to another

1. Use visual cues (e.g., *Stop* signs or red dots) on the paper when the student must change operations. Have the student raise his/her hand when reaching *Stop* signs, and provide instructions for the next problem.

2. Use color coding (e.g., make addition signs green, subtraction signs red, etc.). Gradually reduce the use of colors as the student demonstrates success.

3. Reduce the number of problems on a page (e.g., five problems to a page with the student being required to do four pages of work throughout the day).

4. Make certain the student recognizes all math operation symbols (e.g., +, -, ÷, ×).

5. Have the student practice recognizing series of math symbols (e.g., +, -, ÷, ×).

6. Use a written reminder beside each math problem to indicate which math operation is to be used (e.g., division, addition, subtraction, etc.). Gradually reduce the use of reminders as the student demonstrates success.

7. Make the math operation symbols, next to the problems, extra large in order that the student will be more likely to observe the symbols.

8. Require the student to go through math assignments highlighting or otherwise marking the operation of each problem before beginning to solve the math problems.

9. Work the first problem or two of a math assignment for the student in order that he/she knows which operation to use.

10. Use a separate piece of paper for each type of math problem. Gradually introduce different types of problems on the same page.

11. Recognize quality work (e.g., display the student's work, congratulate the student, etc.).

12. Teach the student direction-following skills: (a) listen carefully, (b) ask questions, (c) use environmental cues, (d) rely on examples provided, (e) wait until all directions have been given before beginning.

13. Assess the quality and clarity of directions, explanations, and instructions given to the student.

14. Make certain the student knows why he/she is learning a math concept. Provide the student with concrete examples and opportunities for the student to apply those concepts in real-life situations.

15. Have the student talk through math problems as the student is solving them in order to identify errors he/she is making.

16. Develop a math reference sheet for the student to keep at his/her desk (e.g., steps used in doing subtraction, multiplication, addition, and division problems).

17. Have the student check his/her math assignments using a calculator. The calculator can also be used to reinforce the learning of math facts.

18. Make certain the student is not required to learn more information than he/she is capable of at any one time.

19. Provide practice in math by using a computer software program that gives the student immediate feedback.

20. Reduce the amount of information on a page if it is causing visual distractions for the student (e.g., fewer problems, less print, etc.).

21. Evaluate the appropriateness of a task to determine: (a) if the task is too difficult and (b) if the length of time scheduled for the task is appropriate.

22. Speak to the student to explain: (a) what the student is doing wrong (e.g., adding instead of subtracting) and (b) what the student should be doing (e.g., adding addition problems, subtracting subtraction problems, etc.).

23. Reinforce the student for correctly changing from one math operation to another: (a) give the student a tangible reward (e.g., classroom privileges, line leading, passing out materials, five minutes free time, etc.) or (b) give the student an intangible reward (e.g., praise, handshake, smile, etc.).

143 Does not understand abstract math concepts without concrete examples

1. Have the student practice the concept of regrouping by "borrowing" and "carrying" from manipulatives arranged in columns set up like math problems.

2. Have the student use "sets" of objects from the environment to practice addition, subtraction, multiplication, and division problems.

3. Use actual change and dollar bills, clocks, etc., to teach concepts of money, telling time, etc.

4. Make certain all of the student's math problems have concrete examples associated with each one (e.g., 9 minus 7 becomes 9 apples minus 7 apples, etc.).

5. Work the first problem or two with the student, explaining how to associate concrete examples with each problem (e.g., 9 minus 7 becomes 9 apples minus 7 apples).

6. Have a peer tutor assist the student in solving math problems by providing concrete examples associated with each problem (e.g., 9 minus 7 becomes 9 apples minus 7 apples).

7. Use a scale, ruler, measuring cups, etc., to teach math concepts using measurement.

8. Make certain to use terms when speaking to the student which convey abstract concepts to describe tangible objects in the environment (e.g., larger, smaller, square, triangle, etc.).

9. Use concrete examples when teaching abstract concepts (e.g., numbers of objects to convey more than, less than; rulers and yardsticks to convey concepts of height, width, etc.).

10. Review, on a daily basis, those abstract concepts which have been previously introduced. Introduce new abstract concepts only after the student has mastery of those concepts previously presented.

11. Provide the student with computer software which uses graphics associated with math problems.

12. Have the student play games with colored chips, assigning values to each color to learn the concept of one, etc.

13. Make sure that the student is taught concepts such as "square" and "cube" separately. To introduce both concepts at the same time may be confusing.

14. Provide physical objects of math concepts to teach these concepts (e.g., when referring to a yard, provide the student with a yardstick to make it concrete for him/her, etc.).

15. Provide the student with money stamps to solve money problems (e.g., penny, nickel, dime, etc.).

16. Provide the student with clock stamps that he/she fills in when practicing the concept of telling time.

17. Introduce all new abstract math concepts with a concrete example (e.g., to introduce the concept of liquid measurement, use a liquid and measuring cups with ounces indicated).

18. Have the student use concrete manipulatives in real-life problems (e.g., use measuring cups to prepare a recipe, use money to purchase items from the store).

19. Only after a student has worked with the concrete manipulatives and mastered the concept, should the abstract symbols and terms be introduced (e.g., ounce, oz.; cup, c.; pint, pt.).

20. When introducing an abstract concept, use the following steps: concrete, practice, abstract, practice, review, test (e.g., concrete/cups and liquid, practice/using cups to solve problems, abstract/word problems with cups, practice/prepare a recipe, review, test; or concrete/cups and liquid, practice/prepare a recipe, abstract/symbols for cups, practice/word problems, review, test).

21. Have the student draw pictures to illustrate math problems.

144 Fails to correctly solve math problems requiring regrouping

1. Evaluate the appropriateness of the task to determine if the student has mastered the skills needed for regrouping.

2. Provide the student with many concrete experiences to help learn and remember regrouping skills. Use popsicle sticks, tongue depressors, paper clips, buttons, base ten blocks, etc., to form groupings to teach regrouping.

3. Provide practice in regrouping facts by using a computer software program that gives immediate feedback to the student.

4. Use daily drill activities to help the student with regrouping (e.g., written problems, flash cards, etc.).

5. Have the student perform timed drills to reinforce regrouping. The student competes against his/her own best time and score.

6. Find opportunities for the student to apply regrouping to real-life situations (e.g., getting change in the cafeteria, figuring how much items cost when added together while shopping, etc.).

7. Develop a regrouping reference for the student to use at his/her desk when solving math problems which require regrouping.

8. Have the student solve half of the math problems each day and use the calculator as reinforcement to complete the other half of the math assignment.

9. Reinforce the student for attempting and completing work. Emphasize the number correct, then encourage the student to see how many more he/she can correct without help. Have the student maintain a "private" chart of math performance.

10. Make certain the student understands number concepts and the relationship of number symbols to numbers of objects before requiring him/her to solve math problems requiring regrouping.

11. Make certain the student knows the concepts of *more than, less than, equal,* and *zero.* The use of tangible objects will facilitate the learning process.

12. Have the student practice the concept of regrouping by *borrowing* and *carrying* from objects in columns set up like math problems.

13. Provide the student with opportunities for tutoring from peers or a teacher. Allow the student to tutor others when he/she has mastered a concept.

14. Make certain that the language used to communicate with the student about regrouping is consistent (e.g., *borrow, carry,* etc.).

15. Provide the student with shorter math assignments, but more of them throughout the day (e.g., 4 assignments of 5 problems each rather than one assignment of 20 problems).

16. Work the first problem or two of the math assignment with the student in order to make certain that he/she understands the directions and the operation necessary to solve the problems.

17. Have the student talk through math problems as he/she solves them in order to identify errors the student is making.

18. Require the student to check subtraction problems by adding (i.e., the difference plus the subtrahend equals the minuend). Reinforce the student for each error corrected.

19. Make certain the student has a number line on his/her desk to use as a reference.

20. Develop a math reference sheet for the student to keep at his/her desk (e.g., steps used in doing subtraction problems, addition problems, etc.).

21. Have the student check his/her math assignments using a calculator. The calculator can also be used to reinforce the learning of math facts.

22. Use manipulative objects (e.g., base ten blocks) to teach the student regrouping.

23. Make certain the student understands the concept of place value and that place values move from right to left beginning with the ones column.

24. Make certain the student is not required to learn more than he/she is capable of at any one time.

25. Make certain the student has mastery of math concepts at each level before introducing a new skill level.

26. Have the student solve math problems by manipulating objects to experience regrouping.

27. Reduce the emphasis on competition. Competitive activities may cause the student to hurry and make mistakes in regrouping.

28. Reinforce the student for solving math problems that require regrouping: (a) give the student a tangible reward (e.g., classroom privileges, line leading, five minutes free time, etc.) or (b) give the student an intangible reward (e.g., praise, handshake, smile, etc.).

145 Fails to correctly solve math problems involving fractions or decimals

1. Make certain the student understands that 8/8 equals a whole, 10/10 equals a whole, etc.

2. Make certain the student understands the concept of regrouping (e.g., changing mixed numerals into improper fractions, etc.).

3. Identify a peer to work with the student on problems involving fractions or decimals.

4. Have the student solve math problems involving fractions and decimals using computer software.

5. Have the student solve math problems involving fractions by using tangible objects (e.g., pennies which are one-tenth of a dime, inch cubes which are one-twelfth of a foot, etc.).

6. Provide the student with many concrete experiences to help him/her learn to use fractions (e.g., cutting pie-shaped pieces, measuring ½ cup, weighing 1/4 pound, etc.).

7. Make certain the student understands number concepts and the relationships of number symbols to numbers of objects before requiring him/her to solve math problems involving fractions.

8. Provide the student with enjoyable math activities involving fractions which he/she can perform for drill and practice either alone or with a peer (e.g., computer games, math games, manipulatives).

9. Work the first few problems of the math assignment with the student in order to make certain that he/she understand directions and the operation necessary to solve the problems.

10. Cut pieces of paper into equal numbers (e.g., fourths, sixths, tenths, etc.); have the student add fractions together, subtract fractions, etc.

11. For math problems involving fractions with unlike denominators, have the student use a tangible object such as a ruler to help him/her solve the problem (e.g., compare 3/4 to 7/8).

12. Have the student solve fraction problems by using real-life measurement such as ounces, inches, pounds, etc., to determine weight, length, volume, etc.

13. When the student is solving fraction problems, provide the student with manipulatives which represent the fractions involved.

14. Provide the student with paper to solve decimal problems which has blank boxes and decimal points in order to help guide the student to proper placement of decimal numbers.

15. Have the student solve money problems to practice decimal problems.

16. Have the student solve math problems involving decimals by using tangible objects (e.g., two dollar bills and one 50 cent piece equals $2.50, etc.).

17. Provide the student with many concrete experiences to help him/her learn to use decimals (e.g., use money, determine mileage (5.2 miles to school), etc.).

18. Have the student use a calculator when learning to solve problems involving decimals.

19. Provide the student with enjoyable math activities involving decimals which he/she can perform for drill and practice either alone or with a peer (e.g., computer games, math games, manipulatives).

20. Provide the student with a daily shopping list of items with a corresponding list of the cost of each item (each involving a decimal point). Have the student determine the cost of his/her purchase.

21. Bring a selection of menus to the classroom to have the student select items for a meal and compute the cost of the items (each involving a decimal point).

22. Have the student use a newspaper or catalog to make a list of things advertised which he/she would like to purchase. Have the student determine the total cost of the items selected using decimals.

23. Have the student earn a hypothetical income and engage in money-related math problems using decimals (e.g., taxes, social security, savings, rent, food, clothing, auto payments, recreation, etc.). The degree of difficulty of the problems is matched to the student's ability level.

1. Beginning with the addition and subtraction facts, separate the basic facts into "sets," each to be memorized successively by the student.

2. Use the tracking technique to help the student learn math facts. Present a few facts at a time. Gradually increase the number of facts the student must remember as he/she demonstrates success.

3. Have the student use a calculator to reinforce learning to solve problems involving money. Have the student solve several money problems each day using the calculator.

4. Provide practice in solving money problems by using a computer software program that gives the student immediate feedback.

5. Use real-life situations for the student to practice money problems (e.g., paying for lunch in the cafeteria line, making purchases from book order clubs, purchasing a soft drink, etc.).

6. Use actual coins in teaching the student coin value (e.g., counting by ones, fives, tens, etc.; matching combinations of coins; etc.).

7. Make certain the student recognizes all coins (e.g., penny, nickel, dime, quarter).

8. Make certain the student recognizes common denominations of paper money (e.g., one dollar bill, five dollar bill, ten dollar bill, twenty dollar bill, etc.).

9. Have a peer work with the student every day practicing coin values, paper money values, combinations, etc.

10. Have the student match equal values of coins (e.g., two nickels to a dime, two dimes and a nickel to a quarter, five nickels to a quarter, etc.).

11. Make certain the student understands all math operation concepts involved in using money (e.g., addition, subtraction, multiplication, division, decimals, etc.).

12. Make certain the student can solve the necessary math problems involved in the use of money (i.e., the student can solve math problems of the same difficulty as those involving money).

13. Make certain the student can count by pennies, nickels, dimes, quarters, and half-dollars.

14. Have the student use actual money to simulate transactions in the classroom (e.g., purchasing lunch, groceries, snacks, clothing, etc.). Have the student practice acting as both a customer and a clerk.

15. Provide the student with math word problems involving the use of money, making certain the appropriate operation is clearly stated.

16. Provide the student with a daily shopping list of items and a corresponding list of the cost of each item. Have the student determine the cost of his/her purchase.

17. Bring a selection of menus to the classroom to have the student select items for a meal and compute the cost of the items.

18. Have the student use a newspaper or a catalog to make a list of things advertised which he/she would like to purchase. Have the student determine the total cost of the items selected.

19. Have the student earn a hypothetical income and engage in money-related math problems. The degree of difficulty of the problems is matched to the student's ability level (e.g., taxes, social security, savings, rent, food, clothing, auto payments, recreation, etc.).

20. Have the student talk through money math problems while solving them in order to identify his/her errors.

21. Using money stamps, make individual work sheets for the student with only a few problems on each page.

22. Make certain the student is not required to learn more information than the student is capable of at any one time.

23. Make certain the student knows why he/she is learning the concept of money. Provide the student with concrete examples and opportunities to apply those concepts in real-life situations.

24. Review, on a daily basis, those skills, concepts, tasks, etc., which have been previously introduced.

25. Reduce the emphasis on competition. Competitive activities may cause the student to hurry and make mistakes in solving problems involving money.

26. Reinforce the student for correctly solving problems involving money: (a) give the student a tangible reward (e.g., classroom privileges, line leading, passing out materials, five minutes free time, etc.) or (b) give the student an intangible reward (e.g., praise, handshake, smile, etc.).

147   Fails to correctly solve problems using measurement

1. Find opportunities for the student to apply measurement facts to real-life situations (e.g., cooking, measuring the lengths of objects, etc.).

2. Develop a measurement reference sheet for the student to use at his/her desk when solving math problems.

3. Call on the student when he/she is most likely to be able to respond successfully.

4. Provide the student with enjoyable activities during free time in the classroom (e.g., computer games, math games, etc.).

5. Make certain that the language used to communicate with the student about measurement is consistent (e.g., meters, grams, etc.).

6. Make certain the student has mastery of math concepts at each level before introducing a new skill.

7. Work the first problem or two of the math assignment with the student in order to make certain that he/she understands the directions and the operation necessary to solve the problems.

8. Have the student practice basic measurement concepts (e.g., pound, ounce, inch, foot, etc.) using everyday measurement devices in the environment (e.g., rulers, measuring cups, etc.).

9. Have the student practice measuring items in the environment to find their length, weight, etc.

10. Make certain the student knows the basic concepts of fractions before requiring him/her to solve problems involving measurement (e.g., 1/4 inch, 1 ½ feet, etc.).

11. Have the student practice using smaller units of measurement to create larger units of measurement (e.g., twelve inches to make one foot, three feet to make one yard, eight ounces to make one cup, four cups to make one quart, etc.).

12. Assign the student measurement problems that he/she will want to be able to perform successfully (e.g., following a recipe, building a model, etc.).

13. Have the student begin solving measurement problems which require same and whole units (e.g., 10 pounds minus 8 pounds, 24 inches plus 12 inches, etc.). Introduce fractions and mixed units (e.g., pounds and ounces, etc.) only after the student has demonstrated success with same and whole units.

14. Have the student use a calculator to solve measurement problems, check the accuracy of problems worked, etc.

15. Have the student use software programs to practice measurement skills on the computer.

16. Have the student begin to solve measurement problems by using measurement devices before solving the problems on paper (e.g., 5 inches plus 4 inches using a ruler; 3 liquid ounces plus 5 liquid ounces using a measuring cup; etc.).

17. Let students use dry ingredients such as macaroni, beans, rice, etc., to measure cup fractions.

18. Make certain the student knows why he/she is learning measuring concepts. Provide the student with concrete examples and opportunities to apply those concepts in real-life situations.

19. Make certain the student is not required to learn more information than the he/she is capable of at any one time.

20. Provide practice in solving measurement problems by using a computer software program that gives the student immediate feedback.

21. Review, on a daily basis, those skills, concepts, tasks, etc., which have been previously introduced.

22. Have the student participate in an actual "hands-on" experience by following simple recipes (e.g., making Jell-O, cookies, etc.).

23. Evaluate the appropriateness of the task to determine: (a) if the task is too difficult and (b) if the length of time scheduled for the task is appropriate.

24. Assign a peer to act as a model for the student to demonstrate how to solve measurement problems.

25. Discuss and provide the student with a list of words/phrases which usually indicate measurement problems (e.g., pound, inches, millimeter, kilogram, etc.).

26. Reduce the emphasis on competition. Competitive activities may cause the student to hurry and solve measurement problems.

27. Reinforce the student for correctly solving problems involving measurement: (a) give the student a tangible reward (e.g., classroom privileges, line leading, passing out materials, five minutes free time, etc.) or (b) give the student an intangible reward (e.g., praise, handshake, smile, etc.).

1. Reduce the emphasis on competition. Competitive activities may cause the student to hurry and make mistakes in math problems.

2. Provide the student with concrete experiences to help him/her learn and remember math facts. Use popsicle sticks, tongue depressors, paper clips, buttons, etc., to form groupings to teach math facts.

3. Have the student use a calculator to reinforce learning math facts. Have the student solve several problems each day using a calculator.

4. Provide practice in place value using a computer software program that gives the student immediate feedback.

5. Have a peer tutor work with the student each day on place value activities (e.g., flash cards).

6. Use manipulative objects (e.g., base ten blocks, connecting links, etc.) to teach the student place value and to provide a visual image.

7. Make certain the student has the prerequisite skills to learn place value (e.g., counting, writing numbers to 100, etc.).

8. Make certain the student knows the concepts and terminology necessary to learn place value (e.g., *set, column, middle, left, digit*, etc.).

9. Make certain the student understands that the collective value of ten "ones" is equal to one ten and that ten "tens" is equal to one hundred.

10. Provide the student with learning experiences in grouping tangible objects into groups of tens, hundreds, etc.

11. Have the student practice labeling columns to represent ones, tens, hundreds, etc.

12. Have the student practice regrouping a number in different positions and determining its value (e.g., 372, 627, 721).

13. Make certain the student understands the zero concept in place value (e.g., there are no tens in the number "207" so a zero is put in the tens column).

14. Money concepts will help the student learn place value association (e.g., $1.26 is the same as six pennies or six ones; two dimes or two tens; one dollar or one hundred).

15. Use vertical lines or graph paper to help the student visualize columns and put a single digit in a column.

16. Make certain the student understands that math problems of addition, subtraction, and multiplication are worked from right to left beginning with the ones column.

17. Make certain the student knows why he/she is learning a math concept. Provide the student with concrete examples and opportunities for the student to apply those concepts in real-life situations.

18. Have the student talk through math problems as he/she is solving them in order to identify errors in place value the student is making.

19. Develop a math reference sheet for the student to keep at his/her desk (e.g., steps used in doing subtraction, multiplication, addition, and division problems).

20. Have the student check his/her math assignments using a calculator. The calculator can also be used to reinforce the learning of math facts.

21. Make certain the student is not required to learn more information than the student is capable of at any one time.

22. Make certain the student has mastery of math concepts at each level before introducing a new skill level.

149 Confuses operational signs when working math problems

1. Evaluate the appropriateness of the task to determine: (a) if the task is too difficult and (b) if the length of time scheduled for the task is appropriate.

2. Have the student practice recognizing operational symbols (e.g., flash cards of ÷, +, -, ×).

3. Use a written reminder beside math problems to indicate which math operation is to be used (e.g., addition, subtraction, multiplication, division). Gradually reduce the use of reminders as the student demonstrates success.

4. Make the math operation symbols next to the problems extra large in order that the student will be more likely to observe the symbol.

5. Color-code math operation symbols next to math problems in order that the student will be more likely to observe the symbol.

6. Require the student to go through the math problems on each daily assignment, highlighting or otherwise marking the operation of each problem before he/she begins to solve them.

7. Work the first problem or two of the math assignment for the student in order that he/she knows what operation to use.

8. Use a separate piece of paper for each type of math problem. Gradually introduce different types of math problems on the same page.

9. Place the math operation symbols randomly around the room and have the student practice identifying the operation involved as he/she points to the symbol.

10. Provide the student with a math operation symbol reference sheet to keep and use at his/her desk (e.g., + means add, - means subtract, × means multiply, ÷ means divide).

11. At the top of each sheet of math problems, provide a math operational symbol reminder for the student (e.g., + means add, - means subtract, × means multiply, ÷ means divide).

12. Have the student practice matching math operation symbols to the word identifying the operation using flash cards (e.g., +, -, ×, ÷; add, subtract, multiply, divide).

13. Have the student solve his/her math problems using a calculator.

14. Have a peer work with the student to act as a model and provide reminders as the student solves his/her math problems.

15. Make certain the student knows why he/she is learning a math concept. Provide the student with concrete examples and opportunities for the student to apply those concepts in real-life situations.

16. Have the student check his/her math assignments using a calculator. The calculator can also be used to reinforce the learning of math facts.

17. Make certain the student is not required to learn more information then he/she is capable of at any one time.

18. Provide practice in operational signs using a computer software program that gives the student immediate feedback.

19. Make certain the student has mastery of math concepts at each level before introducing a new skill level.

20. Highlight operational signs so that the student is sure to notice the signs before beginning the operation.

1. Make certain when speaking to the student to use terms which convey abstract concepts to describe tangible objects in the environment (e.g., larger, smaller, square, triangle, etc.).

2. Identify tangible objects in the classroom with signs that convey abstract concepts (e.g., larger, smaller, square, triangle, etc.).

3. Use concrete examples when teaching abstract concepts (e.g., numbers of objects to convey "more than" or "less than," rulers and yardsticks to convey concepts of "height" or "width," etc.).

4. Play *Simon Says* to enhance the understanding of abstract concepts (e.g., "Find the largest desk." "Touch something that is a rectangle." etc.).

5. Conduct a scavenger hunt. Have the student look for the smallest pencil, tallest boy, etc., in the classroom.

6. Teach shapes using common objects in the environment (e.g., round clocks, rectangle desks, square tiles on the floor, etc.).

7. Evaluate the appropriateness of having the student learn abstract concepts at this time.

8. Teach abstract concepts one at a time before pairing the concepts (e.g., dimensionality, size, shape, etc.).

9. Provide repeated physical demonstrations of abstract concepts (e.g., identify things far away and close to the student, small box in a large room, etc.).

10. Review, on a daily basis, those abstract concepts which have been previously introduced. Introduce new abstract concepts only after the student has mastered those previously presented.

11. When introducing abstract concepts, rely on tangible objects (e.g., boxes for dimensionality, family members for size, distances in the classroom for space, cookie cutters for shape, etc.). Do not introduce abstract concepts by using their descriptive titles such as square, rectangle, triangle, etc.

12. Have the student match the names of abstract concepts with objects (e.g., triangle, square, circle, etc.).

13. Give the student direction-following assignments (e.g., "Go to the swing that is the farthest away." "Go to the nearest sandbox." etc.).

14. Have a peer spend time each day with the student pointing out abstract concepts in the classroom (e.g., the rectangle-shaped light switch plate, the round light fixture, the tallest girl, etc.).

15. Have the student question any directions, explanations, instructions, he/she does not understand.

16. Have the student physically perform spatial relationships (e.g., have the student stand *near* the teacher, *far* from the teacher, *over* a table, *under* a table, etc.).

17. Call attention to spatial relationships which occur naturally in the environment (e.g., call attention to a bird flying *over* a tree, a squirrel running *under* a bush, etc.).

18. For more abstract concepts such as left and right, north, south, east, and west, have the student follow simple map directions. Begin with a map of the building and progress to a map of the community, state, nation, etc., with more complex directions to follow.

19. To teach the student relationships of left and right, place paper bands labeled *left* and *right* around the student's wrists. Remove the paper bands when the student can successfully identify left and right.

20. Use actual change and dollar bills, clocks, etc., to teach abstract concepts of money, telling time, etc.

21. Use a scale, ruler, measuring cups, etc., to teach abstract concepts using measurement.

22. Make certain to use the terms *right* and *left* as part of the directions you are giving to the student (e.g., refer to the windows on the left side of the room, the chalkboard on the right side of the room, etc.).

23. Have the student practice following directions on paper. Instruct the student to make a mark or picture on the right, left, middle, top and bottom parts of the paper according to the directions given.

24. Avoid the problem of mirror images by standing next to the student when giving right and left directions.

25. Have the student sort left and right gloves, shoes, paper hand and foot cut-outs, etc.

26. Be certain to relate what the student has learned in one setting or situation to other situations (e.g., vocabulary words learned should be pointed out in reading selections, math problems, story writing, etc.).

27. Make certain the student is attending to the source of information (e.g., eye contact is being made, hands are free of materials, etc.) when delivering directions that involve abstract concepts.

28. Label abstract concepts throughout the classroom (e.g., triangle shapes and names on the walls, left and right sides of a desk, directions on the wall, etc.) to help the student understand abstract concepts.

29. Make certain the student is not required to learn more abstract concepts than the student is capable of learning at any one time.

VI. Appendix

Preventing Behavior Problems

- Determine reinforcer preferences

- Determine academic ability levels

- Determine social interaction skills

- Determine ability to remain on task

- Determine group behavior

- Monitor and limit contemporary determinants of inappropriate behavior such as having to wait, task length, task difficulty, peer involvement, etc.

- Base seating arrangements on behavior

- Base group involvement on behavior

- Maintain teacher mobility in classroom

- Maintain teacher/student contact: visual, verbal, and physical

- Use criteria for expectations based on observed behavior and performance

- Use shaping, fading, and imitation procedures to gradually change behavior

- Maintain variety in reinforcers

- Use the Premack Principle in arranging schedule (i.e., a more desirable behavior can be used to reinforce the completion of a less desirable behavior)

- Use curriculum as reinforcement

- Use rules, point cards, and schedules of daily events as discriminative stimuli

- Use contracting to individualize, specify expected behavior, and identify reinforcers

- Arrange seating so all students have visibility to and from the teacher and teacher can scan the entire class

- Maintain a full schedule of activities

- Use language that is positive and firm, not demeaning, insulting, or harassing

- Intervene early when any form of conflict occurs

- Do not ignore behavior as an excuse for not intervening

- Use time-out to help the student resolve problem behavior

- Use removal to prevent contagion, destruction of property, and danger to others

- Communicate and coordinate with other teachers

- Communicate with home to prevent students playing one adult against another

Typical Methods of Modifying Academic Tasks

- Reduce the number of problems on a page (e.g., five problems to a page; the student may be required to do four pages of work throughout the day if necessary).

- Use a highlight marker to identify key words, phrases, or sentences for the student to read.

- Remove pages from workbooks or reading material and present these to the student one at a time rather than allowing the student to become anxious with workbooks or texts.

- Outline reading material for the student at his/her reading level, emphasizing main ideas.

- Tape record material for the student to listen to as he/she reads along.

- Read tests/quizzes aloud for the student.

- Tape record tests/quizzes for the student.

- Make a bright construction paper border for the student to place around reading material in order to maintain his/her attention to the task.

- Make a reading window from construction paper which the student places over sentences or paragraphs in order to maintain attention.

- Provide manipulative objects for the student to use in solving math problems.

- Rearrange problems on a page (e.g., if crowded, create more space between the problems).

- Use graph paper for math problems, handwriting, etc.

- Rewrite directions at a more appropriate reading level.

- Tape record directions.

- Have peers deliver directions or explanations.

- Allow more time to take tests or quizzes.

Reinforcer Survey

Name: _____ Age: _____

Date: _____

1. The things I like to do after school are _____
   _____

2. If I had ten dollars I would _____
   _____

3. My favorite TV programs are _____

4. My favorite game at school is _____

5. My best friends are _____

6. My favorite time of day is _____

7. My favorite toys are _____

8. My favorite record is _____

9. My favorite subject at school is _____

10. I like to read books about _____

11. The places I like to go in town are _____

12. My favorite foods are _____

13. My favorite inside activities are _____

14. My favorite outside activities are _____

15. My hobbies are _____

16. My favorite animals are _____

17. The three things I like to do most are _____
    _____

The Reinforcer Survey may be given to one student or a group of students. If the students cannot read, the survey is read to them. If they cannot write their answers, the answers are given verbally.

Reinforcer Menu

REINFORCER MENU

Reinforcer	Points Needed
Working With Clay	30
Peer Tutoring	25
Using Colored Markers	30
Using Colored Chalk	30
Feeding Pets	20
Delivering Messages	15
Carrying Wastebasket	20
Operating Projector	30
Playing a Board Game	35
Leading the Class Line	25
Passing Out Materials	20
Using a Typewriter	25

CLASS REINFORCER MENU

Reinforcer	Points Needed
See a Film	30
Class Visitor	25
Write and Mail Letters	30
Field Trip	30
Lunch Outdoors	20
Pop Popcorn	35
Take Class Pictures	30
Tape Songs	15
Put on a Play	25
Have Adults in for Lunch	30
Work with a Peer All Day	25

The Reinforcer Menu is compiled from information gathered by having a student or students respond to the Reinforcer Survey.

Rules For School Environments

GENERAL SOCIAL RULES....

- BE QUIET
- REMAIN IN YOUR SEAT
- WORK ON ASSIGNED TASK
- RAISE YOUR HAND

HALLWAY RULES....

- WALK IN THE HALL
- WALK IN A LINE
- WALK ON THE RIGHT
- WALK QUIETLY

CAFETERIA RULES....

- BE QUIET IN THE CAFETERIA LINE
- WALK TO YOUR TABLE
- TALK QUIETLY
- REMAIN SEATED

OUTDOOR RULES....

- TAKE PART IN SOME ACTIVITY
- TAKE TURNS
- BE FRIENDLY
- LINE UP WHEN IT IS TIME

ACADEMIC RULES....

- FINISH ONE TASK
- MEET YOUR CRITERIA
  TO EARN 5 POINTS

These rules, except for perhaps the outdoor rules, are applicable to all grade levels and have been used in public schools for general behavioral expectations.

Point Record

ACADEMIC POINTS

Monday

1	2	3	4	5	6	7	8	9	10	11	12	13	14

Tuesday

1	2	3	4	5	6	7	8	9	10	11	12	13	14

Wednesday

1	2	3	4	5	6	7	8	9	10	11	12	13	14

Thursday

1	2	3	4	5	6	7	8	9	10	11	12	13	14

Friday

1	2	3	4	5	6	7	8	9	10	11	12	13	14

SOCIAL POINTS

Monday

Tuesday

Wednesday

Thursday

Friday

The Point Record form provides for Academic Points, top section, for each task completed with criteria met; and Social Points, bottom section, for demonstrating appropriate behavior in and around the classroom. The Point Record is kept with the student at all times, wherever he/she may be, in order that points may be given for following any school rules.

Point Card

TIME	DAYS OF WEEK				
	M	T	W	T	F
8:00 - 8:50					
9:00 - 9:50					
10:00 - 10:50					
11:00 - 11:30					
11:30 - 12:20					
12:30 - 1:20					
1:30 - 2:20					
2:30 - 3:20					

Name: _____

This is a Point Card for secondary level students and may be used in special education classes or in regular classes. Teachers assign points, give checks, or sign initials for appropriate behavior demonstrated by the student while in the classroom. These points are relative to rules of the classroom, expected behavior, a contract developed with the student, etc. The card is a 3 x 5 inch index card which is easily kept in a shirt pocket and is small enough to reduce embarrassment for some students who would prefer to keep their behavioral support program more confidential.

CONTRACT

I, __Eric Johnson__ ,

HEREBY DECLARE THAT I WILL __finish my math__
__assignments on time__

THIS JOB WILL BE CONSIDERED SUCCESSFUL __this job will__
__be considered successful when I finish 3__
__assignments in a row on time__

NAME __Eric Johnson__

FOR THE SUCCESSFUL COMPLETION OF THE ABOVE JOB
YOU MAY __use the computer for 15 minutes__

DATE SIGNED __12/10__

DATE COMPLETED _____

__Ms. Cummins__
(SIGNED)

The contract is one of the most idividualized and personalized approaches of intervening to improve behavior. This component contributes to the personal aspect of the individual reinforcement system due to the private manner in which teacher, student, and parents may work together for behavior improvement. The contract should specify:

1. Who is working toward the goals
2. What is expected (i.e., social behaviors or academic productivity and quality)
3. The amount of appropriate behavior that is expected
4. The kind of reinforcement that is being earned
5. The amount of the reinforcement
6. When the reinforcement will be made available

CONTRACT

I, _____,

HEREBY DECLARE THAT I WILL _____

_____

_____

THIS JOB WILL BE CONSIDERED SUCCESSFUL _____

_____

NAME _____

FOR THE SUCCESSFUL COMPLETION OF THE ABOVE JOB

YOU MAY _____

_____

DATE SIGNED _____

DATE COMPLETED _____

_____

_____
(SIGNED)

GROUP CONTRACT

WE, _____ ,

HEREBY DECLARE THAT WE WILL _____

_____

_____

THIS JOB WILL BE CONSIDERED SUCCESSFUL _____

_____

NAMES _____

FOR THE SUCCESSFUL COMPLETION OF THE ABOVE JOB

WE MAY _____

_____

DATE SIGNED _____

DATE COMPLETED _____

_____

_____
(SIGNATURES)

Schedule of Daily Events

SCHEDULE OF DAILY EVENTS

NAME: _____

	#1	#2	#3	#4	#5	#6	#7	#8	#9	#10
Monday										
Tuesday										
Wednesday										
Thursday										
Friday										

SCHEDULE OF DAILY EVENTS

NAME: _____

	#1	#2	#3	#4	#5	#6	#7	#8	#9	#10
Tuesday										

Each individual student's Schedule of Daily Events is developed for him/her and attached to his/her desk for a week at a time or for one day at a time. This schedule identifies each activity/task the student is assigned for the day, and the schedule is filled in by the teacher one day at a time. Students tend to know what they are to do next when the schedule is provided, and teachers can expect fewer interruptions for directions when students refer to their schedules.

Schedule of Daily Events Sample

SCHEDULE OF DAILY EVENTS

NAME: _____

	#1	#2	#3	#4	#5	#6	#7	#8	#9	#10
Monday	Reading	Art (Clay)	Math	Art (Paint)	Science	Creative Writing	Social Studies	Listening	Music	P.E.
Tuesday										
Wednesday										
Thursday										
Friday										

Parent Communication Form

Teacher: _____ Date: _____

Parent(s): _____ Student: _____

Grade or Level:_____ Type of Class:_____

Other School Personnel: _____

———••••—

TYPE OF COMMUNICATION: Letter _____ Note _____ Telephone _____

Parent Visit to School _____ Teacher Visit to Home _____

Out-of-School Location _____ Other _____

———••••—

Initiation of Communication: School Scheduled Meeting _____

Teacher Initiation _____ Parent Initiation _____ Other _____

———••••—

Nature of Communication: Information Sharing _____

Progress Update _____ Problem Identification _____ Other _____

———••••—

Communication Summary (Copies of Written Communications Should Be Attached): _____

_____

_____

_____

_____

_____

_____

———••••—

Expectations for Further Communication: _____

_____

_____

———••••—

Signatures of Participants (If Communication Made in Person): _____

_____

_____

_____

The Parent Communication Form is a record of communication made with parents in person, by telephone, or by notes or letters.

Student Conference Report

Student's Name: _____

School Personnel Involved and Titles: _____

_____

Date: _____ Grade Level of Student: _____

—————••••••—————

Initiation of Conference: Regularly Scheduled Conference _____

Teacher Initiation _____ Other Personnel Initiation _____

Student Initiation _____ Parent Initiation _____

—————••••••—————

Nature of Communication: Information Sharing _____

Progress Update _____ Problem Identification _____

Other _____

—————••••••—————

Conference Summary (Copies of Written Communications Should Be Attached): _____

_____

_____

_____

_____

_____

_____

_____

—————••••••—————

Expectations Based on Conference: _____

_____

_____

—————••••••—————

Signatures of Conference Participants: _____

_____

_____

_____

—————••••••—————

The Student Conference Report is used for recording conferences held with the student to identify problems, concerns, progress, etc.

A List of Reinforcers Identified by Elementary-Aged Students

1. Listen to the radio
2. Free time
3. Watch favorite program on TV
4. Talk to best friend
5. Listen to favorite tapes
6. Read a book
7. Candy, especially chocolate
8. Play sports - baseball, kickball, soccer, hockey
9. Ride a bike
10. Do something fun with best friend
11. Go to the zoo
12. Build a model plane or car
13. Go to the arcade and play video games
14. Camping trip
15. Play with pets
16. Go to a fast-food restaurant
17. Pop popcorn
18. Go to a movie
19. Play in the gym
20. Play outside
21. Help clean up classroom
22. Play with puppets
23. Play with dolls and a doll house
24. Ice cream
25. Cookies
26. Go shopping at a grocery store
27. Tacos
28. Hamburgers and french fries
29. Pizza
30. Money
31. Making buttons
32. Parties
33. Teacher's helper
34. Field trips
35. Eat lunch outside on a nice day
36. Recess
37. Student-of-the-month
38. Honor roll
39. Buy sodas
40. Work on puzzles
41. Write on the chalkboard
42. Gumball machine
43. Race cars
44. Use colored markers
45. Roller skating
46. Puppet show
47. Water slide
48. Stickers
49. Pencils
50. Use the computer
51. Fly model airplanes
52. Visit the principal

A List of Reinforcers Identified by Secondary-Aged Students

1. Free time

   - Doing nothing

   - Reading magazines (from home or library)

   - Reading newspapers

   - Writing a letter (to a rock star, favorite author, politician, probation officer, friend)

   - Peer tutoring (your class or another one)

   - Listen to records (from class, library, home)

   - Visit library

   - Work on a hobby

   - See a film

   - Draw - Paint - Create

2. Acting as teacher assistant (any length of time)

3. Acting as principal assistant (any length of time)

4. Have class outside

5. Field trip

6. Go to a movie

7. Have a soda

8. Have an afternoon for a sport activity (some students play and some watch)

9. Play a game (Bingo, cards, board games)

10. Use a camera (take pictures and have them developed)

11. Play Trivia games

12. Time off from school

13. Coach's assistant (any length of time)

14. Picnic lunch

15. Run errands

16. Extra time in high interest areas (shop, art, P.E.)

17. Do clerical work in building (use copy machine, run office errands)

18. Library assistant (any length of time)

19. Custodian's assistant (any length of time)

20. Watch TV

21. Earn a model

22. Typing

23. Attend a sports event

24. Food or treat coupons

25. Iron-on decals

Note Taking

1. For note taking from lecture or written material, follow:

   - **Outline Form**
     (e.g., Who, What, Where, When, How, Why)

   - **Mapping Form**
     (e.g., Who, What, Where, When, How, Why)

   - **Double-Column Form**
     (e.g., Who, What, Where, When, How, Why)

2. For note taking from directions, follow:

   - **Assignment Form**
     (e.g., What, How, Materials, When)

   - **Assignment Sheet**

   - **2-Week Project Outline**

♣ **(See Appendix for the above forms.)**

Outline Form

SUBJECT: _____

Topic: _____

	General	Specific
What:		
Where:		
When		
How:		
Why:		
Vocabulary		

Outline Form (Alternative)

SUBJECT: _____

Topic: _____

	General	Specific
What:		
Why:		
How:		
Vocabulary		
Example:		

Mapping Form

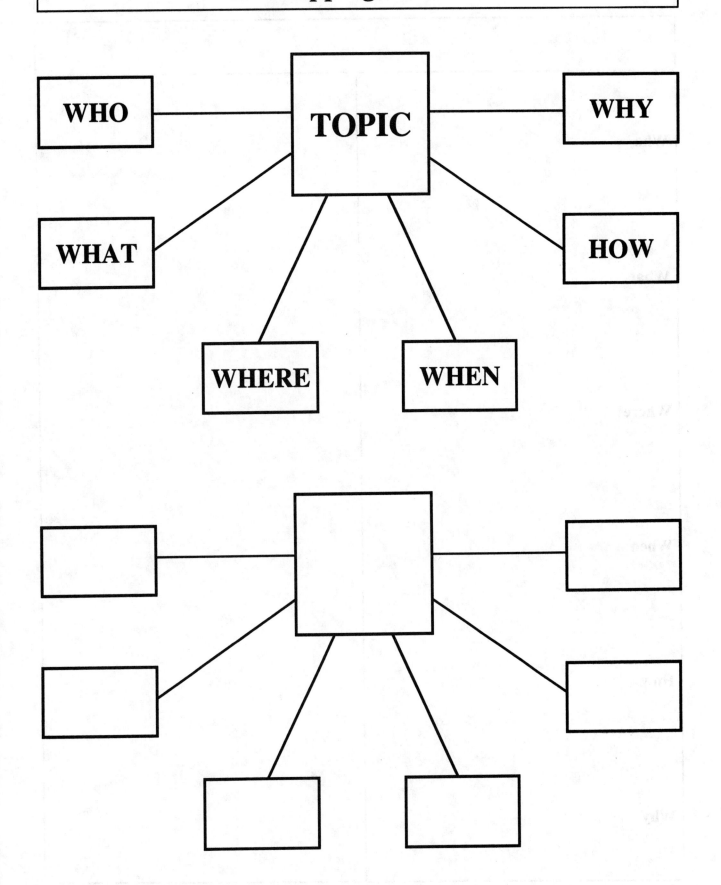

Double-Column Form

Who

What

Where

When

How

Why

Assignment Form

Subject: _____

	General	Specific
What:		
How:		
Materials:		
When:		

Subject: _____

	General	Specific
What:		
How:		
Materials:		
When:		

Assignment Sheet

ASSIGNMENT SHEET

DATE _____

SUBJECT	ASSIGNMENT	DUE DATE	TEACHER SIGNATURE
Math			
Reading			
Science			
Social Studies			
Spelling			
Other			

_____   Comments:
PARENT SIGNATURE

ASSIGNMENT SHEET

DATE _____

SUBJECT	ASSIGNMENT	DUE DATE	TEACHER SIGNATURE
Math			
History			
Science			
English			
Fine Arts/ Practical Arts			
Other			

_____   Comments:
PARENT SIGNATURE

2-Week Project Outline

DAY 1   **Determine exactly what the assignment is**
- **Identify due date**

DAY 2-4   **Project Preparation**
- **READ ASSIGNED MATERIALS**
- **RESEARCH RELATED MATERIALS**
- **GATHER NECESSARY MATERIALS**

DAY 5   **Summarize reading material by answering:**
- **Who, What, Where, When, How, Why**

DAY 6   **Preliminary project construction**
- **Make sketches, determine scale, make revisions**

DAY 7-11   **Project construction**
- **Lay out all materials**
- **Prepare materials to scale**
- **Draw/color**
- **Cut**
- **Glue**
- **Paint**

DAY 12   **Touch up work**
- **Label, check that all items are secure, etc.**

DAY 13   **Write paragraph from summary (Day 5)**

DAY 14   **Turn in!**

Test-Taking Skills

1. Survey entire test for the kinds of items that are included (e.g., true-false, multiple- choice, fill-in-the-blank, etc.).

2. Read all directions.

3. Underline or circle all key words in directions (e.g., locate, write, choose the best answer, identify the main idea, etc.).

4. Do not answer any items until the directions are thoroughly understood (i.e., ask the teacher for clarification if directions are not thoroughly understood).

5. Respond to all items for which the answers are known, skipping remaining items to answer later (some items may provide clues or reminders for items the student could not answer the first time through the test).

6. For those items which are difficult to answer, underline the key words (e.g., who, what, where, when, how, why) and then respond.

7. For those items still not understood, ask the teacher for clarification.

8. Go back and check all answers for accuracy (e.g., followed directions, proper use of math operations, no careless errors).

ADDITIONAL SUGGESTIONS

● In order for a statement to be true, all of the statement must be true (e.g., note words such as all, never, always, etc.).

● When matching, first answer items that are known, crossing off answers that are used, then go back to remaining items and make the best choice.

● Some items may provide clues or reminders for items the student could not answer the first time through the test.

● When writing an essay answer, construct the answer around Who, What, Where, When, How, and Why.

● On multiple-choice items, read all choices before responding. If any of the choices look new or different, they are probably not the correct answer.

● If a true-false item looks new or different, it is probably false.

Studying for a Test

1. Identify the information to be covered on the test.

2. Identify and collect all necessary materials (e.g., textbook, notebook, etc.).

3. Identify major topics.

4. Under each topic identify major headings.

5. Under each heading identify Who, What, Where, When, How, and Why.

6. Write this information on the Outline Form
      or
   underline this information
      or
   highlight this information.

7. Make study aids such as flash cards. (See Appendix.)

8. Memorize information using the Outline Form and/or mnemonic devices

ADDITIONAL SUGGESTIONS

● Study with a friend.

● Write practice questions from the Outline Form and answer the questions.

● If study questions are provided, answer all questions.

● Make certain that all information in the summary is thoroughly understood.

Flash Card Study Aid

Questions   **Topic:**_____

Who:

What:

Where:

When:

How:

Why:

Questions   **Topic:**_____

Who:

What:

Where:

When:

How:

Why:

Fiction Frame

TITLE: _____

AUTHOR: _____

This story takes place _____. An important character in this story

is _____ who _____.

A problem occurs when _____

_____.

Next, _____

_____.

The problem is solved when _____

_____

_____.

At the end of the story, _____

_____

_____.

Selected Abbreviations and Symbols

ab.	about		$	money
add.	addition		mo.	month
&	and		natl.	national
bk.	book		no.	number
bldg.	building		#	number
cap.	capital		oz.	ounce
c/o	care of		p., pg.	page
cm.	centimeter		pd.	paid
cent.	century		par.	paragraph
ch., chap.	chapter		pop.	population
co.	company		lb.	pound
cont.	continent		pres.	president
cont.	continued		qt.	quart
corp.	corporation		rd.	road
dept.	department		rep.	representative
dict.	dictionary		Rev.	Reverend
educ.	education		sch.	school
enc.	encyclopedia		sc.	science
Eng.	English		sig.	signature
fig.	figure		s.s.	social studies
geog.	geography		sp.	spelling
govt.	government		sq.	square
gr.	gram		subj.	subject
ht.	height		subt.	subtraction
hist.	history		syn.	synonym
ill., illus.	illustration		temp.	temperature
in.	inch		t.	ton
intro.	introduction		treas.	treasurer
lab.	laboratory		U.S.A.	United States of America
lang.	language		univ.	university
lat.	latitude		v.	verb
leg.	legislature		vs.	versus
lib.	library		v.p.	vice-president
liq.	liquid		wk.	week
max.	maximum		wt.	weight
meas.	measure		w/	with
mi.	mile		yd.	yard
min.	minute		yr.	year
misc.	miscellaneous			

The above list only serves as an example. The student should further develop his/her own list.

VII. Index